1995

The Trade Union Question
in British Politics

Making Contemporary Britain Series

General Editor: Anthony Seldon
Consultant Editor: Peter Hennessy

The Trade Union Question in British Politics

Government and Unions since 1945

Robert Taylor

BLACKWELL
Oxford UK & Cambridge USA

First published 1993

Blackwell Publishers
108 Cowley Road
Oxford   OX4 1JF
UK

238 Main Street
Cambridge, Massachusetts 02142
USA

British Library Cataloguing in Publication Data
A CIP catalogue record for this book is available from the British Library.

Library of Congress Cataloging-in-Publication Data
Taylor, Robert, 1943–
    The trade union question in British politics : government and unions since 1945/Robert Taylor.
        p.   cm. — (Making contemporary Britain)
    Includes bibliographical references and index.
    ISBN 0–631–16626–2 (alk. paper). — ISBN 0–631–16627–0 (pbk. : alk. paper)
        1. Trade-unions—Great Britain—Political activity—History—20th century.
    2. Great Britain—Politics and government—1945–
    I. Title.   II. Series.
    HD6667. T394   1993
    322'. 2'0941—dc20
                                                                92–39484
                                                                        CIP

Typeset in 10 on 12 pt Ehrhardt
by Graphicraft Typesetters Ltd., Hong Kong
Printed in Great Britain by T.J. Press, Padstow, Cornwall

This book is printed on acid-free paper

To the memory of Ann

Contents

Acknowledgements

I should like to thank Anthony Seldon first and foremost for his patience and encouragement throughout the protracted period required for the completion of this book. The *Financial Times* was kind enough to allow me to take two months' leave of absence in the spring of 1992 from my post as the newspaper's Nordic correspondent based in Stockholm, in order to further the book's progress. I should also like to thank Cornell University at Ithaca in New York State for appointing me as a visiting scholar in its Western Societies program. The university's Industrial and Labor Relations library remains one of the best in the world and I found it invaluable in the preparation of this book.

My stay at Cornell was made particularly stimulating and enjoyable – thanks to Nick Salvatore and Ann Sullivan, the kindest of hosts. They were even invaluable over the cross-Atlantic telephone link to Sweden in resolving certain teething troubles I experienced with my laptop computer.

I would also like to thank Nuffield College, Oxford where I spent three happy years as a post-graduate student in the late 1960s. Its library was invaluable in the preparation of this book. The chairman of the Conservative party gave his permission to quote from the Conservative Party Archives in Oxford.

The book has grown like Topsy since its modest beginnings, mainly because the subject is central to an understanding of post-war British politics and little has been written specifically on it. For nearly fifty years the trade union 'question' dominated the public debate. My account is based on primary printed sources as well as on the voluminous literature on both industrial relations and British politics.

Oxford
February 1993

General Editor's Preface

The Institute of Contemporary British History's series *Making Contemporary Britain* is aimed directly at students and at others interested in learning more about topics in post-war British history. In the series, authors are less attempting to break new ground than presenting clear and balanced overviews of the state of knowledge on each of the topics.

The ICBH was founded in October 1986 with the objective of promoting the study of British history since 1945 at every level. To that end, it publishes books and a quarterly journal, *Contemporary Record*; it organizes seminars and conferences for school students, undergraduates, researchers and teachers of post-war history; and it runs a number of research programmes and other activities.

A central theme of the ICBH's work is that post-war history is too often neglected in British schools, institutes of higher education and beyond. The ICBH acknowledges the validity of the arguments against the study of recent history, notably the problems of bias, of overly subjective teaching and writing and the difficulties of perspective. But it believes that the values of studying post-war history outweigh the drawbacks, and that the health and future of a liberal democracy require that its citizens know more about the most recent past of their country than the limited knowledge possessed by British citizens, young and old, today. Indeed, the ICBH believes that the dangers of political indoctrination are higher where the young are *not* informed of the recent past.

Robert Taylor's book is one of the longest in the series, which is itself settling down to fuller books than the comparatively thin early volumes. The expanded length of titles in the series is a development to be welcomed, given that the volumes frequently cover more than half the century's history, and considering the paucity of published literature on many of the subjects covered.

The fuller text is particularly welcome with Robert Taylor's volume, as it covers such a critical aspect of post-war history, namely the relations of trade unions with British governments. Every British Prime Minister and his or her Cabinet since 1945 has been necessarily heavily preoccupied with the management of organized labour. For good or ill, trade unions have had immense influence on the nation's economic and social policies, at least until Margaret Thatcher became premier in 1979.

To write such a book requires not only mastery of the extensive secondary literature and primary sources, but also deep knowledge of the workings of the unions themselves, their principal leaders, and the reality of life on the shop floor. Robert Taylor, one-time academic and then long-serving and acclaimed Fleet Street labour correspondent, is uniquely qualified to have written this book.

It is published at a time when relative tranquillity on the industrial scene affords an opportunity to be able to assess the often stormy and always controversial trade union question in British politics with a degree of historical detachment and perspective. The book also reminds us that experience has shown that the tranquillity is unlikely to last throughout the 1990s.

Anthony Seldon
June 93

Introduction
Britain's Trade Unions: Scapegoats of National Decline

Unions: Too strong or too weak?

It gradually became almost a conventional wisdom from the middle of the 1950s to blame Britain's trade unions for a large part of the country's relatively poor economic performance after the end of the Second World War. As Sir Denis Barnes, Permanent Secretary at the Department of Employment and Productivity between 1968 and 1972, wrote (with Eileen Reid):

> Since 1945 all governments have been concerned about the consequences of trade union power. They have regarded the wage increases produced by collective bargaining as impeding their attempts to maintain full employment, stable prices and a satisfactory balance of payments and to increase the rate of economic growth and generally manage the economy. They have been concerned also about industrial relations – the effect on the economy of strikes, restrictive practices, demarcation and overmanning.[1]

From the strategic outlook of his office in London's St James's Square, Barnes was ideally placed to assess the nature of what came to be known as the trade union 'problem' during the 1960s. As he asserted: 'Between 1969 and 1979 three successive Prime Ministers have been prevented by the industrial and political power of the unions from pursuing policies they declared essential in the national interest. All lost the elections which followed the defeats of their policies.'

In *Industrial Relations in the 1990s*, a triumphalist White Paper published in July 1991, the Department of Employment also criticized in succinct and forceful language what it regarded as the malignant role that the trade unions played in the development of the post-war British economy. The document declared that:

It was a widely held view in the 1960s and 1970s that the severity and damaging consequences of Britain's industrial relations problems were exceeded only by their intractability. Nothing did more to damage the reputation of the British economy abroad or to undermine confidence at home in the possibility of economic recovery than the belief that these problems were beyond any real or lasting solution.

It went on to argue:

Britain's poor industrial relations were generally acknowledged to be a fundamental cause of the weakness of the British economy. British industry's record of strikes, restrictive practices and overmanning seriously and persistently damaged its ability to compete in the markets of the world. The balance of bargaining power appeared to have moved decisively and permanently in favour of the trade unions. In many cases union leaders were seen to be both irresponsible and undemocratic in exercising their industrial power. British industrial relations were increasingly disfigured by scenes of intimidatory picketing and by strikes aimed directly at the life of the community.[2]

In fact, the issue of trade union power was always much more complex than such intransigent and sweeping assertions might suggest. Here was a subject that aroused impassioned polemic but until the 1980s produced very little empirical evidence to justify the odium heaped upon organized labour. The lurid picture of obstructive and tyrannical trade unions as the bovine obstacles to the achievement of an economic miracle enjoyed, however, the potency of a national myth and it coloured as well as polarized attitudes across the entire political spectrum.

The demise of the British Labour Movement after May 1979, with the marginalizing of the trade unions as an influence on the state and the Labour party's four successive general election defeats, contrasted starkly in the popular mind with the position of the trade unions in the post-war period as having been over-powerful, an Estate of the Realm that exercised – as Conservative Prime Minister Stanley Baldwin once said of Fleet Street newspaper proprietors – 'power without responsibility'. Criticism of trade union power in Britain, however, began long before 1945. Indeed, from the early origins of trade unions during the eighteenth century, they were denounced by politicians, employers and above all lawyers as threats to economic freedom and the social order. In the gloomy words of former Conservative party leader Arthur Balfour in 1912: 'The power they [the unions] have got, if used to the utmost is, under our existing law, almost limitless. And there is no appearance that the leaders of the movement desire to temper the use of their legal powers with any consideration of policy or of mercy'.[3] Such views became commonplace, especially in Conservative party legal circles, after 1945 and they were to be influential in the formulation of the comprehensive labour law reform programme carried through 'step by step' under Margaret Thatcher's government during the 1980s.

But other observers argued quite the reverse: that far from being all-powerful, the trade unions in post-war Britain were actually much too weak to be effective in their relations both with employers and the state. Allan Flanders, the influential Oxford scholar of industrial relations in the 1960s, insisted they could not 'determine the greater part of the experience to which their members reacted'.[4] Operating for the most part on a financial shoe-string in a highly competitive market place, trade unions were unable either to broaden the agenda of collective bargaining or to exercise an effective influence over governments and, more importantly, on corporate strategies at company or industry level, in the interests of their often disparate and divided memberships. 'One of the striking contemporary features of British collective bargaining is the poverty of its subject matter, the limited range of substantive issues regulated by written and formally signed agreements', argued Flanders.[5] As insecure, reactive and defensive bodies, trade unions were often the hapless victims of the destructive competitive structure of multi-unionism as they fought with each other for members and bargaining recognition. It was more their lack of authority and control over their own members rather than any dictatorial power that union leaders might wield that caused so much difficulty in the post-war years.

The confused perception of whether trade unions were strong or weak dominated much of the post-war national industrial relations debate. Often governments acted as if they believed organized labour was too powerful in its dealings with employers while the trade unions failed to safeguard the individual freedom of shopfloor workers. But on many other occasions ministers thought the trade unions were much too weak and needed to be provided with effective legal sanctions so they could reassert a lost control and authority. The ill-fated 1971 Industrial Relations Act was motivated by a mixture of both perceptions in its bold but futile attempt both to strengthen trade unions as organizations and protect individual workers from closed shops.

This book examines the evolution of the tangled, often unsatisfactory relationship that developed between British governments and the trade union movement from the summer of 1945 until the aftermath of the

1992 general election. Its purpose is to trace the transformation of the trade unions over the passage of time as seen through their dealings with governments.

From being sought after by the state as social partners in the management of the economy and regarded as virtually an unquestioned Estate of the Realm, the trade unions came to be seen as a sizeable part of the problem itself – of why Britain fell into economic decline relative to its main competitors on world markets. 'Industrial relations have been closer to the heart of economic policy in the United Kingdom than in almost any other country in the world in the post-war period', noted one recent academic observer.[6] But no consensus exists about what role (if any) the trade unions have played in the country's undoubted economic malaise since 1945.

The subject of British governments and the trade unions in the post-war period is vast and controversial. My basic purpose has been both to describe and explain the complex relationship between governments and organized labour and narrate the flow of events in which both of them took part from the end of the Second World War to the early 1990s. It is also an attempt to bridge the wide gulf that has existed in so much of the contemporary literature between the world of national politics and that of shopfloor realities. More often than not, employers, trade unions and workers have seemed to go on practising their collective bargaining in a highly pragmatic way, keeping the state as far as possible away from their activities. For governments – impatient with the slow, messy and essentially reactive labour world of custom and practice – such insouciance looked complacent and irresponsible. As they wrestled with the tenacious post-war economic ills of an over-valued currency, balance of payments deficits, low productivity and high unit labour costs, many came to believe that the radical reform of industrial relations was a necessary prerequisite for national economic revival. The subject was apparently far too important to be left to capital and labour to resolve across the bargaining table. It needed the active and permanent involvement of the state.

Legal immunities and voluntarism

At the outset, it is important to understand the peculiar underlying characteristics of the British industrial relations system. Without an appreciation of the ethos that shaped collective bargaining and union–state relations before 1945, it is much more difficult to recognize the deeply held convictions that continued to dominate trade union attitudes into the 1980s and beyond. This does not mean that we must retrace all the steps along organized labour's 'magnificent journey' (as the Labour journalist Francis Williams once called it) back to the country's first industrial revolution, but certain fundamental features of the post-war labour scene can only be appreciated within a long historical perspective.

In its 1968 report, the Donovan Royal Commission on Trade Unions and Employer Associations provided an authoritative and widely accepted description of the relationship between the British state and organized labour. As it explained:

> Until recent times it was a distinctive feature of our system of industrial relations that the State remained aloof from the process of collective bargaining in private industry. It left parties free to come to their own agreements. It imposed some, but few, restrictions on the right of employees to strike or of employers to resort to a lock-out. The parties to the collective agreement themselves rarely intend that their bargain shall be a legally enforceable contract, but rather that it shall be binding in honour only. The law goes out of its way to provide that such bargains between employers' associations and trade unions shall not be directly enforceable. This abstentionist attitude has reflected a belief that it is better in the long run for the law to interfere as little as possible in the settlement of questions arising between employers and workmen over pay and conditions of work.[7]

The traditional voluntarist system of industrial relations was not merely accepted by the state, but in the immediately post-war years successive governments sought to safeguard and strengthen it. The Ministry of Labour and National Service acted as an impartial body between capital and labour that would offer its own conciliation services to settle disputes but intervene only when both sides agreed to allow the state to intervene. Sir Godfrey Ince, who was the Ministry's Permanent Secretary during part of the 1950s, described its role in a study published in 1960:

> It is the traditional policy of the Government that industry should be given the fullest encouragement to settle its own affairs and that the State should take action only when there is no effective bargaining machinery in an industry or when negotiations through an industry's machinery have broken down. This general policy has been written into all legislation in this sphere.[8]

As the TUC explained in its 1966 written evidence to the Donovan Royal Commission, 'Virtually all the traditional activities of the Ministry of Labour in the field of industrial relations can be described as complementary to free collective bargaining.'[9]

The trade unions themselves recognized from their very beginnings that they needed the state's support to help them to protect their autonomous activities from attack by judges. Legislation was passed in 1871 and 1875–76 and reinforced much more substantially in 1906 to protect the trade unions from the ravages of judge-interpreted common law that tended to treat organized labour as a threat to property rights for their attempts to restrain trade. Up until 1871 trade unions were regarded by the law very much as conspiracies and strikes as criminal acts. Thereafter, those workers involved in industrial stoppages did not face the threat of criminal prosecution. After a number of adversely anti-union legal judgements from the early 1890s onwards, the newly elected Liberal government in 1906 agreed to a settlement that appeared to establish a permanent and settled legal framework for industrial relations. In fact, the resulting Trade Disputes Act went much further than the government had envisaged in extending the protection of the law to trade unions. They were provided with legal immunity from action in tort for acts that were done 'in contemplation or furtherance of a trade dispute'. This negative approach meant there was no legal right to strike in Britain but in lawful strikes union funds were safeguarded from the depredations of the courts and aggrieved employers.

To liberal economists like Friedrich von Hayek and constitutional lawyers such as Professor A. V. Dicey, the 1906 Act was a dangerous measure that gave organized labour enormous privileges that they believed threatened the well-being of the market economy. Theoretically this may have been so, but without legal immunities trade unions would have enjoyed no security at all from the law and faced the prospect of emasculation. This may have been a minimalist use of state power but without the backing of such statute law trade unions would have found it virtually impossible to operate freely. Britain's trade unions had to operate in a hostile environment 'where the stakes were very high and where the dice might well be loaded'. As Dr Pelling observed, 'It is not very surprising that union leaders were inclined to steer clear of the law whenever they could.'[10]

The hostility of the law towards organized labour shaped the fundamental attitudes of the trade unions because it ensured they had an 'uncertain legal status'. As the 1981 government Green Paper on Legal Immunities explained, 'Trade unions came into existence in the nineteenth century despite the law and not under its protection.'[11] Their ability to act came from the collective power they were able to establish to offset the power of employers to hire and fire. In other European countries, trade unions pressed for and eventually won from the state positive rights to guarantee their freedoms but this was not so in Britain.

But the British industrial relations system was never pure voluntarism in practice. The state – even in the nineteenth century – was not entirely abstentionist in industrial relations, concerned only to provide a limited legal framework. Under the 1896 Conciliation Act the British government also intervened in a positive manner by introducing a system of arbitration administered by the Board of Trade which could be used by employers and unions through mutual agreement. However, the purpose of such conciliation was to foster the development of collective bargaining in a voluntary framework, not to provide a dominant role for the state in the conduct of industrial relations. The Board of Trade's Labour Department, created in 1893, was supposed to be impartial between employers and unions, providing the means for the settlement of disputes. Under the exceptional conditions of the First World War the state banned strikes and lock-outs and introduced compulsory binding arbitration in industries crucial to the war effort, though this proved impossible to enforce in the face of disruptive shopfloor action in the engineering and coal industries. More lasting was the emergence of the so-called Whitley Council system in 1917, the state's response to shop steward unrest in the war industries. This encouraged the development of joint industrial councils made up of employers and unions on a voluntary basis. The state itself developed this approach in dealing with its own employees and accepted trade union organization and negotiation in the civil service from the 1920s. Indeed, governments took a benevolent view of voluntarism. In the words of the Ministry of Labour's industrial relations handbook of 1953, 'For 80 years the state has recognised "collective bargaining" as the normal means of settling wages and working conditions and more recently has actively encouraged the establishment of jointly agreed machinery in industry.'[12]

But state power was also seen as vital by trade unions not simply in reinforcing voluntarism in collective bargaining through a defence of legal immunities and the institutional provision of arbitration, but also in providing statutory minimum protection for all workers in areas like health and safety at work and low pay as a complement to their own bargaining efforts. For the most part, governments of whatever political persuasion accepted this. At a time when a Conservative government strongly resisted a directive from the European Community laying down a maximum 48 hour working week for workers, it is worth remembering those Tory Reformers of the 1840s like Lord Shaftesbury and Richard Sadler, who championed the passage of the 1847 Factory Act that established a ten hour a day statutory limit on working time for women and the young, and the Conservative administration of Benjamin Disraeli that enforced a consolidated measure that was seen as the first modern Factories Act. It was Lord Salisbury's Unionist government in 1891 that passed the Fair Wages Resolution obligating the state to ensure the current comparable level of wages was paid to workers employed on all government contracts in a move to counteract the exploitation of labour in the sweated trades. In 1909 the young Winston Churchill, as President of the Board of Trade in a reforming Liberal administration, established the wages council system with the power to fix minimum wage rates that were legally enforceable throughout the industries covered.

But state action was regarded by the trade unions as only second best to the practice of collective bargaining between employers and themselves in achieving satisfactory conditions of employment for workers. Little enthusiasm existed among the trade unions in support of the state playing a more interventionist role in industrial relations through the legal provision of positive rights for trade unions and workers. The unions did not view state action as an alternative or substitute for voluntarism. After all, with rights went responsibilities and this would – it was feared – ensnare organized labour in a more regulated and legalistic system that could work to their disadvantage in the face of hostile courts. The defence of trade union autonomy from the state was regarded as an overriding objective by the leaders of organized labour. They were satisfied with a highly minimalist view of the state when it came to industrial relations. Len Murray, General Secretary of the Trades Union Congress (TUC), reflected this tenacious and accepted tradition in his 1980 Granada Guildhall lecture when he quoted the words of Frederick Rogers, the General Secretary of the Bookbinders' union in the 1890s who sought to differentiate the objectives of trade unionism from those of Socialism:

> We shall enlarge the frontiers of the State and control, so far as Government can control, the power of the capitalist over the labourer more and more. But there must be an independent life within the state to prevent Government becoming tyranny and the Trade Unions will be chief among those who shall bring that independent life into being.[13]

In its written evidence to the Donovan Royal Commission in 1966 the TUC gave cogent expression to its sceptical, suspicious and limited view of the role of the state in industrial relation. It explained:

> No state, however benevolent, can perform the function of trade unions in enabling workpeople themselves to decide how their interests can best be safeguarded. It is where trade unions are not competent, and recognise that they are not competent, to perform a function, that they welcome the state playing a role in at least enforcing minimum standards

but in Britain this role is recognised as the second best alternative to the development by workpeople themselves of the organisation, the competence, the representative capacity, to bargain and to achieve for themselves satisfactory terms and conditions of employment. In general, because this competence exists, the state stands aside, its attitude being one of abstention, of formal indifference.[14]

The continuing need to defend the autonomous life of the trade unions from the demands of the modern state lay at the tangled heart of the relations between organized labour and British governments that developed after 1945. It helped to explain the severe limitations the TUC imposed upon itself at the behest of its affiliated unions in most of its dealings with governments. There was only ever a half-hearted belief among trade unions in the virtues of any form of corporatism in post-war Britain. Despite the aspirations of Sir Walter Citrine, its finest General Secretary, to ensure that the TUC was the main representative body of organized labour in relations with the state, it remained essentially a loose confederation of divergent sectionalist interests hampered in its search for unity by the pace of the slowest. It is true that from time to time in a crisis (1948–50, 1965–6, 1975–8) Congress House could act decisively and bind together its disparate forces behind a common position of wage restraint in support of a Labour government in economic difficulties. But it was always much more successful being defensive than innovative, as the crisis of June 1969 over legislation taken from the *In Place of Strife* White Paper and the TUC's campaign against the 1971 Industrial Relations Act were to underline.

Increasingly after 1945, however, governments tried to bring the TUC and its affiliated unions into playing a much more positive role in the management of the economy, a process that culminated in the far-reaching but abortive talks with Edward Heath's government in the summer of 1972 and the notorious Social Contract with the Labour party during the 1970s. The state's wish for more direct involvement in industrial relations and collective bargaining reflected increasing government concern with the intractable problems of the stagnating British economy relative to its main foreign competitors from the mid-1950s onwards. For its part, the TUC said that it would like to bargain with the state over a wide area of policy beyond industrial relations. Like it or not, the trade unions recognized that if they wanted to influence the economic and social environment in which they acted as bargainers they needed to create a harmonious relationship with governments. This is what the Trades Union Congress had sought to achieve since its formation in 1868. But the TUC was the first to acknowledge the complexity of that relationship. It wanted to deepen and strengthen its voice in the corridors of government without losing its distinctive sense of independence. In its 1966 evidence to the Donovan Royal Commission Congress House asserted that governments treated the TUC 'as a sort of industrial parliament',[15] from which they benefited in drawing up and developing legislation from trade union expertise and in securing TUC consent for broad changes in the law that influenced the work of the trade unions. There was, of course, never in any sense a dialogue of equals. But after the Second World War until May 1979 successive governments, both Labour and Conservative, took the TUC's avowed aspirations for a bigger say in public life at their face value. Ministers sought cooperation with national trade union leaders, although very much on government terms, and under persistent economic pressure they tried to coax the TUC to shoulder burdens in the labour market that exceeded the ability of either Congress House or its affiliated unions to deliver.

Governments were convinced that they needed organized labour's co-operation to ensure the maintenance of full employment by moderating wage rises. The dangers of pay-push inflation troubled the Treasury continually and the need for a national incomes policy (however defined) was seen as almost a *sine qua non* for post-war social and economic advance. Most government policy-makers from the 1940s to the end of the 1970s believed Britain needed to develop some kind of national understanding between the state, the employers and the trade unions on what the economy could afford in wage increases to ensure the survival of the post-war social settlement.

But beneath the pressing imperatives demanded by an economy which seemed to be in almost permanent crisis, the old trade union insecurities remained almost as strong as ever. As George Woodcock, the TUC's General Secretary, explained in 1968: 'Trade unions are bodies to which the state gives no rights and from which the state has consequently removed most of the legal restrictions which unions came up against in the course of their normal activities'.[16] However, most trade union leaders – at least until the late 1980s – were content with what was essentially an uncertain and ambivalent role. From time to time when adverse legal judgements appeared to threaten the freedom of unions to act as autonomous organizations, trade unions used the TUC's political lobbying influence on governments to try and restore what they saw as their traditional position in the framework of law. But they demanded the protection of their legal immunities in industrial disputes, not any radical change in the substance and structure of industrial relations law. The remorseless erosion of trade union immunities during the Conservatives' sweeping legal offensive of the 1980s convinced a growing number of trade union leaders that they needed to reappraise their attitude to the idea of positive rights in a codified legal framework on the model of continental Europe, but their sudden discovery of a possible alternative to voluntarism was belated and confused.

It is not just the complex legal relationship between the state and organized labour, however, that is necessary in any understanding of Britain's post-war industrial politics. Another important underlying theme that also needs to be stressed, if we are to understand the evolution of the trade union 'problem' in the years that separate Clement Attlee from John Major, concerns the lingering and underlying hostility towards organized labour displayed inside a political and legal system dominated by the divisive consequences of class.

Official anxieties about the dangerous threat of trade union 'power' did not emerge suddenly in post-war Britain as the fond memories of the Worker's War gradually faded away. From their very origins in the early nineteenth century, trade unions were regarded by governments as potential threats to the established order. During the 1860s, in the years immediately before the outbreak of the 1914–18 War with the sudden emergence of industrial syndicalist ideas, and above all during the early 1920s in the period before the General Strike, British governments grappled with varying degrees of success with what they saw as the menace of organized labour both to the well-being of the economy and the maintenance of the constitution.

The Conservative party in particular always disliked the close political connection between the trade unions and the Labour party which the TUC helped to form in 1900 initially as an independent political voice for workers, though even then Conservatives accepted that workers could belong to trade unions and tolerated a modest if subordinate function for the TUC in public life. For its part, the Labour party believed the trade unions were its natural partners, despite the real tensions that existed between a Socialist ideology glorifying in the collectivist power of the state to transform society and a pragmatic acceptance by trade unions of the market economy for resolving differences of opinion with capital through the practice of collective bargaining.

In the years after 1945 neither the Conservatives nor the Labour party were able to secure a lasting and peaceful coexistence with the trade unions. Under conditions of full employment until the mid-1970s, governments of all persuasions found it hard – if not impossible – to secure the acquiescence, let alone the TUC's warm-hearted approval, for economic strategies that required some measure of state control over wage determination. The attitudes of the trade unions were not as negative or irresponsible as the politicians might suppose. Indeed, the TUC's own economic policy-makers tended to adopt prudent and reasonable proposals which they wanted governments to implement. Certainly, Congress House was not at the forefront in the 1950s and 1960s in calling for a devaluation of sterling as a way of reviving the country's industrial competitiveness. It was not until 1968 that the TUC even established its own public independent assessment of economic prospects outside the Treasury's influence with the emergence of its annual economic reviews.

Post-war British governments treated the TUC as if it was an Estate of the Realm, an impressive and respected organization that could act as a partner or at least an ally of the state. By doing so they ignored the lack of power in the TUC, its genuine weakness in the face of union autonomy. They also overlooked the internal weaknesses of the trade unions themselves. Union leaders might seek to order and demand but their ultimate power rested on the need to persuade and argue with their members to achieve consent, if not acquiesence. After 1945 the distribution of power grew increasingly more diffuse than ever inside the trade unions with the re-emergence of a cadre of self-reliant and articulate shop stewards operating effectively in conditions of full employment. As a result, it became harder year on year for the TUC to deliver or maximize what strength it could gain from its members in its dealings with the state.

As in so many other ways, Britain's trade unions were simply not equipped to become centralized corporatist institutions, capable of introducing the kind of admirable methods of jointly regulated employer–worker cooperation that seemed to work so well in West Germany, Austria and Sweden. Perhaps Len Murray put it best when he explained in his 1980 Granada lecture:

> Unions emphasise the necessity and the advantages of securing consent to change: this is the essence of democracy. Governments tend to deal in absolutes. Their typical instrument is the law; the typical instrument of unions is the agreement, sometimes written, often verbal, which can be applied and interpreted by custom and practice to accommodate the constantly changing needs of industry and used to solve problems on an agreed and therefore mutually acceptable basis. We see the law itself as summing up and generalising practices which are generally accepted as good and relying not on the use of sanctions – though sanctions may exceptionally be needed to deal with deviations – but on acceptability.[17]

Nevertheless, governments took tentative but cumulative steps forward before the Second World War to draw the trade unions – mainly through the TUC – into accepting a more participative role in public affairs beyond the limited parameters of the voluntarist collective bargaining system. In its evidence to the Donovan Commission, Congress House instanced the example of the National Government's request for TUC general council representation at the 1932 Ottawa Imperial Conference on trade as a first important occasion when the trade unions were given official public recognition by the state. But during the First World War, after the so-called Treasury Agreement of March 1915 between David Lloyd George, then Chancellor of the Exchequer, and the TUC, organized labour gained an enhanced position in its relations with government. As Chris Wrigley has pointed out: 'During the war [of 1914–18] the bulk of the trade union movement was prepared to forgo making full use of its strength and to co-operate in the war effort. In doing this union leaders became accustomed to walking the corridors of power and being consulted on all matters affecting their members'.[18]

Unfortunately this sustained and close relationship between the state and organized labour did not really outlast the end of the war. During the period of Lloyd George's peacetime coalition from 1918 to 1922 serious tensions developed. It was only after the 1926 General Strike that the way opened for the development of a more fruitful relationship, as syndicalist tendencies declined inside the unions and governments saw the value of trying to reach accommodation with the leaders of organized labour. After 1929, TUC nominees were provided with representation on consultative bodies in economic policy-making such as the Economic Advisory Council. Their specific influence on government was limited, however, because ministers were not really prepared to concede a collective and accountable voice for organized labour through the TUC in the formulation of their own policy-making. Many outside the Labour Movement expressed their alarm at the alleged role played by the TUC's General Secretary Walter Citrine and the TUC economic committee during the August 1931 crisis, when it looked as if the TUC's leaders were trying to dictate an alternative economic policy to the Labour government. Nevertheless, the TUC's attitude towards the National governments of the 1930s was not as negative as might be supposed. The TUC's more pragmatic and modest objectives after the 1926 General Strike, coupled with the undoubted increase in its internal authority and prestige with affiliated unions, helped to reassure the state that the TUC was a force for stability and moderation. Ernest Bevin, general secretary of the Transport and the General Workers' Union, was able to claim by 1937 that the TUC had 'now virtually become an integral part of the State and its views and voice upon every subject, international and domestic, heard and heeded'.[19] But this was a serious exaggeration. The TUC's desire for government recognition depended to a very great extent on the personal attitude of the Prime Minister of the time. Neville Chamberlain became a hated figure in the Labour Movement despite his commitment to social reform, and his succession to Baldwin brought a distinct chill and uneasy formality into TUC–government relations. As Middlemas explained: 'It became far harder to achieve genuine government recognition after 1937 in the era of Neville Chamberlain than it was to win modest sops to TUC status'.[20] It is true that Chamberlain sought the TUC's assistance in 1938 and early 1939 in the belated preparation of the government's plans for boosting armaments production, but the TUC opposed the introduction of military conscription. Nor did union leaders gain much influential access to the Treasury during the period. While trade unions were no longer regarded by ministers as subversive institutions, they had not yet really become an Estate of the Realm. The obvious respectability of the trade union leadership in the 1930s under Citrine and Bevin, however, did much to convince the policy-makers that a closer relationship with the TUC was a sensible course of action, even if the TUC recognized that its best hopes of achieving its economic and industrial objectives were more likely to occur through a greater direct influence over the Labour party where the trade unions had become a dominant force in policy-making after the 1931 disaster.

Notes

1 D. Barnes and E. Reid, *Governments and Trade Unions: The British Experience 1964–1979*, Heinemann, 1980, p. ix.
2 *Industrial Relations in the 1990s*, Cm 1602, HMSO, 1991, p. 1.
3 Quoted by H. Phelps Brown, *The Origins of Trade Union Power*, Oxford University Press, 1983, p. 73.
4 A. Flanders, *Management and Unions*, Faber & Faber, 1975 p. 293.
5 Ibid., p. 158.
6 N. Richardson, 'Trade Unions and Industrial Relations', in N. F. R. Crafts and N. W. C. Woodward (eds), *The British Economy since 1945*, Oxford University Press, 1991, p. 440.
7 Royal Commission on Trade Unions and Employer Associations, Cmnd 3623, HMSO, 1968, p. 10.
8 Sir G. Ince, *The Ministry of Labour and National Service*, Allen and Unwin, 1960, p. 21.
9 Trades Union Congress, evidence to the Donovan Commission, 1966, p. 140.
10 H. Pelling, *Popular Politics and Society in Late Victorian Britain*, Macmillan, 1979, p. 71.

11 Department of Employment, *Legal Immunities*, Cmnd 8128, January 1981, p. 2.
12 Ministry of Labour and National Service, *Industrial Relations Handbook*, HMSO, 1953, p. 1.
13 W. Wedderburn, *The Worker and the Law*, Penguin, 1986, p. 404.
14 Trades Union Congress, evidence to the Donovan Commission, p. 141.
15 Ibid., p. 138.
16 G. Woodcock, *The Trade Union Movement and the Government*, Leicester University Press, 1968, pp. 7–8.
17 L. Murray, *The Role of the Trade Unions*, Granada Lectures, 1980, p. 85.
18 C. Wrigley, in C. Cook and B. Pimlott (eds), *Trade Unions in British Politics* (second edn), Longman, 1991, p. 83.
19 Quoted in R. M. Martin, *TUC: The Growth of a Pressure Group*, Oxford University Press, 1980, p. 243.
20 K. Middlemas, *Politics in Industrial Society*, Deutsch, 1979, p. 219.

1 Trade Unions and the Making of the Post-war Settlement, 1940–1945

The relationship between Britain's trade unions and the state was transformed during the years of the Second World War. 'The unions could claim to have influenced – almost decided – manpower policies vital to the war effort and worked in partnership with Government to administer those policies', argued Barnes and Reid.[1]

During the period of the Phoney War from 3 September 1939 until Hitler's attack on France and the Low Countries in May 1940, only a limited change took place in government–TUC relations. It is true that TUC leaders were invited and sat as of right on the newly formed tripartite National Joint Advisory Council alongside employer representatives, but this produced no real sense of urgency and the old atmosphere of mutual mistrust continued. As Prime Minister, Neville Chamberlain did little to modify his hostility towards the TUC. He refused outright to consider the TUC's demand for a repeal or at least a suspension of the hated 1927 Trade Union and Trades Disputes Act as a gesture of goodwill by the government in smoothing the way to closer cooperation with the TUC in the war effort.

It is true that the TUC failed to achieve that objective during the rest of the war despite persistent lobbying, but in May 1940 the state's attitudes changed perceptibly towards organized labour with the creation of the all-party coalition government under Winston Churchill as Prime Minister. His inspired appointment of Ernest Bevin, the TGWU's General Secretary, to be Minister of Labour and National Service signified a much more determined mood to bring the trade unions fully into the mobilization for total war against Hitler.

To Bevin the conflict provided the supreme test for the British manual working class: 'I have to ask you virtually to place yourself at the disposal of the state', he told the assembled TUC affiliated union executives in Central Hall, Westminster on 25 May 1940, at the perilous moment of the British army's evacuation from the beaches of Dunkirk. And he went on: 'If our Movement and our class rise with all their energy now and save the people of this country from disaster, the country will always turn with confidence to the people who saved them'.[2]

In their officially authorized study of the government's post-war reconstruction plans, Gowing and Hancock wrote about the existence of what they called 'an implied contract between the Government and the people'. As they explained: 'The people refused none of the sacrifices that the Government demanded from them for the winning of the war – in return they expected that the Government should show imagination and seriousness in preparing for the restoration and improvement of the nation's well-being when the war had been won.'[3] 'The critical moment in the forging of this new 'social contract' was not 1945 but 1940. The major readjustment resulted not from a shift in the electoral balance of power but from a shift in the balance of economic power', explained Professor Samuel Beer.[4]

This is not the place to examine in great detail the Worker's War and the innumerable ways in which the influence of the TUC and its affiliated unions at all levels grew between May 1940 and July 1945, but the close relationship of that time was of vital importance to the post-war understanding between governments and trade unions that lasted until the mid-1950s. Union leaders sat on the Joint Consultative Committee chaired by Bevin which was the executive arm of the state for manpower mobilization and employment planning, as well as on the National Production Advisory Committee. Trade union expertise was also vital in the development of joint consultation machinery that was established on the shop floor and in the regions, especially in the joint production committees in the armaments industry. As MacDonald asserted, 'There was hardly a facet of the war effort with which the unions were not directly associated'.[5]

Citrine was keen to establish what he described as a 'watchful though cordial collaboration' between the TUC and Churchill's government. Certainly, the pages of Congress's annual reports for the war years reveal a widening network of power and influence that the TUC was able to construct in its cooperation with the state. Just how much real influence trade union leaders at any level actually achieved over the government's decision-making remains difficult to assess but there was no doubting their determination to exercise a strong voice. John Price, head of the

TGWU's political department, wrote in a Penguin Special in 1940 on the role of the trade unions in the war:

> Organised labour will henceforth be satisfied with nothing less than full partnership in the state. The war has brought out more clearly than ever before the country's dependence upon the mass of working people. At a critical moment the call for that assistance went forth. By helping to save the country they will find their own salvation too.[6]

For his part, Bevin was keen to avoid as far as possible any resort to coercive methods to maximize the war economy. Although an authoritarian figure in his own union, he refused to believe it was necessary to resort to compulsion to encourage workers to work hard for victory. Instead, he appealed to their patriotic sense of duty as well as their common sense and reasonableness. He disliked having to use methods of state coercion in manpower planning and mobilization. In his opinion it was far better to gain the active consent of trade unions and workers in order to increase production and accept necessary changes, like skill dilution and the removal of demarcation lines, to limit restrictive labour practices, as well as the employment of women. In his speech to the 1943 Congress, Bevin contrasted the British and Nazi methods of mobilizing for the war effort. He explained:

> Their manpower problem is dealt with by the overriding power of fear, concentration camps, the knout, the gun, mass murder, the denial of self-government in industry. As soon as I took office I realised that that policy had to be matched and I proceeded to match it with the institutions which we had developed in this country, including the use of that magnificent joint relation machinery which had been built up so patiently over so many years.[7]

Bevin claimed that British workers had produced 'both in fighting and working a far greater result by the maintenance of these great unions and cooperative movements than any nation can accomplish by their destruction'. He hoped, he added to some laughter from his audience, that British labour would 'emerge stronger and more virile out of the war with a willingness to accept greater and greater responsibilities and if I may say so at times impose a little more discipline'.

In fact, the undoubted extension of trade union power and influence during the war strengthened rather than weakened union leaders' instinctive and traditional conviction in the merits of the voluntarist industrial relations system. Despite enormous Treasury pressure – at its most intensive during the early months of 1941 – Bevin successfully resisted official attempts to either abolish or suspend collective bargaining for the duration of the war. 'With a little less democracy and a little more trust', the Minister of Labour was keen to maintain 'intact the peace-time arrangements, merely adapting them to suit extraordinary circumstances'.[8]

It is true that under wartime conditions voluntarism in some areas was drastically modified by legal regulation. The Emergency Powers Act passed in the critical days of late May 1940 gave the Minister of Labour the theoretical power to order anybody to do what he might require, but Bevin was reluctant to use his powers of compulsory labour direction. He was also able to issue Essential Work Orders which required factories to engage in essential national work for the war effort. Women were mobilized in the labour market and demarcation lines suspended. Albert Speer, Hitler's Minister of Armaments, later recorded in his autobiography that Britain put its domestic economy on a total war footing much more effectively than Germany was able to do with its dependence on slave labour and unwillingness to bring women into productive employment.

Inevitably this meant important erosions of the voluntarist principle. The state also acquired legal powers to outlaw industrial disputes. Order No. 1305, issued in July 1940 by the government under Defence Regulation 58A, made all strikes illegal. If trade unions and employers were unable to settle their differences, they were compelled under the Order to refer them with 21 days' notice to the Minister of Labour who would seek to either settle the threatened dispute himself or call upon the newly formed National Arbitration Tribunal to resolve potential conflict through the imposition of compulsory arbitration awards. Strikes or lock-outs taken in defiance of such an award or in breach of the 21 days' notice were outlawed. But these potentially draconian adjustments to collective bargaining, taken under the pressure of events, fell short of the direct statutory control of wages that many in the Treasury would have liked to impose on the labour market. Moreover, Bevin was extremely reluctant to make use of Order No. 1305 against unofficial strikers if he could avoid having to do so. Certainly, its deterrent effect seems to have proved to be much stronger than its actual application against recalcitrant workers. Only 109 workers and two employers were prosecuted under its provisions throughout the entire duration of the war. Faced by an outburst of unofficial strikes in the coal industry in April 1944, the government did rush through Defence Regulation 1 AA by an Order in Council, with its draconian sentence of five years maximum jail sentence and large fines of up to £500 against workers who struck, or who instigated or fomented trouble in an essential industry. At the same time, picketing was also outlawed. But the measures were never used by the government, although the number of unofficial stoppages rose dramatically in 1944 and 1945.

Despite all the difficulties and setbacks in the early part of the war, Britain's unions continued to operate with relative freedom. Indeed, the turn of the tide after Germany's defeat at El Alamein in November 1942 appeared to vindicate Bevin's wisdom in so stoutly defending the autonomy of organized labour through the exigencies of war. This is not to ignore or play down the inflationary wage pressures that hit the British war economy. The introduction of food subsidies in the 1941 Budget helped to keep cost of living increases down to only 31 per cent between September 1939 and September 1945, while the average wage rate rise was 43 per cent over the same period, due mainly to the long hours worked and the extra money acquired through the introduction of payment-by-results systems in the war industries. 'On balance the decision of the Government not to introduce direct control of wages appears to have been right', concluded Barnes and Reid. 'Wage controls might well have been impossible to enforce and – if enforced for a period – might have ultimately been rejected with disastrous inflationary consequences and serious industrial unrest'.[9]

But by the end of 1943 a national debate had begun on what kind of policy government should adopt towards collective bargaining after the war in the hoped-for conditions of full employment. It was Sir William Beveridge – fresh from the triumph of his social insurance report – who raised the issue in an important discussion he held with the TUC's economic committee on 10 November 1943. On that occasion he questioned union leaders on whether it was 'inevitable' that there would be a 'rising spiral of wages and prices leading to inflation' in conditions of full employment.[10] In its 1944 interim reconstruction report, the TUC tried to reassure Beveridge and others that there would be no problem. It insisted that 'in all circumstances trade unions should retain their personal freedom from legal restraints upon their right to frame policy and pursue activities in support of that policy and should even be given greater legal freedom in those respects than they now possess.' But the TUC stressed that formal trade union freedom was of less importance than the 'use' to which unions put their freedom in contributing to the existence of full employment. As the document explained,

> It is clear to us that no Government can guarantee full employment unless they can be assured that the steps they are taking or propose to take, will not be rendered ineffective by the failure of the quite legitimate but powerful interests, including the trade union movement, to make their actions conform to the achievement of that objective.[11]

The TUC insisted in 1944 that the trade union movement 'would not be found unwilling, where it is shown to be necessary, to adapt its policies and its practices to the means of achieving full employment'. In short, the TUC argued it was by no means inevitable that there would be the 'rising spiral of wages and prices leading to inflation' in conditions of full employment that Beveridge had feared if the government could

> convince the Movement that in genuine pursuit of a policy of full employment it was determined to take all other steps necessary to control prices and could convince the trade union movement of the need to secure equivalent guarantees that wage movements would not be such as to upset the system of price control. It would be the duty of the trade union movement to give suitable guarantees about wage settlements and reasonable assurances that such guarantees should be generally observed.

The TUC added, however, that this did not mean that it would 'in any circumstances invite the state to impose a system of compulsory arbitration in wage disputes or make it a criminal offence on the part of workmen to refuse to accept the terms and conditions of a wage settlement'. Compliance should be left for the trade unions themselves to acquire over their own members without any need to resort to outside interference by the state or any public agencies.

There was no doubting the TUC's sincerity in 1944 in its expressed willingness to respond positively to a peacetime government that achieved and maintained full employment with its own self-regulation to prevent a resurgence of inflationary wage-push pressures. After all, under war conditions, workers' earnings had not risen to intolerable heights in the absence of state controls. But the TUC's response to Beveridge also indicated that the trade unions were as determined as ever to defend their own autonomy and not give up authority over their own activities to anybody else under external pressure. The experience of the Second World War helped to convince the British trade union movement that the voluntarist system of industrial relations was near to perfection. The TUC's desire to play a much more influential and permanent role in the management of the economy was coupled with a clear determination to uphold the existing forms of collective bargaining that had survived the Nazi threat. In the victorious summer of 1945 such a trade union attitude was by no means as complacent as it sounded.

However, Beveridge was unconvinced by the TUC's response to his questions about the dangers of wage-push inflation to its economic committee. In his view the trade union commitment to unfettered collective bargaining under conditions of full employment would inflict severe inflationary damage on the economy, partly because of the competitive structure of British trade unionism. As he explained insightfully in his book, *Full Employment in a Free Society*, published in the autumn of 1944:

> Particular wage demands which exceed what employers are able to pay with their existing prices and which force a raising of prices, may bring gains to the workers of the industry concerned, but they will do so at the expense of all other workers, whose real wages fall owing to the rise in prices. The other workers will naturally try to restore the position, by putting forward demands of their own. There is a real danger that sectional wage bargaining, pursued without regard to its effects upon prices, may lead to a vicious spiral of inflation, with money wages chasing prices and without any gain in real wages for the working class as a whole.[12]

Beveridge argued that there was 'no inherent mechanism' in the bargaining system that could 'with certainty prevent competitive sectional bargaining for wages' leading to inflation under full employment. He suggested two ways of dealing with the problem. One was for the TUC itself to coordinate the pay bargaining of its affiliated trade unions. 'Organised labour in Britain has sufficiently demonstrated its sense of citizenship and responsibility to justify the expectation that it will evolve, in its own manner, the machinery by which a better coordinated wage policy can be carried through', he asserted. Beveridge's alternative solution was voluntary arbitration so that wages could be determined by 'reason, in the light of all the facts and with regard to general equities and not simply by the bargaining power of particular groups of men'. Unions and employers would accept in advance in their collective agreements that they would honour such arbitration and not resort to strikes or lock-outs to thwart it. Beveridge did not want to see the state used to coerce both sides of industry into responsible wage bargaining in the national interest. He accepted 'primary responsibility' for preventing full employment leading to wage-push inflation rested with the union bargainers. But he also argued that the state could help by ensuring price stability through controls and subsidies, and that employers could assist by revealing their financial position so that reason could prevail.

In fact, by the last stages of the war a national consensus had emerged that in peacetime the state should strive to prevent any return to the kind of mass unemployment that had scarred so much of the inter-war period. The 1944 White Paper on Employment Policy made it clear in the bold first sentence of its foreword that governments accepted 'as one of their primary aims and responsibilities the maintenance of a high and stable level of employment after the war'. 'Government policy will be directed to bringing about conditions favourable to the maintenance of a high level of employment', it asserted while adding that jobs could not 'be created by Act of Parliament or by Government action alone'. Stability of prices and wages was one of the essential prerequisites for achieving success with a dynamic manpower policy. 'It will be essential that employers and workers should exercise moderation in wages matters so that increased expenditure provided at the onset of a depression may go to increase the volume of employment', it added.[13] The White Paper said this did not mean 'every wage rate must remain fixed at a particular level', for there had to be room for flexibility and the removal of pay anomalies within and between industries. But it warned 'the principle of stability' did mean 'increases in the general level of wage rates must be related to increased productivity due to increased efficiency and effort'. The government believed this could only be achieved by joint efforts between the state, employers and unions. The White Paper suggested the government would do what it could to stabilize prices but it was also the 'duty of both sides of industry to consider together all possible means of preventing a rise in the costs of production or distribution and so avoid the rise in prices which is the initial step in the inflationary process'.

There was no question of any direct state interference in the industrial relations system to prevent inflation in a tight labour market. Ministers accepted it would need moral exhortation, appeals to reason and responsibility and to the shared values of the country to ensure restrained pay bargaining in the national interest. Compulsion was out of the question.

Yet Beveridge was right to worry that the structure of the British trade union movement would exacerbate the dangers of wage-push inflation in conditions of full employment. These concerns stemmed from a tradition of insecurity in a harsh, unregulated labour market. The resolute determination of workgroups and craft unions to defend restrictive practices like limited entry into skilled trades and demarcation lines between particular jobs stemmed from an understandable reaction to the fear of the dole queue. A state commitment to full employment could only succeed if those sectionalist shopfloor attitudes of mind were eradicated.

But such a necessary change would require a radical reform of trade unions. Unfortunately, in 1944 the TUC was in no mood to carry out any internal reforms of a fundamental nature to modernize trade union structures and organization. Organized labour was growing dramatically without any apparent need to adapt. The war years witnessed a strong upsurge in trade union membership from 6,298,000 in 1939 to 8,087,000 in 1944, 38.6 per cent of the workforce. Yet union leaders seemed timid and highly conservative in their response to the possibility of structural adjustment. In 1944 the TUC's interim report on trade union structure and closer unity amounted to little more than a virtual repetition of its 1927 inquiry into the same subject which had concluded little could be done. The document recognized that the 'prestige and efficient working' of the trade union movement was impaired 'by the overlapping and competition' caused by inter-union conflict.[14] In 1944 there were as many as 781 registered trade unions in Britain of which 190 belonged to the TUC. As the report argued, the existence of so many unions was 'confusing and irritating and the reason for it is even beyond the comprehension of many members and most non-unionists'. But the TUC accepted it lacked any centralizing powers to do anything that would rationalize trade union structures. 'It is not always recognised that the TUC cannot compel its affiliated unions to make substantial changes in their organisation', confessed the 1944 report. 'Each union is autonomous and is at liberty to accept or reject the advice of the TUC general council as it may feel disposed.' 'In the absence of power to enforce structural changes', the TUC accepted it was pointless to draw up blueprints for reform like the creation of single industry-based unions, which stood no chance at all of being accepted by the large general manual unions like the TGWU and the GMWU that dominated the TUC. All that could be hoped for was a greater coordination between trade unions through the development of joint advisory committees and industry-based federations that could bring unions closer together in the same industry. This was hardly a clarion call for action in a post-war world where the TUC expected to exercise considerable power and influence over the making of government policy.

The TUC's document on post-war industrial reconstruction was not particularly radical either. Many of its proposals were drawn from earlier TUC decisions made in the early 1930s. The TUC favoured establishing 'some measure of public control over industry and trade'.[15] Indeed, the TUC asserted that a 'controlled economic system' was a 'modern necessity in advanced industrial communities'. It favoured the nationalization of a range of industries including coal, gas, electricity, the railways, civil aviation, road transport, iron and steel and 'ultimately' the cotton industry. The TUC also wanted a wide range of state controls which would enable the government to control the supply and availability of cash and credit, the supply of capital for investment, foreign trade, the location of industry, as well as prices and monopolies. The document went on to propose the creation of tripartite Industrial Boards responsible for the internal regulation of each industry including general planning, standardization, research and marketing. The TUC repeated its 1932 demand for the creation of a National Industrial Council made up of union leaders, employers and others with the aim of providing the government with 'detailed industrial experience upon which to draw in the formulation of policy'. In its views on finance the TUC repeated its call of 1930 for the creation of a National Investment Board to stimulate industrial restructuring as well as state control of joint stock banks, public control of the money supply, and the maintenance of price stability.

The corporatist system envisaged by the TUC in 1944 would have given the state enormous powers of control and intervention in industry and finance. But in the same document the TUC re-emphasized its continuing commitment to voluntarism, on keeping the state at arm's length when it came to collective bargaining and industrial relations practices. The 1944 report rejected any schemes for direct worker participation or co-determination in nationalized enterprises. The TUC was anxious to ensure that trade unions 'maintained their complete independence' in the state industry sector by insisting they should play no part in company decision-making. The proposed public corporations would be accountable to Parliament through government departments, not to their employees or the trade unions. However, the TUC did favour recommending names of suitable candidates to sit on nationalized industry boards as a way of ensuring the views of the industry's own workers received full consideration. But the TUC was determined to keep separate the managerial and trade union functions in a state-owned enterprise. On the other hand, it acknowledged the value of the joint production committees and works councils created in industry between 1940 and 1944, and it wanted to retain them as 'a permanent feature of our industrial organisation'. The TUC was also enthusiastic about the spread of joint consultation machinery in industry as long as this was not ensnared in collective bargaining which the trade unions insisted must remain free and unfettered.

It is surprising, however, just what little new thought was contained in the TUC's 1943/44 reconstruction programme. Its content was made up of a ritualistic defence of union autonomy and self-regulation coupled with a highly statist view of how Britain's post-war economy should develop.

In the late 1940s the TUC was to play an important part in the revival of free trade unionism in the western part of occupied Germany. The establishment of the *Deutsche Gewerkschaftsbund* (DGB) in 1949 and the creation of single industry-based trade unions in West Germany owed much to the British influence, even if works councils and the concept of co-determination in industry derived mainly from the German Labour Movement's own traditions. Unfortunately for the British unions, there was no *tabula rasa* in their country on which to construct a more effective, streamlined and stronger trade union organization. As the TUC's 1944 report confessed:

> It is one thing to plan an entirely new structure on unoccupied ground; it is another to plan and rebuild where so many institutions already exist. Examination has always led to the same result viz that basic structural changes are impracticable and that the best that can be done is to adapt the trade union movement so as to meet the new requirements of modern times.[16]

In fact, the reality of workplace life during the war years suggested it would have been difficult to stimulate the kind of reforms needed to establish the British trade union movement as a radical and effective voice of organized labour. Behind the potent myth of Bevin's patriotic working class lay a familiar picture. Correlli Barnett in his *Audit of War* (1986) pointed to the stubborn resistance on the shop floor to the lifting of restrictive labour practices, and to the rigidity of demarcation lines between workers, the jealously guarded sectionalism in the face of pressure for skill dilution, and above all the tenacity of the 'them' and 'us' class war mentality. In contrast to Bevin's working class saviours of the nation, Barnett drew attention to the inadequacies of the industrial response to conditions of total war: 'In the high technology industries as in the old Victorian staples the war, with its soothing drug of lavish but only partly earned wages and secure jobs, served as the midwife of the bogus full employment and the notorious low productivity of the postwar era'.[17] Barnett believed the main reason for the resilience of such negative shopfloor attitudes lay in 'that deep reservoir of resentment and hostility which impelled the workforce to take as much as it could while giving as little as it could get away with'. This lamentable attitude of mind apparently persisted in vital war industries like shipbuilding and aeroplane production throughout the conflict, despite the passage of the 1940 Restoration of Pre-War Trade Practices Act with its firm promises that the craft unions would regain their lost privileges on the shop floor once the war was won.

However, in the heady days of 1945 such observations would have seemed churlish and irrelevant. To most of the British people the country's trade unions had become cherished national institutions. Certainly, there was no fear of the power of organized labour in the ruling Establishment as there had been during the period of Lloyd George's peacetime coalition government from 1918 to 1922. A broad social consensus insisted there must be no return to the bad old days of the inter-war years with its dole queues and means tests even if that was only a partial view of the realities of 1930s Britain. After the People's War would come the People's Peace with a firm commitment to social justice, full employment and a dynamic role for government in the management of the economy. The trade unions were widely regarded as an integral part of that emerging national settlement, underlined by the Labour party's landslide general election victory in July 1945. But as Kenneth Morgan wrote, the war left Britain with 'an ambivalent legacy' which contained elements of unity and division.[18] This was true certainly for organized labour. At the national level, Bevin and Citrine had brought the trade unions and the TUC a long way forward into a semi-corporatist role even if the reality never measured up to the ideal. As partners in the running of the war on the Home Front, the trade unions were no longer insecure outsiders in a class society dominated by the power of capital. But the very success of the war effort had reinforced negative, complacent tendencies inside the trade unions. As Attlee and his Cabinet colleagues met for the first time to assess the unhappy legacy of a victorious but exhausted and economically shattered nation, they might have expected their trade union allies to recognize they must now shoulder wider responsibilities for the common good. Yet beneath the social patriotism and the mixture of mutual regard and ideological conviction that dominated the Labour Movement in the summer of 1945 lay what was to become an increasingly decentralized, fragmented shop floor that would not respond without question to the demands of the national interest. It was the resulting tension between the economic demands made on organized labour by successive post-war British governments up to 1979 and the parochial but nonetheless potent force of an increasing atomized and deregulated labour market, that brought the so-called trade union 'problem' to the forefront of the political agenda after 1945.

Notes

1 D. Barnes and E. Reid, 'A New Relationship: Trade unions in the Second World War', in C. Cook and B. Pimlott (eds), *Trade Unions in British Politics*, Longmans, 1991 edition, p. 152.

2 A. Bullock, *The Life and Times of Ernest Bevin*, Vol. 2, Heinemann, 1967, p. 20.

3 M. Gowing and K. Hancock, *The British War Economy*, HMSO, 1949, p. 541.

4 S. Beer, *Modern British Politics*, Faber & Faber, 1965, p. 215.

5 D. F. MacDonald, *The State and the Trade Unions*, Macmillan, 1976, p. 125.

6 J. Price, *Labour in the War*, Penguin, 1940, p. 173.

7   TUC Congress report, 1940, p. 233.
8   TUC Congress report, 1943, p. 154.
9   D. Barnes and E. Reid, 'A New Relationship', p. 147.
10 Ibid., p. 159.
11 TUC Congress report, 1944, p. 195.
12 W. H. Beveridge, *Full Employment in a Free Society*, Allen & Unwin, 1944, pp. 199–201.
13 *Employment Policy*, Cmd. 6527, HMSO, May 1944, pp. 1, 18–19.
14 TUC Congress report, 1944, pp. 420–1.
15 Ibid., pp. 348–50.
16 Ibid., pp. 398–410.
17 C. Barnett, *The Audit of War*, Macmillan, 1986, p. 156.
18 K. Morgan, *The People's Peace*, Oxford University Press, 1992, pp. 10–11.

2 Labour and the Honourable Alliance, July 1945 to October 1951

War heroes

Britain's trade unions emerged from the Second World War as a recognized and accepted Estate of the Realm. 'The strength of Britain has been that of free men and women, working as they have never worked before and willingly accepting the restraints which were necessary to win the war. This Trades Union Congress of 1945 takes its place among the victory parades of the Forces of the United Nations', declared the recently elected Labour Prime Minister Clement Attlee to exultant delegates in Blackpool.[1]

This was also Churchill's opinion. When still Prime Minister, he was asked in the House of Commons about the 'exact status' held by the TUC delegation which went to San Francisco for the United Nations founding conference in May 1945. While he acknowledged that the union leaders on the trip enjoyed 'no official' position at the conference, Churchill assured MPs that the government would 'take advantage' of their presence 'to consult them as and when necessary on labour matters'. And he added for good measure: 'We have all got along pretty well together in this hard war; we owe an immense debt to the trade unions and never can this country forget how they have stood by and helped.'[2]

Indeed, the period between May 1940 and August 1945 had seen the arrival of organized labour as an important force in British public life. 'Without the co-operation of the trade unions the war effort of the British people could have been neither so sustained nor so intense', wrote John Price from the TGWU in a pamphlet for the Ministry of Information at the end of the war.[3]

'We have passed from the era of propaganda to one of responsibility', claimed Sir Walter Citrine at the 1946 Congress, in his valedictory speech on departing after twenty years as the TUC's General Secretary. He spoke of the 'revolution' which had taken place in Britain with a widespread recognition that workers had 'a right to participation and consultation in the conduct of industry and the public services'.[4] Citrine's avowed aim of transforming the TUC into a necessary partner in the management of the economy seemed nearer to achievement in the immediate aftermath of 1945 than ever before. 'In Britain today the trade unions are regarded as competent to take part in the affairs of industry and the state', asserted Price. 'They began as organisations on the defensive, fighting for the narrow interests of a limited class. They have grown into a constructive force, helping to shape the country's destiny and working for the welfare of the whole community'.[5]

The positive change in the TUC's status in its relations with the state was graphically described by *The Times*'s labour correspondent J. V. Radcliffe at the 1945 Congress. He told the delegates:

> How very far away are those days when a few top-hatted frock-coated gentlemen made a promenade of government offices in Whitehall respectfully carrying resolutions passed by Congress, leaving them at the door, extremely happy if they saw a permanent secretary and most handsomely flattered if by accident they stumbled across a Minister. I cannot imagine that in these days you yourselves or Sir Walter Citrine will be content to stand on anyone's doorstep. The only place I can think of in which Sir Walter Citrine would defer to authority is Transport House [then TUC headquarters] and at Transport House he exercises the authority himself. The days of your humiliation are gone but not the days of your power. You do not now go to 10 Downing Street but 10 Downing Street comes to you. The Minister of Labour and National Service also came to unburden his soul to you on the problems which afflict him as well as you. Even the military authorities on the Continent invite you to tell them how to do things which are beyond their comprehension and their knowledge. You have no longer any need to thunder; you have only to whisper and Ministers tremble and Field-Marshals bend their knees.[6]

Such claims were a considerable exaggeration but there was no doubting the TUC's self-confident mood in the autumn of 1945. Citrine and his colleagues on the TUC general council had a heightened awareness of their own importance after their close cooperation with the coalition government through the war, and they expected as of right and without question to play an important role in the peacetime reconstruction. The TUC complained about the way in which the trade unions were being ignored in the preparation of the first draft of Labour's general election manifesto. It was suggested a number of reforms should be promised – notably the introduction of a 40 hour working week, two weeks' holiday with pay and the introduction of a legally guaranteed working week. The omission was quickly remedied by a Labour leadership keen to placate the TUC.

A strong harmony of interest and outlook existed between the political and industrial wings of the Labour Movement in 1945. The 'contentious alliance' had never seemed more at ease with itself. It is true that Attlee was keen to insist that the Labour government must govern the country unbeholden to the TUC or any other interest group, but he was never openly hostile to the trade unions in the way in which Labour's inter-war prime minister Ramsay MacDonald had often been. In his 1937 study *The Labour Party in Perspective*, Attlee had written with shrewdness about the role of the trade unions in politics. In his view, an obvious dualism existed in union practice. On the one hand, unions worked within 'the framework of capitalist society' in order to defend their members' interests as wage-earners from injustice and to gain better material rewards from employers, but on the other the unions were 'an opposition to the existing system of society' which they sought to change.[7] Attlee acknowledged that a trade union could 'not subordinate the immediate interests of its members entirely to the attainment of its ultimate aims or for purely political ends'. Yet he also believed a trade union could 'not sacrifice its ideals for society as a whole in order to obtain some transient advantages for a section of its membership or even its entire membership'. The answer to this genuine conundrum lay through achieving a 'balance' between the two aspirations. As Attlee explained:

> It is useless and harmless to look at the trade unions purely as a revolution-ary force to be subservient to the demands of the political leaders. It is equally dangerous for the trade unions to regard the politicians merely as an agency for obtaining particular advantages for organised labour.

More than most Labour politicians of his generation, the party's leader recognized the practical and narrow limitations that made it difficult for trade union leaders to deliver their side of any political bargain. He was also conscious of the position that the trade unions held inside the party. Attlee described them as 'the backbone of the movement' but he also insisted the party 'represented something more than the needs of organised labour'. This meant that while Labour needed to support the 'demands' of the trade unions it also had to 'have due regard to the interests of all sections of the workers and of the nation as a whole'. After all, he maintained the party was 'the partner not the servant' of the TUC. 'The party had no right to expect the TUC to do its work for it or to take the burden of decisions which it ought to bear itself.'[8]

The TUC–Labour alliance before 1945

'It was not Keir Hardie who formed this party, it grew out of the bowels of the Trades Union Congress.'[9] Bevin chose to use such crude imagery during his scalding speech against Labour leader George Lansbury at the party's 1935 conference. Many constituency party delegates disliked what he said but he was merely asserting a self-evident if usually unmentioned truth. Without the organizational and financial support provided by the trade unions, the Labour party would have remained little more than a sect or pressure group on the fringes of British politics. It was a resolution moved by the Amalgamated Society of Railway Servants at the 1899 Congress that led to the famous meeting at the Memorial Hall in London's Faringdon Street in February 1900. Here was formed the Labour Representation Committee (LRC) with its stated aim of electing independent Labour candidates to Parliament. Only after the Taff Vale judgement in 1901 with its clear threat to the security of trade union immunities did a large number of unions affiliate to the LRC. The vital role of the trade unions in the Labour party before the First World War was underlined by the consequences of the Osborne judgement in 1909 which outlawed the political levy. As a result, there was a steady decline in affiliated membership to the party which imperilled Labour's future. The passage of the 1913 Trade Union Act revived the party, though the subsequent union ballots over establishing political funds revealed a sizeable minority of rank and file trade unionists who remained hostile to the idea of supporting Labour representation.

In 1918 Labour acquired a new constitution and the party moved into joint headquarters with the TUC. Two years later under the direction of the party's chairman Arthur Henderson the industrial and political wings of the Labour Movement came to share research facilities. In the early 1920s the Labour party was still very much an ill-formed alliance between trade unions, Socialist intellectuals and an increasing number of former Liberals, held together by a vague commitment to Socialism. But it was the trade unions who remained vital to the party's existence. In his 1929 study of the Labour Movement, the German Social Democrat journalist Egon Wertheimer emphasized the crucial importance the trade unions still enjoyed inside the party. He pointed out that the party's 'fluctuations

in strength and organisation had always been dependent upon the
fluctuations in trade union membership and to all intents and purposes
on that alone'.[10] Wertheimer pointed out that the trade unions met 90 per
cent of Labour's administrative expenses through its affiliation fees and
paid directly for a third of Labour candidates in parliamentary general
elections.

It was the 'collective allegiance' of the trade unions that gave the
Labour party its particular ethos. 'The trade union connection brought
both strength and weakness to Labour's claim to be a national challenger
for power', argued Kenneth Morgan. 'It provided financial security through
the political levy. It provided of course a solid foundation of identification
with the mass proletariat.' During its formative years the Labour party
continued to give the impression that it was not much more than 'a
defensive pressure group designed simply to fight for the living standards of the working class' rather than being 'a dynamic party anxious
to capture power and to reach out to all classes and sections of the
community'.[11]

But then Labour was never to be a mass party based solely on an
individual membership like other social democratic parties in continental
Europe. Structurally it remained a federation of diverse interests, with
the trade unions in the dominant position if they wished to exercise their
power. As Ross McKibbin wrote, 'Union predominance was felt at all
levels. . . . For the most part, the unions and their officials made up the
deficiency of individual members. They provided the volunteer workers,
the local party officers and the money.'[12]

The importance of the trade union link for the Labour party was
emphasized in the August 1931 crisis when Labour Prime Minister Ramsay
MacDonald was confronted by the TUC's implacable opposition to his
government's austerity proposals which involved substantial cuts in the
size of the unemployment insurance fund. 'The TUC undoubtedly voice
the feelings of the mass of workers,' noted MacDonald in his diary. 'They
do not know and their minds are rigid and think of superficial appearances
and so grasping at the shadow lose the bone.'[13] In his view, if the Labour
Cabinet had bowed to the pressure being exerted by Bevin and Citrine
not to cut the size of the unemployment insurance fund they would
'never be able to call our bodies our own'.[14] To MacDonald, the national
interest as defined by the government must come before any sectionalist
concerns from a trade union dominated party. The majority of the Cabinet
– led by Foreign Secretary Arthur Henderson – disagreed with him, but
only after the TUC had made clear its total opposition to the Treasury's
proposed economy measures. The events of the summer of 1931, which

culminated in Labour's catastrophic election defeat and the loss of its senior leaders (MacDonald, Philip Snowden, Jimmy Thomas) to an all-party National government, left deep wounds inside the Labour Movement that continued to colour attitudes well into the 1970s.

As a result of the 'great betrayal' the trade unions played a much more important and direct role inside the Labour party during the 1930s than they had done in the previous decade. The National Joint Council (NJC) – first created by Henderson in 1921 and renamed the National Council of Labour in 1934 – became a crucial forum for discussions between the industrial and political wings where Bevin and Citrine took a prominent part in the shaping of domestic policy and in the emerging campaign against the menace of Fascism abroad. The TUC General Secretary told the November 1931 meeting of the NJC that while the TUC 'did not seek in any shape or form to say what the party was to do, they did ask that the primary purpose of the creation of the party should not be forgotten. It was created by the trade union movement to do those things in Parliament which the trade union movement found ineffectively performed by the two-party system.'[15]

In December 1931 the TUC secured seven seats on the revamped NJC, with the parliamentary Labour party and the National Executive Committee only receiving three each. In the aftermath of the 1931 debacle it looked as though the trade unions intended to take over the direction of the party both tactically and strategically. In 1933 the Labour conference passed a resolution that insisted no future party leader could form a government after an election victory until he sought the NJC's advice on what to do. It also proposed that a Labour government would appoint a Cabinet minister to attend TUC general council meetings 'in a consultative capacity'.[16] But despite this, the NJC's power was exaggerated. Attlee insisted in 1937 that the work of the NJC was 'essentially co-ordinating and not mandatory'. 'It is not a super-authority with the right to enforce its decisions on its constituent bodies', he pointed out. 'The most it can do is recommend. The industrial and the political sides keep each other informed of their respective activities but there is no intrusion into one another's spheres.'[17] As Ben Pimlott has pointed out: 'The main function of the National Joint Council was to give weight to party pronouncements by demonstrating that the Movement spoke with a united voice. It was never out of step with the majority view on the NEC.'[18] This was not really so apparent during the early 1930s when the party went through a left-wing phase in which it argued for the end of capitalism and showed little interest in the practicalities of reform. Tensions between the party and the TUC ran high on occasions. But then from the mid-1930s onwards, the party shook off its post-1931 extremism. With cautious and practical men like Attlee, Morrison and Dalton in charge there was no real need for Bevin and Citrine to intervene from a trade union point of view into the actual details of policy-making.

Indeed, the evolution of the party's domestic agenda in 1937 as formulated in Labour's 'Immediate Programme' raised no difficulties for the TUC, as it was clear that the party now accepted the TUC's general outlook on economic and industrial questions. The policy document proposed the introduction of paid holidays and the 40 hour working week, which were both key TUC demands. The only potential issue for division between the political and industrial wings of the Movement concerned the role of workers in newly nationalized industries. But the party policy-makers agreed with the TUC that the concept of the public corporation ruled out any notion of industrial democracy or workers control of industry that might breach trade union autonomy in collective bargaining. Bevin may have disliked Morrison intensely for personal reasons but the two men shared similar views on what organizational form state-run industries should take under Labour, once Morrison had conceded in 1933 that organized labour should have some form of representation on nationalized industry boards. Moreover, there was a general tacit agreement that a future Labour government would not seek to question the voluntarist system of industrial relations.

It is true that some of Labour's younger economists, notably Hugh Gaitskell, Evan Durbin, Douglas Jay and Barbara Wootton raised awkward questions about the economic role of the trade unions under a Labour government pledged to planning and socialization of the economy. They believed that the sectionalist self-interest of the trade unions could endanger Socialist planning by creating wage-push inflation in a tight labour market. But they failed to make any impact on mainstream party thought before the war on the sensitive question of wages policy. There was a fairly close cooperation at the top on economic policy-making. Dalton and Morrison sat as Labour party representatives on the TUC's economic committee during the 1930s.

In fact, the balance of influence inside the Labour Movement by the late 1930s was weighted firmly towards the trade union presence, not least because of the effective manner in which Bevin and Citrine developed a coherent TUC strategy. The vociferous left in the party may have disliked it but there seems little doubt that the trade unions provided Labour with a strong dose of realism, particularly on foreign policy questions. Many constituency party activists at the time favoured both unilateral disarmament and opposition to Fascism, a view which found little sympathy among potential working class Labour voters. It was Bevin who gave fierce voice to a patriotic Labourism that flourished in the People's War after May 1940 and that led on to the great 1945 general election victory.

Not all in the party were concerned about the trade union presence just because it was hostile to Socialist fundamentalism. The Labour intellectual G. D. H. Cole wrote in 1937 that he thought the trade union influence had grown markedly during the decade and this was going to hurt the party's electoral appeal. 'The trade unions have always had the power when they have chosen to exercise it, to call the tune to which the party must dance', he argued. 'But until quite lately their mass power was very rarely used'.[19] Now Cole claimed that the TUC under the influence of Bevin and Citrine had been 'transformed into a positive instrument of policy making' so that the annual Congress had become

> largely a political assembly which meeting only a few weeks before the Labour party conference could define the trade union point of view and marshal the trade union battalions behind the official policy. That done, the decisions made at the TUC could be re-registered at the party conference with the aid of the massed trade union vote.

Cole believed this development raised serious questions about Labour's electoral viability. He pointed out that in order to win, the party would have to make gains in industrial areas where trade unionism was weak like the West Midlands – the stronghold of Chamberlainite Unionism – as well as make organizational inroads into the ranks of the white-collar salariat and the manual workers in the new industries of southern England. If the party failed to widen its popular appeal and was seen by voters merely as a mouthpiece of the trade unions, it would fail to win a general election, argued Cole. But the alleged trade union dominance of the Labour party during the 1930s was over-stated. The key policy-making body was really the NEC's Policy sub-committee, established in November 1931, and this was influenced most of all by two senior party figures – Herbert Morrison and Hugh Dalton. It is true Bevin's public excoriation of George Lansbury at the 1935 party conference which led to Lansbury's resignation as party leader highlighted the brutal power trade union bosses could wield when they chose to do so, but for the most part they preferred to avoid any suggestion that they dominated the party with their block votes. Although the trade unions had direct control of the NEC itself until 1937, through the election of its entire membership by block vote, they did not pack the NEC with first-rank union leaders. Instead, only the second tier of union officials were nominated for NEC places in what was a tacit admission by the trade unions that they did not want to maximize their strength inside the party.

In 1937 the constituency activists achieved a surprising success when they won enough support among many trade unions to push through important constitutional changes at party conference that gave them their own slate of separate constituency section representatives on the NEC to be elected by them alone. That important reform did not make any dramatic impact on the power balance inside the party until the early 1950s when Bevanism was in the ascendant but it was a clear sign that the trade unions as a whole did not want to overwhelm the party's supreme body. As Richard Shackleton concluded in his study of Labour and the trade unions in the 1930s, 'By 1938 the union leaders were taking a strongly proprietary attitude towards the Labour party and trade union power in the party was at its apogee.' In his opinion, union leaders began to see an 'increased significance' in the development of the party as a 'medium for the achievement of trade union policies', as slowly but surely Labour dropped its millenarian tendency and recognized the need for 'practical and limited reforms'.[20]

As we have seen, during the war years both the TUC and the Labour party acquired the experience of power and influence. Under Citrine the trade unions grew both in self-confidence and public esteem. But it was also clear that Attlee and his senior colleagues had done so as well. Indeed, their years in the wartime coalition had shown that they were highly capable of ministerial responsibility and of keeping their union allies in a friendly but subordinate position.

Consensus at the top

'In the war, so in the period of reconstruction, close collaboration by the government with great organisations such as the TUC is essential if changes are to be carried through with the goodwill of all', Attlee assured the 1945 Congress.[21] When in November 1946 a TUC delegation to 10 Downing Street urged the Prime Minister to remind his ministers about their need to use the existing joint consultation machinery with union leaders, after complaining that some ministers had not been doing so, he agreed to act. In the ensuing circular he sent out, Attlee urged his Cabinet colleagues to be 'vigilant in ensuring that the TUC and in suitable cases individual unions' were 'fully taken into consultation wherever appropriate at the earliest possible stage'.[22]

For the most part, the highly effective personal network of power and influence established in the 1930s, which had strengthened enormously under wartime conditions, ensured the Labour government kept in close touch with the views and moods of the trade union leaders. Here the role of Ernest Bevin continued to be of crucial importance. Although Foreign Secretary in the Labour Cabinet, he remained in constant contact with the senior trade union leaders and acted as their vital go-between. As Lord Bullock, Bevin's official biographer emphasized:

> The importance of union support to the government extended beyond the industrial and economic sphere; it was an essential element in enabling Bevin to carry out his foreign policy and the key to holding steady behind the government the political support of a party which was liable to ideological division.[23]

The appointment of George Isaacs, the elderly former General Secretary of the print union NATSOPA (the National Association of Operative Printers and Assistants) as Minister of Labour was also regarded as a strong indication that Attlee intended to try and maintain a fraternal liaison between his government and the TUC. It is true that only 120 out of the 393 Labour MPs were sponsored by a trade union, but six of Attlee's 20-strong Cabinet came from trade union backgrounds and 29 out of the 81 posts in the government went to union sponsored MPs. Moreover, the trade union section on Labour's NEC and the mighty union block vote at annual conference provided an impressive bulwark of loyalty in support of almost all the government's policies.

The union leaders at the top of the TUC in the years immediately after 1945 were tough, dependable right-wingers who often treated the opposition in their own ranks as nothing less than subversion. Arthur Deakin, who formally succeeded Bevin as the TGWU's General Secretary in 1945, was an able self-made man of Shropshire with a short temper and an authoritarian style of running the union. Hated by the Left as the epitome of the union boss, he remained a fiercely loyal champion of the Labour government. Contrary to his own instincts, he even persuaded himself to accept the need for a national wages policy in 1948, though his conversion was derived more from a sense of loyalty to the government than genuine conviction. His natural allies on the TUC general council were Tom Williamson, who was elected General Secretary of the General and Municipal Workers' Union (GMWU) after the retirement of Charles Duke in 1946, and the robust National Union of Mineworkers' (NUM) president Will Lawther, who articulated all the powerful emotions of a late convert to the anti-Communist cause after years inside the Communist party. This triumvirate dominated the TUC for most of the first ten years after the end of the war. By contrast, Vincent Tewson, who replaced Citrine officially as TUC General Secretary in September 1946, was a rather mediocre figure, a consolidator rather than a source of new ideas or an inspiration. He lacked the authority and presence that Citrine had been able to achieve. To a very large extent, it was the so-called junta of Deakin, Williamson and Lawther that provided the TUC with what collective sense of direction it possessed in the years immediately after 1945. This was no slavish, unthinking obedience to whatever the Labour government wanted, but at the same time there was a recognition that on the broad range of economic and social policy no genuine division of opinion existed between the Attlee Cabinet and the TUC Establishment.

During the years of the Labour government the TUC consolidated and expanded its important role in providing nominees for the plethora of public bodies established for consultation and advice. The tripartite National Joint Advisory Council continued its work, as did the Joint Consultative Committee, while the TUC was represented on the newly formed Economic Planning Board after 1947. In areas like rationing and price controls, production and supply, productivity, regional policy and technical education, the TUC continued to man committees alongside employer representatives and civil servants. Just what all this work achieved is more difficult to assess. There was limited reporting back to the TUC on the activities of the public bodies, and complaints were made to the TUC by the Ministry of Labour and National Service about the lack of effort and attendance by some trade union worthies. Nonetheless, the TUC was able to capitalize on its cooperative activities with government during the war to maintain its presence in the corridors of Whitehall, even if its influence was often hard to detect.

But then both sides of the Labour Movement after 1945 shared a mutual understanding of what needed to be done. The war years had shaken up the social system and given the organized working class a crucial role to play. In retrospect, we can see this did not amount to anything as dramatic as a social revolution, let alone Socialism, but in the words of Lord Bullock it did represent 'a major shift in the relationship between the classes in Britain, as a result of which the working class majority of the nation began to exercise in the political system a power much more commensurate with its numbers'.[24]

As Lewis Minkin argued, it was the 'imprint' of the unions 'that lay on many key features of the post-war settlement'.[25] The government's firm commitment to the maintenance of full employment reflected TUC concerns that there must be no return to the dole queues of the 1930s. Labour's plans for the nationalization of gas, water and electricity and the key industries of coal, steel and the railways also owed a great deal to

TUC influence. The creation of a more comprehensive welfare state based on universalist principles of provision and a redistributive tax system were also to the liking of trade union leaders. In its carefully organized demobilization of the armed forces and the development of a dirigiste regional policy to counter any threat of mass unemployment in the former depressed areas of Britain, the Attlee government acted with the TUC's positive support. Moreover, trade union leaders expressed an understandable delight in 1946 when Labour repealed the hated 1927 Trade Union and Trade Disputes Act. A mean-minded if ineffective measure passed by the Conservative government in the aftermath of the 1926 General Strike, the Act had outlawed sympathetic strikes, prevented civil service unions from belonging to the TUC, banned the closed shop in the public sector, made so-called secondary picketing illegal and introduced the principle of 'contracting in' to payment of the political levy by trade unionists rather than 'contracting out'.

But it would be quite wrong to suggest that the Attlee government was a mere transmission belt for the implementation of TUC policy. As Norman Chester pointed out in his official study of nationalization, 'the TUC and the unions found that the fact that a Labour government was in power did not eliminate the need for formal consultative machinery. Indeed, at first they had to fight hard for the principle of being consulted on those matters which were directly within their sphere of interest.'[26] Labour ministers did not concede, for example, any general right for the TUC to be consulted on the drawing up of legislation for taking private industries into state ownership. Union leaders were particularly concerned at what they regarded as the high-handed behaviour of Emmanuel Shinwell, Minister of Fuel and Power, who did not take easily to working closely with them. But for the most part the TUC and government ministers established and maintained harmonious relations.

What about the workers?

The affinity of common purpose between the Attlee Cabinet and the TUC general council was coupled with a surprisingly similar tough-minded attitude towards unofficial strikes. Throughout the lifetime of the Labour government, ministers displayed little hesitation in confronting and defeating industrial disputes when they believed the national interest was being endangered. On a number of occasions troops were used to maintain essential supplies and services during strikes. Twice the Cabinet declared a State of Emergency under the 1920 Emergency Powers Act in

Table 2.1   Strikes under Labour, 1945–1951

	Stoppages	*Workers involved*	*Working days lost*
1945	2,293	531,000	2,836,000
1946	2,205	526,000	2,158,000
1947	1,721	620,000	2,433,000
1948	1,759	424,000	1,944,000
1949	1,426	433,000	1,807,000
1950	1,339	302,000	1,389,000
1951	1,719	379,000	1,694,000

Source: *British Labour Statistics 1886–1968*, HMSO, 1971, p. 396.

Table 2.2   Unemployment and trade union membership penetration, 1945–1951

	Unemployment		*Trade unionists*	
	(%)	*(number)*	*(%)*	*(number)*
1945	1.3	159,970	38.6	7,875,000
1946	2.6	394,100	43.0	8,803,000
1947	2.0	498,300	44.5	9,145,000
1948	1.6	331,300	45.2	9,362,000
1949	1.6	328,400	44.8	9,318,000
1950	1.6	332,100	44.1	9,289,000
1951	1.3	264,100	45.2	9,535,000

Sources: *British Labour Statistics 1886–1968*, HMSO, 1971; G. Bain and R. Price, *Profiles of Union Growth*, Basil Blackwell, 1980, p. 38.

response to unofficial dock disputes. The severe economic troubles facing post-war Britain did much to unite Labour ministers and the TUC in their strong resistance to shopfloor unrest. This was particularly true after the onset of the Cold War in 1947 when Communist agitation was blamed by government and trade union leaders for many outbreaks of industrial militancy.

Ministers did not hesitate to act forcefully in the face of unofficial industrial stoppages. In 1950 the Cabinet even decided to prosecute, under Order 1305, 1,700 gas maintenance workers who went on unofficial strike despite trade union anxieties. The men were each sentenced to one month in prison which was reduced to fines on appeal. In February 1951 seven TGWU dockers were charged under Order 1305 for taking part in alleged unlawful disputes. Other dockers struck in sympathy and the prosecutions were dropped hastily.

Hugh Gaitskell, the young Chancellor of the Exchequer in 1950–1, worked in alliance with Citrine, by then chairman of the British Electricity Authority, to crush unofficial strikes in the power supply industry – though not without some difficulty. As he recorded in his diary for 27 January 1950 on receiving a warning from Citrine of unrest ahead,

> I asked for a meeting of the Cabinet emergency committee and got authority to put troops in immediately if necessary. Again the trouble blew over and then ten days later on a Monday morning – this time without warning – the strike began at four London power stations. We put the troops in at once and this made a favourable impression on the public. Unfortunately however it proved impossible to get the stations to anything like full capacity owning to the inexperience of the troops and the shortage of people to train them.[27]

Gaitskell believed that once the 1950 general election was out of the way the government should 'face up to the issue of power station strikes and decide whether they can afford to treat them as ordinary industrial disputes. In my view they cannot.' Nor was such a robust attitude from Labour cabinet ministers towards industrial conflict confined to right-wingers like Gaitskell. Aneurin Bevan, for example, did not show much sympathy for unofficial strikers either. As Jeffrey and Hennessy wrote:

> Increasingly during the 1940s and early 1950s the government became almost obsessed with the domestic threat of Communism. After five years in power Attlee's Cabinet, which began its emergency planning with such careful deliberation, had convinced itself that virtually all industrial unrest stemmed from a subversive challenge to established order. In these circumstances, detailed and systematic emergency planning seemed both necessary and desirable. Ironically fear of revolution or at least subversion, which had been the initial stimulant for the establishment of a strike-breaking machine after the First World War, did much to sustain the development of a similar organisation after the Second.[28]

Many national trade union leaders shared the Cabinet's views about the menace of shopfloor unrest and the need to combat shop steward power. As early as the 1946 Congress Charles Duke, retiring as GMWU General Secretary, warned that it would be 'fatal to the future development of the trade unions as a responsible and constructive force in national life if their unity was undermined by irresponsible and headstrong minorities which tried to usurp the elected and representative leadership of the move-ment'.[29] Tom Williamson, his successor at the head of the GMWU, moved a resolution at the 1948 Congress that denounced the 'disloyal activities of small factions' in the trade unions who ignored their leaders and were 'undermining trade union solidarity and responsibility'. 'In no circumstances whatsoever can any unofficial stoppages be defended', as-serted Williamson. 'No government can stand aside and see the progress of its economy interfered with when by the exercise of common sense and reason, stoppages and dislocation can be avoided.'[30] Lawther of the NUM used his 1949 TUC presidential address to excoriate shopfloor militants: 'In our trade union policy and procedure the time has come to say unofficial strikes must be outlawed. Union discipline must be enforced against those who promote, organise and lead unofficial strikes', he declared. 'Very few of the stoppages in industry in the last four years has been sanctioned by the unions but they have been against the advice and direction of the unions whose members have been involved'.[31]

The TUC was prepared to accept the peacetime continuation of Order 1305, which had been passed by the Churchill coalition in the crisis of 1940 to prohibit strikes. The Order was not in fact revoked by the government until August 1951, only two months before Labour lost office, but this did not lead to complete freedom. The Cabinet decided to replace it with Order 1376, which maintained the system of compulsory arbitration and sought to uphold the authority of full-time union officials against the rise of shop steward power. It was not until October 1958 that a Conservative government decided to abolish Order 1376.

In the political atmosphere of the late 1940s many union leaders regarded shopfloor militancy as nothing less than national treason. The Cold War between the Soviet Union and the Western world unleashed a strong outburst of hysterical anti-Communism inside the TUC. In October 1948 the general council accused the British Communist party of pursu-ing a strategy of industrial disruption on orders from Moscow. 'Communist influences are everywhere at work to frame industrial demands for pur-poses of political agitation and to magnify industrial grievances and bring about stoppages in industry', alleged the TUC. It warned that the Communist party through its use of 'underground methods' was exercising 'in certain trade union organisations a degree of influence which is out of all proportion either to its membership or support'.[32] By a crushing 6,746,000 votes to 760,000 the 1949 Congress backed the TUC's anti-Communist position.

The simplistic crudity of the attack on Soviet Communism inside the British unions reflected the understandable mood of the time, in the aftermath of the Soviet take-over in Czechoslovakia in April 1948 and the Berlin airlift of 1948–9, when rightly or wrongly, many in the West feared that Stalin harboured aggressive military intentions to occupy or subvert the whole of Europe. But trying to pin the blame on Communists for the outbreak of unofficial strikes focused attention on the effect not the cause of industrial disruption. No doubt, Communists were able to exploit rank and file grievances but they did not manufacture those discontents. As K. G. J. C. Knowles explained in his seminal book on strikes published in 1951:

> The history of the dock strikes between 1945 and 1948 revealed not only a resentment by the dockers of the tighter discipline necessitated by decasualisation but also an enduring suspicion of their own main union [TGWU] which seemed to have been aggravated by the union participation – however defensible – in the managerial function of the Dock Labour Board. Against this background the Communists have won their influence by default.[33]

Indeed, Knowles believed that far from being a menace to the established order, unofficial stoppages came to be 'tacitly recognised by the public if not by the unions as an essential safety valve under a system of national collective bargaining.'

The constant anxiety and often irrational attitude displayed by both Labour ministers and the TUC towards the outbreak of wild-cat strikes tended to obscure the undoubted fact that the vast majority of workers did not take militant action in pursuit of their wage claims during the late 1940s. On the contrary, despite the successful maintenance of full employment, an extraordinary degree of social self-discipline was maintained inside the ranks of organized labour throughout the duration of the Labour government. 'The trade unions today could, if they chose, demand almost anything and in a great number of industries at any rate, no power could resist them if their members were really determined to have their way', observed the Socialist academic G. D. H. Cole in February 1947. He claimed that the rank and file in the trade unions were 'in instance after instance deliberately refraining from pressing demands which they know could not be refused'.[34] Cole believed it was the 'fewness' not the 'frequency' of unofficial strikes that was most 'astonishing'. In his opinion the reason for the moderation inside the unions was the deep sense of responsibility that existed not just with the leaders but among most of their members as well.

But Cole also drew attention to the important shift in the locus of trade union power which was already taking place – away from the national and even district machinery of collective bargaining between unions and employers' associations to the company and workplace level. This trend, he believed, would have to be heeded by the unions nationally through more formal recognition and acceptance of the devolution of power from their full-time officials to shop stewards. There was certainly more than a touch of romanticism about Cole's acclaim for the changing power balance inside a growing number of trade unions with large memberships in private manufacturing. In fact, it is easy to gain the impression from the activities of the trade unions during the years of Labour government up to October 1951 that leaders and members were of one mind and that the 'implied social contract' at the centre reflected not just a widespread acquiescence on the shop floor but a positive rank and file enthusiasm for the 'new Jerusalem'.

But there were signs throughout the period that national union leaders were finding it difficult either to represent or influence the views of their members, while the problems for the government in convincing trade union members of the wisdom of its economic policy remained enormous. PEP's 1949 study of trade unionism argued: 'Government policy can still be – in fact for the vast majority of trade unionists still is – something remote, laid down and executed by a distant central authority and for most of the rank and file is not regarded as "their" policy'.[35]

Despite the idealistic rhetoric of the alliance between the TUC and the Labour government, basic and traditional working class attitudes of insecurity and suspicion about authority remained widespread on the shop floor. As PEP's report observed, 'Much of the old distrust is still very much alive and still hampers the execution of government policy in the economic field.'

Moreover, an enormous gulf remained between the perceptions of full-time union officials and their mass memberships. This was well established by Joseph Goldstein, a young American doctoral student of the time, who discovered during his pioneering research into the internal structure of the TGWU that the union was 'an oligarchy at every level of its structure, failing to elicit the active participation of its members'.[36] 'In treating the rank and file as cogs in the union's administrative machinery, the psychological nexus between the member, his union leader and official union policy has been broken', declared Goldstein. In his opinion, the TGWU needed urgently to integrate its shop stewards more formally into the existing organization because it was they and not the local branch activists who represented the union in action in the eyes of the rank and file. At that time, union headquarters in London's Transport House maintained that the responsibilities of shop stewards should remain limited essentially 'to deal with minor matters arising at the place of employment'. Goldstein wrote that the shop stewards had 'in practice become a new level in the structure of the government of the union, wedged firmly though unofficially between the rank and file and the branch'. As he argued:

> The failure of the union to integrate the shop steward unit within the formal structure of its organisation has served to hinder rather than encourage membership participation at branch level and to maintain rather than bridge the gap between leader and rank and file.[37]

Ferdynand Zweig's perceptive study of the British worker, published in 1950, also exposed the genuine difficulties facing the trade unions as they sought to reconcile the demands of their own members for higher pay and better benefits with the needs of a Labour government. 'The unions have changed their character. The times of struggle are over – theirs is the time of achievement and fruition. They have grown not only big but fat', explained Zweig. ' "Let us sit quietly and enjoy the fruits of victory" is the spirit now.'[38] In Zweig's opinion, Britain's trade unions by the end of the 1940s had grown into bulwarks of 'industrial peace and lawfulness'. But the new more secure status of organized labour as an Estate of the Realm coexisted with a nagging doubt among trade union leaders about what their function should be. Zweig quoted the words of an unnamed local full-time trade union official who articulated the post-war dilemma for the industrial wing of the Labour Movement, at least until Margaret Thatcher rejected any suggestion that trade unions should have a role to play in the management of the economy. 'This close co-operation with the government is a golden opportunity for us', the official told Zweig,

> But it deprives us of our independence. Our movement is basically a sectionalist movement for the benefit of small sectionalist interests but now we are expected to give them up for the benefit of the nation. How can we do that without being disloyal to our members and giving up the tasks for which we are appointed? We were not meant to be public servants to guard the interests of the nation. We were appointed to protect our members and to further their interests within the framework of the law. Does anyone ask the employer to have the national interest in mind instead of the interest of his firm? It is all right having the national interest in mind but we are not the right people to have it.[39]

Leave wages alone

The internal problem of maintaining discipline and order in the trade unions was certainly made much more difficult by the initially successful attempt by their leaders after 1948 to try in line with government policy to restrain their members from pressing for higher wage increases. The clear erosion of the voluntarist system of industrial relations put a severe strain on the unity of the Labour Movement because it ran contrary to the whole practice of the trade unions, who were always eager to press for a planned economy just as long as the improved wages and fringe benefits they wanted could be achieved through free collective bargaining.

Almost from their first days in office, however, a number of ministers in the Attlee Cabinet believed pay restraint was a crucial necessity if Britain hoped to resolve its enormous post-war economic troubles. The pressure for the introduction of a national wages policy was already apparent in government circles as early as October 1945 when Herbert Morrison, the Lord President of the Council, argued that 'in the long run a proper relationship between the nation's needs and distribution of the labour force' could 'only be secured by a rational and effective wages policy'.[40] An official ministerial working party which looked into the subject came up with a number of suggestions for government action, including the creation of a tripartite National Wages Commission with sweeping powers, but the proposed measures were dropped from consideration under pressure from the Ministry of Labour and National Service which continued to resolutely defend the voluntarist industrial relations system. The only tangible result of the inter-departmental debate was a decision to reinvigorate the National Joint Advisory Council so that it could take a more direct interest in wage determination.

Other ministers who favoured direct government action on wages were Emmanuel Shinwell, who proposed the establishment of a Central Wages Tribunal, and Ancurin Bevan, the Minister of Health. Shinwell, as the minister responsible for the nationalization of the coal and electricity supply industries, believed the government would be 'unable to escape ultimate responsibility for the determination of wages in the field of socialised industry'.[41] But both Ernest Bevin and George Isaacs were opposed strongly to any direct governmental interference in the wage bargaining process. Bevin told a special TUC conference of trade union executives on 6 March 1946 that the government's policy was 'to leave the trade unions and the state to settle wages where the state was the employer and to leave trade unions to settle wages with the employers where they were dealing with private employers'.[42] For his part, Isaacs assured the same audience that the government would 'continue to rely on the existing system of negotiation in industry to settle all wage problems'. 'There would be no change in the present system unless the TUC came along and asked for it', he added.[43] Isaacs went out of his way to reject any notion of a 'national wages policy', suggesting the arguments used in favour of it were 'academic and unconvincing' and out of touch with the realities of British industrial relations. At the 1946 Trades Union Congress the Minister of Labour and National Service also told delegates that the government still 'adhered to the policy of leaving all negotiations on wages and working conditions to industry'. He assured them that he believed there was 'enough common sense' among the trade unions to ensure they would do the best for their own members' interests without injuring the community.[44]

But at the Labour party conference a few weeks later, Herbert Morrison told delegates that Britain would show the world that it was possible to reconcile 'democratic freedom and economic planning'. 'We have turned our backs on the economics of scarcity', he declared. Morrison assured the party faithful that the government was against any 'arbitrary inter-ference with wages'[45], but he was keen to dispel any trade union com-placency about wage bargaining. He warned at the 1947 party conference that the greatest dangers to the achievement of the government's objec-tives came increasingly from workers themselves. 'In Britain today the battle for Socialism is the battle for production', he told them. 'Anything that delays or lessens production is a blow in the face for the organized workers and their cause. Today any avoidable strike – whether caused by employers or workers – is sabotage. And an unofficial strike is sabotage with violence to the body of the Labour Movement itself.'[46] Morrison was fearful in particular that workers were not prepared to restrain their collective power for the greater needs of the economy. 'Higher wages and lower hours before the goods are there to be bought – that is far worse than useless', he declared. 'They give no more real income and by inflation and financial strain, they may wreck the whole structure we are trying to build.' He warned that trade unionists 'could not live indefinitely on overdrafts without heading into an economic and financial smash which would damage the workers and smash the Labour party'.

The trade union mood over the issue of a 'national wages policy' had been clear from the short, sharp debate at the 1946 Congress on a resolution moved by the National Union of Vehicle Builders (NUVB) calling on the TUC general council to draw up a report for the establishment of a single national minimum wage for all workers enforceable by law, as well as the replacement of the present wage bargaining system by a new one which would achieve a 'more satisfactory, lasting and equitable wage standard'. Deakin warned delegates that the proposal was 'an attempt on the part of vested interests and the Tories to force the government to declare a wages policy which would bring it into conflict with the unions'.[47] He asserted that the unions would go on drawing up their pay claims 'in conformity with the needs of the people we are representing'. 'Any attempt to interfere with that position would have disastrous results', he asserted. The NUVB motion was defeated by 3,522,000 to 2,657,000, though the surprisingly large size of the minority vote suggested many trade unions were less enthusiastic about the virtues of free collective bargaining than Deakin was willing to recognize.

Ministers were increasingly concerned about what they saw as the growing wages problem in a tight labour market. In the first five months of 1946 the annual wage rate rose by as much as 11 per cent – twice the average for the last four years of the war. An official government steering committee, which was preparing the 1947 Economic Survey, suggested that 'the urgent immediate task' was to discover a way of 'exercising restraint against a further general increase of wage rates or other labour costs without an appropriate increase in productivity'.[48] But as Sir Alec Cairncross explained, the majority of the committee 'shrank from the industrial unrest' that might follow any proposed direct governmental intervention in wage fixing'.[49] Ever sensitive to trade union feelings on the pay issue, ministers toned down references to wage restraint in the government's own January 1947 *Statement on The Economic Considerations Affecting Relations Between Employers and Workers*. It noted that the TUC had 'remained throughout firmly convinced that it is impracticable and would in any case be undesirable to impose specific limits and restrictions on wage increases', but went on to urge the trade unions 'to exercise even greater moderation and restraint than hitherto in the formulation and pursuit of claims for wage increases'.[50]

The government's 1947 Economic Survey also urged trade unions to limit their wage claims to rises that could be justified only be improved productivity. It warned of the dangers of rising costs on industrial production that could make it impossible for Britain to pay its own way in the world. But while the TUC was keen to help the government as far as it was able, it refused to accept any suggestion that free collective bargaining should be curbed in the national interest. 'Nothing in the White Paper was to be taken as restricting the rights of unions to make claims through the normal bargaining arrangements. Such claims should be considered on their merits', argued the TUC.[51] While it agreed that the Ministry of Labour might establish a new department to collect information on wages as a guide to help the work of the wage tribunals and negotiating bodies, the TUC was still opposed to any government intervention in pay determination. Deakin made the position crystal clear in his speech to the American Federation of Labor's 1947 convention, where he told delegates the British unions were unwilling 'to tolerate control of wages by government machinery' and would resist any attempt by the government 'even to offer an opinion as to whether a particular wage claim should be conceded or turned down'.[52]

But continuing trade union resistance to government pleas for wage restraint came at a time when the economy was heading into trouble. The sterling convertibility crisis of July 1947 precipitated a huge outflow of capital from the country. The resulting diminution of what remained of the American loan negotiated two years earlier exposed the fragile conditions of an over-burdened British economy and forced the government into austerity measures with cuts in both food imports and subsidies. In a further sign of the gravity of the economic outlook, Attlee himself felt compelled on 6 August publicly to urge workers to refrain from pushing for higher wages, especially through their efforts to restore eroded pay differentials. But when Isaacs wrote in the following month to joint negotiating bodies asking them to keep in mind the Prime Minister's statement when they came to pay bargaining, the TUC general council protested to 10 Downing Street at his ministerial interference. Attlee agreed under TUC pressure to withdraw the Minister of Labour's letter but in his further discussions with the TUC general council it was agreed that union leaders would 'give very serious consideration to the possibilities of securing some greater stability in wages' in their pay bargaining.[53]

However, the conversion of senior union leaders to some form of national wages policy was slow and uncertain. Old voluntarist attitudes remained strong. Deakin said, for example, as late as the 1947 Labour party conference, that 'under no circumstances at all' would he accept that 'the responsibility for the fixation of wages and the regulation of conditions of employment was one for the government'. 'The question of wages and conditions of employment are questions for the trade unions and the sooner some of our people on the political side appreciate that and leave the job to the unions the better for the battle of production', he added. Deakin made it clear there was no way his members were going to 'play second fiddle'. Any attempt by the government to improve the pay of the miners to meet a labour shortage in the pits, he warned, would 'destroy confidence in our negotiating machinery and create chaos and conflict amongst the rank and file'.[54] He was joined in his unequivocal stance by Williamson, who said he was 'amazed that we should have had delegates advocating that the government should take control of wages'. 'This policy if passed could do no more than usurp the authority of the trade union movement', he claimed.[55]

In December 1947 the TUC general council still took the view that it was 'impracticable and undesirable to impose specific limits and restrictions on wage increases'. The TUC would only go so far as to recommend to union leaders that they 'exercise even greater moderation and restraint than hitherto in the formulation and pursuit of claims for wage increases'. 'Any attempt on the part of an outside body to regulate or directly control wage movements would have disastrous effects in undermining the industrial authority of trade unions', warned the TUC. 'If there was to be greater restraint upon wage movements it could only come from within the trade union movement itself.'[56] In its opinion, 'the continuing stability of prices and the comparative absence of industrial unrest' in Britain had 'provoked the wonder and admiration of the whole world'. As the TUC argued, 'No other country has been able to leave its trade unions free and at the same time keep the prices of essential commodities remarkably stable.'

The wages policy

The form of words on voluntary wage restraint proposed by the TUC did not go nearly far enough to satisfy the Cabinet. Reluctantly, ministers decided they could no longer delay taking action over the pay issue. Without the TUC's prior consent and even consultation, the government published a White Paper, *Personal Incomes, Costs and Prices*, in February 1948. It was drawn up under Attlee's name to emphasize its importance. The document stressed the government's clear determination to introduce restraint into wage bargaining as a way of preventing the 'development of a dangerously inflationary situation'.[57] 'There is no justification for any general increase of individual money incomes without at least a corresponding increase in the volume of production', it said bluntly, since this would simply add to costs and push up prices. The government ruled out a freeze on all pay rises, and companies anxious to fill labour shortages were to be allowed to make necessary pay adjustments. But the White Paper made it clear that the national interest and not just market forces would have to determine future wage levels. 'Each claim for an increase in wages or salaries must be considered on its national merits and not on the basis of maintaining a former relativity between different occupations and industries', it declared, making it clear that the government would observe its own principles in future wage bargaining where it was the employer.

Union leaders were assured by ministers that the government did not believe it was desirable to interfere directly to determine the level of personal incomes except through the use of taxation, but this continuing reluctance for wage fixing by the state would depend on the trade unions and employers observing the White Paper's principles in their future pay bargaining. The document's recommendations fell far short of the proposals that ministers had been considering, which had included making the National Joint Advisory Council responsible for taking a view of major wage claims, imposing a tax on all workers to deter pay rises, introducing a statutory wage freeze or at least one covering the public sector, and bringing a government representative into all major wage negotiations. Ministers hoped the TUC itself would be able to carry out a policy of self-regulation to lower wage demands without the need for any draconian decisions having to be taken by them. But Gaitskell for one was sceptical about the new policy's chances of success. 'I don't know how much it will achieve', he noted in his diary. 'There is very little room between the two horns of the dilemma. To leave things alone so that there is a wage inflation and maldistribution of labour or on the other hand to regulate wages. Probably this represents the best plan.' 'I think on the whole there is bound to be some restraint', he added. 'Probably to act as a brake is all that the statement could have done. But of course, there is a real danger that it will strengthen the Communist power in the unions.'[58]

After the TUC's initial and understandable protest about the lack of prior government consultation over the contents of the 1948 White Paper, and trade union complaints that its provisions to restrain company profits were too 'weak and limited', the TUC general council agreed to back the government's policy. In intense negotiations with the ascetic Sir Stafford Cripps, who had replaced Hugh Dalton as Chancellor of the Exchequer in November 1947, TUC leaders were assured that the government intended to maintain price stability directly through subsidies, controls and moral exhortation. Cripps also told them there would be a limit set on the level of dividends, and employers would be told not to take advantage of the policy to increase their profits. The TUC's support, however, appeared to be hedged around by a formidable list of conditions. These would have enabled workers' pay rises to go to those whose wages were 'below a reasonable standard of subsistence' which was undefined as well as to the defence of 'differentials based on craftsmanship, training and experience.'[59] The TUC added that the government's White Paper was 'not a law imposing rigid and specific restrictions upon wage claims and negotiations' but 'a request to unions to restrain wage claims'. It also sought to reassure that it was the 'responsibility' of affiliated trade unions 'to determine their own wages policy', though 'for the time being' doing so 'solely from the standpoint' of the TUC's declared policy.[60] On the face of it, the TUC's proposed grounds for exceptions in pay increases did not seem to suggest that a wage freeze was about to be imposed on its affiliated members. Indeed as Professor Ben Roberts pointed out, 'It would not be difficult, in practice, for any union to find one reason or another to justify a wage claim'.[61]

At a special Congress of TUC affiliated trade union executives held on 24 March 1948, the TUC general council's position on wages policy was accepted decisively by 5,421,000 votes to 2,032,000. The main unions who opposed what was in fact voluntary pay restraint by the TUC were the AEU, the Communist-controlled ETU, and USDAW, the Shop-workers' union. For all its apparent caveats and hesitations, Congress had embarked on conditional wage restraint to try and help the government through a difficult economic period. But the TUC was keen to emphasize from the beginning that this was not a policy being imposed crudely on the trade unions through any government fiat. When the George Isaacs sent out a letter to the Wages Boards and Wages Councils asking them to take note of the White Paper's contents in their wage award deliberations, the TUC demanded the letter's withdrawal on the grounds it gave the impression that 'some duress' was involved in the government's policy. Union leaders were keen to shoulder the burdens of self-restraint in order to prevent the government from going ahead with any national approach on pay which might threaten the voluntarist system. They had in mind a temporary pause to help the government through what they saw as its transient economic troubles.

'Such a remarkable abdication of their roles by the unions was unique in times of peace', argued Kenneth Morgan. 'The general effect of the wage freeze policy was remarkably successful in the fragmented, adversarial world of British labour relations and a political triumph for Cripps'.[62] Cairncross pointed out that the 1948 wage freeze 'undoubtedly slowed down the rise in wages and prices'.[63] From June 1945 to June 1947, hourly wage rates went up by 9 per cent in the first twelve months and then by 8.5 per cent in the second. Over the first nine months to March 1948 the rise continued at an annual rate of nearly 9 per cent. From then on until sterling's devaluation in September 1949, the annual wage rate increase dropped to about 2.8 per cent, though the retail price index climbed by 3 per cent over the same period. In fact, workers achieved a slight rise in their real weekly earnings because of the impact of overtime, piecework and bonus payments on the size of their wage packets.

At the 1949 Trades Union Congress Attlee assured the delegates that he had 'never believed in lowering wages as a means of reducing costs' but added that 'increases of wages unmatched by increases of production' would 'gravely impair' the country's chances of rapidly recovering from its economic difficulties.[64] The Prime Minister told the TUC that there was a 'danger' when workers claimed their entitlement to pay rises as a way of maintaining their wage differential against the lower paid. 'Our Labour Movement has an ethical basis', he declared. 'We are trying to get away from the old scramble for competitive advantages. As we move into a juster social order there is need for a higher conception of social obligation.'

For its part, the TUC tried to argue that in fact there was no wage freeze nor a pay standstill in existence. It reported to the 1949 Congress that in the first six months of the year 3,913,000 workers had received pay increases, more than 600,000 higher than in the first half of 1948. Its report, *Trade Union Policy and the Economic Situation*, explained:

> The necessity for the continuation of collective bargaining was specifically recognised by the general council as was the justification for wage increases in certain cases associated with increased output, a reasonable standard of subsistence, the need to attract sufficient manpower to undermanned essential industries and the need to safeguard essential differentials.[65]

The 1949 statement even suggested that it was 'important not only that the adjustments that are required from time to time should be negotiated but that they should be negotiated without unnecessary delay'. But the document also underlined the TUC's recognition that the economy was experiencing severe difficulties and admitted that 'the inevitable consequence' of any departure from the general council's current policy of 'moderation and restraint' would be 'disastrous'.

The TUC was attempting to hold back union wage demands through moral exhortation while at the same time admitting the need to ensure flexibility, but there were increasing signs by the early autumn of 1949 that the TUC's wage stabilization strategy was coming under strain. Bryn Roberts, General Secretary of the National Union of Public Employees (NUPE) warned that an 'indefinitely prolonged policy of restraint' would create 'conflict within the unions and between the unions'. 'It will transform the old class struggle from one between the worker and the employer into one between the trade unionist and his own executive council', he told delegates. 'I know of no policy better calculated to create dissension within the unions, to undermine the position of the leaders and to provide glorious opportunities for disruptive elements to exploit.' He suggested that the wage restraint policy would not only 'damage' the mechanism of collective bargaining but also 'completely destroy the workers' confidence in it' as well as 'bring into complete disrepute the machinery of arbitration'.[66]

But his views failed to convince delegates, and the 1949 Congress voted to continue support for the wage freeze policy by a substantial vote of 6,485,000 to 1,038,000. However, only a fortnight later on 18 September the government was forced to devalue the pound, whose dollar parity was cut from $4.03 to $2.80 due to the continuing drain on the country's gold reserves and dollar balances. On this occasion the TUC moved swiftly to back up the government's position. In November 1949 the general council agreed almost with unanimity not only to continue with the wage restraint policy but actually to tighten it up – though it argued its recommendations should be seen within the context of the maintenance of the 'right of free collective bargaining', that 'the government must not impose wages policy and that the existing machinery of voluntary negotiation must be preserved'.[67] The TUC statement also accepted that it could not under its own constitution 'impose a wages policy on affiliated unions' and emphasized there was 'no suggestion of a standstill on wages earnings'. But it also argued that the 'dangerous inflationary tendencies which devaluation inevitably intensifies must be counteracted by vigorous restraints upon all increases of wages, salaries and dividends', and that even with the low paid 'regard had to made to the general economic problems necessitating rigorous restraint'. The TUC statement called on its affiliated unions to 'reconsider' existing wage claims and sliding-scale arrangements, with a view to holding agreed wage rates stable whilst the interim index of retail prices which then stood at 112 remained between an upper and lower limit of 118 and 106. If the index figure reached either limit, then the TUC general council argued that both sides of any industry would 'be entitled to resume the normal consideration of wages questions in accordance with the provisions of their agreements and that cost of living agreements would again operate'. It was argued that the unions 'must pay regard to the realities of the economic situation in framing their policy and act loyally in conformity with the policy now recommended by the general council'. The general council also stipulated the proposed policy should last until 1 January 1951 when it would 'be reviewed in the light of the then existing facts'.

However, the special TUC Congress of union executives called on 12 January 1950 to approve the new proposed twelve month wage standstill revealed widespread unease and opposition to the suggestion of further wage restraint, and the general council's position was only narrowly upheld by 4,263,000 votes to 3,606,000. A formidable number of unions were now lining up against further wage restraint including the NUM and the National Union of Railwaymen (NUR), as well as the ETU and the AEU. The strongest sign of rank and file discontent against pay restraint was seen in the NUM, where a secret pithead ballot in May produced a vote of 518,000 against the pay policy and only 147,000 miners in support.

The end of the wages policy

Within a few weeks of the NUM's rejection of the wages policy it became clear that trade unions were no longer prepared to accept the temporary suspension of sliding scale pay agreements, many of which contained backdated adjustments to cover rises in the cost of living. There was also mounting discontent among skilled manual workers who opposed the erosion of their wage differentials compared to the unskilled and semi-skilled under the pay restraint policy.

Through the spring and early summer of 1950 one trade union conference after another rejected the TUC's wage freeze policy. It is not hard to understand why this happened. The trouble was that the retail price index was rising at a much faster rate than the level of earnings. Between September 1949 and June 1950 food prices rose by 7 per cent while wage rates for men increased by only 1 per cent. The policy of pay restraint was becoming impossible to maintain in such conditions. In June 1950 the TUC general council acknowledged this by deciding to abandon the pay standstill policy it had begun six months earlier. In a statement it acknowledged the strains had grown too great and there was now the need to recognize 'a greater flexibility of wage movements in the future'. But it also acknowledged there was 'no formula' that could be devised to indicate just how that flexibility could operate in practice. 'Its operation must be left to the good sense and reasonableness which has been displayed by the unions', declared the TUC.[68]

Even this anodyne statement was too strong for the majority at the 1950 Trades Union Congress. The delegates refused by 3,898,000 votes to 3,521,000 to endorse the TUC general council's June position and instead they backed an anti-wage-restraint composite motion moved by the Communist-controlled ETU, which was passed by a majority of 222,000. Deakin held the line in the TGWU despite widespread rank and file discontent in his own union's ranks. He accused the general council's opponents of advocating a policy of smash and grab. 'Let those who can, get what they can and let the rest do as they may'.[69] Tewson also did his best to salvage something from the wreckage but admitted that 'the rigorous nature of the restraint' had to be removed and in future reliance would have to be placed on 'the good sense and reasonableness' of the unions 'in their normal conduct of collective bargaining to ensure national stability was maintained'. But Deakin and Tewson ran up against the irresistible and implacable mood of Congress. Only one speaker – Douglas Houghton from the Inland Revenue Staff Federation (IRSF) – suggested that the wages problem required a permanent system of pay determination to ensure the maintenance of full employment, but he could not even find a seconder for his motion on the need for such a national wages policy.

The demise of the Labour government's two and a half year long pay restraint strategy was not really unexpected. After all, there had never been any question of the government imposing penal sanctions on either the unions or employers to enforce it. Labour ministers might have failed to appreciate the problems facing union negotiators in a tight labour market with almost full employment, but there was no possibility that the TUC itself could establish the unifying authority to coordinate any semblance of a national incomes policy. The impressive display of voluntary national restraint by union leaders loyal to the needs of a Labour government in crisis could not hold in check indefinitely the demands of their own members for wage increases at a time of rising prices. As Professor Ben Roberts argued,

> Wage restraint failed because the unions were unable to resist the temptation to press for higher wages. It would hardly be fair, however, to blame the unions for carrying out the wishes of their members. Since it was apparent that employers were willing to pay more to obtain the labour they required, and since some unions were quite willing to exploit this situation, even if the rest had been paragons of virtue they would probably have given way to such seductive encouragement. So long as the demand for labour exceeded the supply and employers could pass on increased costs in one way or another, there was no barrier to wage increases and no union could stand aside for long in these circumstances without endangering its viability as an institution.[70]

In retrospect, it is perhaps surprising that the 1948–50 wage freeze strategy lasted as long as it did. As Gaitskell himself recognized in his 1951 Budget speech, 'During the past four years of labour scarcity and the seller's market the workers have been in a position of unexampled strength and bargaining power. Had they considered only their own immediate interest, they could have pressed their advantage home.' Moreover, as he admitted there was 'little compulsion on employers to resist claims for improvements in wages and conditions which they knew that they could recoup themselves out of prices'. Apparently, between those pressures and the 'menace of runaway inflation stood only the voluntary joint bargaining machinery' of the industrial relations system.[71] The sense of solidarity may have becoming increasingly hard to sustain but it had provided an order and cohesion to the industrial relations system, albeit only temporarily.

The collapse of the national wages policy over the summer of 1950, however, aroused deep anxiety in Whitehall. Many in the government were convinced that a permanent system of pay determination was needed to prevent the onset of a dangerous inflationary wages free-for-all. Under the code name 'Operation Prospero', the Treasury sought an alternative mechanism that would ensure that collective bargaining in conditions of full employment did not lead to self-destructive inflation. By the end of 1950, details had been worked out for the creation by the government of a tripartite Wages Advisory Council made up of employers, union leaders and independents. This would not be empowered to force wage deals on unwilling workers but would act as an independent and voluntary body. Indeed, ministers and civil servants were keen to ensure that voluntarism was preserved. The proposal for such a Council was presented tentatively to the TUC in February 1951, but union leaders expressed little enthusiasm for the idea which was then dropped by Gaitskell.

The new Chancellor of the Exchequer, however, warned in his April 1951 Budget statement of the dangers of a lack of financial confidence in the economy due to the pressure of higher wage demands on costs. He revealed that he and his officials were examining various schemes like the creation by the government of a 'central independent authority' to control wages, while acknowledging that this implied 'greater changes than either side of industry' was 'at present willing to contemplate'.[72] At the 1951 Congress, Gaitskell tried unavailingly to educate his trade union activist audience on the need for further wage restraint. 'If incomes go up more than production goes up, then prices will rise', he explained. 'I would like to see those words hanging as one of those old texts on the wall of every office of negotiators.' 'So long as we have full employment, it is a real problem which cannot just be pushed on one side as though it were a kind of unpleasant spectre that we did not want to have anything to do with', he added.[73] Variants on his homily were to be repeated by many anxious and exasperated Chancellors of the Exchequer over the next thirty years. While it is true that the end of the TUC wage restraint in the summer of 1950 did not detonate a pay–push explosion, there was a 10 per cent increase in pay rates between September 1950 and September 1951 – mainly due to pressure caused by the sharp rise in prices as a result of the needs of the Korean war – though there was no improvement in real wages.

But by the summer of 1951 the TUC had returned to its complacent belief in the merits of voluntarism. Its report to the 1951 Congress insisted that:

> In a period like the present it is all-important to maintain the health and status of the trade union movement and of the voluntary negotiating machinery which trade unionists have fought so hard and long to establish. Our system of collective bargaining is the envy of the world and it has served – and is serving under present conditions – the interests of working people in a way which no alternative system could approach.[74]

As long as trade unionists were guided by 'reason and good sense', provided they honoured agreements voluntarily reached and were on their guard against the minority of wreckers in their midst, all would be well.

The deceptive mood of contentment in the TUC reflected a clear withdrawal from any desire to shoulder responsibilities in support of the government's overall economic strategy, but at least this seemed to be more in tune with the attitude of the shop floor, impatient for an end to all controls and restraint. Unfortunately, the trade unions turned away from any further consideration of formulating a permanent wages policy but the troubles of wage inflation in a labour market of full employment were too easily brushed aside by the TUC. In *A Policy for Wages*, a path-breaking Fabian Society pamphlet published in 1951, Allan Flanders argued that collective bargaining could no longer simply be left to the voluntarist traditions. As he wrote so elegantly:

> The contents of a collective agreement can no longer be regarded as being only of concern to its signatories. *Laissez-faire* cannot be abandoned in other vital sectors of our economic life and retained on the wages front. Least of all can the trade unions, whose very nature has compelled them to seek an increasing measure of public regulation over the free-for-all scramble of each for himself which characterized economic activity in the last century, now claim that their own preserves should be exempted from the application of those principles which they have urged upon the nation.[75]

Flanders insisted that there was a 'public interest' in the outcome of wage negotiations. While he accepted that trade unions could not seek to avoid state intervention in industrial relations 'by themselves becoming formally or informally instruments of the state', because this would 'imperil their freedom and independence and lose the confidence of their members in the process', he was also convinced that the state itself would have to take responsibility for formulating and applying a national wages policy with the cooperation and consent of both trade unions and employer organizations. Flanders argued:

> The essential problem is that of bringing national policy to bear on individual wage settlements without weakening the trade unions or sacrificing that flexibility which is the great merit of the British system of organised industrial relations.[76]

In his view the reconciliation of freedom with planning was 'the very essence of the social experiment of Britain's Labour Government'. But Flanders was very much alone at the time in his passionate advocacy of a wages policy. Under pressure from their members, union leaders were keen to restore the lost world of 'free' collective bargaining as quickly as possible.

Yet despite this the TUC did behave for the most part in a responsible and effective manner during the six years of Labour government. To a very real extent those bonds of loyalty and affection that bound the Labour Movement together between 1945 and 1951 remained strong. Moreover, for most trade union activists the record of the Attlee years justified their strong support for his government. Future Labour governments were to be humbled when they tried to push through economic policies that threatened the autonomy of organized labour, but this did not really happen in the years immediately after the war. However, the experience of the 1948–50 wage freeze also underlined that for all its wider ambitions the TUC was unable as well as unwilling to do anything that conflicted with the ultimate purpose of its affiliated unions, even in an 'implied contract' with a Labour government whose ideals and views it shared. As Professor Jean McKelvey wrote in 1953,

> What the British experience indicates most sharply is the essentially conservative nature of the trade union movement. This is not meant as either praise or criticism but simply as a statement of fact. So long as unions remain independent interest groups in a free society, they must function as associations whose primary concern is that of protecting their own members. No matter how much rhetoric is used about the new functions of the trade unions, the fact remains that they are sectional bodies pursuing special interests.[77]

This was more than just a problem for the industrial and political wings of the Labour Movement. It went to the heart of the government's efforts to reconcile freedom with planning. Trade union resistance to any direct state interference in collective bargaining made it impossible for ministers to manage the ailing economy in the way they wished. If Labour had won the 1951 general election, Gaitskell and the Treasury may well have sought to establish some form of national incomes policy, but it seems unlikely that they would have achieved the TUC's consent for such a development, despite the goodwill of the trade unions for a Labour government. The wages problem had, indeed, created 'an impasse on the road to the New Jerusalem'.[78] No union leader could really contemplate surrendering his freedom to bargain for some Socialist objective. The logic of wage planning by the state involved a measure of coercion, for moral exhortation alone could not be expected to make more than a transient impact. Evan Durbin, who in 1949 drowned tragically at the age of 42, accepted that this might be necessary for the greater good of democratic Socialism. As he wrote in his posthumously published *Problems of Economic Planning*:

> Perhaps the most important requirement of efficient planning is the supersession in the trade union and labour movement in practice as well as in theory of the last elements of Syndicalism. All partial groups of workers by hand and brain – lawyers as well as bricklayers, postmen as well as dockers – must be prepared in the last resort to allow their own interests to be subordinated to the interests of the workers as a whole.

He recognized that the interests of people as workers conflicted with their interests as consumers:

> What is required for efficiency is that the interests of all should be served by a continuous process of concession on the part of particular groups. We must all mitigate our claims in order that others may mitigate their claims against us and that by compromise we may all live.[79]

For Durbin, success depended on 'the breadth and consistency of the Socialist faith which animates us'. In high minded vein he went on:

> The interests of the whole are sovereign over the interests of the part. In society we are born; by society we must live. To the centralised control of a democratic community our livelihood and our security must be submitted. It is the business of society to secure the welfare of all. To do so it must be able to set limits to the welfare of each one of us.

Such a benevolent Leviathan, or what Durbin called vaguely 'some kind of Central Authority' with the power to fix prices and output, as well as to control banking and investment, was necessary to ensure full employment, equality and the creation of a Socialist economy. This required, however, as Durbin explained, 'a willingness on the part of organised labour to adjust itself to the new conditions of national control'. Moreover, he also believed that the 'vested interests of the workers in any particular industry must never be allowed to prevent contraction of employment if it is making losses or expansion if it is making profits'.

Durbin went further than his political colleagues in his efforts to try and reconcile trade union autonomy with economic planning but there could be doubting the authoritarian – if well-meaning – solution he advocated. No doubt, he was very much a man of his times, when many believed that objective and public-spirited planners could create the good society. However, Durbin's prescription lacked political credibility. Trade union leaders were not going to emasculate themselves in the interests of a Labour government no matter how much they might agree with its economic and social aspirations.

It is also clear just how limited the TUC's aims were in the years immediately after 1945. Tewson and his colleagues on the TUC general council had no desire to challenge the right of the government to govern; nor, perhaps more importantly, were trade unions in the mood to question the unilateral prerogative of the employers to manage. Unlike in the Western-occupied zones of Germany, where TUC influence played a part in the introduction of co-determination between labour and capital in industry, there was little pressure from the trade unions to establish effective forms of worker or union participation even in the management of Britain's newly nationalized industries. For all Citrine's earlier claims of a new legitimacy for the TUC as an Estate of the Realm, there were severe limitations on just how far the trade unions as a collective force wanted to go in their activities beyond the defence of traditional collective bargaining based on the voluntarist tradition. As far as they were able the union leaders of the 1945 generation sought to reinforce the post-war social settlement. They also worked diligently at national level on important issues like manpower planning and productivity, particularly through the prestigious Anglo-American Productivity Council. There was even TUC enthusiasm for state-inspired campaigns for the cause of higher industrial production, though all these good intentions foundered on the inability to translate them into positive action on the shop floor.

But there was little sign of any structural reform inside the TUC that would have brought greater centralizing power and authority and rationalized trade union organization to make it more effective. The TUC after Citrine's departure in 1946 seemed to lack a clear and cohesive view of what it wanted to do. In fact, its aims were increasingly modest and defensive. The underlying tensions in Britain's industrial politics that were to grow much sharper over the next thirty years had already become manifest in the immediate post-war period. Not even the existence of the TUC–Labour alliance could disguise the fundamental problem of the tensions between the desire to uphold free collective bargaining and extend the rights and responsibilities of trade unions through the creation of a more dirigiste economy. In the complex entanglements of *laissez faire* and statism the TUC was unwilling to accept the need for the planning of wages.

However, it was the unexpected arrival and maintenance of full employment, not the menace of Soviet Communism among the shop stewards, that provoked a more fragmented and unstable labour market. For a limited time, national trade union leaders like Deakin and Williamson tried, with some success, to subordinate the bread and butter demands of their members to the needs of a Labour government in trouble, but even they recognized this could only go on for a short period without provoking severe conflict with their members inside their increasingly fossilized union structures. The Labour party's defeat in the October 1951 general election postponed for thirteen years any further attempt to resolve the problem.

Notes

1   TUC Congress Report, 1945, p. 263.
2   Hansard Parliamentary Debates, vol. 410, 2 May 1945, c. 1405.
3   J. Price, *Trade Unions and the War*, Ministry of Information, 1945, p. 16.
4   TUC Congress Report, 1946, p. 269.
5   J. Price, ibid., p. 32.
6   TUC Congress Report, 1945, p. 451.
7   C. R. Attlee, *The Labour Party in Perspective Gollancz*, 1937, pp. 62–3.
8   Ibid., p. 66.
9   Labour Party Conference Report, 1935, p. 180.
10 E. Wertheimer, *Portrait of the Labour Party*, Putnam, 1929, pp. 2–3.
11 K. Morgan, *Consensus and Disunity*, Oxford University Press, 1979, pp. 220–1.
12 R. McKibbin, *The Evolution of the Labour Party 1910–1924*, Oxford University Press, 1974, p. 242.
13 D. Marquand, *Ramsay MacDonald*, Jonathan Cape, 1977, p. 621.
14 Ibid., p. 625.
15 Ibid., p. 634.
16 Labour Party Conference Report, 1933, p. 8.
17 C. R. Attlee, *Labour Party*, pp. 72–3.
18 B. Pimlott, *Labour and the Left in the 1930s*, Cambridge University Press, 1977, pp. 18–19.
19 G. D. H. Cole, *The People's Front*, Gollancz, 1937, pp. 292–4.
20 R. Shackleton, 'Trade Unions and the Slump', in B. Pimlott and C. Cook (eds), *Trade Unions in British Politics*, Longman, 1991, pp. 134–5.

21   TUC Congress Report, 1945, p. 264.
22   TUC Congress Report, 1946, p. 299.
23   A. Bullock, *Life and Times of Ernest Bevin*, Vol. 3, Heinemann, 1983, p. 215.
24   Ibid., p. 267.
25   L. Minkin, *The Contentious Alliance*, Edinburgh University Press, 1991, p. 72.
26   N. Chester, *The Nationalisation of British Industry, 1945–1951*, HMSO, 1975, p. 79.
27   P. Williams (ed.), *Diaries of Hugh Gaitskell*, Jonathan Cape, 1983, p. 55.
28   K. Jeffrey and P. Hennessy, *States of Emergency*, Routledge & Kegan Paul, 1983, pp. 220–1.
29   TUC Congress Report, 1946, p. 13.
30   TUC Congress Report, 1948, p. 337.
31   TUC Congress Report, 1949, p. 285.
32   Ibid., p. 275.
33   K. G. J. C. Knowles, *Strikes*, Oxford University Press, 1952, p. 243.
34   G. D. H. Cole, Introduction to N. Barou, *British Trade Unions*, Gollancz, 1947.
35   *Trade Unionism*, PEP, 1949, pp. 150–1.
36   J. Goldstein, *The Government of British Trade Unions*, Allen & Unwin, 1952, p. 271.
37   Ibid., p. 243.
38   F. Zweig, *The British Worker*, Pelican, 1952, p. 180.
39   Ibid., pp. 182–3.
40   A. Cairncross, *Years of Recovery*, Methuen, 1987, p. 396.
41   Ibid., p. 387.
42   N. Chester, *Nationalisation*, p. 517.
43   TUC Congress Report, 1946, p. 170.
44   Ibid., p. 175.
45   Labour Party Conference Report, 1946, p. 179.
46   Labour Party Conference Report, 1947, p. 137.
47   TUC Congress Report, 1946, pp. 421–2.
48   A. Cairncross, *Years*, p. 403.
49   Ibid., p. 401.
50   Ibid., p. 404.
51   TUC Congress Report, 1947, p. 152.
52   American Federation of Labor Congress Report, 1947, p. 236.
53   TUC Congress Report, 1948, p. 289.
54   Labour Party Conference Report, 1947, p. 32.
55   Ibid., p. 36.
56   Ibid., pp. 290–1.
57   A. Cairncross, *Years*, p. 404.
58   P. Williams (ed.), *Diaries of Hugh Gaitskell*, p. 126.
59   TUC Congress Report, 1948, p. 166.
60   Ibid., p. 184.

61 B. Roberts, *National Wages Policy in War and Peace*, Allen & Unwin, 1955, p. 37.
62 K. Morgan, *Labour in Power 1945–1951*, Oxford University Press, 1987, p. 378.
63 A. Cairncross, *Years*, p. 405.
64 TUC Congress Report, 1949, p. 245.
65 Ibid., p. 188.
66 Ibid., p. 234.
67 TUC Congress Report, 1950, p. 215.
67 Ibid., p. 366.
68 Ibid., p. 269.
69 Ibid., p. 214.
70 Roberts, *National Wages Policy*, p. 44.
71 Hansard Parliamentary Debates, Vol. 486, 10 April 1951, c. 830.
72 Ibid., c. 831.
73 TUC Congress Report, 1951, p. 369.
74 Ibid., p. 284.
75 A. Flanders, *A Policy for Wages*, Fabian Society, 1951, p. 15.
76 Ibid., p. 18.
77 J. McKelvey, 'Trade Union Wage Policy in Post-War Britain', *Industrial and Labour Relations Review*, 6, 1952, p. 19.
78 S. Brooke, 'Problems of Socialist Planning: Evan Durbin and the Labour Government of 1945', *Historical Journal*, 34 (3), September 1991, p. 686.
79 E. Durbin, *Problems of Economic Planning*, Routledge & Kegan Paul, 1949, pp. 56–7.

3 The Conservatives and the Industrial Relations Consensus, July 1945 to November 1955

Party traditions

During their years in opposition after their defeat in the 1945 general election the Conservatives came to accept most of the so-called post-war social settlement. 'We are not the party of unbridled, brutal capitalism and never have been', Sir Anthony Eden assured the 1947 National Union conference. 'Although we believe in personal responsibility and personal initiative in business, we are not the political children of the *laissez-faire* school. We opposed them decade after decade.'[1] Under the influence of R. A. Butler as chairman of the Conservative Research Department, the party tried to convince the electorate that modern Conservatism was not a heartless creed dominated by selfishness and greed. There would be no return to the dole queues and means testing of the 1930s. Indeed, the Conservatives insisted that the state should in future play an active role in ensuring the maintenance of a 'high and stable level' of employment through managing the market economy, as well as encouraging the development of a welfare state based on universalist principles of provision and funded through redistributive taxation.

The party's diverse traditions provided strong enough evidence of its willingness in the past to encourage and defend the voluntarist industrial relations system. It was a Conservative government and not a Liberal one which carried through the legal settlement of the trade union question in the 1870s that lasted for nearly a quarter of a century. A delighted Benjamin Disraeli claimed the passage of legislation to provide the trade unions with legal security in their activities would 'gain for the Conservatives the lasting affection of the working classes'.[2] 'We have settled the long and vexatious contest between capital and labour', he told Lady Bradford.[3] Union leaders of the time were appreciative of what had been done to protect organized labour. George Howell, the TUC's parliamentary secretary, admitted that the 1875 Employers and Workmen Act coupled with the Conspiracy and Protection of Property Act had 'conceded all, and more than all the demands made by successive Congresses'.[4] As Dr Paul Smith pointed out, 'The labour legislation of 1875 was a remarkable stroke and easily the most important of the government's social reforms. It gave the working class everything for which they had striven at the 1874 general election and which Gladstone's ministry had steadfastly refused them.'[5] It enabled trade unions involved in strikes not to be restricted in their behaviour by fear of legal action being taken against them on grounds of being a conspiracy. Picketing was also permitted. 'The unions had secured a charter which, until the legal decisions of the late 1890s seemed to guarantee them in the free and effective exercise of their functions', noted Smith.

But Conservative party attitudes towards the trade unions were not always to be so consistently conciliatory. From the late 1890s onwards the party began to adopt a much more cautious and increasingly negative view of the activities of organized labour, especially after the trade unions became more politically partisan after they helped to form the Labour Representation Committee in 1900. A number of legal judgements which were adverse for the trade unions brought the permanency of the 1875–6 industrial relations settlement into serious question. These culminated in the famous Taff Vale case of 1902 when the House of Lords judged that the Amalgamated Society of Railway Servants 'could be sued in a corporate capacity for damages alleged to have been caused by the action of its officers'.[6] The trade unions feared their position was fatally threatened by the judgement and campaigned for further legislation from the state, designed to safeguard their freedom.

Under Arthur Balfour's leadership the Unionist government in the early 1900s set up a Royal Commission to look into the legal position of the trade unions. But it did not respond in a sympathetic way to the TUC's growing anxieties. In opposition after their election defeat in 1906, the Conservatives took a pragmatic view of the Trade Disputes Act in that year which provided the trade unions with wide-ranging legal immunities from actions in tort taken against them under the civil law in trade disputes. Balfour, speaking on that crucial measure's third reading, admitted he 'did not like great powers given to any body of men without any power of making them answerable for the results of their action'. But he added that it was the 'best hope that Englishmen had on the whole shown themselves so far capable of exercising great powers with moderation'. 'There was a natural good sense and moderation about the race in its corporate dealings which might be able to resist the temptation given even by a wide act of Parliament', he argued, while acknowledging that 'they had reached a stage in the discussion when it was only on such hopes that they could rely'.[7]

After 1911, as Alan Sykes has argued, the party was on 'the high road to reaction' in its policy towards the trade unions. 'Fundamentally the Unionists were not prepared to tolerate labour as an independent force, particularly an independent political force', he added. 'The party under Andrew Bonar Law's leadership did not devise and did not want a constructive social policy towards industrial labour.'[8] Even Stanley Baldwin – the originator of One Nation Toryism in its modern guise – oscillated between conciliation and restriction in his attitude towards the trade unions. In the aftermath of the 1926 General Strike he succumbed without much difficulty to pressures from his party's right wing to curb the power of organized labour. In a speech in the Commons in 1927 he even blamed the 1906 Trade Disputes Act for placing the trade unions in what he called 'a position of irresponsibility' because they had ceased to be liable under the law 'in certain circumstances for wrong actions which they might commit'.[9] Baldwin claimed that the Act contained 'certain seeds of trouble' which had developed in subsequent years. He painted a luridly bleak and frightening picture of the growth of organized labour in the years since the end of the First World War. Apparently trade unions were now moving from 'industrial to political action' and there was also a tendency for them 'to proceed from constitutional to direct action', reflected in their use of mass picketing. Baldwin suggested the 1906 Act had ensured that 'when once a strike was declared, anything that a man on strike did was legal'. He warned: 'Whereas previously the trade union forces have moved in regiments and brigades, in recent years they have moved in armies.'

In the event, the 1927 Trade Union and Trade Disputes Act was a much milder measure than the TUC's own rhetoric suggested. It fell far short of an emasculation of the 1906 legal settlement but it continued to remain an irritant to the trade unions for nearly twenty years until its repeal by the Labour government in 1946. Baldwin's biographers admit the Act was 'primarily restrictive and repressive and it must be concluded that if Baldwin had wished otherwise, he would have tried harder to amend it'.[10] Even Churchill was not prepared to repeal or suspend the measure during the Second World War despite pressure from the TUC and his Labour coalition Cabinet colleagues to do so.

But relations between the Conservatives and the trade unions were more cordial between the wars than the bitter debate surrounding the General Strike and the 1927 Trade Union and Trade Disputes Act might suggest. During the 1930s, the TUC was treated with formal respect by the National Governments of Ramsay MacDonald and then Baldwin. Union leaders were appointed by the state to committees of inquiry and quasi non-governmental organizations though not in any systematic way. It is true that the TUC failed to make much of an impact as a lobbying force on the National Government's economic strategy. Trade union calls for economic controls, higher public expenditure and labour market measures to deal with mass unemployment were unacceptable to the Treasury.

The industrial charter

Conservative leaders believed that the party would have to reappraise its post-war attitude towards organized labour if it hoped to recover lost electoral ground. Coming to terms with the trade unions was therefore seen as an important part of the party's revival strategy. It is true that the party opposed the Labour government's repeal of the 1927 Trade Union and Trade Disputes Act in 1946, particularly the provision to replace the right of 'contracting in' to the payment of the political levy by 'contracting out' – a change that improved Labour's finances dramatically as the number of affiliated trade unionists to the party rose as a result from 2,917,000 in 1945 to 5,613,000 two years later. But at the same time the Conservatives were anxious to avoid any suggestion that they were hostile to trade unionism. Most of them in the late 1940s believed trade unions were a vital force in Britain's economic revival, not monopolistic threats to the success of the free market economy.

It was the 1947 Industrial Charter which provided the most significant evidence of the more conciliatory Conservative approach towards the trade unions. The 40 page document sought to dispel any fears that the party stood for an 'unbridled capitalism'. 'Rarely in the field of political pamphleteering can a document so radical in effect have been written with such flatness of language or blandness of tone', wrote R. A. Butler, who as chairman of the party's Industrial Policy Committee was its main author. 'This was not wholly unintentional. We were out-Peeling Peel in giving the party a painless but permanent face-lift; the more unflamboyant the changes, the less likely were the features to sag again.'[11] The Industrial Charter sought to reconcile the Conservatives to the 1944 White Paper policy objective of maintaining 'high and stable' employment. It promised that when the party returned to government it would 'remove as far as lies within human power the fearful dread of enforced idleness'.[12]

The document expressed support for an interventionist role for the state in the management of the economy. In its section on trade unions entitled 'The Workers' Charter', the Conservatives emphasized their important historic role in providing organized labour with legal protections from the common law. The Charter welcomed the arrival of trade union leaders in the corridors of power and accepted that they had acquired 'an important status as members of many advisory committees attached to government departments'. 'We recognise this status and believe that it opens up a wide field of public service in which the unions can make their contribution to the national welfare', it declared. Apparently, the Conservatives attached 'the highest importance to the part to be played by the unions in guiding the national economy'. 'The effective working of this machinery depends upon the participation of union officials at all levels', added the Charter.[13]

The document was not entirely uncritical of contemporary trade union practice. It condemned 'unofficial' strikes on the grounds that 'they undermined the voluntary machinery of collective bargaining and weakened trade unions' and it also deplored what it saw as 'the tendency for some unions to fall into the hands of a small clique because of apathy'. But the Charter gave its unreserved blessing to the extension of trade union membership in hitherto unorganized sectors of the labour market. 'It is right that the unions, large and small alike, should aim to organise all workers in unions so that they are fully representative', it declared. While the document expressed its belief that the 'voluntary' nature of trade union membership was 'best', it did not go on to denounce the closed shop – though it admitted that the Labour's government repeal of the 1927 Trade Union and Trade Disputes Act had left 'some features' of current labour legislation 'in a most unsatisfactory state'. The Charter also promised the Conservatives did 'not intend to indulge in a game of political tit for tat', though it suggested the party would amend the 1946 Trade Disputes Act both to bring back 'contracting in' to payment of the political levy and to ensure no worker lost his job with a public sector employer for refusing to join a trade union in a closed shop.

What really marked a break with the recent Conservative past in the party's document was the conciliatory language used towards organized labour. The way to resolve shopfloor problems was not through the introduction of restrictive legal regulation to change rank and file and union leadership attitudes, but by management taking a more humane attitude towards the workplace so that capital and labour could be transformed into partners unified by a sense of common purpose. Here employers would have to play a crucial role, argued the Charter. It insisted they must provide three 'general rights' for workers – their right to security in their job; the incentive to 'do the job well and to get a better one'; and to have an improved 'status as an individual however big the firm or mechanised the job may be'. The Workers' Charter that enshrined those rights envisaged their extension through voluntary employer initiatives not by the use of legislation. 'The conditions of industrial life are too varied to be brought within the cramping grip of legislation', it explained. 'We do not share the Socialist belief that the world can be put right if only there are enough Acts of Parliament. We desire to work by example and precept as much as or more than by penalty or sanction.' The aim was to establish a 'series of standards' in industrial relations practice to which employers 'must conform'. Parliament was to be asked to vote its approval for the Workers' Charter, which would then operate in a manner similar to the Highway Code for motorists.[14]

But the Charter was much more than a mere verbal exhortation for employers to treat their workers with fairness and dignity. The document also took a positive view about the merits of collective bargaining. It actually proposed public contracts put out to tender by central or local government authorities should be withheld from any company that failed to practise the proposed fair labour standards within a reasonable period. The document also recommended that workers should receive a statement from their employer laying down the terms and conditions of their employment. It was proposed that a worker who had 'done well in a job should not lose it without some longer period of notice than that applicable to a newly engaged man'. The specific proposals embodied in the Industrial Charter were to form the framework of Conservative industrial relations policy towards the trade unions for the next seventeen years.

As party leader, Winston Churchill took no direct personal interest in the formulation of the Industrial Charter, but he appeared to give his vague blessing to the document over a convivial dinner with Butler at London's Savoy Hotel on the eve of its publication in May 1947. However, just before the National Union conference in the autumn he confessed to the young Reginald Maudling that he 'did not agree with a word' of the Charter. Nevertheless, he said he would express approval of it in his end of conference speech. As Maudling wrote later, Churchill's remarks on the Charter were made with 'the calculated coolness' reserved for the rare passages in his speeches that he had not written himself.[15] But Churchill was not really hostile to the Charter's sentiments. As party leader he was quite willing to make the necessary compromises in order to return the Conservatives to the mainstream of British politics. Certainly, he harboured no desire to see any return to the bitter industrial climate of the early 1920s with an anti-union strategy.

The endorsement of the Industrial Charter by the leadership was not the only strong indication of a more sympathetic Conservative party attitude towards the trade unions than had been evident during the inter-war years. David Clarke, director of the Conservative Research Department, expressed some remarkably sympathetic views about the role of organized labour. In a pamphlet for party members, he explained:

> Collective bargaining is now the accepted method of settling industrial wages in this country and it implies organisation on both sides. A few firms – it is true – do not recognise trade unions but usually at the cost of offering higher wages and better conditions. In large-scale industry there is in fact no real alternative to collective bargaining. If unions did not exist, it would be necessary to create some industrial leadership among employ-ees. Unofficial strikes notwithstanding, it is generally true that agreements made by the unions are honoured by their members. Trade unionism is making an important contribution to the orderly conduct of industry.[16]

He pointed out that trade unions now exercised an influence that stretched far beyond the mere practice of collective bargaining. 'They are the con-sultants of the government in administrative as well as legislative action and no narrow interpretation is given as to what are or are not industrial subjects', he wrote. Party members were also told that the often defensive and negative attitudes of the unions were 'naturally and excusably con-ditioned by the haunting fear of unemployment and falling wages which they experienced so harshly between the two wars'.

In *The Worker in Industry*, a pamphlet published by the Conservative Political Centre in 1948, Michael Fraser, who would succeed Clarke as the research department's director three years later, revealed an under-standing of the plight of Britain's manual workers. 'The more irregular a man's employment, the greater is the temptation for him to develop irregular habits', he wrote:

> Conversely regular employment and wages tend to develop self-respect and other qualities valuable both to the worker himself and to his em-ployer. At present the manual worker is picked up and dropped again by industry to suit the circumstances of the moment. He is paid by the hour and everything in his working environment tends to emphasise the funda-

mental insecurity of his position. This is a situation which does not accord well with our idea of the common interest of workers and management.[17]

The first priority in any Conservative industrial relations strategy, argued Fraser, must be to minimize the existing sense of insecurity experienced by manual workers. He proposed that every worker should be given a written contract of employment by his employer with clearly stipulated terms of service. He also favoured a fair procedure to cover redundancy so that compensation payments should be made to workers for the loss of their jobs based on length of time in employment in the company. Fraser championed payment-by-results wage systems, particularly piecework and incentive bonus schemes linked to individual effort. While he rejected the idea of 'worker directors', Fraser backed the idea of 'a proper merit system of promotion' which could cut through rigid demarcation lines. He advocated joint consultation throughout industry in firms employing more than 150 workers. 'There should be no attempt to enforce joint consultation by Act of Parliament', he accepted. 'But the provision and use of suitable formal joint consultative machinery should be made a definite condition for all firms receiving government contracts.'

The party's July 1949 policy statement, *The Right Road for Britain*, indicated a slight retreat by the leadership from some of the implications of the Industrial Charter. It would not make an explicit commitment to seek the maintenance of 'full' employment, for example. But the Conservative policy-makers continued to enthuse over the voluntarist system of industrial relations and called for its improvement by fostering 'new forms of co-operation' in dealing with industrial production problems. 'The Conservatives hold the view that the trade union movement is absolutely essential to the proper working of our economy and industrial life', it argued. The government ought to 'give a lead in securing the establishment of the idea of a common interest and common task' between capital and labour, asserted the statement, but it added that this did not require any reforms 'enforced by law'.[18] The party said its industrial relations policy was based on the idea that the 'prosperity of employers and employed is indivisible'. It welcomed piecework pay systems, profit-sharing and joint consultation as ways of furthering class harmony in the workplace. The document also supported the concept of equal pay for women for equal work done. But the 1949 policy statement also suggested the Conservatives wanted to take party politics out of trade unionism. The close partnership between the TUC and the Labour government at the time was criticized strongly by the party leadership. *The Right Road for Britain* made it clear that a future Conservative government would seek to resolve the sensitive issue by replacing the principle of 'contracting out' of payment of the political levy by that of 'contracting in'. It also suggested that the 'compulsory unionism' question in the form of closed shops would also need to be dealt with through future talks with trade union leaders aimed at reaching 'a friendly and final settlement' of industrial relations problems.

The party's overwhelmingly benevolent if paternalistic post-war attitude towards industrial relations reflected the Conservative leadership's recognition that the new power and authority of the trade unions acquired during the 1940s could neither be denied nor reversed. The influential One Nation group of younger Conservatives believed a new sense of social responsibility must be established between employers, trade unions and workers, aided by a strong role for government in shaping attitudes on both sides of industry. 'Government should leave industry under private ownership but should use the power of the state to make it conform to definite standards', the group argued in October 1950 in a pamphlet edited by Ian Macleod – a future Minister of Labour – and Angus Maude with assistance from Edward Heath, Enoch Powell and Robert Carr.[19] It suggested the 'first responsibility' of a new Conservative government must be the 'maintenance of full employment, for workers require a sense of security so that they can react to the opportunities and accept the responsibilities of liberty'.

The One Nation group went much further than the Industrial Charter in calling for legislation to improve shopfloor conditions. It favoured a new Factory Act to deal with smoke and noise abatement, better lighting, ventilation and decoration of workshops, and improved safety services and training for the factory inspectorate with an 'extra emphasis on preventive health measures'. Special attention was recommended for the training and rehabilitation of disabled workers and it proposed an inquiry into 'the problems of shift work', particularly for women and young people. The group also made it clear it was opposed to any form of incomes policy. 'The fixing of wages must be left to free bargaining between trade unions and employers', it argued, and it favoured much greater rewards for workers based on ability, skill and hard work. The One Nation pamphlet drew attention to what it saw as the malaise in workplace life caused by the spread of technological change that deskilled manual workers. As it explained:

> The increasing scale of production has brought people to work together in larger groups and has made them more subject to the hopelessness of feeling just one of the mass, without individual importance. This is why it

is necessary that the worker should be identified with a larger interest than the performance of his own particular job.

'The success of his own working group and of his firm as a whole must be made a cause for pride and loyalty', declared the One Nation group. It believed 'joint consultation' was the 'most important single technique for achieving' that objective. The group advocated the creation of workplace-based joint consultation committees elected by secret ballot. Macleod and his young colleagues showed a real insight into what was happening at plant level in the post-war conditions of full employment, arguing that:

> Joint Consultation can neither replace nor usurp the prime responsibility of good management. It is part of it. In small factories formal consultation machinery may well be unnecessary. But in small or large factories, whether there are Consultation Committees or not, everybody should be given information about the business as a whole. We believe that employees have the right to know how the company's income is spent, how the profits are used, and something about the prospects for the future.

The group wrote with concern about the rise of the great industrial cities which had 'largely destroyed the old community groups with their individual character and feelings of loyalty, pride and purpose stimulated among their members'. While cures for this problem lay partly in housing and town planning policy, the group also suggested making the workplace 'a new centre of social life' with the development of more sports and social clubs and encouragement for company based non-profit-making housing associations, so companies could build homes for their workers on the Bourneville model pioneered by the Cadbury family.

The conciliatory Conservative approach to industrial relations was emphasized by the party's shadow labour spokesman Sir David Maxwell Fyfe in the run-up to the 1951 general election. He told Conservative union activists that the party would 'uphold and strengthen the position of the unions, where such would be to the advantage of the Nation'. Apparently, there would be 'no attempt to alter Trade Union Acts without full consultation with the unions; but a Conservative government should be prepared to take positive action in regard to the closed shop'.[20] The party's October 1951 general election manifesto, *Britain Strong and Free*, emphasized that

> Conservatives believe that free and independent trade unions are an essential part of our industrial system. . . . We welcome the public endorsement by the trade union movement of the need for an effort to increase production and productivity. We shall consult the leaders of the trade union

movement on economic matters and discuss with them fully and sympathetically any proposals we or they may have for action on labour problems.[21]

While rejecting any form of compulsory trade unionism the manifesto argued it was in the national interest that 'men and women should join trade unions and be active trade unionists'.

Churchill and his colleagues also spoke out strongly in support of the voluntarist industrial relations system. 'We shall retain and strengthen the British practice under which wages and conditions are negotiated by representatives of employers and employed', the 1951 manifesto argued. It is true that criticism was levelled at 'unnecessary restrictive practices' and the party said it intended to 'strengthen the Monopolies Commission and speed up its work' in dealing with shopfloor obstacles to efficiency. But in a personal declaration Churchill promised that the Conservatives wished to create a human as well as an efficient industrial system and they intended to introduce its Workers' Charter 'as early as possible' once elected into government.

The TUC's hostile reaction to the Conservative's persistence in raising the closed shop and political levy questions worried the party leadership, who were keen to avoid any suggestion that they intended to launch an anti-trade-union offensive if they were returned to office at the next general election. But at the same time the leadership remained concerned – as it had been before 1945 – by the close links that existed between most trade unions and the Labour party. The lengths to which the TUC had gone between January 1948 and June 1950 to help Attlee's government combat the economic crisis through a policy of wage restraint strengthened the Conservative party's conviction that the trade unions were too politically partisan and had neglected their proper industrial function of protecting and improving the living standards of their members.

Trade unionists in the Conservative party

The leadership's concern to maintain at least a peaceful coexistence with the trade unions under a Conservative government was paralleled during the late 1940s by the party's attempt to achieve greater electoral support among rank and file trade union members. In March 1947 the Conservatives refurbished their own trade union organization by establishing the Central Trade Union Advisory Committee. Its stated primary aim was to 'free trade unions from Socialist and Communist domination' but it sought also 'to discover, build up and organise the latent forces of Conservative trade unionists and others opposed to political control'.[22] The committee acknowledged from the outset there was a widely held belief that the Conservatives were 'too much associated with wealth and privilege and too much the party of the boss'. It therefore believed the party needed to reassure the trade unions that their future would be safe under a Conservative government. After all, trade unions had 'stood the test of time', even if some of them were to be deplored for having 'gone off the rails in their political associations'. But the party leadership was not particularly keen on publicizing efforts by a handful of Conservative trade unionists to secure shopfloor support. It feared the party's 'capacity for effective work' would be compromised if its trade union section developed too high a public profile. In fact, Conservative leaders faced a genuine dilemma in their strategy towards the trade unions. They wanted to increase electoral support for Conservatism among rank and file trade unionists, but at the same time they wished to establish at least a basis for peaceful cooperation with the TUC as well as stressing the need for non-political trade unionism.

It is indeed highly questionable whether either Conservative policy efforts after 1947 to placate the trade unions or the party's attempt to revitalize its own organizational appeal to workers played any significant part in its electoral recovery in 1950–1. Within months of the Industrial Charter's appearance, Derick Heathcoat Amory, MP for Tiverton and a member of the party's Industrial Policy Committee, was complaining that it had 'not got over to the working man or made an impression on him'. As he explained: 'It has not proved easy to "put over" with any very profound effect on our own people.' Apparently the Charter was 'no red hot gospel' with the party's own rank and file. 'It does not in itself – as it stands – provide that clear concrete alternative policy to Socialism for which there is such an insistent demand', he explained.[23]

In July 1950 a memorandum to the working party established to propagate the Industrial Charter admitted that:

> Many of the difficulties now being experienced are the result of distrust of the motives of the Conservative party and fears of a recurrence of mass unemployment. This distrust is of long standing and it will require patience and persistence in stating our policy and steadfast action in putting it into practice whenever possible before it can be dispelled.[24]

It was even suggested that the party's appeal should be concentrated on 'skilled and intelligent workers who will themselves educate their fellows' as well as on employers to make every effort in influencing shopfloor opinion 'by example and precept'. 'It would not be possible in present circumstances to secure the votes of more than 40 per cent of the industrial workers', confessed the memorandum. The candid document went on:

A proportion put as high as 30 per cent of the working population is of a mentality which will only respond to a 'something for nothing' policy. To offer the sort of policy which would satisfy the shiftless and idlers would be to antagonize the more self-reliant workers. Broadly speaking, the appeal should be to the skilled worker, the type who expects to have to earn his own living and strives to advance as a result of his own efforts. Such men are important not only as intended voters but because of their influence on their fellow workers. A distinction must be drawn however between levels of intelligence and levels of skill. The appeal must include all those, whatever their level of industrial skill who are capable of thinking constructively about their own and their children's future.

Churchill's populist rallying cry of 'Set the People Free' was far more potent in winning back lost Conservative voters than any paternalistic assurance to manual workers that their trade unions would be safe in the party's hands if the Conservatives were returned to power. As Hoffman argued:

By 1951 Conservative policy had redefined the party's attitude towards the role of the state in the direction of a fundamentally free enterprise economy and had absorbed completely the older radicalism of the Tory left. Now fused with the two notions of the 'opportunity state' and a 'property-owning democracy' Conservatives stood poised once again to shape and adapt through gradual change the social and economic structure of Britain.[25]

Indeed, after 1947 much less was heard about the Industrial Charter as the economic neo-liberals inside the party reasserted themselves in reaction to the red tape and controls maintained or imposed by the Labour government – at least in its early years in office. The 'bonfire of controls' carried out by Labour in 1949–1950 helped to lessen that particular criticism but the Conservative appeal for more vigorous free market principles made a favourable impact, especially on many of those middle class voters in suburban southern England who had voted Labour in 1945.

Trade unionists inside the party

Even after their return to power in October 1951 the Conservatives continued to wrestle with the awkward question of how the party should react to the trade unions. In May 1952 yet another committee was established, this time under the chairmanship of Sir Edward Keatinge, the former Conservative MP for Bury St Edmunds. It was given the task of examining the role of the party's trade union organization. Its stated aims were to look at ways the Conservatives could 'free trade unions from political domination'; to 'ensure greater dissemination of the Conservative party among trade unionists'; to strengthen the structure of ward and polling district branches by ensuring trade unions were welcomed as active political and social members; and finally to 'win over the votes of trade unionists and their families to the Conservative party'.[26]

In its confidential report, completed in September 1952, the Keatinge committee admitted that 'Trade unionism is a field where the Conservative influence is weakest and where the Labour party derives most of its strength, its membership and money. Moreover this situation can move even further against us and in their favour'.[27] Keatinge suggested that the 'greatest need' of the Conservatives was to 'attract and hold the support of industrial workers'. He believed the reasons for the party's failure to build up an active base inside the trade unions stemmed from a com-bination of 'fear of intimidation, entrenched Socialism and widespread apathy'. The report suggested 'no sudden and spectacular results' could be expected in trying to win over substantial numbers of trade unionists to support the Conservative cause, though Keatinge pointed out an estimated 40 per cent of trade unionists had not voted Labour in the 1951 general election.

The report recognized what needed to be done. 'We must convince trade unionists that our interest comes from a real desire to make the party inclusive of the whole community and that it is not a class party', it explained. 'There is a need not only to convince newcomers but also to bring a change of heart in some sections of our own organisation. The complaint that wage earners are lionized at party conference is partly counter-balanced by a feeling that they are ignored in their own associations.'

Indeed, Keatinge and his colleagues discovered widespread hostility and indifference inside the party, especially among the constituency as-sociations, about the need to win over trade unionists to the Conservative cause. As their report admitted, this was perhaps not surprising because in many industrial areas local employers were often found to be the backbone of the constituency associations, and they showed little enthu-siasm for an appeal to rank and file trade unionists who also worked for them to join the party.

In fact, the Keatinge report was not well received by the Conservative government either. Central Office was told in no uncertain terms by Sir Walter Monckton, then Churchill's Minister of Labour, that he was 'extremely anxious that no undue publicity should be given to the Keatinge report and expressed his hope that some of its confidential features could be conveyed by word of mouth to whatever body might be charged with examining it'.[28] Ministers also pressed for modification in some passages of the draft document to avoid any 'misrepresentation by the Labour party and the trade unions'. There seems little doubt that the renewed Conservative interest in improving the party's organization and propaganda aimed at trade unionists threatened to upset Monckton's delicate consensual approach to industrial relations, even if the Keatinge report kept well clear of contentious issues such as the closed shop, contracting in or out of the political levy, and the use of secret ballots before strikes.

The Conservative leadership may have been keen to win greater support from rank and file trade unionists at general elections, but at the same time it was not anxious to encourage the spread of party politics onto the shop floor. Harold Watkinson told the 1952 National Union (Conservative party) conference that:

> It is quite true that perhaps a third of the trade union membership supports our party. . . . We certainly hope that this important section will play its full part within the unions but we do not wish it to try to draw them to us but merely to try and make them free and independent to serve the best interests of their members in free negotiations with whatever government may happen to be in power.[29]

Attitudes towards the trade unions did not change much among the Conservative ranks during the course of the 1950s. 'Conservative party associations very seldom ask for advice on trade union matters', it was reported in 1962, 'partly because they do not take a great deal of interest in them and partly because they know nothing about trade union matters – indeed they still have a certain hostility to them in any case.'[30] The occasional trade unionist might be fawned upon by the adoring annual conference as 'an angel in marble', but down in the constituencies active trade unionists, where they existed, were often regarded as a nuisance and given little real responsibility. It was a regular complaint among Conservative trade unionists that they found it hard to win nominations in winnable Conservative parliamentary constituencies. Stalwarts like Sir Edward Brown in Bath and Ray Mawby in Totnes were very much the exception. Indeed, for the most part trade union activists were tolerated with ill-disguised condescension inside the party.

Appeasing the trade unions

The Conservatives might not agree on how they should handle the trade unionists in their own ranks or on whether to campaign actively inside the trade unions for recruits to their cause, but at least after the party's narrow election victory in October 1951 they were united over the need to establish an amicable relationship with the TUC. Churchill was certainly anxious to live down his bogeyman image on the Left as the anti-working-class warrior of the General Strike and scourge of the Labour Movement. During his peacetime premiership, trade union leaders were frequent guests at 10 Downing Street dinners. Lord Moran, Churchill's doctor noted in his diary:

> The PM's friendliness to the trade union leaders is an obvious move but their response to his advances is interesting. They know when they dine with him at No 10 that it will do them no good in the Labour party. But they cannot help liking him. He doesn't seem to them at all like other Tories.[31]

Churchill displayed genuine concern at Deakin's health and insisted that Moran must treat the TGWU leader, albeit in the union's Manor House hospital in Golders Green, London. Sir Tom O'Brien, General Secretary of the Theatrical and Kine Employees' Union, was actually criticized publicly by the Labour left when he sent condolences to the Prime Minister during one of his illnesses.

Churchill's decision not to appoint Sir David Maxwell Fyfe as his Minister of Labour was clearly determined by his desire to avoid giving any unnecessary provocation to the TUC. Maxwell Fyfe had aroused particular criticism among many trade union leaders because of his firm support for a change in the law on the political levy from 'contracting out' to 'contracting in' and his rhetorical attacks on the closed shop. Instead, Churchill chose the arch-conciliator Sir Walter Monckton for the post. Monckton later recalled that 'Winston's riding orders to me were that the Labour party has foretold grave industrial troubles if the Conservatives were elected and he looked to me to do my best to preserve industrial peace.'[32] Monckton was scarcely regarded as a Conservative party politician at all. Having won Bristol West in a parliamentary by-election in February 1951 after a distinguished and varied legal career including a period as adviser to the Nizam of Hyderabad and later King Edward VIII during the Abdication crisis, he was seen as a neutral between capital and labour with a high-minded sense of public service. In the view of Monckton's official biographer Lord Birkenhead his 'virginal political status' in

Churchill's cabinet made him 'a priceless asset' at the Ministry of Labour.[33] Butler wrote later of his 'serene, non-political outlook'.[34] Such was his determination to maintain an impartial bipartisanship in the government's industrial relations policy that Monckton did not even attend the annual National Union conference until 1954, leaving it to his junior ministerial colleague Harold Watkinson to round up the industrial relations debate.

To TUC General Secretary Vincent Tewson, Monckton was an apolitical figure who sought the avoidance of conflict by reasoned compromise. As Tewson told Lord Birkenhead:

> He was not a politician and could take his own incisive down-to-earth line. He was not weak. His legal training was of great value to him as Minister of Labour. It was true that he saw both sides of a question but as minister he had to see both sides and the consequence was that both sides liked and trusted him. If he had been weak he would have offended both. He was a bending cane but he was always on his own axis.[35]

Monckton explained to the House of Commons on one occasion: 'I certainly have no wish to commit myself to any line of policy in advance of consultation with the TUC and the employers.'[36] Trade union leaders were regular guests at Monckton dinner parties and they often lunched with him at his corner table in the Aperitif Grill in London's Jermyn Street just around the corner from the Ministry of Labour and National Service. Monckton also enjoyed a bipartisan political reputation and won the warm respect of Alfred Robens, Labour's shadow spokesman on industrial relations, who had a high regard for his abilities as a conciliator.

His primary concern was to encourage a more humane approach by management to industrial relations problems not through the stimulus of legislation but by moral exhortation. Monckton told the House of Commons in November 1952 that

> What we need today is to encourage the mutual confidence which is being surely developed between workpeople and employers. . . . I have tried in this sphere constantly to do my best to stimulate joint consultation and the spread of works information. I am sure the more workpeople are kept fully informed by the management about the business and the prospects of the undertaking in which they are engaged, the more there will grow up a feeling of common purpose and of confidence.[37]

Although Monckton recognized the need for higher productivity and lower industrial costs, he regarded his department as an impartial, conciliatory force, almost semi-detached from any role in the government's economic policy-making. As he explained the House of Commons in June 1955:

> I have tried during these three and a half years [the time he had been Minister] to deal with all the parties who have come along as fairly and justly as I can and I must go on trying to earn – or at any rate to deserve – their confidence. I have to remember always that my task is not to give judgement but, if I can, to narrow the field of conflict and by trying patiently to understand the best that I can find in all the cases that are put before me, to help towards a settlement – not to impose one: that is not my task.[38]

In recent years Monckton's commitment to the industrial appeasement of trade union power has been denounced as a mistaken strategy that did much to worsen relations in industry in the long run by weakening the authority of employers to resist irresponsible wage demands. Even R. A. Butler admitted in his memoirs that he suffered at the Treasury from Monckton's 'strength to inject his own sweetness and light into the atmosphere' by accepting inflationary wage settlements as a way of buying off the threat of industrial trouble.[39] But Monckton's emollience reflected a widespread recognition in the government that the trade unions must as far as possible be placated and not confronted. In May 1952 Butler himself proposed to the TUC that a joint committee of the National Joint Advisory Council should be set up to look at ways of relating pay more closely to productivity, but his suggestion was turned down flat by union leaders as 'impracticable'.[40] 'Any attempt at interference with existing machinery would threaten the foundations of industrial peace', warned the TUC, which was in no mood in the early 1950s to countenance government attempts to intervene in the conduct of collective bargaining. In July 1952 Monckton referred back proposals from twelve statutory Wages Councils for wage increases on the grounds that they were incompatible with Butler's pleas for wage moderation, but the TUC protested to Churchill at the decision and the Prime Minister had the decision quickly rescinded.

The benign attitude of Churchill and Monckton towards the trade unions was supported strongly by senior officials at what was then still the Ministry of Labour and National Service. They were imbued with the philosophy of voluntarism, believing that their work was to mediate between capital and labour as well as improve the general conditions of working people. In Peter Hennessy's words they were 'the very incarnation of the "New Liberalism" of the Edwardian era'.[41] By the 1950s they were very much in spirit One Nation Tories. Astonishingly, civil servants at the Ministry did not appear to regard their department as being directly involved in the making of the government's economic policy. In Sir Godfrey Ince's study of the Ministry of Labour and National Service at the end of the decade, there is no discussion at all of productivity and wage-push inflation. His department seemed unconcerned by the impact of industrial relations on the wider problems that began to trouble the economy during the late 1950s. Moreover, Monckton displayed no apparent interest in propagating the Conservatives' Industrial Charter. Discussions of a desultory nature were held on the National Joint Advisory Council on the idea of an Industrial Code of good conduct, but both the TUC and the employers were lukewarm and nothing came of it.

In fact, the criticisms – made with hindsight from the 1980s – of Churchill and Monckton for their benevolent policy towards the trade unions ignore the atmosphere of the time. The industrial relations consensus established during the war years still remained intact in the early 1950s. While Conservative leaders accepted the TUC's newly acquired status as an Estate of the Realm, trade union leaders for their part were ready to work with and not against a Churchill government just so long as they did not compromise in any way both their ultimate loyalty to the Labour party and their instinctive belief in the virtues of voluntarism. Butler admitted later that if Monckton had 'gone on for ever, it would have been disastrous', but during his period at the Treasury it was 'extremely convenient' and had done him no harm.[42]

The TUC's determination to avoid putting itself on a collision course with the Conservatives after their return to office was underlined on the very day that Churchill walked into 10 Downing Street. In a statement the TUC general council declared:

> It is our long standing practice to seek amicably with whatever government is in power and through consultation jointly with Ministers and the other side of industry to find practical solutions to the social and economic problems facing the country. There need be no doubt therefore of the attitude of the TUC towards the new government.[43]

In fact, while most trade union leaders were against any form of wage restraint they were not in the mood to push for excessively large pay rises for their members because they realized these would merely fuel the rate of inflation and thereby make their members no better off. Moreover, a strong sense of social obligation still existed inside the TUC that outlived the passing of the Labour government. Deakin exemplified this at the 1952 Congress in his presidential address, when he asserted: 'We – on the trade union side – have a clear duty to act with a full sense of responsibility in this critical period not to make unreasonable demands and to do all we can to avoid interruption of work.' In his opinion, the moral restraints of the 1940s should not be thrown away with the launch of a self-destructive pay offensive. 'It is of the utmost importance to keep our industries going with full employment and with steadily rising productivity at the lowest possible production costs', he declared.[44]

During the early 1950s the TUC displayed considerable caution and sobriety in its attitude to collective bargaining. Sir Lincoln Evans, General Secretary of the Iron and Steel Trades Confederation (ISTC), argued that it was a trade union duty

> to maintain economic stability and avoid unemployment. . . . We know that wage levels do affect prices and we are only misleading our people by encouraging them to believe that all the increases we demand can be met out of profits because that simply is not true. . . . Those who possess power must accept responsibility. Public spirit must always be the mainspring of their behaviour. We want to maintain economic stability and avoid unemployment. but if we price ourselves out of world markets, we automatically create unemployment.[45]

Sir William Lawther, President of the NUM, and Tom Williamson, the General Secretary of the GMWU, took a similar view. The TUC's own economic policy statements up to 1955 also reflected a willingness to pursue modest objectives. Many union leaders still feared there could so easily be a return to the mass unemployment of the inter-war years and they were well aware of Britain's increasingly poor productivity performance and the threats to the stability of sterling from fluctuations in the balance of payments. But the TUC's anxiety about the general economic outlook for the country did not lead the trade unions to reconsider their hostility to any form of wage restraint. Williamson denounced a motion at the 1952 Congress designed to achieve pay coordination and a reform of existing wage negotiating machinery to provide for 'greater equity and fairer relativities'. He called it an attempt to put Congress through 'a preliminary canter directed towards the vague and academic proposal of a national wages policy'.[46] 'I think most unions consider that the negotiating machinery on a voluntary basis which we have been able to build up in this country over the years is second to none', added Williamson.

The TUC's apparent willingness to cooperate with Churchill's government was exemplified in 1953 when four trade union leaders – including Sir Lincoln Evans – accepted government invitations to sit on the new Steel Board designed to run the denationalized steel industry. A motion which condemned their behaviour was defeated by 4,933,000 votes to 2,877,000 at the 1954 Congress. 'The TUC has always taken the line that whenever the interests of our people are involved our people have to be there to do the best they can to protect those interests rather than to leave the members to take the consequences of political policy with which we did not agree', declared Tewson. 'The basic function of the unions is to protect the interests of the people they represent.'[47]

It looked as though the Conservatives and the trade unions had found a way of working together in complacent harmony where both sides appreciated the limitations imposed on the other by the voluntarist system. As the young Anthony Crosland, future Labour Cabinet minister and arch-revisionist, noted in his 1956 classic *The Future of Socialism*, a 'peaceful revolution' had taken place in the relations between the Conservatives and the trade unions:

> One cannot imagine today a deliberate offensive alliance between governments and employers against the unions on the 1921 or 1925–26 or 1927 model with all the brutal paraphernalia of wage cuts, national lock-outs and anti-union legislation . . . [the] atmosphere in Whitehall is almost deferential, the desire not to give offence positively ostentatious.[48]

The government continued to take a benign, hands-off attitude towards industrial relations in the early 1950s. If employers and union leaders found they could not agree over a particular wage claim, then Monckton would step in and appoint a committee or court of inquiry to come up with a satisfactory compromise that invariably split the difference or backed the trade union's demands. Indeed, he acted much more like a conciliator with an open mind than a Cabinet Minister. But Churchill and his colleagues believed that whatever the defects that might exist inside organized labour they were best left for the trade unions themselves to remedy. 'The trade union movement is quite capable today of putting its own house in order providing it has a government that will see fair play in industry', Harold Watkinson told the National Union conference in 1952. He spoke warmly of the constructive attitude of 'the TUC towards the government'. 'There has been give and take on both sides and both sides have been prepared to put the national interest a good way above their own party political factional interest', he added.[49] In his close of conference speech that year, Churchill went out of his way to lavish praise on organized labour:

> We owe a great deal to the trade unions. They are an institution in our land given its original Charter of Rights by the Conservative party. . . . Everyone must recognise the quality, character and courage of the trade union lead-

ers. We do not agree with them on doctrine nor on the part they should play in our domestic politics but we respect them and there is no doubt the country could not get on without them.[50]

Conservative party chairman Lord Woolton agreed with him. 'Since the party came to power we have been gratefully impressed by the statesmanlike way in which so many trade union leaders have sought to gain their legitimate ends', he told the 1954 National Union conference. 'There is no reason why Conservatism and trade unionism should not walk hand in hand.'[51]

Monckton seemed content enough with this benign state of affairs for most of the time as he offered impartial bromides to both sides of industry. He believed in what he liked to call the 'human relations' approach to industrial relations. According to Monckton,

The policy of managements ought to be based on the recognition that a man is not a tool, not a machine but is a complex human personality. A man brings more to his work in his factory than the work of his hands. He brings there a part of his life and he ought to be able to enjoy rights and satisfactions in that working life just as he does in his life as a citizen.[52]

Such high-minded vacuity perhaps did little harm but Monckton was not even prepared to make any innovative moves by implementing the more tangible parts of the Industrial Charter, mainly because such action might offend the TUC's sensitivities.

This national mood of good feelings persisted in industrial relations up until 1955. In a pamphlet published that year the One Nation group suggested that 'in spite of the great weight of resistance to change which is inherent in the trade union structure, the signs of the last few years were by no means without hope'. 'The majority of trade union leaders are becoming increasingly aware of the real needs of the future', it suggested, and it pointed to the emergence of union training schools and the use of modern managerial techniques like time and method study as indicators of progress.[53]

In fact, the persistence of conciliatory industrial relations policies during the early 1950s was based on a relatively stable reality. The economic indicators for those years do not justify the attacks of later critics who regard the period as one of lost opportunity to deal with trade union power. Certainly, there was no pay explosion despite the maintenance of full employment. It is true wages rose sharply by nearly 9 per cent between mid-1951 and mid-1952, but prices also increased over the same period by 10.5 per cent as a result of high world prices due to the Korean war.

Table 3.1   Strikes in the age of Monckton, 1952–1955

	Stoppages	Workers involved	Aggregate days lost
1952	1,174	303,000	1,792,000
1953	1,746	1,329,000	2,184,000
1954	1,989	402,000	2,457,000
1955	2,419	599,000	3,781,000

Source: British Labour Statistics Historical Abstract 1886–1968, DEP, 1971, p. 396.

Table 3.2   Key economic indicators, 1952–1955

	Unemployment (%)	Growth (%)	Increase in real wages (%)	Unit labour cost
1952	2.1	−0.1	−2.0	8.0
1953	1.8	5.0	2.0	2.0
1954	1.5	7.0	5.0	3.0
1955	1.2	4.0	6.0	7.0

Source: Ministry of Labour Gazettes.

With the end of hostilities came a virtual standstill in the rise in living costs, and over the next two years average wages and salaries per worker rose by 4.4 per cent and 4.9 per cent respectively – the lowest for any twelve month period since the TUC's voluntary pay freeze policy in 1948. At the same time, the retail price index rose by 6 per cent in 1952 but by only 1.6 per cent in 1953, followed by 5.3 per cent in 1954. Registered unemployment also remained very low during the period of Churchill's peacetime administration. It averaged a mere 2.0 per cent in 1952 followed by rates of 1.6 per cent, 1.3 per cent and 1.1 per cent over the next three years. Nor was there any sizeable outbreak of labour militancy. Fewer days were lost through stoppages in the 1952–5 period than during the last two years of the Second World War.

It would be wrong, however, to suggest this was entirely a trouble-free period in industrial relations. Monckton might have charmed trade union leaders with his civilized bonhomie but tensions were not entirely absent from the labour scene. The main battlefields were in the engineering and shipbuilding industries and on the recently nationalized railways. In October 1953 the Confederation of Shipbuilding and Engineering Unions (CSEU) submitted a claim for a 15 per cent pay rise for its members to the engineering and shipbuilding employers. After having their demand rejected twice by the employers, the CSEU called a one day strike followed by a ban on overtime and piecework. With the looming prospect of a damaging national engineering stoppage, Monckton intervened and established two Courts of Inquiry to try and resolve the differences, while the CSEU responded by withdrawing its disruption threat. The resulting reports broadly accepted the trade union case for a higher basic rate and in subsequent negotiations a settlement was reached giving rises of just over 6 per cent to skilled workers and slightly more than 5 per cent to unskilled workers in the shipbuilding and engineering industries. The Courts of Inquiry also suggested to the government that the growing problem of wage-push inflation required the creation of 'an authoritative and impartial body' to consider those wider issues of wages, costs and prices and to 'form a view upon their implication for the national economy' as well as providing advice and guidance on what to do about it.[54] Monckton put the idea on the agenda of the National Joint Industrial Council but neither trade union leaders nor employers were keen on such a body interfering with their collective bargaining arrangements.

The railways were also a persistent source of conflict during the early 1950s, mainly because workers in the recently nationalized industry were more badly paid than elsewhere. In July 1953 the three rail unions submitted a claim for a 15 per cent pay rise to the British Transport Commission, who managed the network. This was rejected and referred – according to the procedures – to the Railway Staffs National Tribunal, but the resulting arbitration award from that body was also rejected by the trade unions. At that point Monckton intervened and achieved a settlement with the Cabinet's acceptance. Under its terms the rail unions were promised a further wage increase for their members under an immediate review on top of the agreed arbitration award, though their employers lacked the financial resources to fund it. In fact, the threat of a national rail strike receded for only a few months. In December 1954 all sides were back again at the Ministry of Labour after being unable to agree on the size of the recommended pay rises. Monckton was forced to establish a Court of Inquiry under Sir John Cameron in the face of a strike threat for 9 January 1955 issued by the National Union of Railwaymen. The Court's interim report was ready within just over a week on 5 January. It contained the controversial judgement that railway workers should be paid a 'fair and adequate wage' and that the British Transport Commission's argument that it was not allowed to go into deficit under its articles of association and therefore could not pay the wages demanded by the unions was an argument 'without any real force and substance'.[55]

'Having willed the ends, the Nation must will the means', declared the Cameron report. The Cabinet accepted Cameron's recommendations though with some reluctance and Monckton performed his usual conciliatory magic on the protagonists. With a general election in the offing and widespread public sympathy for the railway workers the government had no desire to face up to a bitter confrontation.

Debating the strike problem

On 5 April 1955 Churchill, at the advanced age of 80, finally decided to step down as Prime Minister to make way at last for his Foreign Secretary, Sir Anthony Eden. The change of guard in 10 Downing Street was followed almost immediately by the calling of a general election. The campaign was punctuated by a number of damaging industrial conflicts. Miners, busmen, printers, dockers and railway workers all went on strike or threatened to do so. In the words of Lord Birkenhead 'a malaise approaching anarchy seemed to have taken possession of the trade union world',[56] and the Cabinet was compelled to call a State of Emergency. Monckton became a virtual prisoner in the Ministry of Labour and National Service as he sought valiantly to resolve the various disruptions. Although the disputes were unrelated to one another they highlighted a number of common problems that were of growing concern to the government.

Inter-union rivalries were a primary reason for the outbreak of labour unrest. In the docks the National Amalgamated Stevedores' and Dockers' Union sought negotiating rights from the port employers but they were opposed in that aim by the TGWU who accused them of poaching its members, an action which eventually led to the expulsion of the Stevedores from the TUC in 1959. A six week long strike in 1955 by the Stevedores' union in pursuit of their claim for recognition crippled a third of the nation's shipping before the union decided eventually to back down. On the troubled railways, ASLEF, the footplatemen's union, brought its members out on strike on May 28 just two days before the 1955 general election in support of maintaining a wage differential *vis-à-vis* other railway workers. The rail dispute was finally called off after seventeen days – thanks to more Monckton conciliation and the TUC general council's constructive intervention. The deterioration in the industrial relations climate also hit the national newspaper industry when Fleet Street electricians and engineers struck unofficially for four weeks before returning to work after yet another Court of Inquiry established by Monckton had improved the employer's final offer.

Eden and his Cabinet colleagues were alarmed at the sudden wave of strikes that had broken out during the spring and early summer of 1955, and they began to discuss whether it might be necessary to introduce legislation to reform industrial relations. 'I feared the nation might drift into sharp antagonisms if no attempt was made to clear the issues and guide opinion', Eden noted in his memoirs.[57] He wanted to initiate a general review into the state of industrial relations, but trade union leaders were quick to reassure him that they too also saw the danger signals and were 'equally concerned at the indiscipline among some trade union members which was aimed in part at them'. They told Eden: 'If the government could strengthen their hand, they would welcome it but they did not want any fresh legislation'.[58]

'I had not much faith in it either', Eden confessed. 'The employers were much concerned to avoid action which would precipitate a collision with the unions. The climate for agreement was therefore pretty good'.[59] However, ministers did discuss the possibility of compelling the unions by law to hold secret ballots before calling strikes, even though they accepted such a reform would be hard to supervise and would do nothing to prevent the outbreak of unofficial disputes, which at the time were a much more serious problem. Such a proposal would, Monckton warned, 'be resisted as an interference with the right to strike and as an interference with the union's management and regulation of its own affairs'.[60] He told the House of Commons that statutory strike ballots would also 'not affect lawful obstruction by going slow or working to rule and one would certainly have to reflect that if a strike had been authorised by ballot, it might be more difficult for negotiators to settle on compromise terms'.[61]

Both the employers and the TUC were opposed to any suggestion that the government should try to outlaw unofficial strikes. Eden admitted that he shared 'their doubts as to whether legislation would be effective', and Monckton agreed with him:

Any attempt to make unofficial strikes illegal raises difficult questions of penalties and enforcement . . . Penal sanctions against individual strikers – there may be tens of thousands of them, as in the recent unofficial coal stoppage in Yorkshire – would be ineffective and dangerous and sanctions could hardly be directed against the funds or the officers of the unions whose authority is being flouted.[62]

Monckton believed that his Ministry could not even intervene with its conciliation services to resolve unofficial strikes, which he suggested were an internal matter for the unions to deal with by themselves. An extension of the use of industrial arbitration was also examined by ministers but without much enthusiasm. Monckton warned that compulsory arbitration would involve withdrawing the right to strike. 'It is not compatible with generally accepted ideas of free negotiation and free contract and is contrary to political pledges given on this subject', he added. Eden thought such reforms could 'hardly be made effective without a general independent inquiry into industrial relations', something which would be a 'slow business and produce no immediate solution'.[63] The Prime Minister personally favoured the idea of a cooling off period or what he called 'a period of reflection'. This would last 21 days between the moment of a trade union's decision to call its members out on strike and the start of the stoppage, to allow 'time for tempers to cool and for every method of conciliation to be tried'. But it was pointed out that this particular measure had made little noticeable impact on the incidence of unofficial disputes before the Labour government had abolished it in 1951.

Indeed, there was little sign of any support in 1955 from either employers or trade union leaders for the state to play a much more active role in resolving industrial relations problems through changes in the existing statute law. At his meeting with TUC general council members at 10 Downing Street on 15 June 1955 to discuss the effects of the docks and railway disputes on the economy, Eden assured the union leaders that 'so far as the Cabinet was concerned, it had not discussed nor had it in mind, the possibility of additional legislation relating to strikes.'[64] He told them that 'he was convinced the best course to follow was to leave the two sides of industry to work out their problems and to continue to make available the machinery of the Ministry of Labour for help in reaching agreements'. Eden added that there had been suggestions 'made in and around Parliament of a general committee of inquiry' into the industrial troubles and he asked the TUC leaders what they thought about that idea – though he added that he could 'see very great difficulties about the terms of reference and the composition of such a committee' and admitted the 'government itself was not greatly enamoured of the suggestion'.

In his reluctance to act, Eden was very much in tune with Monckton's opinion. The Minister of Labour and National Service said he favoured a Royal Commission to look at 'the whole position of trade unions and the system of industrial relations' or even better an authoritative independent committee, but he stressed that any initiative in this area 'should carry the greatest possible measure of TUC approval and concurrence'. 'Unless we carry with us the responsible elements, who are at present in a majority, we run the risk of uniting the whole movement against us', he warned.[65] Despite this negative attitude Eden appointed a cabinet committee in July 1955 to 'consider what action should be taken to check strikes and improve industrial relations'. But Monckton emphasized at its first two meetings that the government could 'not legislate for responsibility'. Indeed, the cabinet committee failed to agree on any proposals and it was wound up in the spring of 1956.[66]

For the most part, the Eden government believed that on balance the trade unions were more of an asset than an obstacle to dealing with the country's economic troubles. As Eden explained to R. A. Butler on 27 December 1955:

> The trade unions do understand that if our costs go on rising we shall inevitably price ourselves out of world markets and they will be the first to suffer. Therefore they will always lend a sympathetic ear to any doctrine aimed at avoiding this danger. If in addition to the measures I have suggested to reduce the cost of living we could call for restraint in dividends and expenditure generally and produce an attractive savings programme, we should have a fair chance of enlisting their help in trying to keep wages steady over the next few years.[67]

However, inside the Conservative party differences of opinion were starting to emerge over what should be done about the trade unions. Some reformers wanted to try and strengthen the power of the central union organizations and work with national union leaders in an effort to contain and defeat inflation. But others thought such an approach too corporatist because it infringed the party's commitment to ensure freedom for workers at the workplace. During the second half of 1955 Butler asked the Conservative Research Department to carry out an inquiry into industrial relations. An interim report was produced in November of that year and although the group responsible for it were divided into those who believed in the need for a state interventionist strategy and those who thought nothing could be done without winning the cooperation of the trade unions, there was general agreement that some action was needed because of the inflationary impact of organized labour on the economy. But all attempts to strengthen party pressure for industrial relations reform was met with firm opposition from the Ministry of Labour and National Service. Watkinson was dispatched to inform the Conservative Research Department that the government would do nothing to upset the TUC. He told them on 8 December 1955 that he 'felt it would be impossible for any Conservative government to introduce legal enforcement unless there was an approach from the TUC'. He was not even prepared to contemplate the establishment of a Royal Commission to examine the state of industrial relations because he believed such a body would be 'filled with lawyers and would inevitably antagonise the TUC'.[68]

In fact, Eden soon dropped whatever vague thoughts he might have harboured for legislative action to deal with the trade unions. Despite the national industrial conflicts of 1955 he concluded that the 'best course to follow was to leave the two sides of industry to work out their problems and to continue to make available the machinery of the Ministry of Labour and National Service for helping to reach agreed settlements'.[69]

The TUC junta's final days

The government's decision to do nothing in its trade union policy that would antagonize the TUC reflected an understandable reluctance to intervene in industrial relations when it was clear to ministers that trade union leaders themselves were keen to do all they could to reassert control over shopfloor discontents. During the strikes of 1955 the TUC did its best to act as a mediating force and it won plaudits from Monckton for its conciliatory attitude. In fact, the growth of unofficial, so-called wild-cat strikes was a direct threat to the power and authority of the unions. In his presidential address to the 1955 Congress Charles Geddes, General Secretary of the Post Office Workers' Union, told delegates that the trade unions could not deny the government's assertion that strikes were a 'contributory factor' to the growing problems of the economy. He spoke of the need to extend the use of arbitration to resolve disputes.[70]

The TUC general council in 1955 indeed did seem ready to take positive action itself by amending Rule 11 of its own rules and standing orders, which would have allowed the TUC to intervene more directly at an early stage of what might turn into a damaging dispute before negotiations had broken down, if the threatened conflict seemly likely to affect workers in trade unions other than those in direct dispute with the employer. It is true that talks were held at the National Joint Advisory Council on 27 July 1955 between Monckton and TUC leaders, as well as private and public sector employers about the summer's industrial conflicts, but all sides agreed no solution lay by 'way of general legislation'.[71] The TUC's report of that meeting showed no support at all for the ideas being floated, such as depriving unofficial strikers' families of national assistance and refusing to pay income tax rebates to those workers in dispute.

The prudent restraint of the government paralleled an equally cautious attitude from the TUC general council. Increasingly during the early 1950s, national union leaders grew worried and angry at what they saw as the dangers to their own power and authority through the emergence of militant shop stewards and the growth of unofficial strikes. To right-wingers like Deakin, Lawther and Williamson the industrial conflict of the time was due in large part to the subversive activities of the Communist party, though more realistically it was far more an indication of the impact of full employment on a decentralized and sectionalist labour market where the demand for labour outstripped supply. By the mid-1950s, national collective agreements were starting to look less and less important, at least in the heartland of manufacturing industry.

The strong shopfloor pressures were concerned to pursue 'short-term, sectional objectives by disorderly, even disruptive methods'. The 'jostling for advantage between groups of workers, paralleled in many cases by employers who competed for labour by bidding up earnings above the nationally agreed basic rates, resulted in wage drift, inflationary pressures and a sharp increase in the number of strikes, the great majority of which were unofficial'. As England and Weekes argued, 'Shopfloor unionism with its protection of restrictive practices and interruptions to production was seen as contributing to the problems of manufacturing industry.'[72] It also placed enormous strain on the internal organization of the unions. Full-time union officials found themselves increasingly confronted by self-confident, articulate shop stewards and a rank and file that had thrown off its fears of unemployment and habits of social discipline.

There was a noticeable growth in the incidence of wage drift, especially in the motor car industry, as employers and union activists at company or plant level negotiated further wage rises for workers on top of nationally agreed minimum pay rates. This development took place in parallel with the increasing fragmentation and sectionalizing of an interdependent shop floor. With no serious threat of any return to the dole queues of the 1930s – as it became conventional wisdom to believed no government could hope to survive in office if it accepted mass unemployment as an instrument of economic policy – workers in the export-oriented industries were in a strong position to maximize their bargaining power for more wages without the need to relate their improved earnings to higher productivity. By flexing their muscles in an acquisitive drive for fatter wage packets, workers were bound to place a severe strain on what were becoming the archaic and fossilized structures of a collective bargaining system which had been established during a time when trade unions were far weaker in their negotiating position with individual employers and when their leaders really believed the shop floor would benefit more from industry-wide level agreements. As an authoritative study of the motor car industry concluded, 'formal union organisations failed to express the expectations in concrete bargaining demands'. It spoke of the emergence of a 'parallel unionism', as the existing institutions of industrial relations failed to adjust to the new realities.[73]

The 1955 Congress passed by just over 2,500,000 votes a motion that condemned unofficial strikes and spoke of the 'small minority of undisciplined and subversive individuals' who the TUC alleged were fomenting conflict on the shop floor. The tone of the TUC was set by Bill Beard of the United Patternmakers' Association in his presidential address when he warned delegates against over-exploiting 'full' employment in wage negotiations. He suggested nobody could 'deny the truth' of R. A. Butler's assertion at that time that strikes were one of the reasons for the country's economic deterioration. 'We cannot and should not try to abolish strikes but we should and must remove as many causes of them as we can', he declared.[74] Bill Heywood of the Dyers' and Bleachers' union suggested that the trade unions must face up to the consequences of their own actions and shoulder responsibilities. 'We must not let our triumphs of the past few years fill our heads with ambition to the point where we destroy our present prosperity', he added.[75] On that issue – for all their differences of emphasis – Churchill's government as well as Eden's shared a similarity of outlook with the TUC.

The Monckton era was regarded with hindsight by many critics as the locust years for wage inflation and the state's appeasement of organized labour. For others it was a Golden Age for industrial relations, a time of growing prosperity, relative tranquillity and benign intentions – the calm before the storm.

Notes

1   National Union Conference annual report, 1947, p. 42.
2   R. Blake, *Disraeli*, Eyre & Spottiswoode, 1966, p. 555.
3   W. F. Monypenny and G. E. Buckle, *The Life of Benjamin Disraeli. Vol 2: 1860–1881*, John Murray, 1929, p. 711.
4   F. M. Leventhal, *Respectable Radical: George Howell and Victorian Working Class Politics*, Weidenfeld & Nicolson, 1971, p. 185.
5   P. Smith, *Disraelian Conservatism and Social Reform*, Routledge & Kegan Paul, 1967, p. 217.
6   H. A. Clegg, A. Fox and A. F. Thompson, *A History of British Trade Unions since 1889*, Oxford University Press, 1964, p. 313.
7   Hansard Parliamentary Debates, Vol. 164, 9 November 1906, c. 911.

8   A. Sykes, *Tariff Reform in British Politics 1903–1913*, Oxford University Press, 1979, pp. 261–2.
9   Hansard Parliamentary Debates, Vol. 205, 4 May 1927, c. 1655.
10 K. Middlemas and J. Barnes, *Baldwin*, Weidenfeld & Nicolson, 1969, p. 449.
11 R. A. Butler, *The Art of the Possible*, Hamish Hamilton, 1971, pp. 145–6.
12 *The Industrial Charter*, Conservative party, 1947, p. 4.
13 Ibid., p. 18.
14 Ibid., pp. 28–34.
15 R. Maudling, *Memoirs*, Sidgwick & Jackson, 1978, p. 45.
16 D. Clarke, *The Conservative Faith in the Modern Age*, Conservative Political Centre, 1947, p. 16.
17 M. Fraser, *The Worker in Industry*, Conservative Political Centre, 1947, p. 15.
18 *The Right Road for Britain*, Conservative party, 1949, p. 3.
19 *One Nation at Work*, One Nation Group, 1950, p. 2.
20 Ibid., p. 8.
21 *Britain Strong and Free*, 1951 Conservative party general election manifesto, p. 6.
22 Central Trade Union Advisory Committee papers, Conservative party archives.
23 Conservative party archives.
24 Conservative party archives.
25 J. D. Hoffman, *The Conservative Party in Opposition*, MacGibbon & Kee, 1964, pp. 213–14.
26 *Keatinge Report*, p. 16. Conservative party archives.
27 Ibid., p. 25.
28 Ibid., p. 32.
29 National Union Conference annual report, 1952, p. 68.
30 Conservative party archives.
31 Lord Moran (ed.), *Diaries*, Weidenfeld & Nicolson, 1965, p. 395.
32 Lord Birkenhead, *Walter Monckton*, Weidenfeld & Nicolson, 1969, p. 276.
33 Ibid., p. 275.
34 Ibid., p. 284.
35 R. A. Butler, *The Art of Memory*, Hodder & Stoughton, 1982, p. 65.
36 Hansard Parliamentary Debates, Vol. 498, 6 May 1952. c. 543.
37 Ibid., Vol. 507, 10 November 1952, c. 624
38 Ibid., Vol. 542, 23 June 1955, c. 1509.
39 Lord Birkenhead, *Monckton*, p. 278.
40 R. A. Butler, *Art of Memory*, p. 183.
41 P. Hennessy, *Whitehall*, Secker & Warburg, 1987, p. 452.
42 A. Seldon, *Churchill's Indian Summer*, Hodder & Stoughton, 1981, p. 204.
43 TUC Congress report, 1952, p. 300.
44 Ibid., p. 81.
45 Ibid., pp. 480–1.
46 Ibid., p. 508.

47   TUC Congress report, 1953, p. 419.
48   A. Crosland, *The Future of Socialism*, Jonathan Cape, 1956, pp. 22–3.
49   National Union Conference report, 1952, p. 68.
50   Ibid., p. 113.
51   National Union Conference report, 1954.
52   Hansard Parliamentary Debates, Vol. 524, 23 June 1955, c. 1526–7.
53   One Nation Group, 1954, p. 8.
54   Court of Inquiry report, 1954, p. 14.
55   Cameron Inquiry report, 1955, p. 20.
56   Lord Birkenhead, *Monckton*, p. 299.
57   Sir Anthony Eden, *Full Circle*, Cassell, 1960, p. 286.
58   Ibid., p. 286.
59   Ibid., p. 290.
60   Ibid., p. 293.
61   Hansard Parliamentary Debates, Vol. 542, 23 June 1955, c. 1525.
62   Eden, *Full Circle*, p. 289.
63   Ibid., p. 287.
64   TUC Congress annual report, 1955, p. 140.
65   Ibid., p. 334.
66   Ibid., pp. 322–3.
67   R. Rhodes James, *Eden*, Weidenfeld & Nicolson, 1986, pp. 416–17.
68   Quoted by J. Ramsden, *The Making of Conservative Party Policy*, Longman, 1980, p. 183.
69   Eden, *Full Circle*, p. 354.
70   TUC Congress annual report, 1955, p. 266.
71   Ibid., p. 273.
72   J. England and B. Weekes, 'Trade Unions and the State: A Review of the Crisis', *Industrial Relations Journal*, 12 (1), 1981, p. 17.
73   H. A. Turner, G. Clark and G. Roberts, *Labour Relations in the Motor Industry*, Allen & Unwin, 1967, p. 343.
74   TUC Congress annual report, 1955, p. 284.
75   Ibid., p. 267.

4 One Nation Toryism on the Defensive, November 1955 to October 1964

Consensus under threat

Although the industrial disputes of 1954–5 failed to bring about any radical change in Conservative policy towards organized labour, and the TUC was reassured that the post-war settlement was not going to be torn up by the government, Britain's union–state relations were coming under severe strain. The TUC was already growing sour with the government as a result of Butler's November 1955 emergency budget with its unpopular increase in purchase tax, hire purchase restrictions and cuts in public investment designed to squeeze domestic demand. Most national union leaders may still have been willing to urge restraint in collective bargaining to ensure full employment, but they were also concerned at what they saw as the lack of social responsibility being displayed elsewhere in the economy, particularly on the stock market where, they alleged, a shareholders' free-for-all had been encouraged by the government. The TUC continued to speak with considerable restraint, arguing that:

> For the last ten years we have had the novel experience of full employment in peacetime. The problems we have been meeting are of a new kind – they are problems of full employment, of economic expansion. They are not insoluble but they will not be solved by trusting to luck or by the government or anyone else relying on outworn economic and industrial policies. Nor can the trade union movement tolerate irresponsible or selfish action whether from other sections of the community or from within its own ranks which would erode the foundations of full employment.[1]

In fact, Eden was keen on trying to establish common agreement with the TUC on the development of a national economic policy. He believed the best way to achieve this was through the establishment of price stability, so the government applied pressure on employers to hold down the level of their price increases – with some success. The Prime Minister met the TUC general council on 5 March 1956 and warned them that the country's financial reserves were low and a balance of payments crisis could provoke a devaluation which would have serious consequences for employment and living standards. For their part, union leaders argued that they disliked what they saw as the government's excessive reliance on general credit restraint in order to reduce demand and they called for import controls and construction licensing as a means of reducing the balance of payments deficit.

But ministers were convinced that the wage bargaining system was at fault. In March 1956 the government published an important White Paper, *The Economic Implications of Full Employment*, in which the Treasury spelt out for the first time publicly in blunt language the dangers of wage-push inflation in a tight, decentralized labour market where unemployment was no longer politically or socially acceptable. As the document explained with painful clarity,

> In order to maintain full employment the government must ensure that the level of demand for goods and services is high and rises steadily as productive capacity grows. This means a strong demand for labour and good opportunities to sell goods and services profitably. In these conditions it is open to employees to insist on large wage increases and it is often impossible for employers to grant them and pass on the cost to the consumer so maintaining their profit margins. This is the dilemma which confronts the country. If the prosperous economic conditions necessary to maintain full employment are exploited by trade unions and business men, price stability and full employment become incompatible. The solution lies in self-restraint in making wage claims and fixing profit margins and prices so that total money incomes rise no faster than total output.[2]

Without such self-restraint being displayed by workers, trade unions and employers, the White Paper argued, the outcome would be obvious enough – both rising unemployment and rising prices, as British industry lost overseas markets because its exports would become uncompetitive. The Treasury believed what was needed was 'an efficient and enlightened system of industrial relations' with 'a full and frank exchange of opinion and information' between management and workers. It also meant the encouragement of genuine productivity bargaining. Above all, the existing industrial relations structures would only work sensibly if there was a greater realism shown in pay expectations on the shop floor. According to the White Paper, it was now time to subordinate 'sectionalist interests' to those of the nation.

The language and tone of the March 1956 White Paper appeared to be a clear break with the well-meaning bonhomie of the Monckton era. But there was no suggestion that some form of compulsory action by the government might be needed to change workplace attitudes. Eden believed – as a convinced One Nation Tory – that moral exhortation and appeals to reason would help to provide the necessary stimulus for a coordinated approach on wage bargaining between trade unions and employers. The Prime Minister tried to encourage the nationalized in-dustries, in particular, to exercise restraint on costs and prices, while at the same time he urged the TUC to 'act with moderation' in wage bargaining.[3]

The government enjoyed some success in achieving price stability through its efforts at persuading employers to hold down price rises, but unfortunately it made little impact on the TUC's attitude and talks be-tween ministers and union leaders were suspended in August as both sides failed to agree on what should be done. The trouble was that the mood was changing inside the TUC. At the 1956 Congress a more mili-tant force erupted onto the public scene in the shape of Frank Cousins, the newly elected left-wing General Secretary of the TGWU. His dramatic first intervention signalled the passing of the right-wing junta that had dominated the TUC since the end of the war. In an uncompromising speech that upset the TUC general council old guard, Cousins articulated the sour post-war mood of shopfloor militancy that was eroding the industrial consensus at the centre. He moved a resolution that rejected any suggestion of wage restraint and asserted 'the right of labour to bar-gain on equal terms with capital' and to use the TUC's strength 'to pro-tect workers from the dislocations of an unplanned economy'. 'We accept that in a period of freedom for all we are part of the all', declared Cousins:

> We are not going out on a rampage. We are not going to use our organ-isational strength to prove that the TGWU are first and the rest can get where they like. What we are saying is that there is no such thing in this country as a place where you say 'Wage levels stop here' and that we ought to be content, even if things remain equal.[4]

Cousins warned Congress that the government had thrown down the gauntlet with its call for pay restraint and he said the trade unions should 'not refuse to pick it up if they were compelled to'. As Geoffrey Goodman, Cousins's sympathetic biographer wrote,

The majority of those in the cabinet and on the TUC general council in 1956 would have preferred to continue the economic truce that had existed since 1951, despite all the difficulties. The emergence of Frank Cousins made that impossible. This was the end of an epoch.[5]

The transformation of the country's largest union from being one of the most right-wing under Deakin into a left-wing monolith did not happen overnight, but there was little doubt that the sudden, unexpected arrival of Cousins on the national trade union scene brought an abrasive unpredictability to the TUC's proceedings and made it even more difficult for the government to secure the kind of trade union cooperation it would have liked in its campaign against home-grown inflation.

One Nation Toryism lives on

The worsening in the national industrial relations climate did not, however, bring any change of direction in government policy. Although temperamentally tougher and more politically incisive than his predecessor Monckton, Ian Macleod, who became Minister of Labour and National Service in December 1955, was also very much a One Nation Tory. He believed in defending the voluntarist tradition, despite the rising anti-union voices being heard inside his party. Indeed, Macleod was keen to revive interest in some of the more tangible but forgotten proposals contained in the party's 1947 Industrial Charter, which Monckton had ignored for fear of giving offence to the unions or employers. He favoured a Code of Practice, for example, to be drawn up by the government, employers and trade unions which would establish voluntary rights for workers, a suggestion that met with open hostility from both sides of industry who disliked such proposed state interference.

Macleod's impatience for action reflected his dismay at the lack of progress that had been made on improving cooperation between capital and labour in the post-war period. The antediluvian character of industrial relations at the time was made apparent by the sudden decision of the British Motor Corporation in July 1956 to make 6,000 of its workers redundant without notice. Men with many years of company service were dismissed with hardly any financial compensation at all. Macleod intervened to prevent a dispute breaking out over the redundancies, and the company agreed to provide cash support for workers who had been employed by the company for more than ten years. At the 1956 party conference, Macleod spoke out in favour of the proposal that workers should receive written contracts of employment with a period of notice related to their length of service. He said he intended to call trade union leaders and employers together to see whether a voluntary agreement could be reached over the issue, but if this failed then legislation would have to be enacted.

However, Macleod remained unenthusiastic about any direct government intervention into the conduct of industrial relations. He told the 1956 party conference that he was not in favour of legal measures to curb strikes and even pointed out that despite the upsurge of labour militancy since 1955 Britain's days lost per thousand workers were still better than most other industrialized countries, including France and Japan. Moreover, Macleod did not believe that the use of secret ballots before strikes would solve the problem of shopfloor militancy. 'The idea of course is that the workers are less militant than their leaders', he explained to the 1956 conference. 'That is not my experience.' 'I believe firmly that the British system of free voluntary negotiation in industry with the minimum of government interference is best and I believe firmly in the trade union system. These views are fundamental to my political beliefs and I have not altered in any way. Nor will I', he declared – though he also had to admit that a growing number in and outside the Conservative party no longer shared his opinion.[6]

The middle way

The arrival of Harold Macmillan as Prime Minister in February 1957, after Eden's dramatic resignation on grounds of ill health in the aftermath of the Suez fiasco, brought no fundamental change in Conservative industrial relations policy. The new Prime Minister had been a progressive Tory advocate of the 'Middle Way' in the 1930s and a staunch social reformer whose memories of his years between the wars as MP for the depression town of Stockton-on-Tees continued to haunt him. Macmillan took an outwardly benign view of trade unions despite his private more pessimistic doubts. During his period in office, inflationary wage-push pressures from the shop floor were to become a regular cause for ministerial anxiety as they threatened to destabilize the economy.

In his very first days as Prime Minister Macmillan was confronted with a potentially dangerous outbreak of industrial conflict both on the railways and above all in the shipbuilding and engineering industries where employers were ready to take the offensive to confront trade union power. 'There seems little hope that the shipyard unions will accept the offer of arbitration', he noted despairingly in his diary on 15 March. 'The unions feel sure that HMG will bring a last-minute pressure on the employers, as they have so often done before. The truth is that we are now paying the price for the Churchill–Monckton regime – industrial appeasement with continual inflation.'[7] For a moment, it looked as though Macmillan would have to confront a putative general strike and he began to reappraise the state's emergency plans that would be involved in using armed forces to run the country's essential services. His worries, however, turned out to be misplaced and the labour troubles were settled without disruption, even if the resulting settlements failed to satisfy him. In the privacy of his diary Macmillan expressed fears over what he described as 'an ugly feeling in the industrial world', which he believed was 'political and inflamed by Communists and left-wingers'.[8] Yet such feelings did not convince him that he should propose changes in the labour laws in order to weaken the unions. On the contrary, Macmillan suggested to Macleod that perhaps the government ought to look at ways of securing trade union cooperation for a productivity drive or even renew a campaign for a 'new industrial charter' that would include the right of workers to have a month's notice before their employment was terminated. But there was no sense of urgency and the issues though raised were left unresolved.[9]

Indeed, to the dismay of the engineering and shipbuilding employers, in 1957 the government seemed unwilling to support them in their conflict with the trade unions. Macleod appointed an arbitrator to resolve the dispute, which threatened to paralyse large tracts of engineering, but when this proposal was rejected by the union leaders government pressure was applied on the employers to improve their pay offer. Both sides in the dispute agreed to cooperate with a government Court of Inquiry. The resulting settlement was seen by employers as a ministerial climbdown. Despite this, ministers went on exhorting companies not to accept inflationary wage settlements, though with varying degrees of vigour.

Much to the TUC's annoyance, the government decided to try and make an institutional response to the problem of pay-push inflation. A three man independent Council on Prices, Productivity and Incomes was created under the chairmanship of an eminent High Court judge, Lord Cohen. This new body emerged from the recommendations made by both Courts of Inquiry reports into the 1954 and 1957 engineering and shipbuilding disputes. These had called for an 'authoritative and impartial examination of the wider problems of wages policy in inflationary circumstances'.[10] The new body was meant to have an educative rather than a regulatory role. It turned out to be harmless, producing a number of hand-wringing and ineffectual reports that exhorted trade unions and workers to restrain their wage demands and ensure any increases in earnings were more closely related to productivity improvements.

In truth, Macmillan was unprepared to take any action to confront the trade unions that would jeopardize the maintenance of full employment and economic growth. He looked askance at the proposal of Peter Thorneycroft, his Chancellor of the Exchequer, to allow no increase at all in nominal government expenditure for the 1958–59 financial year. Thorneycroft's resulting dramatic resignation in February 1958, along with his junior ministerial colleagues at the Treasury Enoch Powell and Nigel Birch, reflected Macmillan's determination not to capitulate to Treasury pressures for too much deflation and austerity. Indeed, the Prime Minister remained always very much an economic expansionist at heart. Moreover, for all his private alarms about the alleged growth of trade union power, he was ready to go a long way to placate organized labour. In the spring of 1958 Macmillan intervened personally to prevent a threatened rail strike when the Railway Staff Tribunal declared that the industry could not afford to pay railway workers any wage increase at all. 'I shared with the public the general feeling of sympathy with the railway workers', he wrote in his memoirs. 'Nationalization had brought them no benefit and all their dreams had vanished into thin air.'[11] The Prime Minister called both sides into 10 Downing Street where amidst a good deal of convivial whisky drinking he revealed that the government was prepared to provide further financial support for railway modernization if the employers were allowed to carry through cost-saving measures and the unions accepted redundancies and an end to restrictive practices. Macmillan recorded that the union leaders had asked many questions in a 'very amicable and reasonable tone' and there was little doubt they knew he was sympathetic to their point of view.[12] Despite Conservative party pressure for a showdown on the railways, Macmillan was keen to reach a settlement, though he admitted later that the eventual compromise of a 3 per cent pay rise for the rail workers was accepted only reluctantly by some of his Cabinet colleagues, more out of loyalty to him than from genuine conviction.

However, much greater Cabinet firmness was on display during the seven week long strike by London Transport busmen in the summer of 1958 in pursuit of a pay rise of 25 shillings per week. The conflict turned rapidly into a real contest of will between Frank Cousins and the government. The strike, which Macmillan described as an 'inconvenience', was avoidable but the days of Monckton-style conciliation were over and the

Cabinet was determined, at least on this occasion, to face down the busmen. In an unprecedented move, the Ministry of Labour's own chief conciliator Sir Wilfred Neden was repudiated by Macleod after he had offered the TGWU and London Transport a face-saving compromise in the form of a public inquiry to examine the busmen's grievances. Neden admitted to Geoffrey Goodman, Cousins's biographer, that his minister had been 'acting on a Cabinet decision to stop rising wage inflation'.[13] What was also evident after the strike ended with the busmen's humiliating defeat was the complicity of senior union leaders in the TUC who assured Macmillan and other ministers privately that the TGWU would secure no support for the busmen's strike from them. In fact, Cousins could find few allies on the TUC general council ready to back him in the strike, and he met strong opposition from other union leaders when he tried to spread the disruption into sectors like petrol distribution and electricity supply as a way of achieving a satisfactory wage settlement for the busmen. Despite this, Macleod's cavalier treatment of Neden during the strike shocked union leaders, who feared the traditional industrial impartiality of the Ministry of Labour and National Service was being undermined as a result.

But Cousins's very public humiliation in the London bus dispute did not herald a change in direction for the government's strategy towards the trade unions, even if it did help to improve the Conservatives' standing in the public opinion polls. On the contrary, Macleod continued to persist with his belief in the merits of the voluntarist system and a minimalist government role in the conduct of pay bargaining. 'We do not believe in a national wages policy', he told the 1958 party conference. 'Nor do we believe in a wage freeze. What we want is a steady increase in the real earnings of all the people.'[14] Macleod even described 'independent voluntary arbitration' as a 'precious part of our industrial system', though he also made it clear that it was the duty of ministers to 'speak out clearly on the economic facts' so that those involved in industrial negotiations might know what the government thought. Yet he insisted that 'only in a partnership independent of politics between the three great partners – government, trade unions and employers – was there any real lasting hope for good, sound industrial relations'. Despite the 'setbacks' and 'sneers', he assured the Conservative faithful that he was determined to 'promote the fellowship, the understanding and the partnership on which in the end all sound human and industrial relations must rest'. At least as far as he was concerned the spirit of the Industrial Charter lived on in the Ministry of Labour and National Service.

Anti-unionism in the ranks

However, by the late 1950s discontent was growing inside the Conservative party at the government's benign policy towards the trade unions. Criticism found its fullest and most stringent expression in an 86 page study published in June 1958 by the Inns of Court Conservative and Unionist Society under the title *A Giant's Strength* in words taken from Shakespeare's *Measure for Measure*: 'O it is excellent / To have a giant's strength; / but it is tyrannous / To use it as a giant.'[15]

The Conservative lawyers drew up a number of specific proposals for reform that struck a quite different note to the One Nation rhetoric that had for so long dominated the party's industrial relations policy. In the summer of 1958 *A Giant's Strength* did not make much of an impact, even inside the party, but many of its recommendations were to find their way into the new Conservative labour strategy, formulated after the party's general election defeat in October 1964. The study emphasized the crucial role that should be played by the Registrar of Friendly Societies, responsible for the supervision of trade unions. As a way of ensuring greater discipline in the unions, it proposed that they would lose all their legal privileges under the existing laws if a strike took place in defiance of union rules or went ahead before an independent tribunal had conducted an inquiry into the threatened stoppage and the elapse of a 14 day cooling off period between the publication of the tribunal's report and the calling of a strike. The Registrar was to be empowered to refuse registration to any trade union that included provisions in its constitution allowing the trade union to prevent somebody who wanted to join from doing so. The study suggested that the Registrar should also refuse registration if there was no rule in the union's constitution to enable a member to enjoy right of appeal from any branch decision before an independent body, and that at the hearing the member was entitled to representation and the hearing 'should be considered in accordance with the rules of natural justice'.

Unions were called upon to incorporate the TUC's own 1939 Bridlington rules into their constitutions under threat of losing their registration if they did not, and they were to have rules in their constitutions which would not allow them to expel a member unless a case of serious misconduct was involved. The Conservative lawyers also favoured making restrictive labour practices a matter for the courts. It would be up to the workers or trade unions operating them to justify why it was in the public interest that they should continue. It was proposed in addition that the envisaged restrictive practices court would adjudicate on inter-union disputes. Lastly, the study favoured recognition for trade unions by employers if a 'substantial proportion of the workers in a particular grade of industry' wanted this.

After victory

Such radical proposals failed to gain much sympathy in the party leadership as the Conservatives prepared for the October 1959 general election. Macmillan basked in what seemed to be a strong economic recovery and carried the party to its third successive general election triumph, winning 44.3 per cent of the vote and a majority of 107 seats over Labour. However, within only a few months of his personal triumph, the Prime Minister came under renewed Treasury pressure to cut the government's spending programmes, restrict bank lending and deflate the economy, in the face of returning economic troubles which began to threaten the value of the pound and increase the size of the balance of payments deficit. Macmillan was still unconvinced by the demands for restraint coming from the Treasury and he urged Sir Derick Heathcoat Amory, his Chancellor of the Exchequer, to prepare a 'standstill', not an austerity budget, for the spring of 1960. But by June of that year, while he rejected the 'panic measures' of full-scale deflation he had come to accept the need for what he called a 'touch on the brake' as the bank rate was raised from 5 to 6 per cent.[16]

Over the next twelve months the British economy continued to worsen with a rapidly rising balance of payments deficit and the resulting vulnerability of sterling to foreign speculation. In his end of session pep-talk to the 1922 Committee on 15 July 1961, Macmillan grumbled about the 'two internal difficulties' the government faced – 'the utter irresponsibility' of labour in the new industries like cars and aerospace and the 'hopeless conservatism' of labour in some of the old industries such as shipbuilding.[17] Ten days later Selwyn Lloyd, who had replaced Heathcoat Amory as Chancellor of the Exchequer, introduced a package of deflationary measures designed to reassure the outside world. Macmillan accepted the need for restraint with cuts in government expenditure, a rigorous enforcement of exchange controls, increases in indirect taxation and a rise in the bank rate to 7 per cent. Above all, he agreed reluctantly that there had to be what Lloyd called a 'pay pause', which was to last for seven months. 'Our difficulties were not due to an attempt to run the economy at too great a rate or to the strains upon government expenditure whether at home or overseas', explained Macmillan. 'They were primarily due to the simple fact that rising personal demand was not being met by rising productivity. The desire to consume started to outrun the willingness to produce.'[18] Over the twelve months up to Lloyd's July 1961 measures, wages and salaries increased by 8 per cent but national productivity by a mere 3 per cent.

The pay pause was initially seen by Macmillan as an 'appeal to the common sense and patriotism of all concerned – employers, employed and the general public'.[19] But he conceded that the temporary expedient would have to be replaced by something more permanent, and this would require the government to grapple for the first time directly with the complexities of the British wages system. The pay pause did not require the passage of any legislation. Instead, the government used its existing powers to curb and delay pay increases in the public sector, where it was the main employer, in the fond hope that the private employers would do the same in their sector. It was agreed that existing arbitration machinery would not be suspended during the period of the pause, but the government made it clear that it reserved the right to decide when and in what stages any arbitration decisions were to be honoured. The government was reluctant to undermine the voluntarist system but it wanted to see employers and trade unions giving much more attention to the wider national interest when they bargained collectively. 'The real need is to preserve our machinery of free negotiation and impartial arbitration and at the same time to ensure that the results do not run counter to the national interest', explained John Hare, the Minister of Labour.[20]

In fact, it was not long before the pay pause was breached by the power workers in November 1961, but the Prime Minister believed he was in too weak a position to prevent their undoubted success in defying government policy. He noted in his diary:

> The likelihood of a strike in the power stations is growing. Foulkes [the Electricians' union leader] has asked for £2 a week immediately. This is intolerable both as to amount and date. But these 150,000 have the whole country to pawn. Owing to the greater interlocking and great complication of these plants, we cannot do what we did in the General Strike of 1926. We could produce little or quite insufficient power to meet the needs of a nation now wholly geared, industrially and domestically to electricity.[21]

In fact, the Electricity Board believed there was no realistic alternative but to capitulate to such powerful trade union pressure and breach the pay pause. Its decision dismayed Macmillan who feared other workers would use the power supply settlement as a precedent to secure the wage increases they were also demanding. There were, indeed, a few further settlements that circumvented the pay pause and it took a mixture of guile and firmness from the government to hold the highly unpopular line through what Macmillan called a 'somewhat ragged and inconclusive battle' into the spring of 1962. But he was satisfied with its outcome. 'The pay pause has been a success', he noted in his diary. 'We have gained a year; rises have been less than they would have been; our "wage structure" is getting nearer to that of France or of Germany (we may even have the edge on them).'[22]

Towards an incomes policy

The Prime Minister was determined – whatever the TUC thought – to introduce a long-term national incomes strategy after the end of the temporary pay pause. But he was so dismayed by the 'lack of any energetic or imaginative suggestions coming from the Treasury' that he decided to take on the task of drawing up the policy himself.[23] For the first time, in the summer of 1962 a post-war Prime Minister wrestled with the difficulties of devising what he hoped would turn out to be a lasting government-inspired policy for incomes. Macmillan's memoirs suggest he had reached the conclusion that the voluntarist collective bargaining system was no longer workable in conditions of full employment without creating a level of inflation that threatened Britain's economic stability. In fact, he believed that 'some permanent form of incomes policy' was necessary if the government was going to maintain its key objectives of maintaining full employment, ensuring stable prices, creating a favourable balance of payments and above all achieving economic growth. As he argued:

> An incomes policy must form part of an overall scheme seen to be fair all round and seen also to be the only fair way. This meant a complete reappraisal of the relative status and conditions of employment of 'workers' and 'staff'. There must be proper contracts of employment for workers and redundancy and retraining arrangements. There must be an impartial source of wage assessment operating over the whole field in place of a series of ad hoc arbitrations when one group after another felt itself to be left behind. Action, if necessary taxation, must be used to prevent profits increasing their share of the national cake. Finally to encourage growth there must be more stimulation of demand as we could not expect all the growth to go into exports.[24]

Table 4.1   Key labour statistics in the age of Macmillan, 1957–1963

	Unemployment (no.)	(%)	Earnings increase (%)	Retail price increase (%)	Union membership (no.)	(%)
1957	327,100	1.6	4.6	3.7	9,829,000	44.0
1958	450,500	2.2	3.5	3.0	9,639,000	43.2
1959	480,200	2.3	4.6	0.5	9,623,000	44.0
1960	377,200	1.7	6.6	1.0	9,835,000	44.2
1961	346,500	1.6	6.2	3.4	9,916,000	44.0
1962	467,400	2.1	5.2	2.7	10,014,000	43.8
1963	558,000	2.6	5.3	1.5	10,067,000	43.7

Source: *British Labour Statistics Historical Abstract*, HMSO, 1968.

The prolonged Cabinet discussions through the early months of 1962 focused on the question of whether or not there should be an element of compulsion in the proposed incomes policy that was to follow the pay pause. Macmillan favoured the creation of an independent Standing Commission on Incomes which would 'examine and pronounce on the relative merits of different wage claims' referred to it by the government in line with the so-called 'guiding light' which related income increases to a rise in national wealth, but ministers were divided over whether it should be supplied with sanctions to ensure compliance with its recommendations. Penal measures against those who breached the policy were examined, including the imposition of a payroll tax on companies or industries that disobeyed the National Incomes Commission, and depriving the trade unions of legal immunities and opening up their funds to civil damages in the event of unlawful strikes. But in the final stages ministers decided to drop any suggestion of providing compulsory powers for the National Incomes Commission. Instead, they agreed to rely for its success on the sanction of 'the power of public opinion'. Macmillan was anxious to ensure that the National Incomes Commission 'should not be thought of as an isolated or temporary measure intended to impose upon an unwilling people disagreeable but short-term restrictions. It was to be represented as closely connected with the expansion of the wealth and strength of the nation.' As he argued, 'The incomes policy must not be an instrument of deflation but a weapon for more rapid growth.' It was a wise maxim that his successors were to ignore at their peril.[25]

Macmillan was now completely exasperated by Lloyd's apparent lack of conviction for what he was doing and decided to replace him at the Treasury with Reginald Maudling, the younger and more expansionist-minded President of the Board of Trade. The so-called July 1962 'massacre' or 'night of the long knives', in which a number of other Cabinet ministers were also summarily dismissed, shocked public opinion by its ruthlessness. But the Cabinet changes cleared the way for the completion of the government's incomes policy, which was presented to Parliament at the end of the month by Macmillan himself.[26] 'An incomes policy is necessary as a permanent feature of our economic life', he told MPs – an 'indispensable element in the foundations on which to build a policy of sound economic growth'. But Macmillan also insisted that it could not be imposed by the state on an unwilling people. To gain acceptance, an incomes policy must be seen to be 'both necessary and fair'. He assured the Commons that the new National Incomes Commission did not mean the end of free collective bargaining. The TUC reacted with predictable opposition to the proposal but Macmillan 'noticed with pleasure that there were a number of the more responsible leaders who said little and from whom I believed we could expect quiet and uneffusive sympathy'.[27] In the event, the National Incomes Commission, which began work in October 1962 was to have a 'short and rather undistinguished life' and 'certainly did not succeed in focusing the wrath of public opinion on excessive wage awards'. As Frank Blackaby pointed out, the body functioned with very limited terms of reference, being only able 'to review certain pay matters where the cost was wholly or partly met from the Exchequer if the Government asked it to do so and to examine retrospectively any particular pay settlement which the Government referred to it.'[28] In its three years of existence the National Incomes Commission received only five references from the government on which to adjudicate. Boycotted by the TUC and treated indifferently by employers, it failed to make much of an impact on wage inflation. However, the Conservatives continued to believe – as they argued in their 1964 general election manifesto – that 'an effective and fair incomes policy' was 'crucial to the achievement of sustained growth without inflation'.[29]

In fact, despite Congress House's outward distaste for the government's attempts at establishing some kind of national incomes policy, the TUC general council was not wholly negative in its attitude to the country's economic troubles by the early 1960s. It agreed after delicate negotiations and persistent pressure from George Woodcock, who succeeded Tewson as TUC General Secretary in September 1960, to join the newly formed tripartite National Economic Development Council (NEDC). The TUC's presence on that voluntary body followed the government's assurance to Woodcock and his colleagues that the NEDC would not be involved in either the creation or administration of any incomes policy and its membership would be confined to national representative institutions. The new tripartite body was very much Selwyn Lloyd's idea, though it appealed strongly to Macmillan's 'middle way' approach to industrial politics. At its first meeting in March 1962 the Council set its sights on expansion by agreeing to examine the 'obstacles' that might be faced by the British economy if it grew at a projected 4 per cent annual rate. Woodcock hoped the TUC's participation in the NEDC would not only increase the influence of Congress House over government economic policy-making but also act as an educative force on trade union thought on economic questions.

More state intervention

By the early 1960s there were clear signs that the Conservatives were beginning to take a much more interventionist attitude to industrial relations. It is true that John Hare as Minister of Labour and National Service (after the end of conscription in 1960 the department reverted to being called the Ministry of Labour) continued to uphold his department's traditional commitment to voluntarism. 'Our main job is to do everything we can to take the initiative to smooth the relationships between employers and unions', he told the 1960 conference. 'We must hold the ring and ensure that each side has no unfair advantage over the other.'[30] Hare welcomed the TUC's decision, at its 1961 Congress, to hold its own inquiry into inter-union disputes and he spoke warmly of the joint union–management strategies which were being followed to try and resolve the underlying troubles of the motor car and shipbuilding industries. 'Our aim must be to strengthen the sense of responsibility of both sides of industry. Weak unions, in my opinion, will be irresponsible unions', he said.

At the 1961 Conservative party conference Hare opposed a resolution that called on the government to carry out an inquiry into the trade unions and legislate any reforms it thought were necessary. He argued that the government must proceed by 'persuasion and by constant appeal to common sense and common interest'. 'There are faults in the way the trade unions conduct their affairs', admitted Hare. 'But their leaders are in the large majority honourable men for whom I personally have a high respect.' 'Over the last ten years we lost fewer working days than any other major industrial power except West Germany', he told the party faithful. 'Many people are also unaware of the fact that 60 per cent of the time lost through strikes last year was lost in four industries employing only 7 per cent of the working population.' Hare also paid tribute to the work of the National Joint Advisory Council in examining areas like joint consultation and communications, training of supervisors, redundancy, and apprenticeship training. It was even looking at restrictive labour practices, he added. 'I believe that the painstaking, though unspectacular ways in which we are trying to remedy weaknesses in our industrial re-lations arrangements are most likely to produce results in the end and therefore in general I am against legislation', Hare declared. 'The legisla-tive answers are not really as easy as they are made out to be. Ultimately they may lead to the sanction of sending thousands of men to jail if they refuse to obey the law.'[31] But he also conceded that if his voluntary self-help policy of better human relations in industry failed then legislation might become 'the only answer', though he was quick to add if it came to that it would be 'a tragic day that would divide and weaken our free society'.

In fact, by the early 1960s the Conservatives were ready to provide some legislative back-up to try and improve the climate of industrial relations in what was a departure from the voluntarist tradition. In 1962 the government passed the Offices, Shops and Railway Premises Act as part of its strategy to improve conditions of employment for workers by giving them a greater sense of job security and an improved status. In the following year, Hare piloted the Contracts of Employment Bill onto the statute book. This was a long overdue measure – first raised in the 1947 Industrial Charter – which laid down minimum periods of notice for the termination of a worker's employment and required employers by law to provide their workers with written statements covering the main terms of their employment contracts. During the Bill's second reading debate Hare told the Commons that the measure was part of the government's wider strategy to provide workers with a greater sense of security. 'The problem of security – of helping the worker to face change with confidence – is basic to our industrial efficiency', he explained. Hare believed the measure would encourage 'co-operation in creating an efficient and flexible economy'. He pointed out to MPs that the vast majority of Britain's manual workers only had the right to a week's notice from their employer before losing their job.[32] The 1963 Act represented a significant departure from traditional state non-interventionism in the same year that Britain opposed a recommendation from the International Labour Office in Geneva that countries should introduce a maximum 40 hour working week. Andrew Shonfield pointed out that a 'hallowed principle' had been abandoned as a result of the measure. By requiring longer terms of notice to be given to workers with more than two years or more of continuous employment in a particular job, the Act 'for the first time in British law recognized the existence of a special right generated by doing a job over a certain period'.[33]

The 1964 Industrial Training act was also another belated Conservative legislative response to deal with one of the innumerable defects of voluntarism. That measure established tripartite Industrial Training Boards, funded by a compulsory levy on employers, in an attempt to provide greater scope and effectiveness for the training of workers. It was also a belated reform after years of official neglect that had ensured a tragic misuse and lack of skilled manpower in industry. The presence of government officials on the statutory boards was an indication that the state intended to play an actively vigorous part in the future development of industrial training. In 1963–4 the Conservatives also looked into the possibilities of introducing legislation to provide redundancy payments to workers who lost their jobs through no fault of their own but as a result of technological change or industrial contraction. Hare informed the House of Commons that only 16 per cent of workers in manufacturing industry were covered by redundancy schemes, but for the time being he hoped employers and trade unions would make voluntary agreements on redundancy compensation. Two years later in 1965 the Labour government introduced the Redundancy Payments Act, which was based to a considerable extent on a draft drawn up by the Ministry of Labour before the Conservatives left office. Sir Joseph Godber, who succeeded Hare as Minister of Labour in October 1963, also favoured the introduction of wage-related unemployment benefit to assist in the encouragement of a shaking-out of labour in over-manned industries in a humane way. The appropriate measure was also implemented by the Labour government in 1965.

A further important piece of positive industrial relations legislation passed by the Conservatives towards the end of their long period in office was the 1964 Trade Union (Amalgamations etc.) Act. This relaxed the voting arrangements for trade union mergers by stipulating that a trade union need not have a 50 per cent turnout and a 20 per cent wide majority in favour to achieve an amalgamation but just a simple majority of the members who voted. The measure helped to stimulate a period of rapid trade union restructuring and merger activity. Apparently, without the 1964 Act 'the expansionary achievements of unions like ASTMS and the TGWU would have been less impressive'.[34]

From Ian Macleod to Joseph Godber, however, Conservative Ministers of Labour between December 1955 and October 1964 continued to reject demands from their party's right wing for a wider reform of industrial relations to cover disputes and trade union behaviour through the use of statute law. But their resistance to legal change was becoming less and less emphatic as the years went by in the face of trade union inertia, growing economic difficulties and a public mood of disenchantment with the behaviour of organized labour, particularly in unofficial strikes. In the early 1960s Hare tried to reassure national union leaders that he believed in the inappropriateness of legislation to reform the trade unions and indicated that he hoped the TUC's own internal review into its structure and purpose launched in 1961 would produce substantial reform. But he also made it clear that if Congress House failed to carry through necessary change itself then the situation would be serious and the government would be forced to intervene. Yet Hare also believed that the best way forward was for 'responsible men on both sides of industry to concert measures' to improve industrial relations.[35]

Unions as a growing problem

Towards the end of the 1950s a perceptible change took place in popular attitudes towards the trade unions as a growing number of influential critics began to denounce them as obstacles to economic progress. In May 1961 the newly formed Organization for European Economic Cooperation (later to become the Paris based OECD) published a particularly critical study of the British industrial relations system in a report on the problem of rising prices:

> Post-war experience suggests the system is less well suited to the new conditions of almost continuous full employment. . . . The haphazard fragmentation of collective bargaining and the weakness of central organisations has facilitated competitive bidding between unions and at the same time political factors bearing on wage determination in the nationalised industries has had a very strong influence on wages in the economy as a whole.[36]

Some of the most influential critiques of the British trade union scene at the time came from journalists. Andrew Shonfield, the *Observer's* economic editor, wrote scathingly in 1958 about the condition of industrial relations in his book *British Economic Policy since the War*. He suggested a 'mood of acute suspicion' had settled over the trade unions since the demise of the 1948–50 wage freeze. Shonfield wrote of the 'new, belligerent mood of labour' of which Cousins was the 'natural leader', and the 'lack of dynamism' on the shop floor where restrictive attitudes impeded necessary change. 'The sort of thing which catches the eye is the ferocious determination to stay put', he observed:

> Right through the economy there are the endless demarcation lines between one job and another, dividing industry into rigid compartments, in each of which a determined effort goes on to maximise costs. And behind all this is the widespread feeling that none of it matters a damn, because whatever is done things are not going to change very much anyhow.[37]

In Shonfield's opinion, trade union structure was the main cause of the problem. He believed the continuing existence of craft unions, the exclusivity of workers in different grades with their insistence on status and hallowed wage differentials, were the reason for debilitating weakness in Britain's industrial performance. Shonfield praised the willingness of American unions like the Autoworkers and the United Steel Workers to work with rather than oppose technological progress, and he came out in favour of single industry based unions where the plant acted as one bargaining unit.

His main complaint was that the TUC and its affiliated unions seemed to lack the strength to come to terms with the workplace challenge as power and responsibility in a period of full employment moved inexorably away from full-time union bureaucracies down to the shop stewards at company and plant level who represented narrow, sectionalist interests. 'No one has the effective power to assert the larger interest of organised labour as a whole, against the blinkered vision of small groups of angry men acting independently on the shopfloor', he asserted.

Michael Shanks, industrial editor of the *Financial Times*, devoted much of his influential 1961 polemic *The Stagnant Society* to a devastating critique of the trade unions. 'They are failing to adjust themselves to the changing pattern of industry and society', he alleged. 'This gives them an increasingly dated, "period" flavour. The smell of the music hall and the pawnshop clings to them'. 'Thrown back for support on the hard core of the older working class, the trade union movement's appeal is increasingly narrowed to the horizons of this declining group, trapped among the slogans and banners of the past.'[38] More seriously, Shanks deplored the persistence of craft unions with their stubborn defence of hallowed wage differentials, the widespread apathy among the rank and file which ensured many unions were run by militants, the lack of trade union professionalism, and their deep sense of insecurity. He enthused by contrast over the progressive character of the Swedish trade union movement and compared the British unions to the decaying Ottoman Empire in the nineteenth century. Shanks wanted to see the TUC transform itself into a 'strong central organisation' which could 'impose its authority on all sections of the movement' with control over wages policy. He favoured the creation of single industry based unions that would break through craft exclusiveness. In an essay published in 1964 in a volume appropriately entitled *Suicide of a Nation?*, Shanks asserted that 'by and large the trade unions have exercised no discernible influence on British social or economic policy in the last decade other than to slow down the process of industrial change and growth'. In his view the 'chaos and defensive mindedness which dominated British industrial relations' reflected 'not union strength but weakness'.[39]

Eric Wigham, the distinguished labour editor of *The Times*, wrote a 1961 Penguin Special entitled *What's Wrong with the Unions?* His criticisms of the trade unions were especially pointed because they came from a friend, not an enemy. 'The unions still do a good job over the greater part of British industry but the movement as a whole has lost its drive and sense of direction', he wrote. 'As a result serious weaknesses and occasional abuses have developed unchecked.'[40] Controversially, he proposed that the government should restrict trade union legal privileges to those who registered under the Chief Registrar of Friendly Societies under accepted rules governing union self-government. He also suggested an inquiry into whether collective agreements should be made legally binding. It is worth noting that both Shonfield and Wigham served on the Royal Commission on Trade Unions and Employer Associations established by the Labour government in 1965.

The party trade union debate

The clear signs of growing public unease about the state of industrial relations in the outside world were also making an impact in the Conservative party outside the government. The evolution of Conservative thought on the subject was uneven, but the minutes of the party's Central Trade Union Advisory Committee provide fascinating evidence of the ebb and flow in the debate among party activists about the trade union 'problem' during the 1950s and early 1960s. For most of the time, the committee concerned itself mainly with the 1947 Industrial Charter, Communist infiltration of the trade unions exemplified by the ballot rigging scandal inside the ETU, and whether a law should be considered for the use of secret ballots before strikes. Occasionally the closed shop

and 'contracting in' to payment of the political levy resurfaced for discussion, but for the most part the Conservative trade unionists remained
unsympathetic to any suggestion of comprehensive industrial relations
legislation.

They took, for example, a hostile attitude to the legalistic arguments
used by the Inns of Court Conservatives in their 1958 Bow group pamphlet
A Giant's Strength. Sir Edward Brown, the Conservative MP for Bath,
wrote a paper in December 1958 that argued forcibly against their proposals to regulate the trade unions through a new legal framework. 'The
right to strike is the basis of all wage negotiations', argued Brown. 'Any
proposal limiting the right to strike must answer the question, how do
you propose to compel a man to work for a wage and under conditions he
is not prepared to accept?'[41] He also suggested that the Inns of Court
Conservatives suggestion that trade union rights should be limited only
to unions who were registered was also mistaken. Brown added that
attempts to ban or severely limit solidarity strikes by workers in support
of others in dispute faced difficulties of definition and enforcement. Even
as late as November 1959 the Conservative trade union advisory committee
was 'unanimous that at the present moment it was still best that the trade
unions should be encouraged to deal with their own problems'.[42]

On R. A. Butler's initiative a new party committee was established in
May 1962 with Brown as chairman to re-examine 'various aspects of
industrial relations'. Its main report was published by the Conservative
Political Centre in September 1963 under the title *Industrial Change: The
Human Aspect*. Its contents were commended by Hare to the party conference that autumn. Some of the proposals resurfaced in the new industrial
relations strategy devised in 1965–6 but the Brown report also provided
strong arguments against any radical change of course in dealing with the
trade union 'problem'. The document opposed the suggestion that unofficial strikes should be banned by law, not merely because the committee
thought it impractical but on grounds of principle. As it argued:

> Legislation to ban unofficial strikes – if by this one means strikes not called
> by a recognised union – would mean denying the fundamental right of the
> individual to with-hold his labour unless he was a trade unionist. It would
> thus be tantamount to forcing work people to join a union regardless of
> their individual beliefs and wishes. It would also assume under law that
> only a union-supported strike can ever be justified. This is nonsense.[43]

The Brown report was equally dismissive of any amendment being made
to the 1906 Trade Disputes Act that would leave trade union funds
unprotected from civil liabilities in unlawful disputes. It pointed out that:

If unions and union officials were made liable for damages in the event of some of their members striking in breach of contract a trade union could be broken overnight. It would thus leave the door open for a small group of militant extremists to bring about the financial collapse of any trade union – perhaps especially those under moderate control.[44]

Nor did the committee believe it was sensible to turn unofficial strikers into martyrs in the courts.

However, the report was not just a defence of the industrial relations status quo. It came down in favour of the principle of secret ballots before the calling of strikes, though it still hoped the TUC itself would encourage such a practice and thus avoid the need for legislation. But Brown and his colleagues acknowledged that if the TUC failed to respond 'the pressure of public opinion' would increase on the government to take the necessary action. The report also favoured new legal powers being given to the Minister of Labour to deal with strikes that the government thought were harmful to the national interest. It recommended the Minister should be able to order a conciliation period if other methods of prevention failed, though it did not support compulsory arbitration. 'It would provide a deterrent against strikes during conciliation partly through pressure of public opinion and partly because in most cases there would be less support for a strike if those concerned felt there was some chance of a reasonable settlement without one', argued Brown.[45] It was also proposed that a system of labour courts should be established on the lines of those operating in continental Europe to provide a form of appeal for workers who felt they had been dismissed unjustly by their employer. The report also favoured a strengthening of the powers of the Registrar of Friendly Societies to deal with cases of internal union abuse.

But the overriding thrust of the Brown document was to reinforce not destroy the voluntarist industrial relations system. Under the heading 'the real answer' the report recommended that the government should 'strengthen the hand of those who are trying to prevent the abuse of the powers the Trade Union Acts confer, to make a man's employment more attractive so that he will not want to lose the benefits he has built up and to establish confidence between management and man'.[46] This was a return to the sentiment of the Industrial Charter and the Monckton era. As Brown concluded:

> We believe the surest way to progress is through the encouragement of responsibility within industry itself. We want to strengthen the hand of management and trade unions in fulfilling functions which are essentially theirs. We do not want to shift their responsibility to the state; indeed, the state cannot enforce better industrial relations.[47]

The need for trade union reform

By the early months of 1964 opinion inside the Conservative leadership was moving inexorably towards the prospect of legislating on industrial relations if the party won the forthcoming general election. Indeed, ministers were being forced – whether they liked it or not – into reviewing the existing condition of labour law. The pressure for reform was coming not just from the Conservative party's right wing but also from the courts, where a number of judgements had introduced considerable confusion and uncertainty over the 1906 legal settlement by throwing doubt on the extent to which trade unions enjoyed legal immunities in strikes. The most notorious and important was the case of *Rookes* v. *Barnard*, which culminated in an important House of Lords judgement in February 1964. A draughtsman at London airport for the BOAC airline, Rookes resigned in 1955 from his union – the Association of Engineering and Shipbuilding Draughtsmen – which operated a closed shop. In response to his action, a meeting of the union's members at BOAC threatened to call a strike if Rookes was not removed from his job within three days, even though BOAC employees had a no-strike clause in their employment contracts. The airline complied with the demand and Rookes was dismissed. But he then sued the union officials who had issued the strike threat to BOAC for conspiracy. Rookes won the ensuing court case and he was awarded 'exemplary' damages, but the Appeal Court overturned the judgement, arguing that Rookes had no cause of action in tort at common law and even if he had the defendants were still protected by the 1906 Trade Disputes Act. But the House of Lords went on to reject the Appeal Court's judgement and found against the defendants. The final outcome of the case aroused deep concern inside the TUC because it looked as though the Law Lords had discovered a means of making trade union officials liable for damages when they threatened strike action that was not only in breach of a commercial contract in a trade dispute but even in breach of a contract of employment. The TUC urged the government to clarify the meaning of the law as soon as possible by amending the 1906 Trade Disputes Act to ensure that in future trade union officials would be protected from legal attack in the way it had been assumed they had been before the *Rookes* v. *Barnard* judgement.

But the TUC failed to secure a clear and satisfactory answer from the government on what it intended to do. Godber was still not keen to make any changes in industrial relations law that could be seen as an attack on the trade unions, but he was also reluctant simply to accept what Congress House wanted. He told the Conservative Research Department in March

1964 that a review of the legal position would 'be most effective if both employers' associations and trade unions' were 'free from the atmosphere of political controversy'.[48] In his memorandum the Minister of Labour expressed the familiar One Nation Tory scepticism about using the law to improve trade union behaviour, explaining that:

> In general the experience of this country for well over a hundred years and of most other industrial countries shows that the law and its apparatus of injunctions, damages, fines, penal sanctions etc. has little to contribute to the solution of problems of industrial relations. . . . Laws attempting to determine when strikes may be held [after a ballot], what labour practices are legal and what illegal have been found from experience to be almost totally unenforceable and to do more harm than good. . . . If fines are imposed when the law is broken, the men will either refuse to pay or it would be impossible to put several hundreds of men in prison – or else there would be a whip-round among the members themselves.

In fact, Godber was doubtful whether there should be a Royal Commission to look into industrial relations on the grounds that it would antagonize trade union leaders 'whose co-operation is essential if progress is to be made'. In words that might have been written by Monckton, he concluded:

> The problem of industrial relations is not one which can be settled by Acts of Parliament or dictatorial intervention by Ministers. It is essentially a human problem – a question of working together, rather than in separate grooves, of getting away from attitudes of mind which think in terms of 'they' and 'us' as if they were opposing camps and of recognizing that fundamentally management, staff and manual workers have an identical interest in the prosperity of industry and the nation as a whole.

His forceful defence of voluntarism was also evident in the party's 1964 campaign guide, which expressed opposition to any suggestion that trade unions should lose their legal immunities in strikes. 'Full liability for damages resulting from a strike could easily ruin a union overnight', it pointed out. 'This would provide an excellent opportunity for the extremists to obtain the power to ruin a union under moderate control. It would also do incalculable harm to industrial relations generally.'[49] In their 1964 general election manifesto the Conservatives also took a studiously non-committal attitude about their intentions towards the trade unions. On the one hand, the document argued that Britain's trade unions had a 'vital responsibility to diminish restrictive practices of labour' and a Conservative government would 'continue to seek their co-operation in matters of common interest and to work in partnership with them through the National Economic Development Council'.[50] On the other, the manifesto pointed out that recent court decisions had 'thrown into prominence aspects of the law affecting trade unions and employers' associations'. 'The law has not been reviewed since the beginning of the century and it will be the subject of an early inquiry', promised the manifesto. But as Godber told the House of Commons in March 1964, such an inquiry should best stay clear of political partisanship if it wanted the cooperation of both sides of industry.[51]

The Labour party in opposition took a more unequivocal position and promised that if it won the general election it would amend the existing labour laws in the way that the TUC wanted in order to restore the threatened immunities of the trade unions. Harold Wilson gave a clear commitment to do this in his speech to the 1964 Congress that launched Labour's election campaign. That decision pleased the TUC but it brought a noticeable hardening of attitudes towards the trade unions among the Conservatives. There was already increasing disenchantment in government circles with the TUC's failure to live up to expectations and modernize itself in response to growing outside criticism. 'What are we here for?', Woodcock had asked the 1961 Congress, but he did not come up with a satisfactory answer. When he succeeded Tewson he had been expected to provide the drive and inspiration necessary to revive the TUC after a long period of relative stagnation. But the hopes were misplaced. Woodcock was a self-made intellectual who had started work at the age of 12 as a loom operator in Preston. A scholarship boy to Ruskin College, Oxford, he went on to secure a first class honours degree at New College, Oxford. But he had toiled too long in the shadows as Assistant General Secretary for fourteen frustrating years. A highly intelligent and articulate man with more than a touch of arrogance and impatience with the less brainy, he seemed to be much more aware of the limitations of being TUC General Secretary than the potentialities of the office. 'The TUC doesn't do anything; it can't tell the unions what to do', he told the journalist Anthony Sampson. 'All I can do is to try and see the way things are going and help them along. I have to try to get the feeling of the general council and then help them to reach a decision.'[52]

But as in 1927 and again in 1944, the reform cause inside the TUC was unable to overcome the structural immobilism of a trade union movement dominated by large general unions whose organizations lacked industrial logic. There was no possibility that the TGWU and the GMWU would agree to their own dismemberment in order to create a more rational, industry-based trade union organization. As Woodcock told the 1963 Congress, 'Diversity of structure is a characteristic of British trade unions and always will be.'⁵³ All that emerged from the great reform drive was a round of TUC conferences in the early 1960s to discuss how to encourage more trade union mergers and amalgamations, and the creation of a number of advisory industrial committees. But there was no real dynamic for radical change coming from inside the trade unions themselves: it was not just the Conservatives who had reached the conclusion by the autumn of 1964 that the TUC would only take trade union reform seriously if it was forced to do so under the threat of external pressure from the state.

Notes

1   TUC Congress report, 1956, p. 384.
2   *The Economic Implications of Full Employment*, Cmnd 1417, HMSO, March 1956, p. 17.
3   TUC Congress Report, 1956, p. 265.
4   Ibid., pp. 399–400.
5   G. Goodman, *The Awkward Warrior*, Eyre & Spottiswoode, 1981.
6   National Union Conference report, 1956, p. 76.
7   H. Macmillan, *Riding the Storm*, Macmillan, 1971, p. 346.
8   Ibid., p. 347.
9   Ibid., p. 352.
10   H. Macmillan, p. 707.
11   Ibid., p. 711.
12   Ibid., p. 712.
13   G. Goodman, p. 169.
14   National Union Conference report, 1958, p. 58.
15   *A Giant's Strength*, Inns of Court Conservatives, 1958.
16   H. Macmillan, *Pointing the Way*, Macmillan, 1972, p. 226.
17   Ibid., p. 375.
18   Ibid., p. 360.
19   Hansard Parliamentary Debates, Vol. 644, 5 June 1961, c. 105.
20   H. Macmillan, *At the End of the Day*, Macmillan, 1973, p. 44.
21   Ibid., p. 44.
22   Ibid., p. 45.
23   Ibid., p. 68.
24   Ibid., p. 70.
25   Ibid., p. 88.
26   Hansard Parliamentary Debates, Vol. 663, 26 July 1962, c. 1757.
27   Macmillan, *At the End of the Day*, p. 108.
28   F. Blackaby (ed.), *British Economic Policy, 1960–1974*, Cambridge University Press, p. 364.
29   Conservative party general election manifesto, 1964, in F. W. S. Craig (ed.), *British General Election Manifestos*, Dartmouth, 1990, p. 31.
30   National Union Conference report, 1960, p. 74.

31 Ibid., 1961, pp. 117–18.
32 Hansard Parliamentary Debates, Vol. 671, 14 February 1963, c. 1504.
33 A. Shonfield, *Modern Capitalism*, Oxford University Press, 1969, p. 113.
34 R. Undy et al., *Changes in Trade Unions*, Hutchinson, 1981, p. 322.
35 Hansard Parliamentary Debates, Vol. 652, 29 January 1962, c. 733.
36 *The Problem of Rising Prices*, OEEC, 1961, p. 8.
37 A. Shonfield, *British Economic Policy since the War*, Penguin, 1958, p. 14.
38 M. Shanks, *The Stagnant Society*, Penguin, 1961, p. 44.
39 A. Koestler (ed.), *Suicide of a Nation?*, Blond, 1964, p. 56.
40 E. Wigham, *What's Wrong with the Unions?*, Penguin, 1961, p. 196.
41 Conservative party archives, Oxford.
42 Conservative party archives, Oxford.
43 *Industrial Change: The Human Aspect*, Conservative Political Centre, 1963, p. 8.
44 Ibid., p. 9.
45 Ibid., p. 18.
46 Ibid., p. 10.
47 Ibid., p. 25.
48 Conservative Research Department archives, March 1964.
49 Conservative party campaign guide, 1964, p. 155.
50 Conservative party general election manifesto, 1964, in Craig (ed.), *British General Election Manifestos*, p. 33.
51 Hansard Parliamentary Debates, Vol. 691, 19 March 1964, c. 1598.
52 A. Sampson, *Anatomy of Britain*, Hodder & Stoughton, 1962, p. 267.
53 TUC Congress report, 1963, p. 316.

5 Harold Wilson and the 'Great Adventure', October 1964 to June 1970

The planned growth of wages

The Labour party under Harold Wilson's leadership came to power in October 1964 with high expectations after thirteen years in the political wilderness. Britain's trade union leaders were particularly pleased to see the return of a Labour government which was committed to economic growth and modernization, and they expressed their determination to do all they could to ensure its success. Indeed, since the late 1950s the TUC and the Labour party had moved closer together in the formulation of a planned economic strategy, designed to bring an end to the years of relative stagnation. The trade unions were expected to play a vital part in the country's economic revival.

However, the crucial question was whether the TUC's affiliated unions were really ready and willing to cooperate in a policy that would require them to compromise with their traditional commitment to 'free' collective bargaining, perhaps as a *quid pro quo* for the implementation of a socially equitable economic growth strategy. Unhappy memories of the 1948–50 wage freeze period were still fresh in the minds of many trade union leaders. As a result, Congress House was compelled to move circumspectly in any public debate over just how far the trade unions would be willing to go in working in alliance with a government – even a Labour one – that sought to restrict trade union autonomy in wage determination.

During the early 1950s Aneurin Bevan was the only senior figure in the party courageous enough to wrestle with the problem, at least in public. No doubt, his attitude was partly conditioned by his dislike for the right-wing domination of the larger trade unions at that time. He complained that Labour policies were being 'determined by an irresponsible group of trade union bureaucrats'. 'We have actually reached the position where it would be true to say that the leaders of the TGWU and GMWU decide the policy of the Labour party', he wrote to one of his supporters.[1] But in his thoughtful political study *In Place of Fear*, Bevan wrote perceptively about the need for the creation of an incomes policy under a future Labour government in partnership with the trade unions. 'Most people who have given their minds to the problem are now convinced that a national wages policy is an inevitable corollary of full employment, if we are not to be engulfed by inflation', he claimed. He called for an indexation of wages and salaries to the cost of living to ensure no wages policy would produce any fall in real earnings. Bevan was well aware of the difficulties involved in such an approach. As he explained:

> The trade union world is involved in a continuous succession of wage negotiations. Each union is naturally disinclined to adopt any general principle until its own particular negotiations have been completed. Before that point is reached, other unions have put in fresh wage claims, so at no stage can it be said that a holding-line has been arrived at.[2]

Bevan believed the wonders of industrial automation would smooth away any difficulties by creating an economic increment that could be distributed over 'the whole system in the form of improved standards'. Prophetically he warned about the consequences of a wages free-for-all:

> In the absence of a policy which strictly relates current adjustments of personal incomes to any surplus which may be available for distribution, mounting paper claims will continue to produce a series of crises both in industry and politics until bewilderment generates despair and despair in its turn sinks into apathy.[3]

The centrist Socialist Union, under the intellectual influence of Allan Flanders and Rita Hinden, also confronted the wages question in its 1956 book *Twentieth Century Socialism*. Concern was expressed that wage–price pressures in a full employment economy threatened union solidarity and Socialist principles of equality. It explained:

> Those who are in the strongest market positions or who are most ruthless in exploiting their bargaining power, can assert their claims and hold the community to ransom. Every section of the community justifies its own demands by reference to the increases enjoyed by others. But each advance is a Pyrrhic victory for it forces the pace all round, and most of what is gained on the swings of increased incomes is lost on the roundabouts of increased prices.[4]

The Socialist Union was well aware that the central issue of wage determination was divisive inside the Labour party, but it believed any future Labour government would need to reach a national agreement with the trade unions and employers on what the general level of wage rises needed to be for the economy as a whole. It argued that the search for wage stability was to be accompanied by restrictions on rises in rents, dividends and interest rates. Barbara Wootton, in her 1954 classic *Social Foundations of Wage Policy*, was also keen to deal with the pay problem. Her devastating critique of collective bargaining emphasized the inequalities of the wages system that reinforced the social hierarchy through income distribution. Like Beveridge she feared the inflationary consequences of an unfettered wage system in a full employment economy.

For understandable reasons of party unity, Labour leaders were reluctant to launch a debate on the incomes policy issue during most of the 1950s. Indeed, they appeared to believe that whatever genuine differences of view might exist on the subject between the political and industrial wings of the Labour Movement could be overcome by a generalized commitment to economic growth. In its 1958 policy document *Plan for Progress*, the Labour party argued that any future growth in money incomes would have to 'broadly keep in step with higher productivity', but party leaders assumed that if they were in government they would be able to rely on the TUC's goodwill to support that aim because a Labour government would 'restore a climate of expansion, maintain fair play between different sections of the community, promote greater equality and create a price truce'.[5]

TUC General Secretary George Woodcock tried, in the early 1960s, to convince his often sceptical if not hostile general council colleagues that they should not take a wholly negative attitude towards the idea of cooperation with any future national incomes policy under a Labour government but it proved to be a difficult task. Opposition from the trade unions to Harold Macmillan's National Incomes Commission was predictable enough, but Woodcock was keen to emphasize that while in the last resort it would be the trade unions themselves who should decide whether or not to restrain the pay demands of their members they would respond in a positive way to any government that was willing to accept the TUC's wider economic objectives. 'No discussions that we can enter can lead to anything like the pay pause or the guiding light with their attempts at precision in terms of amount and terms of period over which you can operate', he explained to the 1962 Congress. 'You cannot have that kind of wages policy. You can at the most induce a mood, a sense of responsibility.'[6] But Woodcock also believed this did not mean trade unions should merely pursue their own sectionalist self-interests without any regard for the views of others. As the TUC argued: 'While condemning the government's proposal the general council did not deny that it is possible for incomes to get so much out of line with output as to raise costs and prices or that at any time some groups of people have a greater claim than others to improvements in their incomes.' Moreover, the TUC declared that no 'group of trade unionists' was 'entitled (or indeed able) to pursue its own interests with complete disregard of the interests of the rest of the community – or of other trade unionists'.[7]

At the 1963 Congress Woodcock found himself in open public conflict over the incomes policy question with Frank Cousins, the TGWU's General Secretary. Reluctantly he was forced to retreat – under pressure from Cousins – and accept a dilution of a TUC economic statement, which had already been approved by the general council, over its willingness to accept involvement in a future incomes policy. But in Woodcock's opinion, the TUC could not avoid shouldering responsibilities in its dealings with the state and this meant it must adopt an attitude towards wages. His characteristically agonized but brilliant speech to the 1963 Congress went to the heart of the tangled problem that strained government–union relations for much of the post-war period. Woodcock pointed out that he knew well enough it was 'entirely foreign to trade union tradition and practice for there to be any interference whatsoever at any time with unions in their right to pursue on behalf of their members claims for improvements in wages and working conditions'.[8] 'It is the tradition of the trade union movement', he added. 'This is why we were formed. This is what we have done all our lives.' Moreover, Woodcock agreed it was 'wrong and certainly dangerous even to attempt to interfere with unions in this bargaining process'. But on the other hand, he told the delegates it was impossible for the TUC to avoid having an opinion on the wages issue in a post-war labour market based on full employment. As a result of the growth in the TUC's own power and influence over governments since 1945, the TUC expected to have its views on economic growth and inflation listened to by ministers. Therefore it was impossible, Woodcock argued, for the TUC to exclude the wages question from any discussions it might have with the government over its economic policy. 'Are we, when these big issues come up, to sit supine and dumb and mute; to have nothing at all to say?', he asked. In his view the days of protest by the TUC on the streets were over. 'We left Trafalgar Square a long time ago', he asserted. Now the TUC should use its influence in the committee rooms, sitting opposite the men with power in government.

The 1963 Labour party conference also debated the question of a possible incomes policy under a future Labour government. By 6,090,000 votes to a mere 40,000 against, a motion from the GMWU was passed calling on the party in consultation with the trade unions to devise an incomes policy which would 'include salaries, wages, dividends and profits (including speculative profits) and social security benefits'.[9] Jim Callaghan, the shadow Chancellor of the Exchequer, spelt out what this would involve for the trade unions. 'We will not attempt to enforce it [the incomes policy] if we got into difficulties', he promised. In his view that would be 'economic madness, quite apart from being bad politics'. Callaghan assured the delegates that the framework for an equitable incomes policy was 'an expanding economy' as well as a government strategy that involved price restraints, action to curb racketeers and rent speculators, and government action against monopolies. In the wider context of economic growth, an incomes policy could not be portrayed in the trade unions as a form of wage restraint.[10] Indeed, Labour party leaders before October 1964 were keen to emphasize that they did not envisage any attempt by themselves when in government to interfere directly with the wage bargaining system in order to hold down pay levels.

The trade unions responded in a positive manner to what Labour was proposing. Jack Cooper, the ever-loyal General Secretary of the GMWU suggested that 'the necessity for an incomes policy or if you like a clear understanding of what is available for distribution from any particular level of output is self-evident', and he called for 'a clear understanding to be achieved between the party and the TUC' before the general election.[11] Even the supposedly most left-wing of union general secretaries like Ted Hill of the Boilermakers' union were able to reconcile themselves to the concept of an incomes policy. He accepted you could not 'get more than a pint out of a pint pot'.[12] Although drawing the line at a pay freeze, Hill told the Labour leadership in 1963: 'If you are in trouble come to us and as long as you do not humiliate us we will assist you.' Frank Cousins laid his emphasis on 'attitudes and intentions', but he pinned his faith on 'a planned growth of wages'.[13]

Labour's 1964 general election manifesto accepted the Cousins view. It promised 'a planned growth of incomes broadly related to the annual rate of production' and went on to assert that the policy would 'apply in an expanding economy to all incomes; to profits, dividends and rents as well as wages and salaries', emphasizing that it would 'not be unfairly directed at lower paid workers and public employees'.[14] In his speech to the 1964 Congress that launched Labour's general election campaign, Wilson enjoined the enthusiastic delegates to become 'partners in a great adventure'.

'We shall consult – and I mean consult not present you with a diktat; we shall listen and we shall say what in our view the national interest demands', he assured them.[15] He insisted a Labour government had 'the right to ask for an incomes policy' but he said this was because the party was 'prepared to contribute three necessary conditions' to ensure its success. These were 'an assurance of rising production and rising incomes' so that the restraint that would be asked· for would be 'matched by an assurance that it will result in increased production and increased rewards; as well as equity and social justice' because Labour's policies would be 'directed to the benefit of the nation as a whole and not to the advantage of a sectional interest'; and finally that what Labour asked for on 'wages and salaries' would apply equally to 'profits, dividends and rents'.

It is true that no jointly agreed detailed economic strategy was hammered out between the Labour party in opposition and the TUC before October 1964, as would happen ten years later with the Social Contract. But an aspiration to achieve common objectives did seem to bind the two sides together beneath a wide understanding of good intentions. The 1964 Congress agreed to a composite motion that declared 'an acceptable incomes policy' would have to 'redress the injustices in the existing wages structure' by being based on 'social justice taking into account all forms of incomes including rent, interest and profit'.[16] But the rhetorical unity achieved by the TUC over this crucial question in the atmosphere of a countdown to a general election could not completely hide genuine differences of opinion. It was Cousins – despite his honest willingness to help – who laid bare the real and clear dilemma that would face trade union negotiators under any voluntary pay agreement reached with a Labour government. 'If we do not fulfil the purposes for which members join unions, to protect and raise their real standard of living, then the unions will wither and finally die', he warned in his union journal in October 1963. 'We can give leadership, we can persuade but basically we must serve trade union purposes.'[17] 'It is not the intention of the trade union movement to hold back its members' wage claims if they are justified', declared Cousins in a speech at Oxford in June 1964. 'It is our purpose to sell our labour and our skill in the open market to the best of our ability while we live under the present system'.[18] In the battle of all, Cousins's members were to be part of the all. But his views were shared by most union negotiators, both on the Left and the Right of the Labour Movement, who were never really convinced by the arguments in favour of a national incomes policy achieved through negotiations with the state. Over the next fifteen years they would often acquiesce in government-imposed pay norms but they continued to preach the virtues of so-called 'free' collective bargaining where labour and capital fought it out in the market place in what was an uneven distribution of the limited spoils of a contracting economy.

In fact, in October 1964 the heady glow of optimism among trade union leaders in the aftermath of the Labour party's narrow general election victory gave a rather misleading impression of the nature of the relationship between the political and industrial wings of the Labour Movement. As Denis Barnes and Eileen Reid noted: 'The close working relationship between governments and the TUC general council which had existed from 1940–50 had disappeared during the thirteen years of Conservative government.'[19] It is true that during the early 1950s the right-wing union junta of Deakin, Lawther and Williamson had wielded their block votes in unison inside the Labour party to keep the Left away from control. Their loyal support for Hugh Gaitskell, expressed through the wielding of their block votes at Labour's annual conference, was important after he was elected party leader in November 1955 by the parliamentary Labour party. But the defection of the TGWU from the right-wing camp after Cousins's surprise election as General Secretary in the spring of 1956, following the sudden deaths of first Deakin and then his moderate successor Jock Tiffin, brought a greater degree of uncertainty to the balance of political power inside the Labour Movement.

But in the immediate aftermath of Labour's third successive general election defeat in October 1959, not even the revisionist Right of the party like Douglas Jay, Tony Crosland and Roy Jenkins questioned openly whether the party ought to maintain its trade union links, though they favoured moves to replace Labour's obsolete and unpopular 'cloth-cap image' with a more modern appeal to the increasingly affluent working class electorate. There was no question of any divorce proceedings to separate the party from the trade unions during the early 1960s. Indeed, the role of the trade unions turned out to be vital in resolving the bitter struggle over unilateral nuclear disarmament that ended in Gaitskell's triumph at the 1961 party conference when the majority of trade union block votes were mobilized behind him on the defence issue. On the other hand, even right-wing trade union leaders were less than enthusiastic about Gaitskell's desire to revise Clause 4, Section iv of the party constitution to make it clear to the voters that the Labour party did not want to nationalize every industry in the country. He was forced to compromise over that question to avoid humiliation at the hands of the trade unions.

However, most union leaders most of the time were anxious not to maximize their strength inside the Labour party. As Labour's main paymasters and controllers of 90 per cent of the votes cast at the party conference with direct control over the majority of the 28 strong National Executive Committee, they could have easily dictated the party's policy and strategy, but in practice they displayed a deep reluctance ever to do so. As Allan Flanders explained in 1961:

> The relationship between the unions and the Party has been governed far more by unwritten assumptions than by its formal constitution. They are usually covered by some such phrase as 'acting responsibly' and for the unions this has meant that they did not abuse the power that was theirs.[20]

For the most part, union leaders wanted Labour's politicians to keep their noses out of their industrial affairs and in return they were happy not to interfere in what they regarded as political questions. In this way, they hoped to ensure the relationship between the party and the trade unions could remain in practice one in which there was a more or less clear-cut demarcation line of responsibilities. Most union leaders disliked having to act as a praetorian guard in defence of the Labour leadership. But in reality it was never possible to keep political and industrial affairs so neatly apart. If the trade unions wanted to play a key role in economic policy-making – as they said they did – then they would have to shoulder some responsibilities in those areas where they exercised some degree of influence, if not control, such as wage bargaining on behalf of their members.

For their part, the Labour party's leaders were not keen to be over-dependent on trade union support. 'We are comrades together but we have different jobs to do', Gaitskell told trade union delegates at the 1959 party conference. 'You have your industrial job and we have our political job. We do not dictate to one another.' While he accepted there were 'common aims' between the two wings of the Labour Movement, and that it was in the interests of both to work with each other, he had 'never known an occasion when any trade union leader or any collective body of trade unionists ever attempted to dictate to the Labour party'.[21]

Woodcock was keen to play down any exclusively political identification of the TUC with the Labour party. He wanted to establish an enhanced role for Congress House as the representative national body for all Britain's organized workers, whatever their political loyalties might be, and he was also determined to win over the unorganized white-collar salariat to trade unionism. Although he reluctantly accepted Congress as the launch-pad for Labour's 1964 general election campaign, Woodcock favoured an arm's length relationship with the party. As the TUC explained in its 1966 written evidence to the Donovan Royal Commission on trade unions and employers' associations:

The growth of the Labour party to the point where it became the Government of the country has entailed a significant divergence of function. The existence of common roots yet distinct functions is therefore the most important feature of the relationship between trade unions and the Labour party. . . . The relationship becomes strained if either attempts to capitalise on the loyalties which exist and the strength of the relationship lies paradoxically in the looseness of the ties.[22]

This dispassionate observation on the historic relationship may have accurately reflected the mood of the moment in Congress House, but even if there was a much less dominant sense of social solidarity binding union leaders and the Labour government together than there had been between 1945 and 1951, the two sides wanted to maintain a working relationship after October 1964. As Martin Harrison noted in his 1960 study of Labour and the trade unions: 'The Labour Party is bound to the unions not just by cash and card votes but by personalities and doctrines, common experience and sentiment – and mutual advantage.'[23]

Indeed, Wilson wanted to include prominent trade unionists in his Cabinet. Although Woodcock made it clear he would not consider joining the new government, Cousins accepted the Prime Minister's offer of a ministerial post and became the country's first Minister of Technology, taking leave of absence from his post in the TGWU. It turned out to be an unhappy experience for Cousins. He was no Bevin and was to spend much of his time in fuming, self-imposed, ineffective isolation. Other trade union voices were to be few in the government and were not particularly influential in the Labour Cabinets of the 1960s. It is true that the combustible George Brown as the first Secretary of State for Economic Affairs had been an official in the TGWU, and Ray Gunter, the Minister of Labour, had once worked for the Transport Salaried Staffs' Association, the white-collar rail union. Jim Callaghan, Chancellor of the Exchequer, could point to sterling work as a young Assistant Secretary in the Association of Officers of Taxes before the Second World War. But none of them was close socially to the current crop of TUC heavyweights.

Loyal brothers

The lack of any powerful go-between binding the political and industrial wings of the Labour Movement after October 1964 played a part in the growing disenchantment and divergence that soured relations close to breaking point five years later. Certainly, the economic inheritance Labour had to face would have tested the alliance to its utmost whoever had been sitting on the TUC general council or in the Cabinet. But the absence in the 1960s of that mutual social solidarity between government and TUC, which had worked so successfully under Attlee and Bevin back in the immediately post-war period, was unfortunate for both sides.

However, the legacy of a huge £800 million balance of payments deficit – mainly caused by a Conservative pre-election consumer spending boom – did little to dampen the euphoria of Labour's first exciting days in office. But from the beginning, Wilson and his Cabinet colleagues were under almost continuous pressure from the international money markets, once the Prime Minister had made the fateful if understandable decision not to devalue the pound as a way of easing the country's economic troubles. As a result, the new government's room for manoeuvre was severely limited, particularly as it remained firmly committed to the maintenance of full employment. The trouble was that any economic policy that was designed to protect the over-valued currency required wage restraint, and the TUC's cooperation was seen as crucial in order to achieve that objective. Within a few weeks of coming to power, ministers had in effect already accepted that an incomes strategy would not be a part of an economic growth policy as promised, but instead an instrument for deflation. This took many months to become apparent. Instead, the TUC enthused in the creation of the 1965 five year National Plan with its unrealistic commitment to achieve an annual growth rate of 3.8 per cent up to 1970.

Brown and Gunter told Woodcock that the government 'desperately needed' an incomes policy with the TUC if it hoped to resolve successfully the country's underlying economic difficulties. At their meeting with the Prime Minister on 26 October 1964 the TUC general council gave its full support to the new Labour government's first efforts to deal with the balance of payments deficit. Union leaders also responded sympathetically to Brown and Callaghan when they met them on 9 November and were told of the need for an effective prices and incomes policy because of the severity of the balance of payments deficit. Indeed, gaining immediate TUC consent to a voluntary curb on wage increases was regarded by the government as a necessity in order to win over overseas financial support to defend the country's currency reserves. Union leaders also lined up dutifully behind the grandiose Joint Statement of Intent with the government and employers' associations, launched in December under the guidance of the energetic Brown. Although the document was concerned mainly with the need to increase exports and improve productivity it also accepted the principle of voluntary wage and price restraint linking pay rises to productivity and cooperation in the creation of machinery 'to keep under review the general movement of prices and of money incomes of all kinds'.[24]

During his negotiations in the early weeks of 1965 Brown fought hard to secure the TUC's cooperation for, or at least its acquiescence in, an immediate 3 to 3.5 per cent pay limit, and despite Woodcock's serious doubts about the wisdom of such a policy the TUC general council accepted the proposed norm – though no sanctions were envisaged to enforce it. Plans were also laid for the creation of a tripartite National Prices and Incomes Board, which was to be a purely voluntary organization without sanction powers. Collective bargaining was to continue unrestricted but particular price rises or wage increases could be referred to the new body after consultation with trade unions and employers. However, the TUC was able to convince the government that exceptions should be permitted to that wage figure if they involved productivity improvements, the low paid, perceived unfair pay differentials between workers, or manpower demands as a result of industrial restructuring. At a Special Congress of the TUC held on 30 April 1965, Brown assured delegates that what the government had in mind had 'nothing in common with the wage restraint policies of previous Conservative governments' but was an attempt to bring together the industrial objectives of the trade unions as wage bargainers with their wider political aims.[25] For his part, Woodcock warned that if the voluntary strategy failed, the government would either have to abandon full employment or restrict free collective bargaining. The general council report was endorsed by 4,800,000 block votes to 1,800,000 against, the latter composed primarily of the TGWU's huge block vote.

But the TUC decision to administer its own voluntary incomes policy failed to bring any obvious success in reducing the high level of wage settlements, a point that began to exercise President Lyndon Johnson's administration in the United States, and particularly Henry Fowler, the Secretary of the Treasury. As Wilson wrote:

> Looking to the future, he [Fowler] was afraid of an inflationary situation developing and in particular doubted whether the voluntary prices and incomes policy which George Brown had negotiated would be able to withstand the pressure for wage increases to which we were subject. While he did not attempt in any way to make terms or give us orders, he was apprehensive that if further central bank aid were required it would be difficult to mount if we had no better safeguard against inflation than the voluntary system. It was in these circumstances that we began first to think in terms of statutory powers.[26]

In July 1965 Callaghan had to introduce a crisis package of austerity measures involving public sector spending cuts and a postponement of cherished welfare benefit improvements. But this was not enough. Wage restraint had now become a political imperative in the eyes of the international money markets.

At a three hour Cabinet meeting on 1 September 1965, Callaghan called for the introduction of a statutory incomes policy with penal sanctions. Eventually a compromise was agreed when Brown made it clear he believed the government could achieve what it wanted through pay restraint, not by a resort to compulsion but through securing the TUC's cooperation for a more effective incomes strategy backed up with reserve powers from the government. Ministers agreed that the National Board of Prices and Incomes should be turned into a statutory body, with the Secretary of State for Economic Affairs empowered to refer any price or wage rise to it and to defer any implementation of a specific wage or price settlement while the Board carried out its investigation. The statutory back-up also involved the establishment of an 'early warning system' for price increases and wage settlements. On the eve of the 1965 Congress Brown travelled down to Brighton where he held twelve hours of talks with the TUC general council to try and browbeat them into acceptance of a compulsory 'early warning' system on pay claims. In his view, union leaders needed 'frequent kicks in the shins'[27] to respond positively to what the government wanted but his bullying style of personal diplomacy failed to impress a moody Woodcock, who believed that an incomes policy only stood any chance of success if it was placed in the wider context of a commitment to economic growth and was not used as an instrument for deflating the economy. Woodcock was also convinced that it was going to take a period of many years of patient persuasion before trade union leaders were willing to accept that they should restrain the wage demands of their members in line with the government's economic objectives. Eventually, the majority of the TUC general council agreed reluctantly by 21 votes to 6 to compromise under government duress and establish a TUC committee to vet wage claims from affiliated unions and settlements, while at the same time the government would go ahead with its plans to prepare for a statutory prices and incomes policy. This would require an Order in Council agreed by Parliament to come into force and this would happen only if the TUC's own self-regulated system failed to work. The general council's decision was endorsed by the 1965 Congress but only by 5,300,000 votes to 3,300,000, with the TGWU once again leading the growing resistance to any government interference with free collective bargaining. However, as Callaghan noted in his memoirs 'the remarkable turnabout of the TUC attracted favourable coverage in many countries and improved sentiment markedly'.[28]

The trouble was that the fragile British economy required a prolonged period of wage restraint to ensure international confidence, and this was hard to achieve with a collective bargaining system that was fragmented and based on voluntaristic principles not legal regulations. Brown in his address to the 1965 Labour party conference emphasized the need for fairness. 'Our present traditional system of negotiation puts a premium on those and gives a bonus to those with great bargaining power', he explained. 'We have been operating the law of the jungle ourselves while condemning it for every other purpose.' He told delegates that to ensure fairness within a 3 per cent pay norm it was necessary that some workers would have to hold back in their wage demands so others could go forward. 'That after all is the basis of Socialist belief anyway', he asserted. Brown tried to reassure his audience that an 'early warning' system on price and wage rises could only work with consent, and involved no coercion. 'We have no intention of supplanting the voluntary system by government action if the former works', he added. 'We are now doing all the things our movement has always said were essential prerequisites for a prices and incomes policy'.[29]

But mere verbal exhortation failed to make much difference to the general level of wage settlements. Trade unions and employers continued to bargain together, almost oblivious to the demands of the national interest. The TUC's own vetting committee turned out to be a complete fiasco, as Gerald Dorfman noted:

> Although it examined more than 600 claims during its first nine months, it questioned only a handful and had no total effect on the course of any of them. . . . The committee often acted on claims at the rate of 50 an hour during its one day sessions each month. It reached decisions to approve claims without making any attempt to measure them against the 3 to 3.5 per cent present norm the TUC had agreed to honour.[30]

In fact, earnings in the period rose by around 7 per cent, far above what the government believed was economically sensible.

Blown off course

The British economy continued to deteriorate during the spring and early summer of 1966. The Labour party won a 97 seat overall parliamentary majority in the April general election but this did little to inspire overseas confidence in the wisdom of the government's economic strategy. A seven week long official strike by the National Union of Seamen (NUS) in pursuit of a 17 per cent wage claim helped to shake foreign business opinion still further. Sterling came under intensive pressure on the foreign exchange markets and substantial sums of money began to flow out of the country. A serious attempt was made inside the Cabinet to convince Wilson that the only way out of the crisis was to devalue, but again that option was ruled out. Instead, after declaring his government had been 'blown off course', Wilson introduced stringent economic measures on 20 July 1966, which included a six month wage standstill followed by a further six month period of 'severe restraint' on pay rises as well as a twelve month price freeze and a plea to companies to hold down their dividends for twelve months. On top of this, higher indirect taxes and tighter controls on hire purchase were introduced. The National Board of Prices and Incomes was given compulsory powers to secure one month advance notification of any price and wage increases to be implemented to be followed by three months' delay. The new law gave the government powers to direct that specified prices, charges or rates of remuneration should not be introduced from a certain date, and also enforced recommendations of the Prices and Incomes Board though this power was never actually used. It would have needed an Order in Council to bring that section of the law into force and this would have lapsed automatically after twelve months.

The TUC general council met Callaghan and Brown four days later to discuss the details of the crisis package. Union leaders were told by the two ministers that the government had had no alternative after the damage caused to the economy by the seaman's strike, the rise in world commodity prices and the rapid increase in earnings of the previous twelve months. Brown said he wanted to try and preserve the framework of the prices and incomes policy for the future, while Woodcock warned that a pay freeze would bring trouble with anomalies and unfairness between work groups and the dishonouring of existing collective agreements. By ruling out wage rises, even for improved productivity, there would be a standstill on economic growth, warned the TUC General Secretary. There is little doubt that Woodcock was in the mood to reject the government's wage freeze. He thought it would serve trade unions little purpose to swallow the government's crisis package if it was then rejected by work groups in strong bargaining positions on the shop floor, over whom neither the TUC nor their affiliated unions would be able to exercise any effective restraint. If a sufficient number of such groups broke through the wage standstill by the threat of unofficial strike action, the sense of injustice among other workers would be so intense that the whole of the government's strategy would disintegrate. Woodcock and his TUC colleagues took their fears to Wilson who told them that if the government had failed to act unemployment would have soared to over two million. In the end, the TUC general council demonstrated its strained but residual loyalty to the government by deciding on 27 July by 20 votes to 12 to 'acquiesce' reluctantly in the government's crisis measures, despite Woodcock's principled opposition. 'There is no doubt the Government had no alternative to taking quick and purposeful action', admitted the general council but it added that the main reason why the TUC had 'decided not to leave the Government to act unilaterally was they believed this was the way in which they could best protect and advance' trade union interests.[31] Cousins resigned from the government in protest at the pay freeze and went back to lead the opposition from his old post at the head of the TGWU as well as securing the succession for Jack Jones. But as Middlemas wrote, 'A period of too-credulous trust in a Labour Government had ended but not in detachment from the Labour party. By the end of the year, talk about a loyalty "trap" became common on the general council.'[32]

At the 1966, Congress support for the government's wage and price standstill carried the day but only by a wafer-thin majority of 240,000 in a card vote of 4,560,000 for and 4,320,000 against. However, Wilson won a standing ovation when he spoke to delegates despite his withering attack on restrictive labour practices, the inadequacies of the apprenticeship system and union opposition to improved productivity measures, as well as warning that wage rises not paid for by higher productivity would lead to unemployment. Nonetheless, much of the moral credit built up by the Labour party and the TUC during the previous five years was wasting away rapidly in defence of restrictive government economic policies, designed to uphold sterling at an unrealistically high exchange rate. The crude measures of July 1966 were also a blow – despite Wilson's assurances – to the deeply held conviction that an incomes policy should be regarded as part of a long-term growth strategy. Here it was instead being used as a short-term crisis measure and a vital element in an austerity package, intended to check the rise in output and consumer spending. In the eyes of an increasing number of workers the government's incomes strategy was becoming identified inevitably with wage restraint and a squeeze on their own living standards.

It is true that the July 1966 measures did not immediately provoke wide-spread shopfloor unrest. Despite the militant rhetoric coming from Cousins, his union failed to spearhead any wage-push offensive. As Wilson wrote later, 'The wages freeze was total and was honoured without exception. More surprising there was not a single strike against it.'[33] In fact, only 14 standstill orders were made by the government under its statutory

Table 5.1 Labour statistics during the years of Harold Wilson, 1965–1970

	Hourly wage rate rise (%)	Unemployment (no.)	(%)	Strikes (Working days lost)	Union membership (no.)	(%)
1965	7.2	317,000	1.4	2,925,000	9,742,000	43.2
1966	5.4	330,900	1.4	2,398,000	10,111,000	42.6
1967	5.4	521,000	2.2	2,787,000	9,970,000	42.8
1968	5.5	549,400	2.4	4,690,000	10,049,000	43.1
1969	5.6	543,800	2.4	6,846,000	10,472,000	44.4
1970	11.6	582,200	2.5	10,980,000	11,179,000	47.7

Source: Department of Employment Gazette; *British Labour Statistics: Historical Abstract 1886–1968*, HMSO, 1971.

policy and these covered a mere 56,000 workers out of a 23 million strong labour force. The government was keen, however, to secure the TUC's support for an incomes policy when the period of 'severe restraint' was due to come to an end in July 1967, but ministers made it clear that any wage increases after that would have to be tied closely to productivity improvements. For its part, the TUC continued to believe that a viable incomes policy had to be part of a plan for economic growth and seen as socially equitable, with a better deal for low paid workers than for others. While Congress House was clear that it wanted an end to the statutory approach to pay restraint as soon as possible, it was also anxious to avoid the suggestion that the TUC itself should try and exercise pay restraint over its affiliated trade unions, though accepting the need to 'adopt a more positive approach to the development of incomes policy' if it was to 'convince the government that the collective actions of unions will not prevent the achievement of national objectives'. The TUC general council's November 1966 statement on incomes policy asserted:

> It is no more desirable or practicable for the TUC to attempt detailed control of wage determination at all levels than it is for the government. Nor does it imply that the aim would be to find an alternative means of perpetuating the policy of overall restraint which has too often character-ised the approach of governments in recent years.[34]

At the 26 April 1967 Special Congress of the TUC executive, members ratified the TUC's proposal for a voluntary incomes policy. This involved a revival of Congress House's wage vetting machinery, which had been suspended after the imposition of the July 1966 freeze, and an assessment of pay claims based on the aim of raising national minimum wage rates to £15 a week as well as pay comparability between workers. Wilson described the decision with characteristic exaggeration as 'historic' and urged the TUC to agree on the idea of an annual appraisal between government and both sides of industry, to be known as the National Dividend, for distribution between all forms of income. The TUC was unenthusiastic about such an idea but continued to accept that an incomes policy had to be part of a growth and redistribution strategy. For its part, the government announced plans for a further stage of statutory prices and incomes control which the TUC suggested should be ignored as 'irrelevant to the real issues'. Woodcock pleaded for much more room for manoeuvre. 'In this business we need flexibility', he explained. 'Room for those shoddy, shabby dirty compromises which are the essence of practical people trying to do a job.'[35]

But the TUC's patience with the government was running out rapidly. At the 1967 Congress a composite motion hostile to the statutory approach was carried by 4,883,000 votes to 3,502,000. Wilson noted laconically:

> The majorities [on the anti-government votes] were not all that large, mainly because the president of the Engineers, Lord Carron, insisted on using 'Carron's law' – where as president of the union he claimed to decide what general union policy meant on any Congress or Labour conference vote – to throw a million votes on the Government side. He would not be there another year.[36]

The 1967 Labour party conference turned out to be a less demoralizing spectacle than Wilson had feared. A motion denouncing the government's prices and incomes policy as detrimental to the 'best interests of trade unionists and lower income groups' was actually defeated decisively by 3,860,000 to 2,535,000. Delegates even voted by a narrow 122,000 majority for a motion that gave general support to the government's economic strategy by 3,213,000 votes to 3,091,000. Wilson won a standing ovation for his conference speech, with Cousins the first man to rise to his feet to clap in appreciation.

But economic events in the real world outside the Labour party conference were less susceptible to platform hyperbole. The French government believed that Britain was planning to devalue the pound and there was a rapid drain on the currency reserves as international speculation mounted in the face of the officially inspired rumours emanating from

Paris. Just over a month after Wilson's conference triumph on 18 November 1967 the government devalued sterling by 14.3 per cent with a fall in sterling's dollar parity from $2.80 to $2.40. The long three year struggle to defend the pound's fixed parity had failed. TUC leaders met Callaghan and Brown on 20 November to discuss the consequences of the devaluation. They were told the aftermath was not going to be a 'painless process' because it would now be necessary to curb domestic demand to make room for an export drive and import savings. The government estimated prices would rise by between 2.5 and 3.0 per cent as a result of the devaluation and ministers warned the TUC that income increases must not try to keep pace with rising prices if the devaluation's full benefits were to be achieved. There would be an 'inevitable' drop in living standards in the short run, union leaders were informed, but the economy would be able to take full advantage of export-led growth with the eventual prospect of renewed prosperity. For their part, TUC leaders argued that policies to improve productivity would be prejudiced unless full employment could be secured, something they said the government's austerity programme would undermine. Gunter told the TUC that tougher legislation on incomes – even another wage freeze – had been considered by the Cabinet but ministers had decided to accept the TUC general council's assertion that 'they were the only people who could deal with incomes policy and looked to the TUC to do its best in the new situation'.[37] In its statement on 22 November the TUC general council gave its support to the government's decision to devalue sterling. The trade unions appeared to accept that 'if a greater proportion of the country's output had to be exported there would have to be a smaller proportion available for domestic consumption'. But the TUC was relieved to know there would be no return to a pay freeze and it suggested its own voluntary incomes policy would prove to be sufficient.

At the 1968 Congress Woodcock sought to down play the TUC's role in seeking pay restraint among its affiliated union members. Apparently, all Congress House sought was 'a moral obligation upon individual unions to let us know what they have in mind and to be willing to discuss it with their colleagues'.[38] But on the other hand, Woodcock did not see himself as a militant leader, intent on the destruction of the Labour government's incomes policy. 'We have to oppose government's policies but there is no future in getting into fights with government in the kind of world in which we live today. In the long run we have to live with governments', he argued. Woodcock could see no future for the TUC in 'keeping away from governments'. At the same time the TUC General Secretary, at what was to be his last Congress, was determined to take a constructive view of the trade union movement's approach to wage determination. He told delegates that what Britain needed was a 'better ordered and more methodical, sensible and more just system of collective bargaining and wage settlement'. 'Trade unions existed as custodians of the principle of collective bargaining', he added, and it is in that context an incomes policy had to operate. To Woodcock, collective bargaining was more than 'simply strengthening little groups to do what they like and to hell with the rest of us'. But his world-weary philosophical attitude was that of a disappointed man and it was out of tune with the growing and aggressive impatience of the newly emerging TUC left. Cousins moved a motion that rejected all legislation restricting wages and salary 'movements' on the grounds that it curtailed basic trade union rights. 'I don't care what political background the government has. It cannot get involved in the detail of industrial negotiation', declared Cousins. 'We are asking the government to keep out before they destroy not only themselves but us'.[39] His resolution was seconded by Hugh Scanlon, the newly elected left-wing President of the AEU, who argued the government's incomes strategy was 'a policy on the old traditional Tory lines, committed and perpetrated with the full approval of the Treasury'.[40] Congress voted by a massive 7,746,000 votes to 1,022,000 for the composite motion that rejected all legislation that restricted wage bargaining. A resolution from the Dyers' and Bleachers' union that merely reaffirmed Congress's support for the TUC's own voluntary incomes policy as 'the only feasible alternative to growing legislative interference in the field of wage negotiations' was carried but only by a wafer-thin majority of 34,000.

The writing was clearly on the wall for the government's prices and incomes policy as delegates gathered for the 1968 Labour party conference, though a serious attempt was made by the party leadership to try and avoid defeat. The debate over the government's economic strategy revealed its fundamental difference of opinion with the trade unions. Roy Jenkins, who was appointed Chancellor of the Exchequer after Callaghan moved to the Home Office following the November 1967 devaluation, was unrepentant in his defence of what the government was doing. He admitted that it would need another 'eighteen months of hard but difficult and ultimately rewarding effort' to restore the economy. 'None of us want to keep on the present restrictive legislation a moment longer than we have to', Jenkins told the delegates. 'We are not masochists.' But he also emphasized that the Government could not have done without it.[41] Jenkins pointed out that without the government's incomes policy rapid wage increases would have driven up consumption and done severe damage to competitiveness. A spending spree would have ensured the accumulation of a large deficit and destroyed the 9 per cent competitive advantage achieved by the devaluation. Moreover, without any statutory incomes restraint the government would have been forced to impose even more austere deflationary measures than they had done already with a resulting sharp increase in unemployment.

The Chancellor's lesson in economic realism made no difference to the attitude of Cousins and Scanlon, who sought to repeat the block vote triumph they had secured at the TUC Congress. 'We are almost getting to the state of accepting that the workers are on one side and the government is on the other', declared Cousins.[42] Although he hastened to add that he did not really believe this had happened yet, he went on to warn the government that 'forcing through laws to restrict the rights of trade unionists to deal with their employers' was not the 'way to solve the problems of Socialism'. In his first appearance as AEU President at the Labour party conference Scanlon received tumultuous applause:

> We reject the philosophy which suggests that Britain's undoubted economic ills stem from the fact that our workers are overpaid and lazy . . . Employers with certain notable exceptions never needed any encouragement to say No. The only reason in our case why we continue in these difficulties is the solace and support that they receive from the government and the iniquitous prices and incomes Act.[43]

'Legislation makes wage bargaining inflexible and this is to the detriment of the nation as a whole', said Tom Jackson, the recently elected General Secretary of the Post Office Workers' union (UPOW). 'It is a self-inflicted wound which is destroying healthy relationships which ought to exist between the two wings of the Movement.'[44] Even Lord Cooper of the GMWU had to back the Cousins motion though without enthusiasm. 'We are not marching forward in the TUC as one army', he admitted. 'This is the great problem. If therefore we cannot grapple with it ourselves, then as I see it the government are bound to do something about it.'[45]

Barbara Castle, the Employment Secretary, faced a hopeless task in summing up the debate but she made some telling points. 'Real wages have advanced every year since this government came into power', she reminded the conference.[46] In its first year the wage rate index went up by 7.3 per cent, much higher than retail prices. 'We paid ourselves in wages and dividends an increase of £1,300 million and we earned by increased production only £600 million', she explained. Mrs Castle pointed out wage costs per unit of output had fallen between April 1964 and April 1967 in France, West Germany and Italy but had risen by 11 per cent in Britain. 'No method of taxation or monetary management can restore

export competitiveness', she argued. 'All it can do is create unemployment by reducing demand and it is only by a direct influence on unit
costs that we can retain export competitiveness that we have endured
devaluation to achieve.' She went on to point out that in the nine months
since devaluation hourly wage rates had gone up by over 4 per cent,
earnings by nearly 5 per cent and prices by 4.4 per cent:

> So what nonsense all those resolutions are that say we have had a wages
> freeze while prices have been allowed to get out of hand. . . . Clumsily,
> perhaps inadequately no doubt, the government has been reaching for
> something better than crude industrial power politics, whether practised
> by industrial tycoons or trade unions. If you kill that without being clear
> what you put in its place, then you will share a very heavy responsibility.

But the party conference took no notice and the government's incomes
policy went down to a resounding defeat by 5,098,000 votes to 1,124,000.

Relations were growing frayed in the 'honourable, open' alliance between the political and industrial wings of the Labour Movement. On the
last morning of the 1968 conference, Scanlon moved a motion that declared support for the government in carrying through its 1966 general
election manifesto and recognized 'the difficulties both at home and abroad'
that it had been confronted with. But the resolution also said that the
support was conditional on acceptance of the TUC's policy decisions.
Moreover, Scanlon made it clear it also did not mean any softening in
trade union hostility to the government's incomes strategy. In his view,
the difference between the government and the conference was concerned
with 'a simple, straightforward Socialist belief of ensuring that less of the
national gross product goes in rent, interest and profit and more goes in
wages and salaries'.[47] The AEU president won applause for his attack on
'the growing practice of pretending that conference decisions do not
matter'. 'Conference decisions are not always a reflection of what the
general electorate may desire but they are a far greater reflection of what
is universally felt than the personal opinion of any trade union leader or
politicians', he observed. The unforgiving mood was underlined by the
defeat of an attempt to omit the words from the motion that made
support for the government conditional on approval of TUC policy
decisions in a card vote of 3,287,000 to 2,722,000.

In fact, by 1968 the whole idea of a national incomes policy had
become discredited across large sections of the trade union movement.
Initially promised by the Labour party leadership as an integral part of an
expansionist economic programme, it had not been used to bring about
any income redistribution to help the low paid or provide the opportunity

for genuine productivity bargaining. The tensions and animosities over incomes policy that soured relations between the TUC and the Labour government for most of the 1965–9 period seem in retrospect to have been out of all proportion to the policy's modest achievement. 'As far as the actual earnings of manual workers were concerned the policy had little overall effect in the period 1965–1969 but slowed down the rate of increase in the first half of the period', was the careful conclusion of Derek Robinson, the Oxford labour economist. In his opinion it was 'an excessive price to pay for merely postponing wage increases'.[48] In fact, by the summer of 1970 Britain was suffering from the consequences of a dangerous wages explosion with an outbreak of industrial conflict on a scale which had not been experienced for more than forty years. The remnants of Labour's incomes strategy had fallen to pieces by the early months of 1970 during the run-up to the June general election as workers demanded wage rises to restore the relative pay position they believed they had lost through nearly five years of freeze and restraint.

It has been argued that the main reason for the upsurge of rank and file shopfloor discontent between 1969 and 1972 stemmed from the emergence of a dangerous wage–tax spiral. Turner and Wilkinson estimated that between 1964 and 1968 gross money incomes for male manual workers increased by 6.6 per cent but their net real incomes rose over the same period by a mere 0.5 per cent. The burden of direct taxation rose during the 1960s to help to pay for Labour's generous public expenditure programmes. In 1960 the average manual workers' tax plus National Insurance contributions accounted for less than 8 per cent of his earnings, but by 1970 that proportion had risen to nearly 20 per cent. According to Turner and Wilkinson:

> It seems to be the fate of Labour governments in Britain to tax employees more heavily or restrain their real wages more effectively. . . . Indeed, it almost appears as if the objective economic historical role of the British Labour party is to do (no doubt despite itself) those things to the workers that Conservative governments are unable to do.[49]

The new unionism

The failure of the government's efforts to achieve a permanent and acceptable incomes policy in the late 1960s stemmed primarily from the decentralizing tendencies inside Britain's collective bargaining system that had first begun to concern national policy-makers ten years earlier. It was really during the 1960s that self-regarding sectionalism gathered pace with the erosion of notions of solidarity and the dominance of the work group with the growing power of shop stewards. John Goldthorpe and his colleagues discovered the new kind of trade unionism in their seminal study of manual workers in Luton during the early 1960s:

> Neither as a way to greater worker participation in the affairs of the enterprise nor as a political force is unionism greatly valued. Rather, one would say, the significance that unionism has for workers is very largely confined to issues arising from their employment which are economic in nature and which are local in their origins and scope.[50]

Apparently, the workers valued union membership solely as a form of meal ticket not as an expression of class feeling, let alone a political identification with a mythical united proletariat. This did not mean that manual workers were suddenly all becoming middle class in their life-styles and ambitions. The embourgeoisement of the working class suffered real setbacks as an ideological concept during the 1960s. But nor were manual workers in any meaningful sense part of a collectively conscious proletariat. 'Instrumental collectivism' was how Goldthorpe described the attitude of the Luton workers towards the trade unions. They found self-fulfilment not with their fellow shopfloor workers but in their family networks and in the community outside the factory gates.

The shift in power and influence to the shop floor may have been uneven between industries, but it reflected a new mood of impatience with authority and the ossified structures of too many trade union organizations. It also brought about in the late 1960s a significant change in the political complexion of the union movement with the coming to power of a new generation of much more militant national union leaders. The election in 1968 of Laurence Daly as the NUM's General Secretary symbolized the growing radicalism among the mass membership. A shrewd and articulate Socialist from the Fife coalfield, he espoused a more uncompromising strategy for the miners after years of retreat and cooperation in the rundown of the coal industry. 'The Labour Movement should formulate ideas about the society it would ultimately like to see and be less satisfied with minimal short-term objectives; more demands and less compromise', he declared in October 1969.[51] Daly did not believe trade unions should settle for piecemeal pragmatism or incorporation into the management of the economy. In his opinion the 'uneasiness' he found inside the trade unions stemmed from the dilemma they found themselves in as being 'at one and the same time organisations of protest and social change and yet participators in pragmatic central government decisions'. Daly left nobody under any doubts about where he stood. He wrote about the 'sense of bewilderment' among the trade union members as their leaders shouldered government responsibilities that made them remote from shopfloor realities. 'The individual wanders in a Kafkaesque nightmare in which a mindless, fathomless social machine manipulates his destiny', he lamented. Daly wanted to revive a sense of moral idealism inside the trade unions.

The most effective and idealistic of the new breed of union leaders was undoubtedly Jack Jones, who took over from Cousins as the TGWU's General Secretary in September 1969 after a landslide election victory. Ever since his days as district secretary for the union in Coventry during and just after the war. Jones had favoured the devolution of power to the shop stewards with less of a role for the full-time union officials. 'Our success – indeed the success of industry itself is going to be determined by the extent to which we can decentralise – spread decision making amongst the work people and above all get industrial agreements settled where they are going to be', Jones told the annual Institute of Personnel Management conference in October 1969.[52] He believed in the virtues of self-help on the shop floor and decried any notion that union leaders should be in any sense boss figures barking out orders to subordinates. As he explained:

> I am working for a system where not a few trade union officials control the situation but a dedicated, well-trained and intelligent body of trade union members represented by hundreds of thousands of lay representatives – every one of whom is capable of helping to resolve industrial problems and assist in collective bargaining and the conclusion of agreements.

Jones said he wanted to create 'trade unionism with a human face'. Through the 'right to participate' workers would achieve the democratic conditions for industrial progress.

Jones's vision was of a decentralization of power that legitimized the position of the shop stewards as the 'greatest instruments for democracy'. No longer should they be treated by full-time union officials as a threat from below. Internal union organizational reforms such as the establishment of industrial delegate conferences, lay representation on trade union bargaining teams in multi-employer and single-employer negotiations, and the drawing up and ratification of pay claims and offers by the rank and file, were all proposed as ways of helping to integrate workplace realities into the more formalized rubric and settled ways of union structures. But was it really possible to reconcile the inevitable parochialism and limited objectives of shopfloor bargainers with the wider idealistic needs and aspirations of trade unionism? The optimistic Benthamite assumption that the sum of diverse and often conflicting self-interests would ensure the harmonious well-being of everybody was hard to reconcile with the virulent outbreaks of sectionalist workplace feeling in the 1960s and 1970s. Far from being concerned with the liberation of a thwarted, frustrated idealism and the emergence of a sense of purpose on the shop floor, decentralization tended to inflame the underlying fragmented tendencies of what were often diverse and competing work groups. Certainly, decentralization failed to generate any sense of worker solidarity or a level of political consciousness that could provide any Socialist perspective to the endless struggle of the annual pay round.

The 1967 broad left election victory of Hugh Scanlon to the AEU presidency was also a significant shift in the trade union balance of power. Reared in Manchester, he cut his teeth at Metropolitan Vickers in Trafford Park where he became chairman of the works committee before his election as a full-time union official in 1947. Scanlon brought a more militant face to the union after the bullying antics of Lord Carron. He was a passionate advocate of industrial democracy which he believed would 'release the dammed up potential of the workers' hard-won experience' in the 'transition to the beginnings of a Socialist society' which could be 'accomplished more swiftly and easily in Britain'. 'The rights of workers to negotiate with management about wages and conditions was not achieved by putting out the begging bowl', he wrote. 'It has been and is being achieved by hard and militant struggles'.[53] A strong advocate of workers' control in industry, Scanlon called for a coordinated trade union offensive against the power of the multinational companies by making them 'open their books'. This did not mean he favoured schemes of worker participation in management:

> Our programme is to actively intervene to make all workers aware of how decisions are arrived at. . . . To cast down the screen that separates workers from the processes taking place in the centres of corporate power. We cannot and will not allow ourselves to be disarmed in the process. We must decisively reject all systems of so-called social partnership, of profit sharing etc. which primarily seeks to divorce the worker from his union and instil only loyalty to the firm.

In fact, the rhetoric of the class war made very little impression on workers during the 1960s. W. G. Runciman in *Relative Deprivation and Social Justice*, an important study published in 1966, discovered that workers retained surprisingly narrow terms of reference when they compared their own earnings and benefits at work with those of other workers. Envy of the rich was not particularly widespread on the shop floor, though there remained a belief in the natural justice slogan of a 'fair day's work for a fair day's pay'. What did tend to stimulate a sense of grievance among workers was a disruption of wage relativities and differentials between workers doing similar kinds of work or who were employed in jobs that were close in proximity to each other. It can be argued that the primary reason for instability and unrest in industrial relations in the 1960s and 1970s stemmed not from the exertion of trade union 'power' or a determination by the low paid to crusade for higher wages, but as the result of often archaic and often arbitrary pay bargaining structures hallowed by time and custom and handled insensitively by unprofessional managers.

Donovan's analysis

The most influential critique of industrial relations during the 1960s came from the report of the Donovan Royal Commission on trade unions and employers' associations, which was published in June 1968. This document was the result of three years of investigation into the British labour scene. Under the powerful influence of the so-called Oxford University voluntarist school of industrial relations reflected in the influential writings of Allan Flanders, Hugh Clegg and Alan Fox, it sought to explain what had happened principally to private sector manufacturing trade unionism during the post-war period. The report argued that Britain had now 'two systems of industrial relations', which it defined as the 'formal' and the 'informal'. On the one side were the official public institutions – the trade unions and the employers – bound together by substantive collectively bargained industry wide agreements. On the other side stood the reality of shop stewards and managers in individual companies bound together by custom and practice and a decentralized autonomy. As Donovan asserted:

> The formal and informal systems are in conflict. The informal system undermines the regulative effect of industry-wide agreements. The gap between industry-wide agreed rates and actual earnings continues to grow. Procedure agreements fail to cope adequately with disputes arising within factories. Nevertheless the assumptions of the formal system still exert a powerful influence over men's minds and prevent the informal system from developing into an effective and orderly method of regulation.[54]

The report suggested that trade unions as much as employers' associations had been 'guilty' of 'sustaining the facade of industry-wide bargaining with its pretence of dealing with everything of importance for collective agreements'. But it also conceded that most trade unions had albeit 'fitfully and haltingly responded to changing conditions by recognising shop stewards and making some effort to equip them'. Donovan explained: 'Thus it is not so much that the unions have lost power as that there has been a shift of authority within them.' But the report also argued that the existence of multi-unionism in most manufacturing workplaces had strengthened the post-war tendency to decentralize industrial relations through an enhancement of the power of work groups and a growth in their independence from any centralized trade union control. Unions continued to operate a local branch structure usually based on geographical area rather than the workplace but increasingly such an organization was little more than an empty shell. Power had moved to shopfloor combine committees that cut across traditional union membership lines. By bringing stewards together from different trade unions to bargain in cooperation with each other meant a further weakening in trade union national authority. The Donovan Report did not believe it was possible to restore the lost power of the full-time union officials outside the workplace. As the report explained,

> Trade union leaders do exercise discipline from time to time but they cannot be industry's policemen. They are democratic leaders in organisations in which the seat of power has almost always been close to the members. For a brief period between the wars the conjunction of industry-wide bargaining and heavy unemployment gave trade union leaders an unusual ascendancy in their own organisations. Before that, however, power was generally concentrated in the branches and the districts. Since then, workshop organisation has taken their place.[55]

Donovan also discovered that employers for the most part did not deplore the re-emergence of workplace trade unionism but on the contrary preferred to work in alliance with the shop stewards. In the popular imagination the shop steward might resemble the nightmarish Fred Kite played by Peter Sellers in the 1959 film *I'm All Right Jack*, who ordered his obedient and work-shy members out on strike at the drop of a cloth cap. But he was a mythological if potent figure who bore little resemblance to the realities of shopfloor life. The report found from its own survey material that only 2 per cent of its cross-section of managers surveyed thought shop stewards were 'unreasonable', compared with 95 per cent who believed they were 'very reasonable' or 'fairly reasonable'. Four out of five managers also thought shop stewards were 'very efficient' or 'fairly efficient' at their job. These benign feelings were reciprocated.

Almost all of the shop stewards surveyed believed managers were 'very or fairly reasonable' in their dealings with them. Indeed, the report suggested that shop stewards were 'rarely agitators pushing workers towards constitutional action'. In the words of one of the Commission's research papers: 'For the most part the steward is viewed by others and views himself as an accepted, reasonable and even moderating influence; more of a lubricant than an irritant.'[56] Apparently, while in some instances they might be the mere mouthpieces of their work groups, quite commonly they were 'supporters of order, exercising a restraining influence on their members in conditions which promote disorder'.

Donovan, however, did not take a complacent view of industrial relations practice. The report admitted that the 'formal' and 'informal' systems were 'in conflict' with one another and went on to argue:

> The assumption that industry-wide agreements control industrial relations leads many companies to neglect their responsibility for their own personnel policies. Factory bargaining remains informal and fragmented, with many issues left to custom and practice. The unreality of industry-wide pay agreements leads to the use of incentive schemes and overtime payments quite different from those they were designed to serve.[57]

The picture painted by the report was mainly drawn from the experience of manual workers in the private sector of manufacturing industry. Donovan admitted only an estimated one-third of the labour force – 6 million workers – was covered by the 'formal/informal' system. The analysis excluded the 4 million workers whose wages were determined by Wages Councils, a further 7 million workers whose pay was still determined by genuine industry-wide national agreements, and 5 million more workers whose wages were decided outside any collective bargaining arrangements at all. Moreover, the analysis also made little sense in the growing heavily unionized public services sector of the labour market, where national agreements were still paramount. But its prescriptions were really focused on private sector manufacturing. The report was concerned to see a return to 'effective and orderly collective bargaining' with greater 'control' over incentive schemes, the number of hours worked, the use of job evaluation, work practices and the linking of changes in pay to changes in worker performance, as well as shop steward facilities, and disciplinary rules and procedures in factory and workshop relations. The Donovan Report favoured the integration of the 'formal' and 'informal' systems through the introduction of flexible but comprehensive company-wide collective agreements covering pay and conditions, grievance procedures, redundancy and discipline, and the rights and obligations of shop stewards. This was the way to 'put an end to the current pretence of industry-wide agreements and the realities of industrial relations'.[58]

Unfortunately, the report devoted little attention to the complex connection between what was going on at shopfloor level and the wider imperatives of an economy in crisis. It acknowledged that the Confederation of British Industry (CBI) had made a valid point when it suggested national planning over incomes was impossible because of the fragmentation of plant bargaining. As Donovan argued in a key passage:

> Incomes policy must continue to be a lame and faltering exercise so long as it consists in the planning of industry-wide agreements, most of which exercise an inadequate control over pay. So long as workplace bargaining remains informal, autonomous and fragmented the drift of earnings away from rates of pay cannot be brought under control.[59]

But it was unclear why the Commission thought that either work groups or trade unions should see any obvious advantage for themselves in voluntarily participating in a more controlled and regulated localized bargaining arrangement if this meant greater disciplines and control being imposed by employers over the pay of the rank and file.

However, Donovan and his colleagues were not entirely willing simply to endorse the voluntarist system. They were prepared to suggest some important legislative action to buttress existing industrial relations. The majority recommended, for example, that companies (initially, those with more than 5,000 on their pay-rolls) should register their collective agreements with the Department of Employment and Productivity as a way of clarifying their importance. An Industrial Relations Commission (the IRC) was proposed complete with a full-time secretariat, which would deal with 'problems arising out of the registration of agreements' as well as other areas referred to it by the government, including incomes policy. While the Commission accepted the validity of the arguments against making all collective agreements legally enforceable, it did suggest that there should be a 'case by case' or *ad hoc* approach in which legal enforcement machinery might be 'inescapable' in 'exceptional situations' for a 'limited period' if the 'persuasive influence' of the Commission failed to improve collective bargaining methods. This power, it suggested, should be in the hands of the Secretary of State for Employment and Productivity and would provide him with the authority to issue an Order through the Industrial Court.

A majority of the Commission also favoured the idea of statutory machinery to protect workers against unfair dismissal by their employers. The existing industrial tribunals were to be renamed 'labour tribunals' to deal with breaches of contracts of employment. The report rejected the suggestion that the closed shop should be outlawed but it backed the creation of an independent review authority, attached to the Registrar of Friendly Societies, with the power to award compensation to individual workers who suffered from any abuse by a trade union of its own rule book. The Commission also favoured the establishment of a special Industrial Law Committee with links to the IRC to 'codify' 'in due course' existing labour law. A majority also supported a recommendation that immunities from civil action 'in furtherance and contemplation of a trade dispute' under section 3 the 1906 Trade Disputes Act should be limited only to trade unions with a new corporate status and employers' associations that registered under the new proposed Registrar.

Donovan was by no means a unanimously agreed report. Indeed, four of its members wrote a 'supplementary note' which urged that the proposed IRC should be empowered to deregister a trade union or employers' association if it failed to comply with its own rules or breached registered agreements with their right to appeal against such a decision to the Industrial Court. More substantially, Andrew Shonfield, the forceful economic journalist, wrote a 15 page 'note of reservation' which read very much like a minority report. In trenchant style, Shonfield suggested the commission had 'barely concerned itself with the long-term problem of accommodating bodies with the kind of concentrated power possessed by trade unions to the changing future needs of an advanced industrial society'. His main argument was that the 'traditional notion of the individual workplace as a separate and largely autonomous estate, where employers and employees are able to conduct their quarrels with little or no regard to the effect of what they do on other workplaces' no longer made any sense in a world dominated by a 'large complex of inter-related industrial operations located in different concerns'. Shonfield favoured a more much 'regulated system' than his colleagues.[60]

The report turned out to be a missed opportunity because it failed to address the fundamental question of what the role of the trade unions should be in a complex, dynamic open market economy. The analysis was too one-dimensional with an over-concentration on the industrial relations system in the engineering industry. It had little to say about the relationship between the state and trade unions at a time when Labour's statutory incomes policy was emphasizing the direct intervention of government in collective bargaining. Nor did the report pay much attention to the effects of trade unionism on the economy. Were the trade unions really to blame for Britain's wage-push inflation, relatively low rise in productivity, over-manning and the other economic ills? No clear or direct answer could be found in its pages because they contained no economic analysis. Moreover, the expanding public services sector and its distinctive and well-developed industrial relations practices failed to win much interest from the Commission either. The dramatic expansion of public services sector trade unionism towards the end of the 1960s, reflected in the membership growth of NUPE and the National Association of Local Government Officers (NALGO), where nationally influenced pay bargaining remained crucial, revealed a new worker awareness among groups of hitherto poorly organized workers of the successful role trade unionism could play in protecting them from the ravages of inflation. The greater strike-proneness of workers beyond the traditional bastions of labour in dockland, the coal industry and car production could also not be easily explained by reference to the rapid spread of unregulated plant bargaining. In fact, the Donovan report was a highly conservative document which lacked any sense of national urgency. It provided a philosophical justification for continuing with the voluntarist system. After three years of patient and methodical work – heavily influenced by the so-called Oxford school – its results fell far short of what the politicians thought was required.

But ministers had only themselves to blame for this. The Commission was a rather curious body in the first place. The TUC had insisted that the trade union members should be nominated by the general council and Woodcock decided to take a place himself on the Commission. Wilson doubted the wisdom of such appointments at the time when Donovan was being established but bowed to Gunter's 'wisdom' over the matter.[61] Certainly, it made it most unlikely that the resulting report would endorse anything controversial that would upset the complacent inertia that tended to dominate TUC general council thinking on the subject of industrial relations reform. Indeed, the value of Donovan is that despite the persuasive arguments in support of marginal and piecemeal changes to existing industrial relations practice, discordant voices were raised within its very own pages. However, the report was sensible in one important respect that the politicians ignored at their peril: it was not based on an emotional response to transient events. So often in the 1960s, as always, governments were obsessed by the instant glare of newspaper headlines about particular damaging industrial conflicts, giving rise to sudden bouts of decision-making that failed to grasp the complexity of workplace realities. At least, the Donovan Commission provided a rich corpus of expert knowledge and argument that was to be understood and acted upon in the 1970s particularly by management in the country's larger private manufacturing companies as a promoter of good industrial relations practices. But for politicians in search of panaceas and instant answers the report proved to be a sad disappointment.

'In place of strife'

Barbara Castle, the newly appointed and first Secretary for Employment and Productivity, was in no doubt that Donovan could certainly not be the last word on the subject of industrial relations reform. Taking over from Gunter in April 1968 as the beneficiary of the Ministry of Labour's transformation, she was impatient for rapid change. To her, the Royal Commission's report read like a prescription for inertia, an endorsement of what she regarded as the TUC's negative attitude to necessary innovation. Her doubts were confirmed by Woodcock's initial response. 'I can't see any revolutionary changes being carried through unless the government is prepared to impose them on an unwilling TUC', she wrote in her diary on 3 July 1968. 'The one I would go for would be compulsory amalgamation of trade unions but we can't even get that.'[62]

Mrs Castle was convinced of the need for urgency and she soon made it clear that the TUC could not be left alone to move along at its own plodding pace. Most of her senior policy advisers at the newly named Department of Employment and Productivity agreed with her. During the early 1960s a more robust attitude began to emerge towards the trade unions in a department famed for most of its life for a stubborn and successful defence of voluntarism. The appointment from outside the department of Sir Laurence Helsby as Permanent Secretary at the Ministry of Labour in 1959 was seen as a clear signal that the government was no longer content simply to promote able civil servants who had spent all their time in St James's Square. Helsby had served in the Treasury, the Cabinet Office and the Ministry of Food, and spent five years as First Civil Service Commissioner before going to the Ministry of Labour. In 1963 he became Permanent Secretary to the Treasury and Head of the Civil Service.

The sharper approach to industrial relations became more apparent in the Ministry of Labour's own written evidence to the Donovan Royal Commission presented late in 1965. What was most noticeable in its 140 page submission was the official belief that the trade unions could no longer be left alone to act merely as defenders of their sectionalist self-interests. As the Ministry explained:

> The position has been reached where the processes of collective bargaining, their traditional activities, have a profound effect on the economy and

in consequence on the national well-being. The question – and it is a question which the trade union movement itself has not declined to face – is whether their policies should be based on a more effective recognition that they are a major economic force and that higher priority in policies should be given to their responsibility for the good of the community as a whole.[63]

The Ministry went on to assert that the 'furtherance of the interests of trade union members has become dependent upon the social and economic advance of the nation'. Senior civil servants argued that it was 'clearly in the interests of trade union members that trade union policies and actions should as far as possible assist the government' in achieving economic conditions 'favourable for increased industrial output and the maintenance of full employment'. The Ministry added that trade unions should also support government policies to control inflation and promote 'efficiency and technological innovation'. Civil servants acknowledged that there was a danger that if unions accepted such wider responsibilities they might risk losing 'influence and authority' over their members to the shop stewards. But they proposed a number of reforms to strengthen the unions so that they could both uphold collective bargaining but also accept those wider obligations. The Ministry of Labour proposed that unions should secure legal rights of recognition from employers, that they ought to be subject to financial penalties if they failed to resolve unofficial strikes involving their own members, and that collective agreements should be legally enforceable.

It was not difficult, therefore, for Mrs Castle to find willing enthusiasts among her senior advisers to prepare a comprehensive reform of industrial relations based on state intervention. Indeed by December 1968 she had made up her mind to legislate. A summit conference of civil servants and academics held at the Civil Service college at Sunningdale that month strengthened her determination for resolute action. She explained: 'We rejected the concept of "collective laissez faire" and were in favour of state intervention in industrial relations. The question to decide was – intervention for what and by what means?'[64] From the start Mrs Castle insisted her intention was not to weaken, let alone destroy, the trade unions but on the contrary to strengthen them. She believed it was 'wrong to assume state intervention always meant using the law against the unions'. Nor should state intervention 'necessarily mean sanctions'. Instead, the state ought to take a 'positive' not a 'negative' view of trade unions.

In her opinion, 'the most pressing need was to reform negotiating and disputes procedures for until there were good practices workers could not be expected to observe agreements'. 'Here the state should intervene to guarantee trade union rights and improve the machinery of collective bargaining', she argued:

> But it was also urgent to persuade unions and workers not to use their bargaining powers in ways which damaged the collective economic interest. If sanctions were to be used (and there were few cases where they would be desirable or effective) they should be specific and not general and should be administered by the government.

Mrs Castle and her advisers found the Donovan report a particularly inadequate response to what she called 'industrial anarchy which was doing so much harm to the economy and the fact that so many strikes seemed to be directed more against the community than the employer'. The problem was how to deal with this problem 'without putting unacceptable curbs on what we called the "primitive power" of workers to defend their own interests'. But everybody agreed at the Sunningdale conference that 'we would never get anything positive out of the TUC and the government would have to risk giving a lead'.

Only a few weeks earlier there had been an appalling example of the kind of industrial chaos Mrs Castle was determined to put a stop to once and for all. Twenty-two machine setters struck at the Girling brake factory in Cheshire in a dispute over which unions members were entitled to turn on an oil supply valve. More than 5,000 car workers were laid off in other plants as a result of the strike. It transpired there had been no less than 57 separate stoppages at the Girling plant over the previous eighteen months. At the same time, a strike by only 10 men at Vauxhall's auto plant at Ellesmere Port on Merseyside led to the lay-off of 15,000 car workers. It was such acts of sectionalist disruption that Mrs Castle and her advisers were determined to end through legal restraints. The time was ripe, they believed, for a bold government initiative which would come to grips with the country's appalling industrial relations.

Mrs Castle's resulting White Paper, *In Place of Strife*, was a coherent and strongly argued document. It began with a critical look at what it described as the 'serious defects' in the British industrial relations system. This had, it argued, 'failed to prevent injustice, disruption of work and inefficient use of manpower'. It had also perpetrated 'the existence of groups of employees who, as the result of the weakness of their bargaining position, fall behind in the struggle to obtain their full share of the benefits of an advanced industrial economy'.[65] The document argued that employers and their workers were able to 'unfairly exploit the consumer and endanger economic prosperity'. It went on to criticize the 'growing number of lightning strikes' and suggested the industrial relations system had 'contributed little to increasing efficiency'.

In Place of Strife proposed a radical, vigorous use of the state in industrial relations to 'help to contain the destructive expression of industrial conflict and to encourage a more equitable, ordered and efficient system', which 'would benefit both those involved and the community at large'.[66]

There was a clear tone of impatience among Mrs Castle's departmental advisers at the voluntarist tradition of industrial relations. The document stressed 'an alternative view' to that contained in the Donovan Report which involved a recognition that 'the periodic readjustment by the state of the bargaining power' between capital and labour was 'not in itself sufficient' and the state must also act at times to contain the disruptive consequences of the struggle of those not immediately affected – especially if non-intervention was likely to result in 'widespread damage to the interests of the community at large'.[67] The White Paper instanced examples of how the British state had not abstained completely in the past from involving itself directly in industrial relations. It pointed to sections 4 and 5 of the 1875 Conspiracy and Protection of Property Act which was 'designed to limit the freedom to strike where it was likely to have undue effects on essential services or on life or property'. The document also drew attention to the Truck Acts which forbade payment in kind rather than in cash, as well as the creation of the Wages Councils and the use of Fair Wages resolutions as evidence that the state in the past had not been indifferent to 'advance objectives which could not at the time be met by collective bargaining'. It emphasized how direct government intervention had grown in industrial relations during the 1960s. The White Paper instanced the examples of the 1963 Contracts of Employment Act, the establishment of the industrial training boards, and the introduction in 1965 of the redundancy payments scheme to help encourage greater labour mobility and ease the pain of job loss.

In Place of Strife pointed to the contradiction between industrial relations theory and practice:

> While often still voicing the doctrine of non-intervention, managements and unions have entered into a positive and mutually beneficial partnership with the state to secure common objectives. . . . In short, the doctrine of non-intervention is not and never has been consistently preached. The need for state intervention and involvement, in association with both sides of industry, is now admitted by almost everyone. The question that remains, is what form should it take at the present time?[68]

In Mrs Castle's opinion the issue was a pragmatic one to be determined by the circumstances of the moment. She did not see it either as an ideological crusade or as a struggle over first principles. Nor did she believe her proposals were hostile to the trade unions. Indeed, she emphasized that most of her White Paper was concerned to promote positive reforms designed to assist not hinder trade union growth and legitimacy. 'The overwhelming preoccupation of the White paper is with the need to improve and strengthen collective bargaining', Mrs Castle told the House of Commons on 3 March 1969. But she added: 'Trade unions in this country cannot advance without the support and help of the Government.'[69] It was proposed to create a new independent body – the Commission on Industrial Relations (CIR) – with the aim of encouraging the spread of good industrial relations practices like the establishment of company-wide procedural agreements, encouraging company recognition of their shop stewards, and carrying out inquiries into the causes of strikes, as well as ways to improve productivity. The CIR was also to have the role of encouraging the reform of trade union structures and services and was to deal with trade union recognition cases. Other suggested reforms were also intended to benefit trade unions and strengthen collective bargaining: one proposal favoured giving trade union representatives access to information from management for collective bargaining purposes; another favoured the appointment of worker representatives onto company boards. There was to be a state funded trade union development programme to assist union education courses. Workers were also to be given protection against unfair dismissal by their employers. What Mrs Castle proposed to do was provide some legal muscle to back up the persuasive powers of trade union leaders so they could enforce their authority over their own members. She was eager to bring a belated sense of order to what she saw as the unacceptable anarchy of the industrial relations system. Perhaps even more importantly, she desired to introduce a feeling of social justice and equity into the workplace.

Mrs Castle opposed the idea of giving employers legal powers to sue unofficial strike leaders for inducing strikers to break their contracts of employment. As the White Paper explained, 'The great majority of employers would refuse to use such legal rights and so such a change would be ineffective in practice, while by creating uncertainty, it would worsen the general atmosphere of industrial relations.'[70] Moreover, the White Paper argued that trade unions would simply declare such strikes official and thereby ensure legal protection for groups of unofficial strikers, while the strike leaders would have no defence for their actions and as a result this would threaten industrial relations stability. However, Mrs Castle was determined to propose legislative means of dealing with unconstitutional strikes. *In Place of Strife* proposed the introduction of 'a conciliation pause' before the calling of unconstitutional disputes. This could be imposed by the Employment Secretary to enable both sides in the threatened strike to have more time to resolve their differences before the disruption began. An Order was to be issued by the Employment Secretary if a strike went ahead in defiance of the 'conciliation pause'; this would tell the two parties to desist from industrial action for a period of 28 days, and require the employers to uphold 'specified conditions or terms during the pause, which normally existed before the dispute'. If either side defied the government Order, financial penalties would be imposed upon them.

However, there were to be no martyrs as a result of the legislation with workers going to prison in defiance of the law. The White Paper suggested there might be a detachment from a defiant worker's earnings or other civil remedies that were used for the collection of debt through County Courts in England and Wales. During the pause before the strike began an inquiry would be held to try and settle the trouble, but there would be no further legal powers to ensure further delay once the period of the pause ended. The purpose of the reform was to increase the authority of trade union officials and ensure they made their members observe agreed procedures before going out on strike. Another controversial proposal in the White Paper was the 'discretionary' power given to the Employment Secretary to compel a union or unions involved in a strike to hold a secret ballot of their members to discover whether they supported the proposed disruption. The actual ballot would be administered by the union or unions concerned but the Employment Secretary was to have the right to approve the form of question on which the members were to vote. The CIR was also to be provided with legal back-up powers to ensure compliance with its recommendations. The White Paper proposed that if unions rejected a CIR proposal about which union should gain recognition from an employer in a disputed sector, the Employment Secretary was to be empowered to produce an Order to achieve obedience. Financial penalties would be imposed on unions that used 'coercive action' to defy what the CIR favoured.

Mrs Castle's proposals won Wilson's enthusiastic endorsement, not least because they promised to bring his demoralized government some badly needed electoral popularity. But from the very outset they aroused deep disquiet inside the Cabinet, where Jim Callaghan as Home Secretary expressed his immediate hostility to the whole suggestion of legislating trade union reform. Callaghan thought the unions should be allowed to put be 'on their honour' to change themselves. 'Barbara galloped ahead with all the reckless gallantry of the Light Brigade at Balaclava and tried to rush the cabinet into publishing the White Paper only nine days after ministers had first seen it', he recalled later.[71] Indeed, it took as many as six Cabinet meetings to secure ministerial support for the White Paper. Crossman noted in his diary that Mrs Castle was 'able and driving but like all the rest of us an amateur, quite new to trade union law and legislation, a tremendously complex subject'.[72]

To Mrs Castle's amazement, Woodcock said he 'did not think there was anything that need alarm the trade union movement' in her White Paper.[73] Indeed, initially the TUC finance and general purposes committee – which had been given prior notice of its contents even before the Cabinet had seen copies – appeared to take a calm and balanced view of what was being proposed. In a statement the union leaders did not reject the White Paper out of hand but said the TUC's aim was 'to reach agreement with the government on ways of improving industrial relations and of strengthening voluntary collective bargaining'.[74] However, the TUC's low-key response was deceptive, even if public opinion appeared to favour what was being proposed. By early March attitudes inside the Labour Movement were hardening rapidly against the whole content of Mrs Castle's ambitious White Paper. As many as 57 Labour MPs voted against *In Place of Strife* in the Commons with a further 30 abstaining. Three weeks later on 26 March the party's National Executive Committee also repudiated *In Place of Strife* by voting 16 to 5 in support of a motion that rejected 'legislation based on all' its proposals. The magnitude of the growing conflict was underlined by Callaghan's decision to vote with the National Executive majority.

It was becoming increasingly clear that if the government decided to push ahead with the White Paper in its entirety it would create severe splits inside the Labour Movement, but neither Wilson nor Mrs Castle were in any mood to appreciate the warning signals. On the contrary, the growing resistance inside both the TUC and the Labour party only seemed to intensify their determination to act decisively. Initially, Mrs Castle's White Paper had assumed a wide-ranging, public debate on its proposals lasting over into the next session of Parliament, with the prospect of legislation reaching the statute book during the summer of 1970 in the run-up to the next general election. But now pressure inside the government for rapid action on the more controversial proposals in the document began to gather momentum. Many ministers thought it would be 'tactically disastrous to wait for a year gnawing at the bone' with the probable defeat of *In Place of Strife* in the autumn of 1969 at both the TUC Congress and Labour party conference.[75] Better, they reasoned, to move forward with legislation at once.

From the start, Mrs Castle had opposed such a hasty approach, arguing that the legislation she had in mind must cover all the proposals in her White Paper because otherwise it might look as if the government was interested only in pushing through penal proposals which dealt with unofficial strikes. As she noted in her diary on 3 January 1969: 'I for one am not prepared to put forward a shorter Bill in which all the emphasis will be on the penal bits. I could not imagine anything more detrimental to my whole philosophy.'[76] But Roy Jenkins, the Chancellor of the Exchequer, and Richard Crossman, the Leader of the House of Commons, now persuaded her that a 'short' Bill should be prepared for immediate implementation. On 14 April 1969 the Cabinet agreed and on the following day Jenkins made the government's intention known in his Budget statement, when he also announced that the government did not intend to seek the renewal of its legal powers to order delays in implementing wage agreements under the 1968 Prices and Incomes Act when it ran out at the beginning of 1970.

'We need to facilitate the smooth working of collective bargaining in industry and to help prevent the occurrence of unnecessary and damaging disputes of which we have seen all too much recently and which are totally incompatible with our economic objectives', Jenkins told the Commons.[77] In fact, the promised industrial relations legislation was seen by the Cabinet as a substitute for the continuation of the statutory prices and incomes policy. Callaghan noted in his memoirs: 'In Place of Strife was suddenly to be turned into instant government.'[78]

The outlines of the proposed Industrial Relations Bill were introduced by Mrs Castle on 16 April 1969. It contained only five proposals from her White Paper but two of them involved so-called 'penal clauses' which were totally unacceptable to the TUC. The measure empowered the Employment Secretary to impose settlements in inter-union disputes with the threat of fines against those who resisted once voluntary conciliation had failed. It also enabled the Employment Secretary to order a 28 day conciliation pause before the calling of an unofficial dispute and to compel the maintenance of the status quo with the back-up threat of financial penalties for those who resisted. The Bill sought to balance those coercive clauses with a statutory right of every worker to belong to a trade union, the provision of power to the Employment Secretary to order an employer to recognize a trade union when recommended to do so by the CIR, and the removal of disqualifications for payment of unemployment benefit to workers laid off because of a strike in which they were taking no direct part. The controversial proposal to enforce secret ballots on trade unions before official disputes was not included the Bill – thanks to some persuasive counter-argument in the Cabinet.

Mrs Castle insisted there was no question of anybody going to prison as a result of defying the new law, and she argued that if the TUC disliked the idea of the civil law device of detachment from earnings as fines on disobedient workers she would be happy to consider any alternative union leaders might suggest. The vital importance of her short Bill was made very clear by Wilson who insisted that it was 'essential' not just to ensure the country's economic recovery but to the government's own 'continuance in office' if the TUC could not provide a credible alternative that could deal with the problems of inter-union and unconstitutional disputes without recourse to penal measures.[79] His personal and firm commitment to Mrs Castle's proposals heightened the magnitude of the issues at stake in the emerging crisis.

Congress House was in no mood to swallow what Mrs Castle and Wilson wanted but on the other hand it was willing to try and find a way of convincing the government to drop the Bill by coming up with its own credible alternative strategy. The search for a compromise by the TUC was already apparent after Vic Feather succeeded Woodcock as General Secretary designate on 1 March 1969. Innumerable private meetings were held over the period between Feather, Wilson and Castle as strenuous attempts were made to resolve what looked like increasingly irreconcilable differences of opinion. However, the TUC – under the ebullient Yorkshireman's direction – was keen to demonstrate that it was prepared to find an alternative way forward and not just rely on negative resistance. Indeed, Feather was keen to devise a TUC industrial relations strategy to deal with the controversial issues of inter-union disputes and unconstitutional strikes. Satisfactory progress was in fact soon made over inter-union disputes during talks between the two sides. At a meeting with the TUC on 12 May Wilson sensed 'a strong desire on their part to avert a split in the movement'. He conceded that union leaders had moved a 'very long way' in their willingness to deal with inter-union disputes.[80] As Wilson explained:

> The general council was to be given power to issue an award in any inter-union dispute it dealt with which would be binding on all unions concerned. Refusal by an individual union to accept such a decision would mean that the general council could either suspend the union from TUC membership or report it to Congress with a view to disaffiliation. This had been accepted by all the unions; Frank Cousins and Jack Jones both stressed to us how far the TUC had gone'.

Mrs Castle agreed, suggesting the TUC had moved 'farther and faster in two weeks than in all the past forty years'.[81] In fact, the TUC's decision over inter-union disputes strengthened the existing Rule 12 in the TUC's constitution. This empowered the TUC general council to adjudicate in inter-union disputes with the right of Congress to suspend and expel any union which refused to accept its judgements.

But unfortunately for both Wilson and Mrs Castle the TUC leaders were not prepared to give a similar unequivocal commitment over how to deal with unconstitutional strikes. Under its new policy *Programme for Action*, the TUC tried to convince the government that it was not adopting a negative attitude to what needed to be done. It proposed to strengthen the powers of the TUC general council by calling on affiliated unions not to authorize strikes before first consulting the TUC and giving them an 'obligation' in unofficial disputes 'to take immediate and energetic steps to obtain a resumption of work'. The TUC general council was also to require affiliated unions to inform it of unconstitutional disputes so it could give its 'considered opinion and advice' on them.[82] The trouble was that neither Wilson nor Mrs Castle was convinced that this went nearly far enough to ensure the trade unions would deal effectively with unofficial strikes. As the Employment Secretary noted in her diary it was a question of 'establishing the will of unions to deal with unconstitutional strikes instead of hiding behind them as a means of extracting concessions on the cheap'.[83] The prolonged discussions between ministers and the TUC over the unofficial strikes problem in the search for what Wilson called a 'copper bottomed' compromise came down to a crucial matter of trust. The question was would the TUC and its affiliated unions – for all their good intentions – really act decisively to deal with what the government regarded as acts of industrial anarchy? What Wilson and Mrs Castle sought was a firm guarantee that sanctions would be imposed on union members who took part in unofficial strikes if they refused to go back to work or failed to accept their own agreed dispute procedures. Wilson complained that the TUC appeared to be providing 'no follow through' for action against unconstitutional disputes.[84]

A secret weekend summit meeting held on 1 June 1969 at Chequers, the Prime Minister's country residence, did nothing to pacify the two sides and emotions began to run high. Indeed, the atmosphere became increasingly tense. At one point in the proceedings Wilson warned Hugh Scanlon, the AEU President, that he had no intention of becoming another Dubcek (referring to the Czech Communist party leader recently toppled from power by the Soviets) and ordered the union leader to take his tanks off his lawn. As Jack Jones explained, 'Wilson and Castle were basically academics and it was difficult to persuade them to see things from a shopfloor angle'.[85] On 5 June in Croydon's Fairfield Hall a TUC Special Congress endorsed *Programme for Action* by an overwhelming

7,908,000 votes to 846,000 and rejected 'statutory penalties on workpeople or trade unions in connection either with industrial disputes or with the compulsory registration by trade unions of their rules'.[86] But that decision failed to impress the government and did nothing to allay the doubts of Wilson and Mrs Castle about the TUC's ability to deliver. A terse and frosty press release from the Department of Employment suggested the TUC's Croydon verdict would not be enough to satisfy the government or allow it to drop its proposed legislation.

The Prime Minister believed that the TUC's position still lacked 'credibility' and pointed out that as many as 241 unofficial disputes had taken place since discussions had begun. But Feather warned him that if the penal clauses of the proposed Bill were not removed the TUC would abandon all of its new policy which included its promise to act in inter-union disputes and its Donovan-inspired structural reforms. In fact, by now Wilson was starting to prepare for a climbdown in the face of mounting Labour Movement opposition to Mrs Castle's Bill. He had been unnerved by Scanlon's warning at the Chequers meeting that fining unofficial strikers would not work because their fines would either be met through a whip-round among sympathetic workers or would provoke further stoppages. 'I knew the militants of Merseyside well enough to know that this would be extremely likely there and no legislation – ours or the proposed Conservative legislation – could deal with it', he noted in his memoirs.[87] On 6 June he told the TUC leaders that he was ready to put all the penal clauses of the proposed Bill 'into cold storage' as had been done with the sanctions in Part IV of the Prices and Incomes Act, so they would never have to be used just as long as the TUC made its own self-regulatory proposals effective. But Mrs Castle was unimpressed with their response. 'The history of the government in the past few months has been one of capitulation – and much good it has done us', she told Cabinet colleagues on 8 June. 'The only way to win victories is to stand up to pressures'.[88]

Feather did his best to try and bridge the gap between the two sides, despite the suspicions of Jones and Scanlon at what they regarded as his over-conciliatory behaviour towards the government. He suggested that the TUC might agree to some form of declaratory statement on unofficial disputes being added to its own rules. For his part, Wilson said the government was ready to drop the penal parts of the proposed legislation on unofficial strikes if the TUC agreed to toughen up its own Rule 11. In fact, it was clear by 17 June that both Wilson and Mrs Castle no longer enjoyed the support of either a majority of the Cabinet or of the parliamentary party for the Industrial Relations Bill. At the Cabinet meeting that day an almost hysterical Wilson threatened to resign on a number of occasions as he faced increasing opposition from his ministerial colleagues. Tony Benn noted in his diary that the Prime Minister 'looked weak and petty' and added that the cabinet was 'completely unmoved' by his threats.[89] For his part, Jenkins recalled that Wilson 'behaved with a touch of King Lear-like nobility. He sounded fairly unhinged at times and there was a wild outpouring of words.'[90] On the following day in what turned out to be a showdown at 10 Downing Street the TUC general council held all the cards but Vic Feather and his colleagues had no wish to humiliate Wilson or drive him from office. As a way out of the crisis they suggested both sides ought to sign a 'solemn and binding' agreement in which the TUC would promise to honour its obligations to try and resolve unofficial disputes. It was Jones who came up with the face saver when he pointed out that Wilson and Mrs Castle 'probably did not understand' that under the TUC's own procedures a 'binding agreement' once endorsed by Congress had the same force as the 1939 Bridlington regulations governing inter-union relations.[91] Scanlon backed him up.

Their initiative proved enough to achieve a settlement and pulled Wilson and Mrs Castle back from the brink of what would probably have been their own political destruction. Early that afternoon both sides agreed to what Wilson called a 'solemn and binding undertaking', a form of words to hide the Prime Minister's humiliation. Jack Jones argued in retrospect: 'A victory had been scored in defence of the right to strike without fear of legal sanctions but the TUC took aboard some big new responsibilities.' However, as Peter Jenkins argued in *The Battle of Downing Street*, his contemporary account of the crisis:

> In terms of industrial relations the outcome was probably the best that could be obtained. It would probably not have made very much difference if the TUC had altered its rules to suit the government. Its ability to deal with official and unconstitutional strikes depended neither on rules nor the wording of declarations but on the strength of its will and the voluntary cooperation of unions. Jack Jones and Hugh Scanlon effectively set the limits on that. Probably it would have made little difference either if the penal clauses had reached the statute book. For the success of Barbara Castle's scheme would have depended no less upon the willingness of unions and their members to observe the law in letter and in spirit. In the long run they might have done so but that would have required a profound change in social attitudes and success in the slow, complex programme of shop floor reform advocated by the Royal Commission. In the absence of voluntary compliance the law would more likely have been brought into disrepute.[92]

What Wilson and Mrs Castle sought would probably not have been achievable in the increasingly militant industrial relations atmosphere of

1969–70, as what remained of Labour's statutory prices and incomes policy disintegrated in the face of formidable shopfloor pressures. Without the active consent of workers themselves the penal clauses in the proposed legislation would have been rendered quickly ineffective. The bold reforming spirit contained in the *In Place of Strife* White Paper ebbed away not just because of TUC and Labour party intransigence but because it seemed irrelevant when confronted by the complex realities of the shop floor. As Wilson himself was forced to admit, 'Strikes did not diminish in number, scale or duration after 18 June 1969', even if inter-union disputes were cut back to a minimum and the indefatigable Feather deployed his enormous energies in a fire-fighting role trying to settle unofficial stoppages up and down the country. 'All the spectacular strikes in which the TUC failed were disputes where our legislation directed mainly against unofficial strikes would have been ineffective', admitted Wilson.[93]

Fresh from his settlement with the TUC Wilson was unable to give a direct reply when confronted by the crucial question thrown across the dispatch box at him by Conservative opposition leader Edward Heath who asked: 'What will happen should unofficial strikers ignore the trade union leaders and go on striking?'[94] But nobody could really provide a satisfactory answer for that situation, including Heath himself. He was also to learn the hard way that dealing with industrial relations through changes in the law did not ensure automatic success.

The controversy over *In Place of Strife* and the short Bill debacle strained relations in the Labour Movement to their limits of endurance. It threatened to bring about what Wilson himself called 'a deep and fundamental split' between its industrial and political wings.[95] In fact, the government had been forced into a humiliating retreat under withering fire from an exposed salient and in doing so it lost much of its already weakened political authority. As *The Economist* cover headline proclaimed, *In Place of Strife* had been replaced by 'In Place of Government'. However, the outcome of the June 1969 crisis was also a lost opportunity for the TUC to demonstrate that it could practise effective self-regulation and disprove its innumerable critics by showing it was capable of solving industrial relations problems without the need for any resort by the state to the external stimulus of statute law. Callaghan, their sturdy champion in 1969, noted in his memoirs – no doubt sobered by his own searing experience at the hands of the unions in the 1978–9 'Winter of Discontent':

> The unions were blameworthy for failing, despite Barbara Castle's warning to make their own programme of reforms effective. In 1969 they still had the opportunity to demonstrate that autonomous self-governing

institutions could respond to adverse public opinion and reform themselves. They failed to do so.[96]

The 18 June 1969 settlement was by no means the end of the story. It was still unclear just how much real power Congress House would exercise as a result over its affiliated unions. Feather tried to reassure the 1969 Congress that the TUC 'never has been and never will be something separated and apart from the unions, sitting in judgement on them'. 'I never talk of TUC authority or union discipline or chain of command', he told delegates. 'Unions are independent voluntary organisations and the TUC is their federal body. We move by discussion, persuasion and argument.'[97] In the ensuing debate Jones made it quite clear that the 'solemn and binding' agreement did not mean the TUC was going to carry out 'the dirty work of the government in lieu of legislation'. 'We now recognise that the corridors of power are not in Whitehall, not even in Congress House but in the streets where our members live, in the factories, on the sites, in the garages and offices where they work', he declared.[98] He argued that the 'new approach' to trade unionism meant involving 700,000 'well-trained, intelligent, well-supported shop stewards and office representatives throughout industry' in decision-making, not 'seven all-powerful leaders at the top of the TUC'.

Wilson's address to the 1969 Congress was received coolly by most delegates and some of his strong words aroused vocal protests. The Prime Minister claimed that the TUC general council under the June agreement would require an affiliated union to discipline its members if they went on strike before exhausting the agreed procedures. 'This means that every union here must be prepared to the full extent of their powers, amended and strengthened as necessary, to take on any who wantonly or unnecessarily endanger industrial peace', claimed Wilson.[99] In his opinion at least, the TUC had accepted an industrial relations strategy based on affiliated unions shouldering the responsibility for disciplining their recalcitrant members. He told the delegates that the government's industrial relations policy was 'based on the acceptance by the trade union Movement of the responsibility for disciplining those of its members who in pursuit of their own interests, however they may feel it to be justified, endanger a wider interest'. And he warned: 'There can be no backsliding now'. 'This was strong meat', Wilson noted. 'I did not expect it to be greeted with enthusiasm, nor was it.'[100]

For her part, Mrs Castle was determined to salvage something from the wreckage of her short Bill by preparing a more comprehensive industrial relations measure based on the whole of her White Paper for the next parliamentary session. She was soon to discover that the TUC was unenthusiastic about that as well. 'Though the TUC had acquiesced somewhat half-heartedly in the setting up of the CIR, it remain deeply suspicious of any interference in the running of union affairs or any hint of sanctions against unions', she complained.[101] Mrs Castle wanted to compel unions to register under threat of losing their legal immunities if they did not. She also favoured enabling trade union members to enjoy a right of appeal to an independent review body if they faced expulsion from a union or were refused membership of one – both of which had been Donovan Royal Commission recommendations. Neither proposal pleased the TUC but Mrs Castle had no wish to prepare legislation that simply strengthened trade union bargaining power and did nothing to tackle deep-seated industrial relations problems. However, the Cabinet was unwilling to endure any repetition of the traumatic showdown it had experienced with the TUC in June 1969, and ministerial colleagues urged the Employment Secretary to prepare a more limited measure that would deal with one or two items like the statutory right to belong to a trade union and appeal procedures for workers against unfair dismissals. Wilson was also unwilling to support Mrs Castle in devising legislation that the TUC would oppose. He rejected out of hand her suggestion that trade unions might be punished by distraint if necessary if they opposed the right of trade union members to appeal to an independent review body. On the other hand, ministers were unenthusiastic about agreeing to the TUC demand for an extension of legal immunities to trade unions so they could induce breaches in commercial contracts in disputes. Mrs Castle admitted later that:

> This was to be part of a balanced package and with the unions now refusing to accept any limitations of any kind on their freedom of action and with unofficial strikes still plaguing us, it had become very difficult politically to include in my Bill this wide extension of the right to bring industrial pressure.[102]

As she told an irate TUC delegation on 25 March 1970:

> The aim of our legislation was to get at the causes of strikes, not to increase them. So we were providing positive alternatives for securing these basic rights. We had worked very hard in the past few months to ensure that anything which was offensive to the unions should not be included in the Industrial Relations Bill. But having built new rights into the measure which would make the vast majority of secondary boycotts unnecessary, it would be electorally disastrous to legalise a whole new range of strikes.[103]

The resulting modest Industrial Relations Bill was eventually published on 30 April 1970 but it was never even to receive a second reading in the Commons. Wilson decided to call a June general election.

Mrs Castle's tumultuous period as Employment Secretary was not entirely barren of legislative achievements. She piloted the Equal Pay Bill onto the statute book just before Parliament's dissolution. The measure aimed through stages up to 1975 to ensure equal wage rates were paid to women and men where both genders were working in the same or broadly similar work in the same establishment, or where through job evaluation it was found a woman's job was the equivalent of a man's of a different nature from her own. The Act was welcomed by trade unions but it did little to pacify the TUC over Mrs Castle's dirigiste activities. Memories of *In Place of Strife* were not so easily erased. The upsurge of labour militancy in the early months of 1970 suggested the next government of whichever party was elected would face severe problems in coming to terms with the trade unions.

In retrospect, it is perhaps hard to see how the TUC and Labour could have worked amicably together in trying to restrain collective bargaining with the arrival of the new Jones–Scanlon left-wing axis of power on the TUC general council. The Wilson years, which had started off with so much optimism and hope that the political and industrial wings of the Labour Movement could work in harmony together through the creation of a voluntary prices and incomes policy backed up by institutional supports, ended in failure as wage-push inflation began to threaten the economic gains achieved by the 1967 devaluation. As in 1951, Britain's trade unions found it impossible to sustain a prolonged period of wage restraint for their members in support of a Labour government. Now nearly twenty years later the outcome was even more disappointing for both sides. Wilson and Callaghan were scarred badly by the industrial troubles of the late 1960s and they drew the conclusion that no incomes policy could ever again be imposed on the trade unions against their will. Once again the demands for wage restraint in the wider interests of resolving the underlying crisis of the British economy had come into conflict with the fragmented character of so much of the country's wage bargaining system, and nobody in the Labour Movement had found a satisfactory way of reconciling such competing objectives. The notable exchange of views made in the 1944 debate between Beveridge and the TUC economic committee remained unresolved. Was it really possible to maintain full employment with low inflation, economic growth and a balance of payments surplus in a country whose industrial relations were based on voluntarist principles? The unhappy experiences of 1964 to 1970 suggested the optimistic assumptions that lay behind the post-war social settlement were of less and less relevance to the messy, almost anarchic realities of workplace life.

But in this respect, Britain was perhaps not much different to other Western European economies at the end of the 1960s. The May 1968 events in France, Italy's 'hot autumn' of 1969, and even a prolonged wild-cat strike by Sweden's iron ore miners at Kiruna in 1969–70 seemed to suggest that worker discontents were widespread. It was felt that the young in particular were growing impatient with the rigours and disciplines of the workplace and demanded not just a greater say but actual control of the means of production. A rather romanticized Trotskyism became fashionable in a brief resurgence of a revolutionary Left, though this was more apparent among the baby boom generation on university campuses than on the shop floor. However, the impatience from below was as much directed at union hierarchies as at employers or the state. Some observers believed they were witnessing the birth of a new humanism in industrial relations which questioned the existing structure of power in industry and politics. In many ways, the Jones–Scanlon generation represented the British example of a wider discontent with the limits of post-war affluence and its inequitable distribution of income. 'The unions must seek for a new political destiny. Union power is once again a full political reality', declared the editors of the *New Left Review*.[104] But the hopes and fears of that brief heady period were much exaggerated. Explanations for the malaise and frustrations could more persuasively be found in the rise of inflation and state spending and their adverse impact on the level of real earnings in full employment economies.[105] The Socialist dimension to industrial action was as illusory in Britain as it was to be everywhere else.

Notes

1   M. Foot, *Aneurin Bevan*, Vol. 2, Davis Poynter, 1973, pp. 439–40.
2   A. Bevan, *In Place of Fear*, MacGibbon & Kee, 1961, pp. 138–9.
3   Ibid., p. 141.
4   The Socialist Union, *Twentieth Century Socialism*, Penguin, 1956, p. 68.
5   *Plan for Progress*, Labour party, 1958, p. 10.
6   TUC Congress report, 1962, p. 638.
7   Ibid., p. 247.
8   TUC Congress report, 1963, p. 391.
9   Labour Party Conference report, 1963, p. 57.
10 Ibid., p. 64.

11   Ibid., p. 61.
12   Ibid., p. 53.
13   Ibid., p. 78.
14   Labour party general election manifesto, October 1964, in F. W. S. Craig, *British General Election Manifestos*, Dartmouth, 1990, p. 50.
15   TUC Congress report, 1964, p. 507.
16   Ibid., p. 437.
17   G. Goodman, *The Awkward Warrior*, Davis Poynter, 1979, p. 369.
18   Ibid., p. 382.
19   D. Barnes and E. Reid, *Governments and Trade Unions*, Heinemann, 1980, p. 51.
20   A. Flanders, *Management and Trade Unions*, Faber & Faber, 1975, p. 34.
21   Labour Party Conference report, 1959, p. 109.
22   *Trade Unionism, TUC's evidence to Donovan*, TUC, 1966, p. 69.
23   M. Harrison, *Trade Unions and the Labour Party since 1945*, Allen & Unwin, 1960, p. 40.
24   TUC Congress report, 1965, p. 312.
25   TUC Special Congress Report, 1965, p. 16.
26   H. Wilson, *The Labour Government 1964–1970*, Weidenfeld & Nicolson / Michael Joseph, 1971, p. 131.
27   G. Dorfman, *Wage Politics in Britain*, Charles Knight, 1979, p. 121.
28   J. Callaghan, *Time and Change*, Collins, 1987, p. 190.
29   Labour Party Conference report, 1965, p. 134.
30   G. Dorfman, *Wage Politics*, p. 138.
31   TUC Congress report, 1966, p. 326.
32   K. Middlemas, *Power, Competition and the State*, Vol. 2, Macmillan, 1990, p. 213.
33   H. Wilson, *The Labour Government*, p. 291.
34   TUC Congress report, 1967, p. 323.
35   Ibid., p. 325.
36   H. Wilson, *The Labour Government*, p. 429.
37   TUC Congress report, 1968, p. 345.
38   Ibid., p. 549.
39   Ibid., pp. 555–6.
40   Ibid., p. 611.
41   Labour Party Conference report, 1968, p. 137.
42   Ibid., p. 123.
43   Ibid., p. 141.
44   Ibid., p. 142.
45   Ibid., p. 139.
46   Ibid., p. 147.
47   Ibid., p. 293.
48   D. Robinson, 'The Labour Market', in W. Beckerman (ed.), *The Labour Government's Economic Record 1964–1970*, Duckworth, 1972, p. 314.

49 D. Jackson, H. A. Turner and F. Wilkinson, *Do Trade Unions Cause Inflation?* Cambridge University Press, 1972, pp. 113–14.

50 J. Goldthorpe, D. Lockwood, F. Bechofer and J. Platt, *The Affluent Worker in the Class Structure*, Vol. 3, Cambridge University Press, 1969, p. 215.

51 *Trade Union Register 1969*, Merlin Press, 1969, p. 46.

52 J. Jones, *Trade Unions in the Seventies*, TGWU, 1970, pp. 5–6.

53 H. Scanlon, in R. Taylor, *The Fifth Estate*, Routledge & Kegan Paul, 1978, p. 213; and in *Trade Union Register 1970*, Merlin Press, 1970, pp. 50–2.

54 Donovan Royal Commission on Trade Unions and Employers Associations, Cmnd 3623, HMSO, 1968, p. 36.

55 Ibid., p. 32.

56 Ibid., p. 29.

57 Ibid., p. 36.

58 Ibid., p. 37.

59 Ibid., p. 52.

60 Ibid., p. 288.

61 H. Wilson, *The Labour Government*, p. 537.

62 B. Castle, *Diaries 1964–1970*, Weidenfeld & Nicolson, 1984, p. 477.

63 Ministry of Labour written evidence to the Donovan Commission, HMSO, 1965, p. 2.

64 B. Castle, *Diaries 1964–1970*, pp. 549–51.

65 *In Place of Strife*, Department of Employment White Paper, HMSO, January 1969.

66 Ibid., p. 21.

67 Ibid., p. 17.

68 Ibid., p. 23.

69 Hansard Parliamentary Debates, Vol. 779, 3 March 1969, cc. 43, 47.

70 *In Place of Strife*, p. 24.

71 J. Callaghan, *Time and Change*, p. 274.

72 R. H. S. Crossman, p. 301.

73 B. Castle, *Diaries 1964–1970*, p. 574.

74 TUC Congress Report, 1969, p. 204.

75 R. Crossman, p. 315.

76 B. Castle, *Diaries 1964–1970*, p. 583.

77 Hansard Parliamentary Debates, Vol. 781, 15 April 1969, c. 1006.

78 J. Callaghan, *Time and Change*, p. 274.

79 H. Wilson, *The Labour Government*, p. 643.

80 Ibid., p. 650.

81 B. Castle, *Diaries 1964–1970*, p. 583.

82 TUC, *Programme for Action*, 1969, p. 15.

83 B. Castle, *Diaries 1964–1970*, p. 658.

84 Ibid., p. 660.

85 J. Jones, *Trade Unions*, p. 204.

86 TUC Congress report, 1969, p. 67.

87 H. Wilson, *The Labour Government*, p. 654.

88   B. Castle, *Diaries 1964–1970*, p. 665.
89   T. Benn, *Office without Power*, Hutchinson, 1988, p. 187.
90   R. Jenkins, *A Life at the Centre*, Macmillan, 1991, p. 290.
91   J. Jones, *Trade Unions*, p. 206.
92   P. Jenkins, *The Battle of Downing Street*, Charles Knight, 1970, pp. 160–1.
93   H. Wilson, *The Labour Government*, p. 662.
94   Hansard Parliamentary Debates, Vol. 785, 19 June 1969, c. 701.
95   H. Wilson, *The Labour Government*, p. 665.
96   J. Callaghan, *Time and Change*, p. 277.
97   TUC Congress report, 1969, p. 551.
98   Ibid., p. 559.
99   Ibid., p. 499.
100 H. Wilson, *The Labour Government*, p. 701.
101 B. Castle, *Diaries 1964–1970*, p. 697.
102 Ibid., p. 711.
103 Ibid., p. 772.
104 R. Blackburn and A. Cockburn (eds), *The Incompatibles: Trade Union Militancy and the Consensus*, Penguin, 1967, p. 11; and also see Solomon Barkin (ed.), *Worker Militancy and its Consequences 1965–1975*, Praeger, 1975, pp. 403–4.
105 R. J. Flanagan, D. Soskice, L. Ullman (eds), *Unionism, Economic Stabilization and Incomes Policies: The European Experience*, The Brookings Institution, 1983, p. 234.

6 Edward Heath and Modernizing the Trade Unions, October 1964 to March 1974

Preparing for change

Within a few weeks of moving into parliamentary opposition the Conservatives began to abandon their previous reluctance to consider the reform of industrial relations through changes in its legal framework. Edward Heath, the former President of the Board of Trade, was appointed Chairman of the party's Advisory Committee on Policy on 24 October 1964, armed with a wide-ranging remit to reappraise the party's entire domestic policy programme. In this exercise the establishment of a new strategy to deal with the trade union 'problem' was given the highest priority. Viscount Amory, the former Chancellor of the Exchequer, was put in charge of a policy group under the umbrella of Heath's Advisory Committee. It was told 'to review the position of the trade unions in our society today and to consider what changes if any in the law relating to the unions were required'.[1]

The policy group's original members included former Ministers of Labour Joseph Godber, Ian Macleod and Lord Blakenham (formerly John Hare), as well as Ray Mawby (the Conservative MP for Totnes), former Attorney General Sir John Hobson and Peter Walker. Geoffrey Howe, who played an important part in drawing up the Inns of Court Conservative's 1958 pamphlet *A Giant's Strength*, joined the policy group later during the spring of 1965. Strenuous efforts were made by the leadership to recruit senior businessmen to become members of the policy group and three eventually agreed to do so – J. R. Edwards, chairman of Pressed Steel; Edward Grint, who soon left the policy group to join the National Dock Labour board; and Stephen Brown, chairman of the

Engineering Employers' Federation. Stephen Abbott from Conservative Central Office, who acted as full-time secretary to the policy group, had worked for Metal Box before becoming a party functionary in 1960.

It was quite clear from the tone of their first meeting that most members of the Amory policy group were determined to press ahead with a fundamental reform of industrial relations. They agreed at the very outset of their work that the group's final proposals should be designed 'to help the economy by discouraging strikes, inhibiting restrictive practices, promoting positive co-operation between workers and employers and reducing the impact of disputes on services not closely involved'.[2] The group added that it was also determined 'to protect the basic rights of individual trade union members, unions and their officials, non-unionists and other third parties including the public'. The stated aims of the policy group revealed the contradictory tensions in the Conservative party's approach to trade union reform. On the one hand, it believed it was desirable to strengthen the central authority of trade union organizations over their members, but on the other it also believed it was necessary to uphold the rights of individual workers against the trade unions.

However, meeting once a fortnight, the Amory group made surprisingly rapid progress. At only their second meeting they agreed 'it would be desirable to provide greater incentives for trade unions to register and that acceptance of model rules should be a condition of registration'.[3] The group wanted to give legal protections only to those trade unions who were registered but they thought further consideration was needed over the issue because they did not wish 'to penalise non-unionists who wished to act collectively in a dispute'. At the same meeting a majority came out in favour of removing all legal immunities from trade unions in actions for tort except where they arose directly from a dispute. But some group members doubted the wisdom of such a drastic move. They believed it 'might well be impractical and politically unwise'. As a result the group agreed not to make the proposal a 'top priority', though believing that it might be reasonable to 'spell out the immunities which unions should have and those they should not'. The group also thought it was 'highly desirable to penalise shop stewards', while recognizing the difficulties because stewards were not paid trade union officials. As the minutes of the meeting explained: 'There was general agreement on the need to curb the activities of people who acted against union authority. However, the meeting reached no firm conclusions as to how best this could be done.' Apparently, the 'main practical problem concerned people who took part in unofficial strikes. Generally speaking trade unions went through the correct procedures before calling a strike.' The group favoured long-term collective agreements with clear-cut dispute procedures which could be written into contracts of employment so that if workers went on strike they 'would be liable to damages as individuals'.[4] The alternative, the group maintained, was to establish a new system of labour courts on the Swedish model, with powers to fine both workers and trade unions for breaches of contract.

At their 13 March 1965 meeting, the Amory group agreed it would be wrong to introduce legislation to enforce pre-strike ballots. However, it favoured giving the Registrar power to require unions who had ballot provisions in their rule books to comply with them. The group concluded at its next meeting that it was 'impracticable' to ban strikes that were called to enforce a closed shop, though it was agreed that where workers lost their jobs for refusing to join a specified union they should receive damages from the courts. By April the group had accepted that all collective agreements needed to be legally enforceable but dismissed the idea of a cooling-off period before a strike as 'not appropriate' and legislation to ban strikes in essential services as 'impracticable'.[5]

The Amory group's interim report was completed by July 1965, only five months after the group had first started its work. The resulting document represented a sharp break from the old voluntarist approach of One Nation Conservatism practised during the thirteen years of Conservative government that had just ended. The first sentence of the report reflected its radical and legalistic flavour: 'The sanctity of agreements must be the basis for industrial peace in a modern economy.'[6]

The group's recommendations were wide-ranging. They included calling for the creation of a new Registrar to supervise trade unions and employers' associations with the power to ensure that fair labour practices were upheld by the unions and to deal with cases of union discipline. Trade union funds were to lose the legal protection of immunities where trade unions remained unregistered. All fixed-term collective agreements were to be made legally enforceable and trade unions as well as employers would be able to sue individuals who broke them. Special labour courts were also to be created. A Registrar of Restrictive Practices was promised to deal with the 'flagrant misuse of manpower' while a Code of Practice was to ensure the closed shop was not used in a tyrannical manner. An independent Industrial Conciliation Board was also promised. Trade unions were to be given the right of recognition by employers when more than half the workers in an establishment voted by secret ballot in favour of such a move. The group was anxious to reject any suggestion that these proposals were motivated by any anti-union prejudices, arguing that: 'We must show we are not out to undermine or destroy but on the contrary to safeguard the legitimate authority of the unions in their own proper field. . . . We think it would be undesirable that the major piece of legislation that we envisage should be capable of being presented as a Bill against the trade unions.'[7] The report argued that the dominant attitude in Conservative industrial relations policy must be seen to be 'fairness' in balancing and safeguarding the reasonable rights of the individual worker and the public as well as trade unions and employer organizations.

The Amory group worked with apparently little self-doubt. The only distinctive notes of scepticism came from the last two Conservative Ministers of Labour. Lord Blakenham wondered whether perhaps 'there were dangers in trying to tackle too many complex problems at the same time',[8] while Godber questioned whether it was sensible to move quite so rapidly in such a comprehensive manner. But by the time Heath succeeded Sir Alec Douglas-Home as party leader in July 1965, the Conservatives were already well on their way to committing themselves to a fundamental new approach to trade union reform as part of the party's wider strategy, designed to modernize Britain's stagnant economy by making it more competitive and efficient.

In their September 1965 statement of aims, *Putting Britain Right Ahead*, the Conservatives endorsed the detailed proposals that had been drawn up by the Amory policy group. 'The dominant aim behind all these proposals is fairness', declared the document. 'This means safeguarding the reasonable rights of the individual and the public as well as of unions and employer organisations.'[9]

In the autumn of 1965 Sir Keith Joseph replaced Godber as the party's employment spokesman in the House of Commons and he also took on the chairmanship of the trade union policy group from Amory. Early in the following year he decided to carry out an appraisal of how the party's new industrial relations strategy was progressing. Joseph was troubled by the fact that so many of the proposals for reforming the way in which the trade unions behaved might prove unpopular if people came to believe that the Conservatives were motivated in their policy purely by a desire to weaken trade union workplace power and influence. 'What we intend is in the public interest', wrote Joseph. 'But we must not allow the trade unions to pose as political victims or martyrs in a class war.'[10] This was why he believed the party needed to make 'at least a gesture' in helping the trade unions in a positive way. At that time he believed one method of doing this was through the introduction of some form of industrial democracy along the lines of the West German works councils system, but this idea failed to find much support among fellow Conservatives.

Conservative policy-makers, however, were determined to reform industrial relations through sweeping legislative change. Despite the party's severe defeat in the 1966 general election the leadership was convinced the Conservatives should remain firmly committed to a radical reform of the trade unions. Over the next two years the party policy-makers refined and added to the earlier groundwork of the Amory group. In the sullen industrial climate of the mid-1960s the Conservative agenda for organized labour seemed – at least to Heath and his Shadow Cabinet – more relevant than ever. It was in March 1968 that the produced their definitive programme under the title *Fair Deal At Work*, just before the publication of the Donovan Royal Commission's report. Its importance to the whole of the Conservative economic strategy was emphasized by the introduction which was written by Heath himself. He placed the proposed industrial relations reforms into the wider context of the party's promised modernization of the economy alongside tax cuts to stimulate competition and initiative, managerial techniques to improve training and a 'ruthless war on waste' in government spending.[11] In Heath's opinion the industrial relations proposals were the 'key element' in the party's strategy to create a high wage, high profit market economy. He claimed confidently that the proposed legal changes would 'be able to withstand the pressures' which had 'defeated previous attempts at an economic breakthrough' as well as 'the difficulty of reconciling the concepts of full employment and free collective bargaining and the menace of rising prices and the inflationary scramble that ensues'. 'Within properly defined rules individuals and organisations can be free to get on with the job without interference by the government', explained Heath. Under the 'new framework of rights and obligations' both sides of industry would be able 'to play their full and vital role in Britain's economic life'.

The avowed aims of the new Conservative approach to industrial relations were highly ambitious. Firstly, the party sought to encourage 'more responsible collective bargaining to improve the content of agreements and to ensure that, once made, they were kept'. Secondly, it aimed to stimulate 'the removal of barriers to industrial efficiency, higher productivity and higher real earnings'. Thirdly, it wanted to achieve 'greater co-operation between management, employees and trade unions in securing industrial peace and progress'. And finally, it favoured providing 'fair and reasonable protection for the basic rights of individuals'.

The proposed changes were indeed far-reaching, but most of them were refinements from the original Amory policy group recommendations made three years earlier. A new Registrar of Trade Unions and Employers' Associations was to be established with substantial powers to ensure that union rules were 'just', based on 'secure fair democratic control' and not 'contrary to the public interest'. Registration with the new body was to be made 'a compulsory condition for any organisation wanting to have full legal status as a trade union'. A National Industrial Relations Court was to be created with lay members drawn from both sides of industry and with legally qualified chairmen. Trade unions were to have corporate legal status 'subject only to immunity against civil proceedings when acting in furtherance of a lawful trade dispute which was not a breach of agreement'. In future, all collective agreements between employers and trade unions were to be legally enforceable except where it was specifically agreed that they would not be. Trade unions were to benefit from a provision that established a legal obligation on employers to recognize and negotiate with registered unions where a majority of workers concerned wanted union representation. A new statutory right of appeal was also to be provided for workers against alleged unfair dismissal by their employer as well as against coercive or disciplinary action by a trade union. Strikes aimed at enforcing closed shops, inter-union disputes, solidarity actions or strikes against employers 'engaging certain types of labour' were to lose all legal protection. New legal safeguards would protect individual workers who did not wish to join a closed shop.[12]

Fair Deal at Work also envisaged a stronger role for the Employment Secretary in dealing with industrial disputes. He was to be empowered with the right to apply for an injunction to the Industrial Court to delay or stop a strike or lock-out if such an action threatened to seriously endanger the national interest. But the minister could only do this if he received a report from an independent committee of inquiry into the dispute. The maximum period that an injunction could last in such an event would be 60 days. Where the injunction was granted, the minister would have the legal power to order a secret ballot during the period it was in force. The ballot would be conducted by the Ministry of Labour itself or an outside body appointed by the minister and this would decide whether or not the workers involved accepted the employer's last offer. Further action to resolve the dispute after that would be left to the parties directly concerned. The Conservatives also proposed the creation of a Productivity Board with the specific aim of rooting out inefficiencies in industry. But no sanctions were envisaged to compel employers and unions to abolish restrictive labour practices. The policy put its faith in public and parliamentary censure if the Board's recommendations failed to bring about change. The body was never in fact created when the party returned to office in June 1970, mainly due to the opposition to the proposal from the Confederation of British Industry.

Critics in the unions regarded the detailed proposals laid out in *Fair Deal at Work* as a serious threat to their traditional freedoms, but the Conservative leadership was anxious to play down any suggestion that such comprehensive reform would make a dramatic impact on industrial relations practice. Robert Carr, who was appointed by Heath as the party's employment spokesman in 1967, assured the Conservative conference in that year: 'If the experience of other countries is anything to go by, the cases which will actually come to court will be few and far between.' He believed that 'the main effect of a proper, comprehensive framework of law' would be 'to influence the way in which management and unions do their business together'.[13] Moreover, Carr was anxious to dispel the widespread belief that what the Conservatives proposed was in any way a measure which was hostile to organized labour. 'This is no pro-employer, anti-trade union policy', he argued. It was to enable employers and trade unions to 'have a better chance by heir own responsible voluntary action' to help in the transformation of the country. 'The need is to strengthen not to weaken constitutional union authority and to extend it down to factory level', he explained. 'Responsible, accountable but also stronger unions – that is the purpose.' In his opinion once the proposals were implemented they would create an industrial relations system where there was 'much less state intervention' and a 'higher degree of discipline and responsibility'. 'It offers the unions a means of re-establishing the independence of free collective bargaining', claimed Carr.

At the 1969 party conference Carr assured the Conservative faithful that the proposals differed markedly from Labour's In *Place of Strife* White Paper because they did not emphasize 'new powers of ministerial intervention nor the sterile and contentious subject of penalising individual workers'.[14] 'In so far as sanctions are needed', explained Carr, 'the main deterrent in our law will be the possibility of civil damages against a company or against a union which fails to honour its obligations or exceeds its legal rights and powers.' In fact, by 1969 the party leadership had extended the scope of the proposed industrial relations legislation. It was suggested that the sensitive issue of inter-union workplace competition for new members should be regulated through the proposed Industrial Court which would define what constituted a 'suitable bargaining unit' and provide the workers concerned with the ultimate right through a secret ballot to decide whether or not they wanted to join a trade union and which one it would be. A new statutory right was also to be introduced enabling every worker to join a trade union as well as one enabling a worker not to belong. It was also proposed that 60 days' notice should be given before an existing collective agreement could be terminated. Greater employment protection was to be given to workers who broke their employment contracts when taking part in lawful strikes. All workers were to be provided by their employer with a written statement of their basic rights and obligations, including what action they could take if they had a grievance. Companies above an unspecified size would also be obliged to provide information on their company's performance to their employees in the same way as they did for their shareholders. Similarly, those companies would also have to establish councils made up of elected workforce representatives.

The new declared rights would not be directly enforceable by law but were to be taken into account as evidence in any proceedings in the Industrial Court connected with a dispute. Despite such wide-ranging additions to the *Fair Deal at Work* proposals Carr still sought to convince the sceptics and opponents that they were wrong to portray the Conservative approach as hostile to free trade unionism. The party leadership tried to suggest that the proposed Industrial Relations Act would have more of an indirect rather than substantial effect. Its purpose was to change attitudes of mind in the workplace by enlightened example not through the use of penal sanctions. As Carr explained to the 1969 party conference:

> Our law will be a beginning and not an end. Utopia will not dawn the day after our Act goes on to the statute book. It will not stop strikes. What it will increasingly do is to make them the means of last resort instead of first resort as they too often are at present. We do not claim that law by its direct action will achieve all that is needed. Its chief benefit will be its indirect and cumulative effect in influencing the way in which employers and unions and individual workers think and act and do their business together. . . . Our present bad law handicaps voluntary action, while the new good law will assist it. Law forms opinion and influences behaviour. A positive code of law does much more than provide sanctions against the transgressors; it is not a matter of compelling people. It puts on record the judgement of the community about what conduct is fair and reasonable.[14]

Indeed, Heath and his colleagues regarded their detailed industrial relations proposals as rational, sensible and essentially modest. The new law would put an end to the existing 'disorderly' character of collective bargaining and in the name of the 'responsible majority' of trade unionists prevent the wild-cat stoppages that had done so much to disfigure industrial relations in the 1960s. The TUC's open hostility to *Fair Deal at Work* did nothing to deflect the party leadership's determination to press ahead with the proposed changes if returned to government. Its authors even suggested that what they proposed was based on the recommendations of the Donovan Royal Commission's report. Heath and Carr were convinced that if the Conservatives stated their aims clearly and precisely enough in a general election campaign they would have secured a democratic mandate from the voters to carry out the proposals once they were in office.

By the end of the 1960s many in the Conservative leadership had come to regard the proposed comprehensive Industrial Relations Bill as far more than just a measure to reform the voluntarist system through the external stimulus of the law. Increasingly, the proposals were also being championed inside the party as a necessary substitute for a statutory prices and incomes policy in the containment of wage-push inflation. 'I think enormous faith was placed in the Industrial Relations Act because really it was the means of bringing about a regulation of the economy without having to go back to the old problems of incomes and prices policy all over again', recalled Jim Prior, a close Heath colleague and future Employment Secretary under Margaret Thatcher.[15] 'The general thesis was that the trade unions had too much power; they exercised that power in a monopoly situation which enabled them to push up wages without pushing up productivity and this was a way of getting rid of it'. Through the introduction of order and cohesion in collective bargaining and a corresponding diminution in the supposed disruptive tendencies of shop stewards, the legislation would apparently make trade union wage claims much more realistic, help eradicate obstacles to genuine productivity deals and match reward and performance in the payment of individual workers. However, such hopes were based more on unfounded optimism than on empirical evidence. Indeed, Conservatives at the time seem to have been surprisingly naive about the likely success of their industrial relations panacea.

The trouble was that there were fundamental flaws at the heart of the proposed measure. Drafted by party professionals and lawyers with no intimate knowledge of shopfloor or even boardroom life and without any recourse to a wider consultation among the employers who would be expected to operate the new legislation once it became law, the Conservative proposals provided contradictory solutions to Britain's industrial relations problems. Heath and his colleagues wanted to encourage full-time union leaders to exercise greater control and authority over their activists and rank and file members. The aim of strengthening the centralizing efforts of the unions was designed to make those organizations less divided by internal uncertainty about where the source of ultimate power lay in their decision-making processes. In the face of the 'challenge from below', trade unions – with the helpful intrusion of the law – were to become disciplined, hierarchical bodies with clear-cut command structures from top to bottom. But even if the unions were to reform themselves in this way to comply with the proposed law, it is unclear why such a change would have produced a more responsible union attitude to collective bargaining. On the contrary, stronger and more self-confident union leaders equipped with greater authority over their own members might prove to be much more effective in mobilizing the rank and file for militant action in pursuit of acquisitive objectives. But if the Conservatives were serious about their desire to turn the unions into much more responsible organizations within a new codified framework of law, the party policy-makers should not at the same time have made gestures in a liberalizing, individualistic direction. By outlawing the pre-entry closed shop and upholding a wide range of individual worker rights, they were proposing to weaken not strengthen the trade unions. Not for the first time in the party's thinking on industrial relations the tensions between collectivism and individualism were apparent. What was even more serious was they were contained within the framework of the same measure.

The passing of the Industrial Relations Act

The June 1970 Conservative general election manifesto promised that the proposed comprehensive Industrial Relations Bill would be introduced in the first parliamentary session if the party won office. 'We aim to strengthen the unions and their official leadership by providing some deterrent against irresponsible action by unofficial minorities', the party promised. 'We seek to create conditions in which strikes become the means of last resort, not of first resort, as they now so often are.'[16] The Conservatives insisted the legislation would 'provide a proper framework of law within which improved relationships between management, men and unions can develop'. In a foreword to the document Heath sought to assure the voters that his administration would introduce a new style of government after what he alleged to be the 'cheap and trivial' way in which Wilson ran his government. As he explained:

> The government should seek the best advice and listen carefully to it. It should not rush into decisions, it should use up-to-date techniques for assessing the situation, it should be deliberate and thorough. What is more, its decisions should be aimed at the long term. The easy answer and the quick trick may pay immediate dividends in terms of publicity but in the end it is the national interest which suffers.

It was a pity Heath did not apply such reasoning to the party's ambitious industrial relations strategy. However, the Conservative leader also went on to declare in the manifesto that once a decision had been made by his government he and his Cabinet colleagues would 'have the courage to stick to it'. 'Nothing has done Britain more harm in the world than the endless backing and filling which we have seen in recent years', declared Heath. He even instanced Wilson's handling of the *In Place of Strife* White Paper as an example of the kind of political manoeuvring he deplored:

> At the first sign of difficulty the Labour government has sounded the retreat, covering its withdrawal with a smokescreen of unlikely excuses. But courage and intellectual honesty are essential qualities in politics and in the interest of our country it is high time that we saw them again.

Apparently, it was not enough that a new Conservative government should 'make a fresh start with new policies'. Heath argued it must also 'create a new way of running our national affairs'.

After his unexpected but decisive victory at the polls in June 1970, Heath believed he enjoyed a mandate to push ahead with the immediate implementation of the party's highly detailed industrial relations proposals. Both the TUC and the CBI were taken aback at the speed with which Heath and Carr, enthusiastically backed by Sir Geoffrey Howe, the Solicitor General, moved to implement their proposed industrial relations legislation. A Consultative Document containing its details was published within a few weeks of the government coming to power, and only a month was set aside for discussion with the interested parties over the precise details. Moreover, when TUC leaders met Carr on 13 October 1970 he told them bluntly that the government had no intention of making any amendments to the central pillars of the Bill, which were based closely on the *Fair Deal at Work* document. The government's refusal to negotiate seriously on any of the exact detail of its proposals led to an immediate breakdown in formal relations with the TUC. It seemed to confirm the view of more militant union leaders who believed Heath and his colleagues had no genuine wish to consult but were hell-bent on provoking a confrontation with organized labour.

The atmosphere between the TUC and the government was already frosty by the early autumn of 1970 as ministers sought to wrestle with what was to be the worst period of industrial unrest seen in Britain since the early 1920s. Douglas Hurd, Heath's political secretary at the time, admitted public sector labour conflicts 'swallowed up' much of his working time in 10 Downing Street.[17] Within days of coming to office Heath found himself having to deal with a damaging national dock strike. He was forced to declare a State of Emergency but the eventual settlement of the dispute was generally seen as a victory for the dockers. In the early autumn of 1970, the low paid local government manual workers launched a pay offensive with a demand for a £30 a week minimum wage. Their disruption made a widespread impact on the community as dustbins were left unemptied. A Committee of Inquiry was eventually established by the government under the chairmanship of the arch-conciliator Sir Jack Scamp as a way of bringing the dispute to an end. This went on to recommend a 14.5 per cent pay settlement, a figure that horrified the government though it was accepted. Ministers may have rejected Labour's discredited statutory prices and incomes policy, but they were trying to bring down the rate of wage increases under a strategy which came to be known as 'N minus one'. This sought rather crudely to ensure that each pay settlement was 1 per cent less than the one before.

N minus one

A growing number of trade union leaders had convinced themselves by the early autumn of 1970 that the new government was impervious to what they regarded as reasoned argument and was intent on destroying the voluntarist industrial relations system. But at the same time, despite their tough rhetoric Heath and his Cabinet colleagues were also beginning to look weak, ineffective and unsure of how to respond to the growth of militant public sector trade unionism. In the winter of 1970 electricity power workers launched a work to rule and overtime ban in pursuit of a 25 per cent wage claim that caused widespread and damaging power cuts. The Cabinet again declared a State of Emergency. But it also agreed – though this time with some misgivings – to the creation of a hastily formed independent Court of Inquiry chaired by Lord Wilberforce, an eminent High Court judge, to examine the merits of the power workers' case. In its remit, ministers insisted that Lord Wilberforce should take the 'national interest' into account in whatever eventual pay award his inquiry made to the power workers. In fact, the Wilberforce inquiry recommended pay rises of between 15 and 18 per cent and although the total was less than the 25 per cent increase the power workers had been originally demanding, it did not augur well for the overall success of the government's much-vaunted N minus one incomes strategy. Heath and his Cabinet colleagues were especially incensed by what Lord Wilberforce and his colleagues had to say about the general pay outlook in the labour market which they used to justify their power workers' award. While the inquiry's report was conscious of the dangers for the economy of unchecked wage-push inflation, it did not believe the power workers alone could be

Table 6.1 Labour market indicators under Heath, 1970–1973

	Unemployment (no.)	(%)	Earnings rise (%)	Union membership (no.)	(%)
1970	582,200	2.5	13.6	11,179,000	47.7
1971	751,000	3.3	10.2	11,127,000	47.9
1972	837,400	3.7	11.7	11,349,000	49.4
1973	595,600	2.6	13.9	11,456,000	49.2

Source: Employment Gazettes.

expected to accept a lower increase in their wages if other workers were not also moderating their own pay expectations. 'The country is at present in a dangerous condition of spiralling inflation', lamented the Wilberforce report, 'a condition in which wages and prices are chasing each other into rises which are far higher than in 1969 and earlier years.'[18] Wilberforce suggested that real wage increases were being undermined and that this created social injustices and resentments as well as threatening the balance of payments and the value of the currency.

It is true the Heath government did not lose all its public sector battles in 1970–1. A clear-cut victory was achieved over Britain's postmen in the spring of 1971 when after a six week all-out strike they were forced to accept a 9 per cent wage settlement. Heath and his colleagues went on calling for a resolute stand in the public sector while encouraging private companies to reject large wage demands made by their workers. But in reality private employers took little notice of government exhortations and continued making pay deals with their workers which were well above the inflation rate.

Trade union leaders were also convinced by the Heath government's industrial strategy that the Conservatives intended to disengage the state from any direct involvement in industry. It is true that no sweeping programme was introduced to privatize the publicly owned industries. Only Thomas Cook, the travel agency, and 200 publicly owned public houses in the Carlisle region were returned to private enterprise during Heath's three and a half years in office. But with former CBI Secretary-General John Davies as industry minister, it looked for a time as if the Conservatives intended to dismantle the panoply of subsidies and cash supports that had been a feature of Labour's industrial strategy in the late 1960s. The abolition of the Industrial Reorganization Corporation – set up by Labour to encourage restructuring – suggested this was their intention. Under the self-proclaimed 'quiet revolution' the frontiers of the state were to be rolled back from private industry which would be left to look after itself in the bracing atmosphere of a free market economy. Apparently, 'lame ducks' of industry were to be sacrificed in the name of managerial efficiency. But the rhetoric belied the reality within a few months. In February 1971 the government felt compelled to save a bankrupt Rolls Royce from collapse by nationalizing parts of the company. Even more significant was the outcome of the crisis at Upper Clyde Shipbuilders. At first it looked as though the Cabinet would refuse to give way to pressure from the workforce, who occupied the shipyards and staged a work-in under the leadership of their shop stewards, but after nine months of argument the government backed down and poured £35 million of taxpayers' money into the enterprise rather than risk the social conflict that threatened to break out if UCS had fallen into liquidation.

The bitterness on the public sector wages front and worker opposition to the government's 'lame duck' industrial strategy certainly worsened the atmosphere which surrounded the passage of the Industrial Relations Bill onto the statute book. The resulting measure was the longest piece of legislation laid before Parliament in the post-war period, containing 163 clauses, eight schedules and 97 amendments. The government was forced to impose a guillotine on debate in the teeth of furious Labour opposition so that only 39 of its 288 clauses were even scrutinized at the Committee stage. Some members of the Cabinet questioned the wisdom of incorporating all the proposals for industrial relations reform into one comprehensive measure, but they failed to convince their colleagues that a more modest approach might be more sensible. 'We tried to do far too much at once, putting our faith in the idea that sweeping changes in the law would rapidly change behaviour on the shopfloor', admitted Jim Prior.[19] 'Apart from Robert Carr scarcely anyone in the party understood industrial relations or knew industrialists, let alone any trade unionists.' But even Carr himself was to admit later that the Industrial Relations Bill had been both too ambitious and too complex. 'I had to have a brief in order to understand the purpose of the clause I was talking about', he admitted with hindsight. 'So if it was complex to me, one of its main authors, what it seemed like to other people I dread to think.'[20]

Carr himself continued to believe that what was being proposed would strengthen and not weaken the trade unions, by making them 'more accountable and more responsible both to their own members and to the community at large'. At the 1970 party conference he highlighted the positive advantages that the proposed Act would provide trade unions – the right of everybody to belong to a trade union; the right to union recognition and negotiation from an employer for his workers if they voted for that in a secret ballot; the right to strike and the right that no striker could be ordered back to work against his will by a court; the right of a worker to appeal, and secure redress for unfair dismissal. All that the government sought in return for what Carr called 'this massive extension and confirmation of the rights that trade unions must have in a free society' were that they must register so that their own rule books could be approved and supervised and that they must accept that 'some kinds of industrial action' were 'unfair to the community at large and therefore accept liability for the harm' which they did to other people against whom they directed such unfair actions.[21]

Despite the intricacies of the measure, Carr was also convinced that the new law would prove in practice to be much less intrusive than the trade unions believed. In fact, the 1971 Industrial Relations Act turned out to be a flawed piece of legislation. For all the attacks on its contents from the Left, who argued it sought to destroy free trade unionism, the measure contained the seeds of its own destruction. The trouble was that it depended for its success in practice not on government action but on the willingness of both trade unions and above all employers to make use of its provisions. Heath and his Cabinet colleagues drew back from the use of compulsion in enforcing the measure. They accepted that trade unions should decide for themselves whether or not they stayed on the existing Register under the Act. Of course, if unions decided to deregister they would become vulnerable to crippling financial damages from the Industrial Court in the event of their involvement in unlawful disputes. The act of deregistration was a clear option open to trade unions if they wished to defy the new law. 'I certainly had a blind spot about this', Carr admitted later. 'I never expected the trade unions would oppose the Bill on the question of registration. And from their narrow short-term point of view it was a damnably effective tactic.'[22] But at the time he was prepared to acknowledge publicly that this course of action was open to the trade unions if they really wanted to avoid any involvement in the new system. 'They do not commit a crime by not registering. Thank heavens there are no crimes in our Act', he explained. Ministers believed that the trade unions would come around eventually to see the advantages to them of registration: 'Unions will register. When some register others will follow', argued Carr. 'In the end they will follow not because they feel coerced into giving way to some oppressive force but because they will know that this is a benefit and a strength to them and to their members'.[23] A late amendment to the Bill by Sir Geoffrey Howe sought to expedite such an outcome by deeming that any union which remained on the newly formed 'provisional' register would be transferred automatically to the permanent register unless it took the positive step of actually requesting its removal. As Moran argued: 'By placing the onus on unions to de-register the Government created enormous problems for the TUC. This single amendment came close to destroying the campaign of opposition to the Act.'[24]

However, there was a second important weakness in the 1971 Industrial Relations Act that helped to make it ineffective. The Cabinet decided that employers and trade unions would not be compelled to make the collective agreements they negotiated legally enforceable if they did not wish them to be so. As a result, in practice both sides agreed to write into any deal between them a final clause that stated it was not legally binding. The willingness of employers to take such an action was actually approved of by the CBI, which was less than enthusiastic about the general thrust of the 1971 Industrial Relations Act than might have been supposed. 'The main effect of the legislation should be to stimulate the improvement of industrial relations by voluntary arrangements', advised the CBI in its guidance to its affiliated company members. 'Resort by employers to the legal processes in the Act may well be less effective than good voluntary practices.' 'Only on rare occasions would you wish to invoke the remedies available under the Act', it added.[25] Indeed, it was the refusal of the overwhelming majority of employers to use the provisions available to them in the new measure that ensured it enjoyed a remarkably short life. What is also significant is that the government itself did not instruct the nationalized industries – over which it could have exercised its authority – to enter into legally enforceable contracts with their recognized trade unions.

But then Heath and most of his colleagues did not regard the 1971 Act as an anti-union measure. On the contrary, as Brendan Sewill, special assistant to the Chancellor of the Exchequer for the whole period of the government, explained later:

> The aim was not to reduce the power of the unions nor to blunt the strike weapon. Some legal protection was removed for certain types of unofficial strike, but nothing was done to reduce the force of official strikes. Indeed, 'the right to strike' was positively expressed in legislation for the first time in history. The Act set out to establish a legal framework for industrial relations (as exists in other countries) in the belief that it would lead to a gradual transformation of the unions into responsible and constructive institutions.[26]

Ministers were taken aback by the fury of the trade unions. According to Sewill:

In opposition, private talks with trade union leaders had led us to believe that, while the unions would be bound publicly to oppose the introduction of legislation on industrial relations, once the law was passed it would be accepted. Where we (and probably they also) went wrong was in not realising that such a head of opposition would be built up that it would become impossible for the law to operate properly.

The TUC fights back

However, despite the loopholes which enabled voluntary deregistration and the non-enforceability of collective agreements by agreement between employers and trade unions, the TUC was by no means convinced in early 1971 that the Industrial Relations Bill could be defeated once it reached the statute book. But at least the trade unions were united in their opposition to what was being proposed. In the face of the government's refusal to bargain, the TUC took to the streets in a massive demonstration. More than an estimated 140,000 people attended the TUC's protest rally against the Industrial Relations Bill in London's Trafalgar Square on 21 February 1971. It was the biggest event of its kind that the TUC had ever organized. A Communist dominated body known as the Liaison Committee for the Defence of Trade Unions called a number of one day unofficial stoppages in opposition to the Bill, but these attracted only marginal rank and file support which was confined mainly to the dockers and Fleet street printers. Such displays of resistance did not in fact reflect accurately the state of public opinion over the government's industrial relations legislation. In December 1970 a Gallup poll found widespread support for the government's industrial relations proposals. As many as 71 per cent believed collective contracts should be legally binding, 65 per cent thought trade unions should be fined if they broke the new laws and 69 per cent favoured secret ballots before workers went on strike. Indeed, throughout the whole period of the Heath government, until its bitter denouement in the three day working week and the second miners' dispute of 1973–4, more people approved than disapproved of the proposals contained in the 1971 Industrial Relations Act.

But the TUC's reasoned opposition to the government's proposals was based on its own trade union perspective not on the findings of national opinion surveys, though it did try to do its best to convince the wider public that it was behaving reasonably in rejecting the legislation. Congress House believed the sweeping changes envisaged by the Conservatives were unnecessary and dangerous and would do nothing to improve

Table 6.2   Public attitudes to the 1971 Industrial Relations Act

'Do you approve or disapprove of the following proposals outlined in the Government's Bill?'

(%)	Approve	Disapprove	Don't know
(a) A 'cooling off' period where a strike harms the national interest?	73	9	7
(b) Fines for unions who break the new rules and commit unfair industrial practices?	65	16	19
(c) A secret ballot of members to be made before holding a strike?	69	17	14
(d) A worker to be able to decide whether to join a union or not?	76	12	12
(e) Agreements between unions and employers to be legally binding unless stated otherwise?	71	10	18
In August 1971 further questions were asked:			
(f) Union members who defied the law and continue to strike may be liable to be fined?	57	25	18
(g) Compulsory recognition of trade unions by employers?	52	23	24

Source: Gallup

the country's industrial relations. The TUC focused its main opposition on the substantial powers which were to be given to the Registrar in the new legal framework. It suggested these would 'impose an alien concept of authority on the internal workings of trade unions'[27] by enabling an external body to determine and alter their rule books. It also argued that the complex provisions of the Bill would be inflexible, time-consuming and would replace voluntary agreements with legalistic restrictions that would cause more frequent and intense disputes.

At a special Congress on 18 March 1971 in Croydon's Fairfield Hall, the TUC debated both its tactics and strategy for opposition to the measure. The TUC general council recommended a number of steps that affiliated unions should take to try and nullify the Act. Unions were 'strongly advised' not to register and urged to 'take steps to ensure' that they did not enter into any legally binding agreements. They were also warned not to use the Act in seeking recognition rights from employers. Trade unionists were told in addition not to serve on the proposed Industrial Relations Court nor on the reconstituted Commission on Industrial Relations. The TUC general council also asked for authorization to assist an affiliated union in meeting the costs of defending any action it took under the Act and promised 'in exceptional circumstances to indemnify the union against damages'.[28] But Congress House was reluctant to instruct affiliate unions to deregister as a condition for remaining a member of the TUC, as the Left was demanding, arguing that:

> To impose on unions such a general condition of affiliation would impose on the TUC the obligation to support unconditionally an affiliated union which put itself in jeopardy by one of its members – by an action that would not have been in contravention of the Act if the union had been registered. . . . The general council could not commit its affiliates to accept such an automatic obligation to each and every member concerned.

The TUC's General Secretary Vic Feather was anxious to preserve the maximum unity of action among affiliated unions in their opposition to the 1971 Industrial Relations Act. But it was soon apparent that Congress House's proposals for resistance to the measure did not go nearly far enough to satisfy the more militant forces inside the TUC who believed the general council's position was far too weak and accommodating. They favoured a much more aggressive strategy of opposition that involved a total non-compliance with all of the measure's provisions. The impetus for strengthening the TUC's attitude came primarily from the AUEW, where the broad left faction enjoyed a majority both on the union's 52 strong policy-making National Committee and its eight man Executive Council. The AUEW was convinced that the TUC would have to move decisively against any errant trade union that made an attempt to comply with the 1971 Act. At the Croydon Congress the militants failed to carry the day and the general council's policy of merely advising affiliated unions to deregister won by 5,055,000 votes to 4,284,000.

However, six months later at the 1971 Congress, the AUEW's President Hugh Scanlon led the successful resistance to the TUC's position when he moved a motion that 'instructed' all trade unions not to register under the Act and to 'take measures to remove themselves from the provisional register'. 'A single scratch can lead to gangrene', he warned. 'Whatever the motives a single step towards implicit co-operation with

Table 6.3   Strikes under Heath, 1970–1973

	Number of strikes	Number of workers involved	Number of working days lost
1970	3,906	1,801,000	10,980,000
1971	2,228	1,178,000	13,551,000
1972	2,497	1,734,000	23,909,000
1973	2,873	1,528,000	7,197,000

Source: J. W. Durcan et al., *Strikes in Post-war Britain*, Allen & Unwin, 1983, p. 133.

the Act by any section of our Movement might give temporary relief but in the long term it would be disastrous to all'.[29] Feather argued against Scanlon's proposed outright defiance, mainly because he feared it would destroy the TUC's own united front if affiliated unions were compelled to deregister. However, much to the surprise and dismay of the majority on the TUC general council, Congress voted by 5,625,000 to 4,500,000 to support the toughly worded AUEW resolution. Three and a half months after that decision as many as 82 of the TUC's affiliated unions, with a combined membership of 5,000,000, had obeyed the Congress instruction and deregistered. But a number of large and important trade unions delayed in making up their minds on whether or not to obey the TUC's deregistering instruction. These included the GMWU, NALGO, ASTMS, the EETPU and USDAW. Both the TUC and the government accepted that if a sizeable union decided to defy Congress and remain on the register in compliance with the 1971 Act it would undermine the TUC's unity and lead to the likely collapse of its opposition. Indeed, the non-registration issue was the hinge upon which the rest of the measure either stood or fell.

The miners' strike, 1972

It was now that a number of unforeseen and uncoordinated external events came to the TUC's rescue in its campaign against the Industrial Relations Act. The first was the six week long miners' strike, which began on 8 January 1972 and dealt a fatal blow to the government's entire industrial relations strategy. The sudden eruption on Britain's coalfields came as a surprise to the National Coal Board as well as to ministers, but it reflected the deep frustration and anger that had been building up among the miners during the enormous wave of pit closures and man-power cuts which had begun in the early 1960s and which had cut the size of the labour force in the coal industry from 700,000 to 290,000 in only twelve years. The union's 47 per cent pay claim with its demand for a new minimum face worker rate of £35 a week and consequential rises for the wage differentials of other miners was based on a widely perceived recognition that the relative real earnings of miners had fallen by as much as a quarter during the period of the coal industry's contraction, with the highest paid face workers only earning £27 a week. Proud and introverted, and outside the TUC mainstream, the NUM was very much an unknown quantity. 'The miners really do walk on their own. We just didn't know the miners', recalled Carr. 'They hadn't been to St James's Square, the old home of the Ministry of Labour for nearly fifty years.'[30]

However, there was little doubting the legitimacy of the miners' strike. The NUM's national executive committee was unanimous in its decision to ballot the rank and file to call a national stoppage, after having imposed an effective national overtime ban for some weeks which had cut coal production dramatically. Under the union's own rules a secret ballot of the members was required before an official strike could be called. This required not just a simple majority of the rank and file to endorse the action but a 55 per cent Yes vote. In an 86 per cent pit head turnout the leadership secured 55.8 per cent rank and file support, which suggested that a sizeable minority on the coalfields doubted the efficacy of an all-out strike. Indeed, if the NUM's ballot had been held only a year earlier there would have been no national stoppage in 1972 at all because then it would have needed as much as a two-thirds majority to sanction strike action. It was the change in the ballot rule in 1970 that ensured the NUM could utilize the strike weapon in pursuit of its demands.

The NUM was in a much stronger position in early 1972 than perhaps even its leaders recognized, with only an estimated two months' coal stocks lying at the nation's power stations. Its strength was soon apparent, however, when the union took the offensive with the use of flying pickets to prevent the movement of undistributed coal to depots and power stations. In the 1926 lock-out most of Britain's miners had sat it out passively on the coalfields before being virtually starved back to work after nine months of stoical misery. Now the NUM's aggressive tactics took the government completely by surprise. 'We were determined to make the battle as short and sharp as possible', explained the right-wing Joe Gormley, who was elected NUM president in June 1971.[31] The union was also undoubtedly helped to ultimate victory by the solidarity action of other workers, most notably the rail drivers in the footplatemen's union ASLEF who refused to move coal from the pit heads to the power stations or anywhere else, and road haulage workers. But the miners also won the battle for public opinion, where there was enormous sympathy for their position.

The showdown finally came at the Saltley coal depot of the West Midland Gas Board in Birmingham. An estimated 15,000 workers led by the Yorkshire miners under the Napoleonic style leadership of the young Arthur Scargill forced the police to close the gates and turn the coal lorries away. 'Here was living proof that the working class had only to flex its muscles and it could bring governments, employers, society to a complete standstill', declared Scargill at the time.[32] The events at Saltley certainly caused a panic among ministers and their civil service advisers as they looked on helplessly at the exercise of brutal industrial force. Indeed, the government was being forced to its knees. Its officials wondered excitedly whether the miners strike would precipitate rioting on the streets, epidemics and a complete breakdown of civil order. 'At the time many of those in positions of influence looked into the abyss and saw only a few days away the possibility of the country being plunged into a state of chaos not so very far removed from that which might prevail after a minor nuclear attack', recalled Sewill.[33] Douglas Hurd noted in his diary: 'The Government is now vainly wandering over the battlefield looking for someone to surrender to and being massacred all the time.'[34] In Gormley's opinion, Heath and his colleagues had been much too slow in reacting to the union's use of flying pickets. He was surprised in particular that it took the government until 8 February – five weeks into the dispute – to call a State of Emergency. 'This gave them wide powers, including the use of troops if necessary', explained Gormley. 'But it was too late. It would have been in practical terms impossible to use the troops because fellow trade unionists had successfully 'blacked' those supplies which under police escort had managed to break through our lines. There was no doubt that any further attempts to break through the lines would have resulted in much wider industrial action.'[35]

On 9 February Robert Carr summoned the NUM's leaders into the Department of Employment and asked them if they would settle for a pay deal longer than 12 months and whether the rest of the trade union movement would treat the miners as a special case. Increasingly confident of victory, Gormley and his colleagues rejected the proposal and stood out for more money and benefits for the miners. The government agreed on 11 February to appoint a public inquiry under the ubiquitous Lord Wilberforce which was asked to report as quickly as possible on the NUM's pay claim. At the same time the Cabinet introduced a three day working week to try and conserve the nation's dwindling energy supplies. After two days of public hearings, which were dominated by an oratorical *tour de force* by the union's General Secretary Laurence Daly in the presentation of the miners' case, the Wilberforce Inquiry published its report. It endorsed the NUM's demands and recommended 20 per cent wage increases for the miners to be phased in over 16 months, and declared:

> We think it an essential part of the present settlement that the miners' basic claim for a general and exceptional increase should be recognised . . . We believe that in general this is accepted by public opinion and if it cannot be paid for out of the NCB's revenue account, in accordance with its statutory obligations, we think that the public, through the Government, should accept the charge.[36]

Ministers might have complained at the size of the award, but they feared they had no credible alternative but to try and settle on its terms. In fact, the NUM executive remained dissatisfied and went on to reject the Wilberforce Inquiry award by 15 votes to 10. The union's leaders insisted on negotiating further humiliating concessions on bonus shift payments, an extra week's holiday and other largess late into the night at 10 Downing Street from harassed Coal Board officials with a defeated Heath and senior Cabinet colleagues waiting in attendance. The end of the miners' strike turned out to be a deep and unforgettable defeat for the government. As Gormley recalled: 'No one could say it had been other than a great victory. We won far far more than even Wilberforce had suggested. All those extra items added up to more than the actual cash offer.' But he also noted that on 28 February – the very day the strike ended – the anti-strike provisions of the Industrial Relations Act came into force, 'provisions which would have made it far more difficult for us to achieve the effect we did'.[37]

From tragedy to farce

The trauma suffered by the government at the hands of Britain's miners early in 1972 brought the beginning of a change in the whole direction of the government's economic policy. Heath declared in a television broadcast that the country needed to find 'a more sensible way to settle its differences'.[38] But the Cabinet was also convinced of the need for a shift in strategy because of the inexorable rise in the level of registered unemployment, the unadjusted total having reached 936,000 in February 1972.

Ministers feared that if the Government failed to take remedial action at once, the registered jobless figure would rise over the one million mark and inflict serious political damage on the Conservatives.

As a result, the 1972 spring Budget was highly expansionary with its well-proclaimed dash for economic growth and in June the floating of the pound. The lame ducks industrial policy had already been dropped with the Cabinet's decision to bow to worker pressure at Upper Clyde Shipbuilders and provide financial aid to the troubled yard. A new Industry Act was rushed through Parliament in the spring of 1972 which provided the government with sweeping powers, enabling it to channel state support into companies that it believed needed financial assistance.

But these economic and industrial policy U-turns did not lead overnight to a more conciliatory government attitude towards the trade unions, despite the onset of wide-ranging talks with the TUC that began in the aftermath of the miners' settlement. The main obstacle to cooperation lay in the existence of the Industrial Relations Act. Indeed, within weeks of the end of the miners' strike its provisions provoked a further dramatic deterioration in relations between the government and the TUC.

The first use of the measure turned out to be more farcical than tragic. Faced in April 1972 with the prospect of a national rail dispute with a crippling work to rule and overtime ban after the rail unions rejected an 11 per cent pay recommendation, Maurice Macmillan, Carr's hapless successor as Secretary of State at the Department of Employment, decided to activate the 14 day cooling off period provision of the Act through the Industrial Relations Court. The rail unions refused to attend the court hearing in line with TUC policy, but they complied reluctantly with the Court's judgement by adhering to the cooling off period. At the end of the 14 days, with no progress to a settlement achieved, the Industrial Relations Court ordered a secret ballot of the railwaymen to find out what they thought about their union's wage claim. The unions lost an appeal against that order and the vote went ahead. The ballot result turned into a humiliating defeat for the government. Over 80 per cent of the railwaymen backed the wage demands made by their union representatives. As a result, the dispute was settled with a 13 per cent wage increase for the railwaymen. Understandably, the ballot provisions of the 1971 Industrial Relations Act were never to be used again.

A far more serious confrontation over the new measure occurred only a few weeks later in Britain's troubled dockland and here the government lacked any means of direct intervention and control. The point at issue in the conflict was regarded by the dockers as fundamental for their very survival. As a result of technological change it was becoming more

efficient and cost effective to load and unload goods required for export
or import in containers, and not in the docks with their restrictive practices
and bad labour relations but well away from the waterfront in modern
inland terminals. The dockers, who belonged to the TGWU, were determined to picket and black the new terminals and the road haulage
companies who used them in order to defend their own jobs. Heatons
Transport, a road haulage firm in St Helens on Merseyside, sought
redress from the Industrial Relations Court for the unofficial blacking
of their goods which was being organized by shop stewards in nearby
Liverpool. On 23 March 1972 the National Industrial Relations Court
instructed the TGWU to stop the blacking of Heatons. In line with TUC
policy, the TGWU refused to attend the Court or obey the order. It was
fined £5,000 for contempt and a further £50,000 on 21 April, after which
the union did make efforts to try and persuade the shop stewards to lift
their blacking action. At that point, the TGWU's executive council,
under a clear threat of the sequestration of the union's funds, decided to
attend the Court. In the subsequent hearing the union argued it lacked
the power to stop the picketing which was unofficial and against the
union's own policy. The Court refused to accept the union's submission
and gave the TGWU 21 days both to put a stop to the blacking and to
repudiate the action of their shop stewards. The TGWU then appealed
to the Court of Appeal against the judgement and to the surprise of many
won its case. Lord Denning, Master of the Rolls, declared on 13 June
1972 that the union was indeed not liable for the behaviour of its shop
stewards. That decision came, in the words of Carr, like 'a torpedo below
the waterline'.[39] It opened up the way to the very outcome that ministers
had believed was impossible under the Industrial Relations Act – the
imprisonment of strikers – because an employer in such a situation could
not seek redress from the union but only from its members who were
carrying out the unlawful action.

Indeed, militant dockers' leaders in London were eager to become the
first 'martyrs' against the hated 1971 Act. It took a good deal of argument
from their union and the TUC, involving the introduction of the Official
Solicitor, to prevent three of them going to jail for contempt of court for
their unlawful picketing at the Chobham Farm container terminal in East
London. But the situation was now deteriorating rapidly with the growing
prospect of a national dock strike. On 4 July 1972 a case involving the
blacking and picketing by dockers of Midland Cold Storage began in the
National Industrial Relations Court. It ended eighteen days later with five
dockers' shop stewards who had been organizing a picket of the company
being committed to Pentonville prison for contempt of court. The trade

union response to their arrival in jail was immediate. The TUC threatened to call a one day general strike in protest and demonstrators gathered outside the prison as thousands of dockers around Britain stopped work. Fortunately for the government, the House of Lords came to the rescue by overturning the Court of Appeal's controversial judgement over Heatons Transport and ruling that it was the TGWU and not the shop stewards who were responsible for the unlawful picketing. With unseemly haste the five 'martyrs' were released from Pentonville on 1 August amidst tumultuous scenes, though they had refused to purge their contempt.

The dramatic events of July 1972 fatally discredited the Industrial Relations Act. In an extraordinarily short space of time it had already become a lingering embarrassment for the government which only a few months earlier had regarded the measure as vital to the modernization of the economy. The imprisonment of the dockers' leaders hardened the attitude of those wavering unions who had initially doubted the wisdom of the TUC's compulsory deregistration strategy. The EETPU, USDAW and ASTMS all announced they had decided to fall into line behind the TUC's militant position as a result of what had occurred in dockland. But the 'victory' of the dockers also chastened Jack Jones, the TGWU's General Secretary, who had been working valiantly with Lord Aldington, chairman of the Port of London Authority, to try and resolve dockland's underlying troubles which were mainly caused by job insecurity bred in the bad old days of casual work. Their inquiry stemmed from a government initiative launched by Maurice Macmillan and John Peyton, the transport minister. The resulting report went a long way to meet the grievances of the dockers over containerization by giving them in effect permanent registered jobs for life, with the abolition of the 'temporary unattached register' and a guarantee of no redundancies. But Jones – the great champion of shop steward power – became the target for the wrath of the militants when he announced the threatened dock strike was being called off in return for the package of reforms. Water was thrown over him in an angry meeting in Transport House.

Searching for consensus

The return of relative industrial calm in the summer of 1972 enabled Heath, the TUC and the CBI to resume in earnest the discussions on achieving an industrial consensus that they had begun cautiously after the end of the miners' strike. The breadth of the tripartite talks that lasted until the beginning of November 1972 was astonishing. After being out in the cold for nearly two years, the TUC found itself encouraged by the Prime Minister to drop its public intransigence against the government and play an active and positive role in the management of the economy. The going was difficult at first, mainly because the TUC kept on demanding the immediate repeal of the Industrial Relations Act and its replacement by voluntary conciliation and arbitration procedures, something the government was unwilling to concede. It took all the guile and finesse of TUC General Secretary Vic Feather to keep the discussions with the government in being during the turbulent summer of 1972, in the face of considerable left-wing trade union opposition. But in September after Congress, formal tripartite negotiations began in what was a serious attempt to reach a common national understanding between government, TUC and CBI on how the economy should be run. Jones was impressed by Heath's conciliatory performance and conceded in retrospect that 'within his limits as a Conservative prime minister' he tried to meet the TUC's point of view.[40] As he wrote graciously in his memoirs: 'No Prime Minister, either before or since, could compare with Ted Heath in the efforts he made to establish a spirit of camaraderie with trade union leaders and to offer an attractive package which mighty satisfy large numbers of work-people.'

In fact, Heath was prepared to move a surprisingly long way politically towards giving the TUC what it wanted. At their meeting at Chequers on 27 September the Prime Minister told the TUC's negotiators he was ready to extend the government's commitment to a 5 per cent growth rate for the next two years, while he urged the CBI to aim at keeping retail price increases within a 5 per cent limit with manufactured goods held to a 4 per cent price rise limit. But he also made it clear he wanted wage restraint as well, with no pay rises of over £2 a week. However, Heath also promised to create a new independent body designed to 'help the traditionally low paid industries to achieve greater efficiency as a basis for higher wages'. Threshold payments were to be introduced with a flat rate amount of 20 pence for every increase of one per cent in the retail price index above a 6 per cent threshold, calculated from the first month that the payments began, an idea the TUC had been pressing for some time. The government calculated that the proposals would ensure average increases of around 8 per cent in earnings over the coming twelve months. Heath also held out the prospect of a better deal for the old age pensioners, something dear to Jones's heart. The Prime Minister continued to remain optimistic that all sides could bargain their way forward to what he called a 'new era of co-operation'.[41]

In its turn, the TUC drew up a veritable shopping list of its favourite demands, a list which seemed to grow longer with each negotiating session with the Government. Congress Houses's demands included the government imposition of statutory price controls; a suspension of rent increases due under the 1972 Housing Finance Act; the renegotiation of the European Community's common agricultural policy; the introduction of a wealth tax and a surcharge on capital gains as well as a government limitation on dividend payments; a substantial increase in family allowances; and a government assurance that it would not use the Industrial Relations Act. In return for all of that the TUC suggested workers should be entitled to wage rises averaging £3.40 a week. By the end of October 1972 even Heath appeared to recognize that the TUC was not really serious about reaching a genuine agreement with a Conservative government except on its own impossibilist terms. Although willing to make a number of concessions, he would not accept the TUC's demand for the suspension of the Industrial Relations Act and the Housing Finance Act. Nor was he prepared to accept the TUC's demand for a freeze on prices. The tripartite talks therefore ended in inevitable failure.

The end of the attempt to establish a new relationship between the government and the TUC came as a bitter disappointment to Heath. As Douglas Hurd argued:

> Of all the charges now made against that Government, the charge that it sought or welcomed confrontation with the trade unions is the most absurd. We had a Prime Minister who believed passionately that realism should prevail if facts were reasonably presented. We had a Cabinet which, representing a modern Conservative party, realized that in no way could that party prosper by setting class against class, however many warlike telegrams its supporters might send.[42]

Far from being obstinately inflexible, Heath tried every way to draw the TUC into accepting a broad based national agreement on running the economy.

Tripartite expansion

The Heath's government's increasingly benign attitude towards the trade unions survived the failure of the Chequers talks. Indeed, the Department of Employment made clear its intentions to legislate on the labour market and to offer the TUC a prominent role in the new institutions which were to be established to promote a more efficient organization of training and manpower planning. The Employment and Training Act that reached the statute book in 1973 established the Manpower Services Commission, a tripartite public agency that was to take over employment and training services from the Department of Employment. The MSC's creation followed extensive government consultation with both the TUC and the CBI who agreed to participate fully in its activities with equal representation. Maurice Macmillan explained to the Commons in his speech on the Bill's second reading that the TUC nominees as well as those from the CBI would 'remain responsible to those bodies which proposed them'. 'I am not suggesting that they are mandated or delegates who must refer back on every major point but they must carry the confidence of the organisations which helped them to be appointed in carrying out their own daily functions', he explained. Macmillan added that as a result of this everybody would have 'an indirect joint responsibility through their members on the commission for developing those services and seeing that they met the real needs of the people who used them'.[43]

A similar approach was followed in 1974 with the creation of the tripartite Health and Safety at Work Commission as well as the Advisory, Conciliation and Arbitration Service. Other such bodies in the 1970s were to cover sex and race discrimination. On all of them the TUC nominated representatives for the boards and committees at local and national level. But it was the Conservatives who pioneered this strategy. Inevitably, it meant the large-scale dismantling of a considerable part of the Department of Employment. The new tripartite public agencies, which were fully operational by 1975, brought a diminution in Department's power and influence. Most of the full-time personnel on the MSC and other bodies were civil servants drawn from the Department of Employment. Sir Denis Barnes became the first chairman of the MSC after his retirement as Permanent Secretary. The spread of industrial tripartism in the early 1970s reflected a political bipartisan attitude. The responsibilities national union leaders were expected to shoulder as a result caused their enemies to accuse them of seeking tyrannical power and many of their own followers to wonder whether they were overstretching their functions. In Whitehall many traditionalists questioned the wisdom of institutional tripartism and lamented the delegation of administrative functions to public agencies. But the substance of the changes that began under Heath in 1973 suggested that despite the public rift between his government and the trade unions, it was never a ministerial intention even at that time to marginalize or ignore the TUC.

Towards a crisis

Reluctantly, the Prime Minister was forced to announce on 6 November 1972 that his government intended to introduce a statutory prices and incomes policy after the immediate imposition of a 90 day freeze on wages, prices, dividends and rents which was to take immediate effect. Two new institutions were also established by the state to administer the economic strategy – the Price Commission and the Pay Board. The government's action, however, did not detonate an industrial confrontation with the trade unions. As Middlemas argued, 'In the end, whatever their previous claims to a share in government, union leaders found it easier to have the terms imposed by the Government than to persuade their own members to accept what the majority of them regarded as necessary'.[44] But even then, Heath still wanted to secure the TUC's cooperation for the working of his statutory incomes policy once the freeze came to an end. However, he was unable to achieve this for Stage 2 of the strategy, which was introduced in January 1973 with a stipulated maximum pay rise per person of 4 per cent plus £1 a week and an average limit of £250 for the next twelve months, with equal pay increases excluded from the limit. Pensions and redundancy payments could be improved and so could cuts in working time and increases in holiday entitlement. Heath stressed that Stage 2 was only to continue until the autumn of 1973, when the next stage of the government's prices and incomes strategy would be introduced – hopefully by then with the TUC's consent. In fact, the unions acquiesced with little but verbal protest at the government's nine month wage norm. The number of days lost through strikes during 1973 actually turned out to be lower than in the previous two years. But the real increase in earnings during the Heath period of statutory incomes policy was also much higher than had been anticipated, not because there was any widespread defiance of its provisions – for only an estimated 6 per cent of workers received wage rises above the limit – but because of those pay settlements coming into force in Stage 2 that had been postponed since November 1972 due to the pay freeze, and incremental awards, overtime increases and rises due to payment-by-results wage systems.

Heath made enormous efforts to prepare with care for Stage 3 of his statutory incomes policy which was due to come into force at the end of November 1973 and last until the autumn of 1974. He was determined to try and avoid any danger of industrial conflict, especially with the NUM whose conference in early July had passed a resolution demanding pay increases for its members of between 22 to 47 per cent. Unknown both to the Cabinet and the union's own executive, Heath and NUM president

Joe Gormley met in the garden of 10 Downing Street on 16 July 1973 to discuss the prospects for miners' pay in the forthcoming wage round. Gormley argued in his memoirs that he gave Heath a clear hint of just how to avoid any conflict with the miners. By accepting that miners could be entitled to extra money for working unsocial hours, the government would enable the miners to exploit a unique loophole which would bypass the Stage 3 provisions but without providing a pretext for other workers to do then same.

Heath launched Stage 3 of the statutory prices and incomes policy on 8 October in the glittering surroundings of London's Lancaster House with a fine attention to detail. The government's aim was to ensure rises of £2.25 a head or 7 per cent with a limit of £350 an individual. It was to be left to each work group to decide whether or not to accept the flat or percentage rate increase. On top of this would be a 1 per cent increase for reforms in wage structures and productivity improvements and where this was not possible 1 per cent to improve sick pay schemes and holiday entitlement. Premium payments were also possible for the working of 'unsocial hours', which appeared to be a gesture to the miners in response to Gormley's big hint in July, and it was accepted that anomalies caused by the wage standstill as well as Stage 2 could also be ironed out. Heath introduced the concept of cost of living protection through threshold agreements, which would involve wage increases of 40 pence a week for each percentage point that the Retail Price Index went above 7 per cent during the twelve month course of Stage 3. 'I hope this safeguard may not be needed', added the Prime Minister.[45] The government had calculated that earnings should rise by between 8 and 9 per cent under Stage 3. At the same time, tight price controls were to continue under the auspices of the Price Commission, the 5 per cent limit on dividends was to remain in force and so were subsidies to the nationalized industries. Heath also announced a £10 Christmas bonus to the old age pensioners and help for first-time home buyers. Stage 3 was to come into force on 7 November. Sir Denis Barnes and Eileen Reid commented: 'The policy was as much an elaborate and comprehensive conciliation exercise to avoid confrontation in the 1973–1974 wage round as it was a counter-inflation operation.'[46]

But it was more an affirmation by the government that it intended to put its authority on the line in support of a prices and incomes policy. As Brendan Sewill admitted later:

> The statutory policy was in a way all bluff. On the pay side the law was never invoked. Indeed because the Government had realized that all hell would break loose if any trade unionist was fined or imprisoned, the law

was so constructed that in normal circumstances it was not actually illegal
to strike. What the policy really meant was that the Government staked its
whole reputation, its whole authority, indeed the authority of Parliament,
in the hope that the unions and their members would accept the law, or
anyway believe that the Government would never allow a strike to succeed.
For 18 months the gamble worked; but when it failed the stakes were
lost.[47]

The miners again

The TUC general council denounced Heath's Stage 3 provisions as 'unacceptable and probably unworkable'.[48] More serious was the NUM's
response. Gormley explained in his memoirs that he was 'not pleased' to
learn that the loophole of special premium payments for miners he had
suggested to Heath in July as a way of avoiding trouble with them was
going to apply to everybody. 'Whether it was through stupidity or deliberate
policy I never knew', he reflected, 'but they had effectively blocked a
loophole by which our position, relative to the rest of industry, could
have been restored.'[49] On 10 October 1973 the National Coal Board negotiators made what they described as their first and 'final' wage offer,
assessed as an average 16 per cent increase with higher rises for the
underground workers, including a 4.4 per cent shift premium. This was
calculated to be the maximum wage improvement possible under the
terms of Stage 3 of the incomes policy. It was turned down at once by the
NUM's negotiators.

In fact, the bargaining power of the miners had been strengthened
enormously by events in the Middle East. The outbreak of war in the
region on 6 October with an attack by Syria and Egypt on Israel was
followed rapidly by the decision of the oil exporting states to cut their
production levels drastically and increase oil prices fourfold. Suddenly,
coal had once again become a vital source of energy. The economic effects
of the Yom Kippur war were to bring an end to post-1945 economic
growth and plunge the Western world into a period of stagflation. But
Heath and his Cabinet colleagues saw no good reason to modify Stage 3
to take account of what had happened to oil prices and production on the
international markets.

The Prime Minister's meeting on 23 October at 10 Downing Street
with the entire 27 strong NUM executive committee revealed a wide
difference of view between the two sides. Once again, as in 1972, it looked
as though the government and the miners were set on a collision course,
but this time the NUM turned out to be much more united than two

years earlier with unanimous support on the executive and a special delegate conference for its militant strategy. Area ballots revealed widespread support for industrial action and from 12 November a national overtime ban was imposed which threatened a 30 per cent cut in coal production. The Cabinet reacted this time without delay by declaring a State of Emergency on the following day and introducing immediate restrictions on the use of electricity. The decision was also taken as a precaution in the face of a threatened dispute by the power engineers over their pay problems. Although the NUM posed the most serious threat to the government's Stage 3 pay limits, ministers were also concerned at what was happening in the electricity supply industry, as well as the on the railways where the footplatemen's union ASLEF insisted it should receive a special pay deal for its members. The rail troubles actually led to a one day national strike on 15 January and disruption on the network, particularly in south-east England, rumbled on through February.

On top of this, Heath and his Cabinet colleagues were also preoccupied with mounting difficulties beyond industrial relations. A fragile agreement had been reached at the end of November to establish a power-sharing executive authority in Northern Ireland between the Protestant and Roman Catholic political parties, but the government was well aware there were serious threats to the new body coming from the Protestants. The aftermath of the Yom Kippur War threatened to plunge the whole world into a severe slump and there were serious differences of opinion between France and Britain over how to establish a common European Community position on what to do. Above all, Britain's economy was overheating rapidly.

Heath was keen to find a way out of the impasse with the miners as long as this did not precipitate the collapse of the government's statutory incomes policy. But further talks held between the NUM's negotiators and the Coal Board proved fruitless despite a marginal improvement in the miners' pay offer. On 28 November Heath called in the NUM's executive committee for a further meeting – this time with the whole of the Cabinet – where he held out hope that the Pay Board's planned wage relativities report might provide the possibility of further money for the miners, and he promised a wide-ranging review of the coal industry with the long-term prospect of better pensions and fringe benefits, but these conciliatory proposals failed to achieve a breakthrough. The NUM executive committee's unyielding attitude was clear when its members voted by 18 to 5, with Gormley in the minority, against putting Heath's offer to the rank and file in a pit head ballot. Ministers began to suspect that the NUM leadership was being driven by political and not industrial motives. Mick McGahey, the Communist Vice-president of the union, told Heath during their Downing Street discussions that he wanted to see the government defeated. According to Gormley's recollection this was to be through the ballot box but ministers were convinced that his remarks revealed that at least for McGahey the looming showdown on Britain's coalfields was organized with an ideological objective of bringing about the government's downfall and not the industrial one of achieving bigger wage packets for the miners. Certainly, the Conservatives sought to exploit McGahey's remarks as evidence that the NUM was trying to use its muscle power to destroy a democratically elected government. But a 'Reds under the Bed' scare failed to appreciate the genuinely wide agreement that straddled the traditional Right – Left spectrum on the NUM executive on the need for a substantial rise for the miners outside what the leaders saw as the inflexible and increasingly obsolete statutory wage limits set out in the government's Stage 3 of its incomes policy.

No way out

On 13 December Heath announced that the whole country would start working only a three day week when industry started back after New Year's Day. This move was made to conserve the dwindling coal stocks at the power stations, which the Prime Minister claimed were falling rapidly as a result of the overtime ban cutting into production levels. But it was also a strong indication that the government intended to convince public opinion that Britain was heading into a grave industrial crisis. However, the Cabinet and the NUM executive committee were not yet completely locked into an inevitable confrontation. Just before Christmas a chance appears to have been missed for a possible settlement of the dispute. Gormley acquired the support of the emollient William Whitelaw – who had just been brought by Heath from what was seen as a successful period at the Northern Ireland Office in the first period of direct rule of the province to take over as Employment Secretary from the exhausted Maurice Macmillan – as well as both the National Coal Board and the Pay Board for the idea of providing extra money to the miners for the amount of waiting and bathing time they needed at the beginning and the end of their shifts. Gormley noted: 'At that point, it was as far as they could possibly go and I felt that we were within only a few days of an agreement.'[50] Unfortunately, the NUM President himself ruined the chance of reaching such a deal. By also making the bathing and waiting time suggestion to Harold Wilson, he enabled the Labour leader to raise it as his own proposal in Parliament and thereby made it politically impossible for the government to accept. In his memoirs, Gormley accused Wilson of deliberately wrecking the prospects of a deal for party political purposes. 'It was completely despicable', he wrote. 'Wilson knew it would inevitably set the miners on another collision course with the Government. If Harold and company wanted an election, they should have forced it another way by parliamentary methods rather than using the union.'[51] In fact, it is doubtful whether that particular loophole would really have defused the conflict as Gormley suggested. Indeed, his memoirs do not provide convincing evidence that he could have really persuaded even enough members of his own executive to accept such a means of avoiding an all-out strike.

Moreover, the Pay Board, after examining the possibility of increasing payments to miners through the device of bathing and waiting time, came to the conclusion that the amount raised would prove to be negligible. Heath always believed that the NUM president betrayed or at least misled him over how a showdown could be avoided with the miners, but it seemed clear that the Prime Minister did not really appreciate that Gormley – like Feather at the TUC during 1972 – was in no position to make secret arrangements with the government that he could have persuaded his NUM executive committee colleagues to accept. The lack of accurate intelligence available to ministers about the thinking of the NUM leadership during the whole crisis was to be a severe handicap for the Cabinet as it weighed the policy options of what to do next.

The TUC was concerned at the adverse impact of three day working and decided to launch an initiative to try and resolve the growing crisis. On 9 January 1974 at the regular monthly meeting of the National Economic Development Council, Sid Greene as chairman of the TUC's economic committee told Tony Barber, the Chancellor of the Exchequer, and other ministers present that the TUC general council would agree that because of the 'distinctive and exceptional situation in the mining industry' it was ready to promise that if the government could give an 'assurance' that it would make 'possible' a settlement between the NUM and the NCB then other unions would not 'use that as an argument in negotiations in their own settlements'.[52] Barber – after a rapid consultation with Sir William Armstrong, head of the civil service, who was with him – rejected the TUC offer outright even as a basis for discussion. A specially convened Congress of TUC affiliated union executives held on 16 January went on to endorse the TUC general council's initiative by a substantial majority but Heath remained unimpressed by what was on offer. He and his senior Cabinet colleagues simply did not believe that the TUC was making a serious proposal on which it could deliver. They were convinced that the electricity power workers would also demand a special deal in breach of Stage 3 of the government's incomes policy if the miners were allowed to secure a large wage increase beyond the maximum level permitted under the legislation.

By the first week of January, Heath for one was convinced that the motive behind the mining dispute had become essentially political. He believed left-wing extremists inside the NUM leadership were trying to provoke a showdown and drive him from office. Moreover, he was deeply suspicious about the manner in which the TUC's peace initiative had been sprung on the government without any prior consultation. Heath missed Feather's bonhomie in negotiations and regarded Len Murray who had succeeded Feather as TUC General Secretary in September 1973 as a cold and calculating partisan figure whom he could not trust. With hindsight, the Prime Minister's repeated refusal to seize the TUC initiative appears to have been at least a tactical mistake. Heath may have been correct in doubting whether the power workers and other groups with proven bargaining muscle who had not already settled under Stage 3 would have been willing to abide by the TUC's position. Ministers claimed that Frank Chapple, the EETPU's General Secretary, had said that while he was willing to make an exception in a pay deal for those coal miners who worked underground this did not apply to the surface workers whose wages were related to those of other groups outside the coal industry. But Chapple in his memoirs suggested that the government was wrong. Certainly, he was angry at the way in which the incomes policy had provoked conflict in the electrical contracting industry where long-standing legal agreements had been torn up. 'My primary aim was the best possible deal for our members, many of them the country's highest paid skilled workers', he argued. But he appeared to support the TUC's initiative of a special deal for the miners and suggested Heath had been 'wrong in every way, politically, industrially, tactically, even morally' by spurning the offer from Congress House. Chapple even accused Heath of exaggerating the crisis and pointed out that there were still enough coal stocks to last ten more weeks from the middle of January. 'Ted Heath's pigheadedness and his refusal to pick up the TUC olive branch in those Downing Street talks was his biggest error', claimed Chapple.[53]

Whatever the truth of the EETPU's real position, it was clear that the government was convinced that the union would not go along with the TUC peace initiative. What ministers failed to appreciate was that the EETPU was not the most important trade union in the electricity supply industry. The GMWU and the TGWU also had a large number of members working in the power stations and they would have been much more willing to back the TUC's position than the EETPU.

Moreover, now the power engineers had secured a pay agreement that was to their own satisfaction they may have been prepared to work normally if the manual workers had attempted to use disruptive action to break Stage 3 of the incomes policy.

The Prime Minister's own political position would certainly have been much stronger if he had been willing at least to test the sincerity of the TUC's initiative and then it had been found to lack credibility. However, the point at issue between the government and the TUC by the end of January had become one of trust. Heath believed he had been patient and reasonable throughout his interminable discussions with the TUC going back over the previous eighteen months and he was in no mood to go any further. Strong anti-union pressures were also building up inside the Conservative party by that stage, and a growing number of Heath's senior advisers were convinced that a general election would be needed to settle the crisis, with the return of a strong Conservative government with a clear mandate from the electorate to stand firm against the misuse of trade union power. His close confidant Sir William Armstrong became so overwhelmed by the pressure of work at this time that he had a nervous breakdown and was forced to abandon the scene.

But Heath hesitated in early January over a decision to call a general election; he still seemed to believe that a settlement could be reached with the NUM that would both satisfy the miners and yet somehow remain within the statutory pay limits of Stage 3. However, when Scanlon, the AUEW's President, asked him outright at a 10 Downing Street meeting on 21 January: 'Is there anything, anything at all, that we [the TUC] can do or say which will satisfy you?', the Prime Minister failed to reply.[54] As the TUC itself recorded: 'The TUC invited the government to state whether there were any circumstances in which it would be prepared to use the powers it had to deal with a claim (like the miner's) on an exceptional basis but no reply to this question was forthcoming'.[55] But in turn Heath asked the TUC leaders whether they could really hold the line if an exceptional pay settlement was conceded to the miners, and ministers made it clear that they did not respond with much confidence that this would indeed be possible.

It was still by no means inevitable that the crisis on the coalfields should have ended in a national strike. On 24 January, the NUM executive decided to ballot the members with a recommendation to vote in favour of an all-out dispute. But on that very same day ministers were presented with another opportunity to achieve a peaceful settlement. The Pay Board produced its report on the relativities problem in which it recommended the creation of a new Relativities Board to examine

Table 6.4   Public opinion and the miners

'Are you sympathies mainly with the employers or mainly with the miners in the dispute which has arisen in the coal industry?'

	Employers (%)	Miners (%)	Neither (%)	Don't now (%)
December 1973	26	41	23	10
January 1974	30	44	18	18
February 1974	27	48	18	7
February 1974	24	52	20	4

Source: Gallup.

Table 6.5   Public opinion: Who is to blame for the 1973–1974 crisis?

'Who do you think is mainly responsible for the present economic situation – the Government or the trade unions?'

	Government	Trade unions	Neither
December 1973	33	36	17
January 1974	31	49	12
February 1974	35	42	16
February 1974	32	39	22

Source: Gallup.

individual cases put to it on their merits. Heath accepted at once that the miners could be the first special group to be examined, but he insisted that this could only happen once the current dispute had been resolved and not before. Similarly, the government was also ready to carry out a full-scale examination of the needs of the mining industry in the light of the renewed importance of coal as a fuel to meet Britain's energy needs after the eventual quadrupling of oil prices. This offered the promise of a new deal for coal, but again Heath insisted it would have to wait for a settlement of the existing conflict.

Defeat and its aftermath

On 4 February 1974 the NUM announced the result of its pit head ballot vote with an 81 per cent support for a strike. The executive decided to begin an all-out national strike from 9 February. On the same day, the TUC leadership met Heath for the last time but it proved to be a fruitless exchange of views. By then the national drama had moved on. Two days before, Heath had announced the calling of a general election with polling day on 28 February. He believed the issue facing the voters would be 'Who governs the country?' His decision to dissolve Parliament and seek a fresh mandate was taken reluctantly but he believed there was now no other way out of the impasse. However, on the very same day, Heath changed his mind about waiting for the coal dispute to end before referring the miners' case for improved relativities to the Pay Board, something he had resisted doing before. This conciliatory move seemed strangely at odds with his parallel decision to seek a fresh mandate for his government from the electorate.

The grim tone of the Conservative campaign was well conveyed by the Conservative party's general election manifesto. Under a sub-heading 'The danger from within' it declared that the choice before the nation was stark. If Britain accepted the NUM's terms for a settlement it would 'mean accepting the abuse of industrial power to gain a privileged position', 'undermine the position of moderate trade union leaders', 'make certain similar strikes occurred at frequent intervals in the future', and 'destroy the chances of containing inflation'.[56] The government argued that while the miners were entitled to have a 'fair' settlement of their wage claim it was also important that any settlement should also be fair to the nearly 6 million workers who had already reached deals within the limits of Stage 3 of the counter-inflation policy and others who were ready to accept similar treatment. The manifesto declared that the Conservatives wanted to see a country 'united in moderation, not divided by extremism; a society in which there was change without revolution'. The party promised amendments to the 1971 Industrial Relations Act 'in the light of experience' after consulting with both sides of industry, which would 'make conciliation a precondition of court action' and 'provide more effective control for the majority of union members by ensuring that they have the opportunity to elect the governing bodies and national leaders of their unions by a postal ballot'.

After the overwhelming democratic verdict of the rank and file of the NUM in support of a strike in February 1974 it was hard to see how such a proposal would really have made much difference to the coal crisis. Moreover, the Conservative argument was based on the widely held but dubious assumption that 'a small number of militant extremists' could 'so manipulate and abuse the monopoly power of their unions as to cause incalculable damage to the country and the fabric of society itself' and that 'the best way of curbing the minority of extremists in the trade unions' was for 'the moderate majority of union members to stand up and be counted'. But the Conservative manifesto also sought to demonstrate that the government was still willing to be fair and reasonable in resolving the coal dispute. It pointed in particular to the fact that the principles of the Pay Board's pay relativities report had been accepted by the Cabinet and the new machinery was going to be used in a thorough examination of the miners' case. Moreover, the government also emphasized that it was 'prepared to undertake' that whatever recommendation the new body made for the miners would be backdated to 1 March.

Most observers believed Heath would win the general election, for the trade unions had grown highly unpopular with public opinion. But a number of fortuitous events occurred during the campaign that severely damaged the Conservative position. The government was not helped first of all by the public demand from Campbell Adamson, the CBI's Director-General, for the repeal of the 1971 Industrial Relations Act, a measure which he condemned for having 'sullied every relationship at national level between unions and employers'.[57] Even more damaging for Conservative electoral prospects was the revelation on 20 February just a week before polling day by Derek Robinson, deputy chairman of the Pay Board, that the wage relativity statistics being used by the NCB to justify their case against the miners were wrong. This appeared to imply that the whole conflict had been based on a false premise and the miners in fact had a much stronger case for special treatment to restore their lost relative position in the national earnings table than had been initially realized. Heath denied the suggestion vehemently but the public controversy over the facts of the miners' case undermined much of the government's credibility. Perhaps the most decisive factor in the outcome of the February 1974 general election, however, was the impeccable self-discipline shown by the striking miners themselves. Gormley had tried unsuccessfully to persuade the NUM executive to call off the strike for the duration of the campaign, but this attempt to lower the temperature was defeated by 20 votes to 6. However, during the second coal strike in two years there were none of the tumultuous scenes of mass secondary picketing outside power stations being displayed across the nation's television screens, as there had been in the 1972 coal strike, to convince the voters that the ugly face of trade union power needed to be dealt with. Moreover, as Heath soon discovered it was very difficult for the Conservatives to fight the whole of a general election merely on a single issue, no matter how overwhelming they believed it to be. Inevitably, as the days of the campaign went by the agenda of the nation's political debate widened to encompass the whole of the government's performance since it came to office in June 1970 and above all to focus on the desperate economic plight of the country with soaring inflation and a record balance of payments deficit.

In the event, the outcome of the general election proved to be indecisive. The Conservatives polled more votes than the Labour party but secured fewer seats, while the Liberals made a dramatic advance. Heath tried to persuade Jeremy Thorpe, the Liberal party's leader, to join him in a coalition government but he was turned down. On 2 March the Prime Minister resigned and Harold Wilson, as leader of the party with most MPs in the new Parliament, was asked by the Queen to form a minority Labour government. A few weeks later the miners' strike was settled very much on the NUM's terms with the backing of the Pay Board's relativities report.

Heath in opposition remained unrepentant about his reluctant decision to call the February 1974 general election and on presenting the issue of trade union power so forcefully to the voters. As he told his party's backbenchers soon after the Conservative defeat, the trade union 'question' would 'certainly recur throughout the lifetime of this Parliament and the party should be neither ashamed of having put it to the electorate in the past nor unready to do so in the future'.[58]

Certainly, the Conservatives drew some bitter lessons from their three years and eight months in office on how they should deal in future with the trade unions. The Labour government moved quickly to repeal the Industrial Relations Act and Heath accepted that there could be no return to such a comprehensive measure. Indeed, in the subsequent October 1974 general election the Conservatives did not campaign on an anti-union platform. The party even accepted Labour's 1974 Trade Union and Labour Relations Act as 'the basis for the law on trade union organisation and as the legal framework of collective bargaining'. 'We hope that our decision will help create a better climate for industrial partnership', declared the Conservatives.[59] The party also acknowledged that the trade unions were 'an important Estate of the Realm' and added that it would 'co-operate closely with them' while promising not to be 'dominated' by them.

Interestingly, under Heath's influence the Conservatives were looking not at draconian plans to crush trade union power but at the possibility of developing employee participation. The election manifesto promised to promote a partnership between both government and industry as well as capital and labour by introducing legislation to require large and mediumsized companies to consult their worker representatives on a wide range of issues, including disciplinary and dismissal procedures, redundancy arrangements, and both profit sharing and share ownership schemes. Although imprecise in details, the Conservatives indicated that in government they would 'set a clear example' in the public sector, and the nationalized industries would be expected to play their part. The programme also included extending worker rights through postal ballot elections for their leaders, government assistance in the training of shop stewards and union officers, ways of regulating the conduct of picketing along the strict lines enforced by the NUM in February 1974, and the right of trade unionists to hold meetings on their employers' premises. The only sting in the tail of the party's new approach to industrial relations was the Conservative determination to make the unions themselves 'accept a significant share of the responsibility for the welfare of the families of men' who went on strike. The positive ingredients of the party's new industrial relations policy were quite different to the legalistic regulations that had become hardened into an inflexible dogma in the late 1960s. But the Conservatives lost the October 1974 general election, though it was not the humiliation they had feared. Four months later Heath was deposed – in an astonishing election among Conservative MPs in what became known as the 'peasant's revolt' – by Margaret Thatcher, his former education secretary. A new era was about to begin for the Conservative party.

The downfall of Heath was a personal tragedy. His government's record became the subject for withering attack and derision not just from the other parties but also among many Conservatives, who believed his corporatist outlook had inflicted enormous damage on the working of the market economy and the party's free enterprise principles, while his prolonged attempt at industrial appeasement after the spring of 1972 had merely stimulated trade union arrogance and self-importance. Many of those judgements were unfair. The warm comments of union leaders like Jones and Gormley for Heath destroy the myth of the unbending anti-trade union Prime Minister who provoked unnecessary industrial conflict. It was clear from the events of 1972 that Heath was no inflexible or brutish ideologue. He believed in rational argument and persuasion, though he lacked the subtler arts of diplomacy. Faced by the prospect of registered unemployment rising and staying above one million, he changed economic course. Unfortunately for him his government was hemmed in by horrendous external events, particularly during its final months in office, over which it could exercise little direct influence, let alone control. More than any other of Britain's post-war governments Heath's was overwhelmed by an unhappy convergence of inter-related troubles.

But one lasting conviction did emerge from those years which was to influence Mrs Thatcher's strategy towards organized labour during the 1980s. Again, Douglas Hurd summed it up well when he wrote that Heath was broken by 'the brutal exercise of trade union power'.[60] This is what Conservatives believed, rightly or wrongly. Heath's critics argued he had been too willing to bend over backwards to placate the TUC, to appeal to the reason and better nature of trade union leaders who were swollen with power and privilege. All sides of the party agreed about the repugnant behaviour of organized labour even when they were unsure of what to do about it.

The brief Heath interlude witnessed some of the most tumultuous scenes in Britain's industrial history. The myths on both sides seemed stronger than the realities. To many Conservatives, trade unions had indeed become 'the enemy within', while to union activists (if not their members) Heath's government, particularly before 1972, was seen as a provocation – a dangerous threat to the post-war social settlement. However, the upsurge of industrial conflict at that time was not limited to Britain. It reflected a pattern that emerged across much of the Western industrialized world. The wider unrest was mainly stimulated by a shopfloor reaction to the impact of inflation and taxation on earnings levels, but it also reflected much of the restless, undefined spirit which was manifest in the May 1968 'events' in France, the peace movement in the United States against the Vietnam war, Italy's 'hot autumn' of 1969, and the student revolt everywhere in the Western world.

The crisis of 1973–4 brought the beginning of the end to that period as the industrialized economies struggled to adapt to a new, more dangerously unstable world with the collapse of the post-war international economic order. The crucial problems discussed between Beveridge and the TUC back in 1944 on how to reconcile wage bargaining with low inflation and full employment were no nearer solution. Indeed, an increasingly influential body of economic opinion began to cast doubt on the wisdom of such devices as incomes policies as a means of moderating wage pressures and the use of demand management by governments to stimulate economic growth. In contrast, they advocated tight control of the money supply, laws to curb trade union power, and supply side measures designed to create a more efficient labour market. Above all, they were willing to accept the abandonment of full employment as a policy objective. These ideological changes did not flow inevitably from the defeat of Heath, but his denouement amidst a welter of debt and inflation coupled with industrial mayhem suggested that the old tripartite ways were no longer realizable in a country where the social solidarity of the war years had virtually disappeared. Like Hurd, many observers regarded the Heath period as being the 'necessary first attempt' to deal with a range of problems that troubled Britain through the 1970s – inflation, unemployment, and 'overweening union power', as well as 'industrial and agricultural stagnation, weakness in Europe and the world'.[61]

Heath's 1970–2 attempt to create a more abrasive free market economy, at least before his so-called policy U-turn was treated very much as a precursor to Thatcherism. More plausibly, Heath can be seen as the last One Nation Tory leader, anxious to modernize the country but through the utilization of what remained of the post-war social settlement. Most union leaders, however, failed to recognize this, which is why he remains Britain's most misunderstood post-war Prime Minister – a conciliator whose government became a byword for industrial confrontation.

Notes

1   Conservative party archives, Oxford.
2   Ibid.
3   Ibid.
4   Ibid.
5   Ibid.
6   Ibid.
7   Ibid.
8   Ibid.
9   *Putting Britain Right Ahead*, 1965, p. 8.
10   Ibid., p. 13.
11   *Fair Deal at Work*, Conservative Party, 1968, p. 36.
12   Ibid., p. 47.
13   National Union Annual Conference report, 1967, pp. 94–5.
14   National Union Annual Conference report, 1969, pp. 35–6, 37.
15   P. Whitehead, *The Writing on the Wall*, Michael Joseph, 1985, p. 70.
16   *A Better Tomorrow*, Conservative party general manifesto, 1970, in F. W. S. Craig (ed.), *British General Election Manifestos*, Dartmouth, 1990, p. 113.
17   D. Hurd, *An End to Promises*, Collins, 1976, p. 95.
18   Wilberforce electricity supply report, HMSO, 1971, p. 6.
19   J. Prior, *A Balance of Power*, Hamish Hamilton, 1986, p. 72.
20   Whitehead, *Writing on the Wall*, p. 71.
21   National Union Conference report, 1970, p. 34.
22   P. Whitehead, *Writing on the Wall*, p. 73.
23   National Union Conference report, 1971, p. 63.
24   M. Moran, *The Politics of Industrial Relations*, Macmillan, 1977, p. 123.
25   *Guidance to Employers on The Industrial Relations Act*, Confederation of British Industry, 1971, pp. 5, 41.
26   B. Sewill, *British Economic Policy 1970–1974*, Institute of Economic Affairs, 1975, p. 33.

27 TUC Special Congress report, 1971, p. 4.
28 Ibid., p. 7.
29 TUC Congress report, 1971, p. 427.
30 P. Whitehead, *Writing on the Wall*, p. 74.
31 J. Gormley, *Battered Cherub*, Hamish Hamilton, 1982, p. 96.
32 A. Scargill, 'The New Unionism', *New Left Review*, 92, July–August 1975, pp. 19–20.
33 B. Sewill, *British Economic Policy*, p. 50.
34 D. Hurd, *An End to Promises*, p. 103.
35 J. Gormley, *Battered Cherub*, p. 106.
36 Wilberforce Inquiry Report, 1972, Cmnd 4903, HMSO, p. 10.
37 J. Gormley, *Battered Cherub*, pp. 117, 118.
38 P. Whitehead, *Writing on the Wall*, p. 77.
39 Ibid., p. 78.
40 J. Jones, *Union Man*, Collins, 1986, p. 259.
41 TUC Congress report, 1973, p. 215.
42 D. Hurd, *An End to Promises*, pp. 104–5.
43 Hansard Parliamentary Debates, Vol. 852, 13 March 1973, c. 1144–5.
44 K. Middlemas, *Power, Competition and The State*, Vol. 2, Macmillan, 1990, p. 357.
45 D. Barnes and E. Reid, *Governments and Trade Unions*, Heinemann, 1980, p. 172.
46 Ibid., p. 175.
47 B. Sewill, *British Economic Policy*, p. 55.
48 TUC Congress report, 1974, p. 234.
49 J. Gormley, *Battered Cherub*, p. 127.
50 Ibid., p. 134.
51 Ibid., p. 135.
52 *The TUC's Initiative*, TUC, 1974, p. 8.
53 F. Chapple, *Sparks Fly*, Michael Joseph, 1984, pp. 136–7.
54 P. Whitehead, ibid., p. 108.
55 *The TUC's Initiative*, p. 10.
56 Conservative party election manifesto, February 1974, in Craig (ed.), *British General Election Manifestos*, pp. 161–5.
57 D. E. Butler and D. Kavanagh, *The British General Election of February 1974*, Macmillan, 1974, p. 85.
58 D. E. Butler and D. Kavanagh, *The British General Election of October 1974*, Macmillan, 1975, p. 67.
59 Conservative party election manifesto, October 1974, in Craig (ed.), *British General Election Manifestos*, pp. 222–3.
60 D. Hurd, *An End to Promises*, p. 150.
61 Ibid., p. 142.

7 Labour and the Social Contract, June 1970 to May 1979

Making the contract

In the aftermath of Labour's unexpected but decisive electoral defeat in June 1970 a short-lived debate immediately broke out inside the party over the issue of incomes policy. The trauma of Mrs Castle's failed attempt to legislate against unofficial strikes had not been forgotten and many trade union leaders remained bitter at what had happened in the summer of 1969. They were also determined not to cooperate in any repetition of the statutory prices and incomes policy that the Labour government had tried to use to impose wage restraint in the national interest. But there were those in the party who did not believe the issue of wage bargaining under Labour could be ignored. They argued that it remained of fundamental importance because it concerned how a future Labour government could hope to achieve its objectives of greater social equality and justice without a close understanding with the trade unions on wage bargaining. The familiar dilemma was once more clear: how was it possible to reconcile the sectionalist and economistic aspirations of trade union members for the good life with the commitment of the socialist activist minority who wanted to create a more rational, equitable and planned economy? Would a future Labour government be able to do any better than its predecessors in managing the national economy, ensuring the maintenance of full employment and preventing further bouts of self-destructive wage-push inflation?

In an important Fabian Society pamphlet published in October 1970, Wilson's former economic adviser Lord Thomas Balogh emphasized the dangers of union militancy to the country's economic well-being. As he explained:

> Once unions, in their wage demands and firms in their investment and other decisions, anticipate further increases in prices, they will take defen-

sive action by increasing their wage demands and prices respectively. This would accelerate and aggravate the process. Should it intensify, the creep of inflation might become a walk, a trot, a canter and eventually a gallop. In the end it would cause unemployment and undermine the currency.[1]

Balogh pointed out that Britain's trade unions were unable, because of their limited power in the economy, to increase the share of total national income that was devoted to wages. As a result, the so-called 'free' collective bargaining they practised tended to widen still further existing earnings inequalities rather than narrow them. 'A free for all in the labour market is incompatible with the achievement either of full employment or of a satisfactory rate of expansion of material resources needed for a better, fuller, more civilised and humane way of life', he argued. Balogh proposed as a way out of the problem that the political and industrial wings of the Labour Movement should establish a '*contrat social*' between themselves to avoid the mistakes and conflicts that had bedevilled their relationship during the later 1960s by breaking the inflationary spiral. In his opinion, a national incomes policy was a crucial element in a much wider Labour strategy designed to strengthen the role of the trade unions.

At the 1970 Labour party conference, speaking in support of a National Executive Committee statement *Building a Socialist Nation*, Callaghan questioned aloud how it was really possible to secure social justice for and between workers in a wages free for all and wondered if there was not a 'better way' to organize the collective bargaining system. 'It is only fair to the next Labour government to know in advance what doors will be shut against them before you get there', he added.[2] The former Chancellor of the Exchequer and Home Secretary was not left in much doubt for long about what senior union leaders thought. In moving a resolution which expressed 'total opposition to restrictions on collective bargaining', Jack Jones, General Secretary of the TGWU, took the opportunity to launch a fierce attack on journalists and 'some politicians' who, he alleged to prolonged applause, 'for the most part had never been covered by a wage claim because frankly they have never worked for a living'.[3] The AEU's President Hugh Scanlon suggested the Labour party could start talking about a Socialist incomes policy 'when we own the means of production, distribution and exchange'.[4] Such strong and unequivocal hostility to any suggestion of a future incomes policy from the leaders of Britain's two largest trade unions made it abundantly clear to Wilson and his senior colleagues that whatever doubts they might have shared themselves over the question of pay determination, it would be impossible for them to advocate a national incomes policy as part of Labour's programme without provoking a severe split inside the party with its trade union allies.

However, if it was virtually impossible to have a serious discussion about an incomes policy inside the Labour Movement during the early 1970s, this did not mean the party–union alliance fell apart or grew more strained. On the contrary, under Jones's powerful stimulus, a genuine attempt was made to heal the wounds inflicted by the 1969 *In Place of Strife* controversy and establish a much closer structural relationship between the two sides of the Labour Movement. Jones launched his initiative at the 1971 party conference. He told delegates:

> There is no reason at all why a joint policy cannot be worked out. But let us have the closest possible liaison. Let us put an end to the stress and strain between the trade union and intellectual wings of the party. This is not just a matter of brainstorming in the back rooms of Congress House and Transport House just before the next election. In the past we have not had the dialogue necessary. The unions and the party leadership perhaps have both been unsure of their own ground but we can make this policy into a great campaign to open up the approach to genuine industrial democracy based on the unions.[5]

The political and industrial wings of the Labour Movement were already beginning to create a new cohesion and sense of purpose through their united opposition to the Conservatives' 1971 Industrial Relations Act, and Callaghan's firm public declaration in April 1971 that the Labour party would repeal that hated measure if it was returned to office at the next general election did much to reconcile differences of view that had festered inside the unions after their unhappy experience with the Wilson government.

The Labour–TUC Liaison Committee met for the first time on 23 January 1972. It grew rapidly into an important policy-making forum inside the party and for most of the 1970s acted almost as a substitute for the National Executive. The 18 strong body consisted of six senior figures from the TUC general council, Labour's Shadow Cabinet and the party's National Executive Committee to work in what it was hoped would be close and effective harmony binding all sides together in support of commonly agreed policies. As Jones admitted it 'took a devil of a lot of pressure' to overcome the objections to the idea from the National Executive Committee, who did not want representatives from the Shadow Cabinet on the new body.[6] During the late 1960s the National Executive Committee had moved to the Left and saw the proposed new committee as a potential threat to its own position. But as Jones argued: 'To most of us at the TUC it would have been a waste of time if the MPs had not been there. We wanted commitments, especially for the repeal of the Industrial Relations Act and only the leaders of the Party could deliver these.' Not since the revival of the National Council of Labour after the Labour party's 1931 election debacle had there been such a formalized attempt to bring all parts of the Labour Movement together in such a regular and systematic way. From the very outset, Jones saw the Liaison Committee as a 'means of ensuring regular consultation with a Labour government when it was in office'.

The new body used to meet on the first Monday of every month, alternating its meetings between Transport House, the House of Commons and Congress House – with a rotating chairman and joint servicing by the TUC secretariat and the Labour party research department. During its first two years of existence the Liaison Committee hammered out what became known as the Social Contract between the TUC and the Labour party. Within six months, its first joint statement appeared on industrial relations policy. It called for the repeal of the 1971 Industrial Relations Act and the creation of a new independent Conciliation and Arbitration Service made up of union and employer representatives together with 'other persons with industrial relations experience' to help in resolving labour problems. The document also proposed an extension of worker rights such as the right of a worker to belong to a trade union and enjoy legal protection against unfair dismissal, as well as shorter qualifying periods of employment for minimum notice, and longer periods of notice from employers. Trade unions were also to be given the legal power to take before an arbitration committee employers who refused union recognition, or who would not disclose company information for collective bargaining purposes; the committee would have the right to make a binding award on employers over individual employment contracts. Trade union representatives were also to be provided with statutory rights in safety and health at work questions. What was clear from the Liaison Committee's first pronouncement was that it would be the TUC itself who would decide what kind of law replaced the discredited Industrial Relations Act. Through the new body, Congress House had secured a substantial direct say in the making of Labour domestic policy in a crucial area. It is doubtful whether Woodcock would have accepted such a development with equanimity because there is little doubt that the TUC's freedom for manoeuvre had been heavily circumscribed as a result. But the emergence of the Social Contract suggested that there would be much a closer and equal relationship between the TUC and the next Labour government than was ever really apparent between October 1964 and June 1970.

In the summer of 1972 the Liaison Committee decided to extend the range of its policy agenda beyond industrial relations issues to cover

Labour's future economic policy. It began to look at the obstacles to future growth prospects, such as inflation and the balance of payments. The Liaison Committee also examined regional policy and new strategies to deal with unemployment. The next policy statement was published in January 1973 when Wilson and TUC General Secretary Vic Feather unveiled their joint approach in *Economic Policy and the Cost of Living*. This amounted to a shopping list of proposals which were to be introduced by the next Labour government, similar in content to that presented by the TUC to Heath in its marathon talks with him during 1972. The document called for a control of basic food prices and public transport fares through the introduction of subsidies, a 'large scale' redistribution of wealth and income, the phasing out of social service charges and an 'immediate commitment' to raise old age pensions to £16 a week for a married couple and £10 a week for a single person. The Liaison Committee statement added that it would be a new Labour government's 'first task' to conclude a 'wide ranging agreement' with the TUC 'on the policies to be pursued in all these aspects of our economic life and to discuss with them the order of priorities for their fulfilment'.[7] There was no reference to any suggestion of having an incomes policy. But the document did indicate the new mutually agreed approach would 'further engender the strong feeling of mutual confidence which alone will make it possible to reach the wide-ranging agreement which is necessary to control inflation and achieve sustained growth in the standard of living'. As Wilson noted later, 'This was widely interpreted as a voluntary agreement to accept restraint in pay demands as part of a wider social agreement.'[8] A further policy declaration emerged from the Liaison Committee in July 1973, which expressed strong criticism of the impact of the European Community's agricultural policy on British food prices and called for an urgent reform of the CAP.

At the same time the left-dominated National Executive Committee under the inspiration of Tony Benn began to formulate a much more sweeping programme of economic and industrial change than anything envisaged by the party leadership. This included plans for the nationalization of the country's largest 25 companies, state intervention into private industry through compulsory planning agreements, the creation of the National Enterprise Board – a state holding company with sweeping powers – and finally a strong dose of industrial democracy. The militant mood among delegates at the 1973 party conference reflected the shift to the Left in Labour's ranks. This was reflected in the party's lengthy new programme which promised 'to bring about a fundamental and irreversible shift in the balance of power and wealth in favour of working people'.[9]

Fighting a belated rearguard action against much of what was being proposed, Wilson was able to veto the nationalization proposals in the run-up to the general election but the party's February 1974 manifesto still remained a highly left-wing document. In fact, its contents made no difference to the outcome of the general election.

Labour minority government

The Labour party became the beneficiary of the mistakes and tribulations of the Heath government. Thanks to Britain's first-past-the post electoral system – Labour actually polled far fewer votes than in 1970 – as a result of a Liberal upsurge it became the party with the largest number of seats in the House of Commons. However, although Labour had 301 MPs it lacked an overall majority. After four days of uncertainty over the outcome Harold Wilson formed a minority Labour government. The new Prime Minister entered 10 Downing Street to face the most critical outlook of any government since 1945. The long post-war period of economic expansion in the Western industrialized world had come to an end with the quadrupling of oil prices in the aftermath of the Yom Kippur War. Britain's balance of payments deficit had risen dramatically to £4 billion in the fourth quarter of 1973, its highest level since statistics were first collected in 1922. In February 1974 alone the deficit amounted to £383 million. The country's inflation rate was moving rapidly upwards with a year on year increase by February 1974 of 13.1 per cent, while the money supply had expanded by 27 per cent during 1973 alone. In the first two months of 1974 Britain's visible trade deficit soared to £800 million. As a result of Heath's dash for growth the Public Sector Borrowing Requirement climbed to over £4 billion in the 1973/74 fiscal year. At the same time industrial output had fallen away sharply.

But without an overall Commons majority, Wilson and his Cabinet colleagues were in no position to bring in the necessary and painful economic policies that were needed. Understandably, they wanted to concentrate on passing short-term popular measures to strengthen Labour's public opinion poll ratings. Most observers believed an early second general election was inevitable and this would give the Labour party a clear working Commons majority as long as the government avoided any austerity measures that squeezed average living standards. In fact, during its seven months in office before the October 1974 general election the minority Labour government carried through most of the Liaison Committee's initial set of proposals under the Social Contract. Indeed, the TUC general council enjoyed a more direct and substantial influence over government policy during that short period of time than it had ever experienced before or would do again.

It was symptomatic of the new relationship that Wilson met the whole of the TUC general council in 10 Downing Street within a few hours of forming his government. The union leaders were delighted at his decision to appoint the veteran left-winger Michael Foot as Employment Secretary instead of giving the post to Reg Prentice who had been shadow Employment spokesman but lacked credibility with the TUC. Union leaders regarded Prentice as hostile to Congress House interests because he had been less than enthusiastic about outright resistance to the Industrial Relations Act and continued to talk about the need for a nationally agreed incomes policy. Foot was able to push through Parliament in rapid time the repeal of the Industrial Relations Act with the resulting abolition of the National Industrial Relations Court. The hated measure was replaced by the 1974 Trade Union and Labour Relations Act (TULRA), which had been mainly drafted inside Congress House with the help of the eminent labour law academic Professor Bill Wedderburn. This brought a return of the familiar legal immunities and an almost complete restoration of the pre-1971 position. Under pressure from the House of Lords, however, the legal immunities were drawn rather more narrowly than the TUC had wanted them to be. It was not until 1976 that the government was able to widen the protection of legal immunities for trade unions through amendments to the 1974 Act. These enabled the trade unions to induce the breaking of commercial contracts in a lawful trade dispute as well as contracts of employment. It was a change the TUC had been lobbying for since the late 1960s.

New industrial relations institutions were also established that were to outlive both the Labour government and the years of Mrs Thatcher. The independent Advisory Conciliation and Arbitration Service (ACAS), formed in 1974 but given statutory powers a year later, was one tripartite body that Mrs Thatcher did not seek to destroy and it continued to thrive during the 1980s in the resolution of potential industrial disputes, dealing with individual worker complaints and seeking to encourage good labour relations practices. The Central Arbitration Committee, the Employment Appeal Tribunal and the Certification Officer (replacing the old Registrar) also sought to implement the new approach.

It is true that the TUC did not achieve everything it wanted through the 1974 Act. It was unable, for example, to insist that only workers of genuine religious conviction could be excluded from closed shops. The TUC disliked the government's suggestion that 'conscientious objectors' should be protected from dismissal if they refused to join a trade union in a recognized closed shop. Union leaders also failed to achieve their demand that pickets must have the legal immunity to stop vehicles and peacefully persuade drivers not to cross picket lines in trade disputes. Foot explained that the government lacked a parliamentary majority to make all the legal changes the TUC wanted. Again it was not until two years later that amendments were made to the Trade Union and Labour Relations Act to satisfy Congress House by making it much more difficult for workers to use legal loopholes as a way of being able to avoid having to join a trade union in a closed shop. There is little doubt that both pieces of legislation helped to ensure the growth of the closed shop during the late 1970s to 23 per cent of the workforce, around 5.2 million workers, compared with a 16 per cent penetration rate in the early 1960s. But what was not given enough emphasis in the debate over the issue of compulsory trade unionism was the positive attitude displayed by many large employers towards the establishment of 100 per cent union membership agreements in their establishments. It has been argued authoritatively: 'To counter powerful shop-floor trade unionism built up over a long period, management sought to involve union representatives on detailed formal regulation of the workplace and saw compulsory unionism as an aid to their joint influence over the workforce.'[10]

There is, however, little doubt that some trade unions grew more intolerant after 1974 in their imposition of the closed shop than they had been before. On the railways, a number of workers were dismissed by British Rail for refusing to join a recognized union, though they had been employed on the railways for many years. The men took their cases to the European Court of Human Rights where they won eventually. But the railway cases were rather exceptional. For the most part, the unions operated post-entry closed shops in a flexible manner. These made union membership a condition of employment. The TUC established an Independent Review Committee in order to deal with particular cases of individual worker grievance in closed shops to allay popular doubts.

In 1974 the Labour government also passed the Health and Safety at Work Act. Drawn up initially by the Conservatives, the measure was strengthened through TUC pressure to ensure its enforcement became much more effective through the introduction of workplace trade union safety representatives and safety committees though these did not come into legal existence until October 1978, delayed at the insistence of employers. Measures were also passed under Labour to deal with sex discrimination and racial discrimination in 1975 and 1976 respectively. Despite their undoubted limitations, these measures provided legal means of redress for individual workers with grievances through the use of the industrial tribunals.

Rapid progress was also made in the first few months of the Labour government in preparing the way for the return of free collective bargaining. The Pay Board was abolished in July 1974 and with it the remnants of Heath's statutory incomes policy, except for the ruinously inflationary monthly threshold payments that expired four months later. But the Price Commission remained in existence and its statutory powers were strengthened. Denis Healey, Chancellor of the Exchequer, won the TUC's warm approval for his first two budgets in March and July 1974 with a £500 million increase in subsidies on basic foodstuffs, a big increase in old age pensions and the value of welfare benefits, a freeze on both public and private sector rents, and higher taxes on the rich coupled with the promise of new taxes on wealth and the transfer of capital. However, Congress House was not pleased with a rise in the price of coal, electricity and postal services, nor the smaller than wished for defence expenditure cuts. For the time being, the minority Labour government seemed content to try and avoid deflation through a strategy of economic expansion and borrowing to finance the balance of payments deficit, as well as statutory price controls and voluntary pay restraint. In his memoirs, Healey admitted his policy of expansion made the balance of payments worse because it was not possible for Britain to grow alone when the rest of the world was contracting. Moreover, his budgets had been devised in the fond hope that the trade unions would 'respond by limiting their wage increases to what was needed to compensate for price increases in the previous year' as he maintained they 'had agreed to do in their so-called Social Contract with the Government'.[11]

At the September 1974 Congress, Callaghan as Labour's fraternal delegate declared that the Social Contract had become a 'means of achieving nothing less than the social and economic reconstruction' of the country.[12] The TUC's enthusiasm for the new Labour government's policies was not hard to understand. Congress House drew up a statement for the 1974 Congress, *Collective Bargaining and the Social Contract*, which was a virtual check list of what the Labour government had achieved since coming to office. It amounted to an item by item implementation of the February 1973 Liaison Committee statement on economic policy. 'Since taking office the government has demonstrated their commitment to implementing the general approach' of the Social Contract, asserted the TUC.[13] As Joel Barnett, Chief Secretary to the Treasury, noted: 'The only give and take in the contract was that the government gave and the unions took'.[14] The one real setback for Congress House came in its failure to secure the release from jail of two construction workers convicted of criminal behaviour during the 1972 national building strike. Here Roy Jenkins, the Home Secretary, remained unimpressed by the TUC's call for clemency and despite internal pressure on him from some of his Cabinet colleagues, notably Foot, he refused to accede to the TUC's demands.

To many people outside the Labour Movement, during 1974 and 1975 it looked as though the TUC had become the dominant political force in the country. There were those – if the lurid revelations of former secret agent Peter Wright are to be believed – in the British intelligence services who regarded Jones and Scanlon as national security risks working to subvert the state. Such reports about industrial subversion were presented to Wilson, who was himself the object of deep suspicion among maverick far right elements inside MI5. In the hysterical atmosphere of the time, anything seemed possible. Preposterous rumours circulated of a possible military take-over to pre-empt what the coup leaders suggested was a Soviet-style revolution, as had happened a year earlier in President Allende's Chile. Union leaders were denounced as cloth cap colonels of the class war. Mocked and feared, they became the enemies of society. The journalist Paul Johnson gave fevered pen to this mood as he moved ideologically from the *New Statesman* Left to the anti-union Thatcherite Right:

> Huge unions, pursuing wage claims at any cost, have successfully smashed other elements in the state – governments, political parties, private industry, nationalised boards – and now find themselves amid the wreckage of a deserted battlefield the undoubted victors. They did not plan the victory and they do not know what to do with it now they have got it. Dazed and bewildered, they are like medieval peasants who have burnt down the lord's manor.[15]

The public perception that trade unions had grown much too powerful by the middle of the 1970s was reflected in the findings of opinion poll surveys. Gallup discovered in January 1977 that 53 per cent of people thought Jack Jones of the TGWU wielded most power and influence in the country, compared to 25 per cent for Jim Callaghan. Rightly or wrongly, the forces of organized labour were regarded by many people as a threat to democracy and the market economy. But this was only a very partial picture. Indeed, the notion of over-mighty trade unions grew into a dangerous myth that distorted the complex realities of industrial relations during the 1970s.

In the same period more and more workers were joining trade unions.

They did so not because they were being dragooned into the unions by militants in the workplace but mainly because they saw trade union membership as a necessary protection for themselves against the ravaging impact of high inflation on their living standards, at a time when the political and legal climate seemed more favourably disposed towards trade union expansion and recognition than ever before. While the cumulative impact of the Social Contract's pro-union legislation turned out to be much less dramatic than seemed likely, it was to have a symbolic importance in giving the widespread, though misleading, popular impression that Britain's trade unions were becoming powerful organizations.

Towards hyper-inflation?

The outward semblance of unity between the TUC and the Labour government throughout 1974 belied serious misgivings and unease among ministers over the vexatious issue of wage bargaining. Throughout all its discussions before January 1974, the Liaison Committee had steered well clear of any discussion about the possibility of whether or not there should be any incomes policy under a future Labour government. After the savage manner in which Callaghan's tentative views on the subject had been rejected so publicly at the 1970 party conference by both Jones and Scanlon, the party leadership was understandably reluctant to raise the question of incomes policy again in the interests of Labour Movement unity. As Barbara Castle explained,

> So bruised and sensitive were the trade unions that any mention even of a voluntary policy was taboo. When at one of the Liaison Committee meetings someone dared to refer to the role of incomes in the management of the economy, Jack Jones jumped in at once to say 'It would be disastrous if any word went from this meeting that we had been discussing prices and incomes policy.'[16]

In fact, it was only on the very eve of the February 1974 general election campaign that the subject was placed on the agenda and then in only a highly tentative way. At the Liaison Committee meeting on 9 January 1974 Wilson asked the union leaders without pressing for a pay norm or 'rigid commitments' whether, 'if the Labour government fulfilled its side of the social compact, the TUC for its part would try to make the economic policy work'. Len Murray, recently appointed as TUC General Secretary, replied that the greatest disservice Congress House could do the Labour party was 'to pretend it could do more than it could and the disillusion from that would be far more damaging than the refusal to make impossible promises in the first place'. This was an interesting observation in the light of his attempt to convince Heath earlier in the very same month that TUC's affiliated unions would not exploit a special wage deal for the miners to further their own pay aspirations. However, Murray assured Wilson that the TUC would 'respond' to what a Labour government did in office to meet its demands and at least the unions would observe the final months of Stage 3 of Heath's statutory incomes policy before its expiry at the end of June. To vigorous nodding from Murray, Wilson emphasized that what they needed was 'more the creation of a mood than a compact'.[17] The sensitive incomes policy issue was in fact left unresolved in February 1974 but it appeared that for the time being the TUC would be given the opportunity to show what it could do in persuading its affiliated unions to exercise voluntary pay bargaining in a responsible way.

A free-for-all

After 1 July 1974 the trade unions were free from any state imposed constraints on their collective bargaining activities. As Callaghan assured the 1974 Congress: 'Rigid wage controls, statutory controls, interference with free collective bargaining have all finished, whistled down the wind, a complete failure.'[18] Now the Labour government was placing all its faith on the trade unions alone to negotiate wage and fringe benefit improvements for their members in a prudent manner. Ministers hoped that the substantial increase they were providing in the so-called 'social wage' for workers and their families through enhanced welfare and other state benefits would lessen the shopfloor pressure for fatter pay packets. The TUC general council agreed unanimously on 26 June 1974 to propose voluntary guidelines to assist the negotiators. 'Over the coming years negotiators generally should recognise that the scope for real increases in consumption are limited and a central negotiating objective in this period will be to ensure that real incomes are maintained', the TUC explained to affiliated unions.[19] But the TUC also emphasized a wide range of priorities, which seemed enough to cover almost every contingency. There was to be a low pay basic minimum rate of £25 a week. Productivity bargaining was encouraged as well as the reform of pay structures, moves to equal pay and improved fringe benefits like better sick pay, improved occupational pensions and longer holidays. The TUC insisted there should be orderly bargaining with a twelve month interval between pay rises.

Congress House did not accept that there was to be a wages free-for-all in the aftermath of the statutory incomes policy. Murray argued that the TUC's guidelines involved 'a degree of self-restraint as a means of breaking the shackles of slow economic growth and social injustice that had for too long bound the trade union movement'.[20]

In November 1974 the TUC sent out a warning circular to all its affiliated unions pointing out that it would be 'far better to get prices rising more slowly, with money wages correspondingly not going up so fast, than to have prices and wages equating with each other at a higher and higher level which would inevitably be self-defeating for most trade unionists'.[21] But few union negotiators took any notice of the TUC's advice during the 1974–5 wage round as average pay rises began to climb to 31 per cent by the second quarter of 1975. The frightening escalation of wage-push inflation was encouraged by the triggering each month of the threshold agreements that had been part of Heath's statutory incomes policy devised in November 1973, before the quadrupling of oil prices. No less than 11 threshold payments were made before the agreements ended in November 1974 and as Ormerod has argued 'they played a major part in the acceleration of the annual rate of increase of earnings from 12.5 per cent in the fourth quarter of 1973 to 25.5 per cent in the fourth quarter of 1974'.[22] But wage-push pressure showed no signs of easing off during the early months of 1975 either. On the contrary, despite occasional public warnings by Murray and Jones of the need for voluntary wage restraint, there was an almost Gadarene-like rush by the trade unions into ever more exorbitant pay demands which employers swallowed in inflationary settlements they passed on in higher prices. The NUM showed that it was just as ready to press for huge wage increases under a Labour government as it had been with the Conservatives in power by securing a 33 per cent pay settlement for its members in March 1975, the biggest percentage rise in the history of the union.

But ministers were growing increasingly alarmed at the rapid deterioration of the economy which achieved a record high balance of payments deficit in 1974 of £3.75 billion and with the rate of inflation rocketing to over 25 per cent. Union leaders seemed powerless to contain the demands of their members for higher and higher money wages which led to pay settlement increases that averaged as much as 29 per cent in 1974. For its part, the TUC kept on pressing through the winter of 1974–5 for more reflation and public spending to counter the growing increase in registered unemployment as it moved remorselessly towards the official figure of one million. But Healey's patience with the TUC was beginning to wear thin by early 1975. In a speech in Leeds in January he warned it was 'irresponsible lunacy to ignore the fact that wages were the main cause of inflation'.[23] None of the wage bargainers took much notice. More than half the pay settlements made in the 1974–5 wage round involved increases that were 8 to 9 per cent or more above the rise in the retail price index. But now slowly and belatedly the government began to reassert some of its long lost authority. Healey's spring 1975 Budget was not to the liking of Congress House. Instead of boosting public expenditure by £950 million as the TUC had wanted he did the opposite, cutting £100 million from public spending programmes and reducing domestic demand by £350 million. Moreover, union leaders were concerned to hear the Chancellor admit that the government would be unable to prevent the level of registered unemployment going over one million for the first time since the 1930s. They also disliked his warning that there might well have to be lower living standards and further cuts imposed on government expenditure if the voluntary incomes policy did not adhere more strictly to the TUC's own guidelines. But neither side wanted to see the collapse of the Social Contract. 'There must be continued co-operation in order to prevent unnecessary misunderstandings and divisions', asserted the Liaison Committee.[24]

In fact, even the TUC was becoming concerned at the high level of wage settlements. In April 1975 it admitted 'there had been undesirable gaps in the observance' of its own pay guidelines and in typical Congress House understatement warned that:

> if settlements in the next round of negotiations were pitched at the level of some of those negotiated towards the middle of the year or if new settlements were made before the due date, the prospect of reducing inflation towards the end of the year and during next year [1976] would be seriously threatened.[25]

The irrational scramble for more money wages in the spring and early summer of 1975 was essentially a destructive process as workers sought desperately to safeguard the size of pay packets whose value was being swallowed up by rising prices. In the second quarter of the year there was actually a decline in real disposable incomes of 2.5 to 3.0 per cent, the largest fall suffered in 20 years. Murray recalled later the feverish atmosphere of the time:

> I remember those union conferences passing resolutions calling for wage increases of 30%–40%. I also remember in tea rooms, in bars, the delegates – the same delegates who were voting the 30% wage increases – saying to me directly; 'Look, we've got to do something about this. We can't go on like this.'[26]

The flat rate policy

By the spring of 1975 it was becoming increasingly clear that urgent government action was needed to stop the pay escalation from triggering a major economic crisis but the Cabinet was slow to respond, mainly because Wilson was anxious to avoid any return to a statutory incomes policy for fear this would provoke damaging TUC resistance. Belatedly, however, Jones began to realize that the irresponsible wage bonanza could not go on through a second twelve month period without inflicting grave damage both on the economy and the Labour government's hopes of political survival. Barbara Castle noticed his gradual change of mood at meetings of the Liaison Committee. Once regarded as 'the archetypal trade union villain' he was transforming himself into 'an almost gentle and certainly benign influence'.[27] The great champion of shopfloor collective bargaining now realized a comprehensive strategy for wage determination was needed in the national interest. Otherwise there was a real danger of an economic catastrophe and the probable downfall of the Labour government. In early May 1975 Jones told a TGWU rally in Bournemouth that a new approach was needed on pay which ought to involve a flat rate wage increase for everybody, related to the cost of living. It was a simple and immediately understandable idea but it also reflected the bargaining interests of the TGWU's unskilled and low paid members and meant an inevitable erosion in the pay relativities and differentials of more skilled workers who belonged to other trade unions. Joe Haines, Wilson's press aide, had also come to the conclusion that a flat rate pay policy was necessary and the Downing Street Policy Unit worked effectively to achieve agreement.

Strenuous negotiations were held between the TUC and the government through May and June to try and reach a firm understanding on pay restraint as the economic outlook appeared to be deteriorating by the day. Healey told an all-day Cabinet meeting at Chequers on 20 June that £1 billion worth of public spending cuts might be needed to reassure the international money markets, as well as a wage freeze. He alarmed his Cabinet colleagues with his fears that registered unemployment might climb to 2 million with a complete collapse of industrial investment and a massive fall in workers' real incomes. The Chancellor believed the country could not afford any wage increases higher than 10 per cent or £5 a week in the next wage round as an 'absolute maximum'. The Treasury disliked the idea of a flat rate pay rise for everybody and believed this could not be achieved without having to resort to legislative enforcement. Instead, it favoured a return to the statutory arrangements of the 1960s with penal sanctions against those companies who defied a 10 per cent maximum wage rise norm. But the TUC and Downing Street opposed such a draconian move and maintained that a voluntary approach stood a much better chance of success. Under the relentless pressure on sterling from the international money markets, with a 28.9 per cent depreciation in its value on 30 June alone, the TUC general council agreed to accept a £6 a week flat wage increase policy with no increases for those earning over £8,500 a year except increments – though only by a troublingly small majority of six, with a vote of 19 in favour to 13 against on the TUC general council. Healey believed this was not sufficient support to ensure pay restraint would work and demanded that the government should promise to legislate reserve powers at once if the TUC initiative failed. The Cabinet agreed reluctantly to the Jones strategy, but as Wilson told the Commons on 11 July 1975 the government had also drawn up the necessary coercive contingency back-up powers needed to secure the compliance of employers if the TUC's own voluntary wage restraint policy failed to work.

Contrary to the gloomy prophecies of failure, however, the £6 a week flat rate voluntary wage policy succeeded in bringing down the level of wage settlements, but its introduction came perilously late and after eighteen months of a self-destructive pay bonanza which neither the Labour government nor the TUC had seemed either able or willing to prevent. During the twelve months of the £6 policy, which lasted until 1 July 1976, the rate of earnings increases dropped from an average of 26.9 per cent to an average of 12.9 per cent while the retail price index rose during the same period by 12.9 per cent. 'Not a free for all but a fair for all – that is our policy', Jones told the 1975 Congress. 'The union I lead and myself personally have never supported the idea that trade unionism is a licence for any group to look after themselves and to hell with the rest'.[28] He added: 'Our policy is to use our general strength and influence to promote social justice.' Delegates at Congress voted to uphold the £6 policy by 6,900,000 votes to just over 3,000,000, while the Labour party conference a month later did so by an overwhelming majority. The Labour Movement had pulled back from the brink of probable disaster and reinforced the Social Contract.

Extending worker and union rights

The government continued to work closely with the TUC in the implementation of its Social Contract programme of economic revival and social justice. The Employment Protection Act reached the statute book in 1975. Described by Jones as the 'shop steward's charter',[29] the measure sought to extend trade union and individual worker freedoms by legal means without undermining the voluntarist system. Its provisions extended workplace rights in a number of specific areas. Guarantee payments were to be provided for workers who were on short time or temporarily laid off. The measure introduced maternity leave and job security for pregnant women workers as well as a legal entitlement to normal pay for workers when under medical suspension. Paid time off work was guaranteed to workers who were carrying out trade union and public service duties as well as those searching for a job after receiving a redundancy notice.

Compensation was to be provided to workers for unfair dismissal, and it was made unlawful for an employer to dismiss a worker for merely belonging to a trade union. Safeguard procedures were to be introduced for workers facing mass redundancies. The Act also laid down provisions for trade union recognition from employers and it imposed an obligation on employers to observe collectively agreed terms and conditions of employment and where no collective agreement existed then the 'general level' of terms in a particular area. Trade unions were also provided with the legal right to access to company information strictly for collective bargaining purposes and in redundancy situations.

Many Conservatives and employers denounced the 1975 Employment Protection Act as a surrender to trade union power, but in practice most of its provisions fell far short of trade union expectations even if they may have looked substantial on paper. As TUC deputy General Secretary John Monks has argued: 'It was modest legislation based on the practices of many good employers. Only in two areas – unfair dismissal and the maternity provisions – was really new ground broken and employers generally pressed to make advances in the interests of their employees.'[30] The 1975 Employment Protection Act suffered from weak enforcement, drafting defects and a narrow judicial interpretation. A study carried out for the Policy Studies Institute in 1978 suggested that the measure had only made a modest impact on the shop floor and its most effective legal provision was that on unfair dismissal, which was a legacy from the hated 1971 Industrial Relations Act.[31] The new unfair dismissal requirements encouraged 'the reform or formalisation of procedures adopted in making disciplinary action and in executing dismissals', while employers became much more careful in their recruitment of new employees and appraising the performance of their existing employees. But as the study pointed out.

Many employers had developed policies and practices which were in advance of minimum standards specified in the legislation. Many others, for whom this was not the case, were able to continue much as before, presumably due to the lack of people at their workplaces with the knowledge or inclination to draw attention to the law or invoke its requirements.

Research at Warwick University into the impact of the disclosure of information provisions for trade union representatives concluded in 1979 that 'the statutory provisions had not been greatly used and their impact appeared slight'. It went on to assert: 'Voluntary disclosure practice varies considerably and in many cases information provision is limited. However, there is little pressure from the unions for greater disclosure.'[32] The Warwick study suggested that 'until trade unions themselves developed policies, priorities and strategies that demanded company information there seemed little prospect of any change'.

The statutory provisions for trade union recognition under the 1975 Employment Protection Act were hardly effective in extending trade unionism either. As another study by the Warwick University Industrial Relations Unit pointed out, the efficacy of the trade union recognition clauses in the measure depended on 'voluntary compliance by employers and trade unions with their spirit as well as their letter. Without it recognition attempts can be sabotaged by obstructing the operation of the procedure or refusing to comply with recommendations for recognition.'[33] The notorious Grunwick strike of 1976–7 revealed the weakness of the trade union recognition procedures when confronted by a determined employer who did not want any trade union presence among his workers at all. A judgement made by the House of Lords in favour of the north London photo-processing company made it clear that a strike over union recognition such as that at Grunwick could be resolved only with the cooperation of the employer concerned. By the end of 1978 it was estimated that collective bargaining had been extended to only 50,000 extra workers through the use of the recognition provisions in the Employment Protection Act. This was during a period when net trade union growth in Britain rose to its historically high water mark with an expansion in density from 49.1 per cent of the labour force in 1974 to 55.6 per cent five years later. Indeed, ACAS chairman Jim Mortimer confessed to Jim Prior, Mrs Thatcher's Employment Secretary in 1980, that ACAS could not satisfactorily operate the statutory recognition procedures as these stood because they lacked any effective means of enforcement and had to rely on persuasion and argument.

Conservatives complained that the Social Contract legislation was a severe hindrance for small firms in their commercial activities because it added to their costs. But there was little evidence to suggest any of the legal reforms made a significant impact on the performance of smaller-sized companies. A Department of Employment commissioned study published in July 1979 found that only 6 per cent of those firms covered in its national survey mentioned employment legislation as one of the main problems facing them, and less than 9 per cent mentioned such issues when asked about government measures that had caused them difficulty. The report added: 'When asked directly if employment legislation had affected them 65 per cent said it had not and only 12 per cent had found particular pieces of employment legislation troublesome when faced with a specific list.'[34]

Despite all the rhetoric surrounding the Social Contract legislation, from its supporters as well as its opponents, there was a clear gap between the potentialities of many of the measures and their practical implementation in the workplace. As Professor William Brown argued, 'It is of limited value to provide employees with rights unless either their employer is willing to comply with them or their trade union is strong enough to enforce compliance.'[35] 'Perhaps the major lesson which emerges from the experience of the 1970s is not to entertain too high expectations of what legislation can achieve in this area', noted Bain and Dickens. 'Legislative procedures cannot substitute for union organising and recruitment activity.'[36]

However, it was true that the legal advances provided for trade unions and individual workers during the Social Contract period represented an important change in the Labour Movement's attitude to the use of the law as an assistance in the growth of union organization and collective bargaining. Union leaders continued to insist that they still believed in voluntarism but the Social Contract reforms at least ensured the creation of minimal legal props or aids to supplement and thereby modify the cherished practice of union autonomy. It was also true, however, that the legislation turned out to be less effective than the TUC had hoped because of 'the problem of weak enforcement, drafting defects and narrow judicial interpretation'.[37] Nevertheless, despite its clear limitations and proven inadequacies, the Social Contract legislation amounted to a clear breach in the voluntarist tradition of industrial relations and revealed a more trusting attitude by the trade unions towards the use of the law in the furtherance of their own objectives.

However, there was one important issue on the agenda of the Social Contract which divided the trade unions. No consensus existed among them over the meaning of industrial democracy. The Labour government appointed a Committee of Inquiry under the chairmanship of the Oxford historian Lord Bullock. It included Jones, David Lea, head of the TUC economic department, the Labour law academic Lord Wedderburn and Clive Jenkins, General Secretary of the ASTMS, as well as three employer representatives. The Committee published a deeply split report in February 1977. A majority, including Lord Bullock, came out in support of a proposal to establish equal numbers of trade union representatives and shareholders on the unitary boards of private sector companies who employed over 2,000 workers. A small group of independents were to hold the balance in what the report called the 2x + y formula. But there was little evidence of enthusiastic rank and file support for what the committee wanted. A number of large and important trade unions, including both the AUEW and the GMWU, opposed the Bullock majority proposals. Some union leaders feared that the autonomy of their organizations would be threatened if they compromised their roles as bargainers by becoming involved in managerial decision-making and the making of corporate strategies. Many ministers in the government were also unimpressed by the notion of industrial democracy – much to Jones's annoyance. 'My worst disappointment was the way in which government ministers treated it, playing for time, failing to think it through, and refusing to face the challenge to the old ways of doing things', he wrote in his memoirs.[38] The Bullock report was in fact referred to a Cabinet committee where it was diluted into a 'puny White Paper' that was closer in spirit and content to the minority recommendations made by the employers on the Committee of Inquiry. Industrial democracy was not translated into legislative form before the government left office in May 1979. It is true that a tentative industrial democracy experiment was launched at the Post Office on the recommended Bullock majority report lines, but it was short-lived and met with widespread rank and file indifference. Worker cooperatives at the Meriden motor-cycle plant, the Fisher-Bendix industrial plant at Kirby on Merseyside, and the Scottish Daily News were championed by Benn when Industry minister but these subsidized experiments failed to achieve commercial viability.

However, the limited and flimsy legislative gains made by Britain's trade unions between 1974 and 1976 were denounced by their enemies as a threat to freedom and a blow to industrial efficiency. Not for the first time in industrial relations the magnitude of the rhetoric belied the modest realities. Indeed, during the late 1970s there was increasing concern inside Congress House over the resurgence of hostile legal judgements against trade unions especially in industrial conflicts. What was particularly worrying for the TUC was the growing use of the interlocutory injunction by judges who were ready to exercise a wide discretion against strikes in support of employers. By seeking an injunction from the High Court against a trade union preparing a strike before the start of the proposed industrial conflict, a company could hope to prevent disruption from breaking out. All the employer needed to do was to convince the judge that there was a serious question to be tried. The plaintiff did not even have to produce prima facie evidence of wrong-doing. At the injunction stage all that judges needed to decide was whether there was a balance of convenience or inconvenience on whether the planned disruption should go ahead or not. An attempt was made in the 1975 Employment Protection Act to prevent this formula from being used in trade dispute cases by suggesting that the court must 'have regard' to the question of whether the party against whom the injunction was aimed would be likely to succeed with the defence that action was indeed 'in contemplation or furtherance' of a trade dispute. In 1975, the Law Lords led by Lord Diplock declared that an applicant's claim for an injunction in an industrial dispute need only satisfy a judge that it was not 'frivolous or vexatious' and there was a 'serious question to be tried' in order to gain it. If a union failed to abide by the injunction imposed on it, it faced proceedings in contempt of court which involved fines and the possible sequestration of union funds. As Professor Griffiths argued:

> For the union, an interim injunction prevents the calling of a strike or other action at a time which the union has decided is the most effective. As the full trial is not likely to take place until weeks or months later, the bargaining position of the union is greatly weakened.[39]

Enemies of the unions in the late 1970s also pointed to the use of aggressive picketing as an indication of the enormous power enjoyed by organized labour. It is true that there were a number of turbulent scenes in some disputes in the period which suggested pickets were using intimidatory tactics to achieve their objectives. But the position was always much more complex than the picture suggested. Under section 15 of the 1974 Trade Union and Labour Relations Act it was lawful for 'one or more persons in contemplation or furtherance of a trade dispute to attend at or near a place where another person works or carries on business' with 'the purpose only of peacefully obtaining or communicating information or peacefully persuading any person to work or abstain from working'. This was hardly a legal licence for the use of obstruction and intimidation in strikes.

Indeed, it was the police who decided in practice when picketing was lawful or not. Their discretionary powers enabled them to determine the outcome. The TUC lobbied hard for the right of strikers to stop moving vehicles on picket lines to picket the drivers but Labour ministers opposed this. Nor did Congress House win the government's support for an extension of the legal immunity to those workers who occupied industrial premises in a lawful trade dispute. Obstruction of the highway, committing a public nuisance, obstructing the police, intimidation, conspiracy and breaches of public order could all be used by the police against pickets. Indeed, the forces of law and order enjoyed a formidable array of legislation to wield in strikes if they chose to do so.

In fact, the TUC found its wider Social Contract with the government growing less and less effective as time went by. The balance of power and influence in the TUC–Labour alliance moved steadily away from Congress House after the summer of 1975, as ministers faced more formidable external pressures on their room for manoeuvre like the International Monetary Fund and foreign governments, most notably those of the United States and West Germany. Wilson and his Cabinet colleagues continued to listen to what the TUC had to say through the winter of 1975–6 and beyond, and the TUC was still consulted in government policy-making but the impact of Congress House was starting to wane perceptibly. Necessary Treasury cuts in government spending plans and the introduction of the controlling mechanism of the Public Sector Borrowing Requirement failed to win the TUC's approval. The Social Contract was meant to be a wide programme of legislative action designed to protect vulnerable groups in society from the threats of inflation and unemployment but through 1976 the dole queue lengthened inexorably. In his April 1976 Budget, Healey rejected the TUC's advice for selective reflation and began to phase out the food subsidies he had introduced two years earlier. Indeed, by the spring of 1976 many union leaders began to despair privately over their apparent lack of impact on the substance of the government's policies. Jones warned that the phasing-out of food subsidies seemed to imply a clear change in policy direction that would take the Labour government towards the neo-liberal market ideas being proclaimed by Margaret Thatcher, the new Conservative party leader, while Scanlon who had mellowed rapidly since Labour's return to office in February 1974 said 'almost pleadingly' that if the 1976 budget did not ensure more investment for industry the TUC's position would become 'almost impossible'.[40]

In fact, it took a lengthy period of patient persuasion and argument to secure the TUC's consent for a second twelve months of wage restraint to follow the successful £6 flat rate policy. The Chancellor of the Exchequer made a bold gambit by seeking to link improved tax allowances with pay moderation in order to achieve trade union consent for further austerity,

Table 7.1   Key labour statistics in the age of the Social Contract, 1974–1979

	Unemployment	Productivity (%)	Earnings rise (%)	Union membership (%)
1974	554,370	−1.79	17.62	50.0
1975	977,900	−1.46	30.02	51.0
1976	1,116,170	2.84	13.01	52.0
1977	1,198,760	2.76	10.37	53.0
1978	1,110,170	2.57	12.81	54.0
1979	1,052,000	1.71	15.53	55.0

Source: Michael Artis and David Cobham (eds), *Labour's Economic Policies 1974–1979*, Manchester University Press, 1991.

after it became clear that the TUC would not agree to any attempt (as the Treasury would have liked) to keep wage rises down to only 3 per cent in the 1976–7 wage round. In the event, a 5 per cent limit with a maximum increase of £4 a week and a minimum of £2.50 a week was eventually agreed, a much tighter formula than in the previous twelve months. The TUC leaders were compelled to admit in public that they had failed to achieve all they wanted from the government in return for their acceptance of a second year of wage restraint. 'I felt terribly dissatisfied because I knew the figures were inadequate', wrote Jones. 'But in the end I felt we should not take the risk of a catastrophic run on the pound and a general election.'[41] Indeed, Scanlon admitted to the special Congress called to endorse phase two of the incomes policy that all the TUC had managed to secure in its negotiations with the government was a deferral of an increase in school meal charges at a cost of £35 million to the taxpayer. But he also warned delegates that the TUC faced no real alternative but to accept what the government wanted. 'We honestly believe then – and still do – that no agreement would have meant a catastrophic run on the pound that would have made what has recently happened look like chicken feed'.[42] Callaghan had also warned the entire TUC general council that failure to achieve agreement on a second year of pay policy would have meant 'the immediate end of the government's life', a prospect that filled the union leaders with understandable gloom.[43]

In fact, phase two of the voluntary incomes restraint policy also turned out to be relatively successful. Between July 1976 and July 1977 earnings rose on average by 8.8 per cent while prices increased by 17.6 per cent. There was a sizeable cut of 6.8 per cent in money wages.

Back to wage freedom

By the time of the September 1976 Congress it was becoming clear to most trade union leaders that there could be no third year of nationally agreed voluntary wage restraint, whatever ministers wanted. Delegates voted overwhelmingly for a 'planned and orderly' return to free collective bargaining from August 1977 when phase two of the incomes policy was due to expire.[44] Union leaders emphasized this meant that they would not provoke an immediate wages free for all but abide by a twelve month interval between pay settlements. However, they also added they were unable to cooperate any further with the government on the creation and enforcement of a wage norm. The TUC's willingness to come to the support of the besieged Labour Cabinet had only turned out to be a temporary expedient conditioned by the gravity of the economic crisis in the summer of 1975. On the other hand for Callaghan, who had been elected Prime Minister in March 1976 after Wilson's sudden retirement, the lesson to be drawn from the attempts at establishing an incomes policy was a recognition that national wage restraint had to become an integral and permanent part of the government's overall economic policy. He tried to interest the TUC in a longer-term approach to the whole problem, but union leaders were in no mood to respond. They looked at the pay issue quite differently from the Prime Minister for they feared a national incomes policy would undermine their own credibility with the members and above all with their increasingly restive shop stewards.

W. W. Daniel in an important piece of empirical research published in December 1976 discovered signs of growing resistance from the shop stewards to any prospect of a further nationally agreed incomes policy, and he warned that 'manufacturing industry represented the most likely detonation point for the pay explosion that would certainly follow the removal of restraint'.[45] The primary cause for the sense of shopfloor grievance in the mid-1970s centred on the squeeze on wage differentials and relativities with resulting 'anomalies and inconsistencies' caused by the tightness of two years of essentially flat rate incomes policy. The well-publicized revolts of the British Leyland toolmakers in 1976 and 1977, with their threat to break away from the AUEW in pursuit of separate bargaining rights, was a bitter forewarning of the corrosive impact national pay limits were having on skilled worker wage differentials relative to the earnings of production workers employed in the same plants. In fact, it was actually much harder to achieve national wage restraint in the mid-1970s through the collective bargaining system than it had been in the 1960s, because of the greater extent of decentralization in the private manufacturing sector with its resulting fragmentation and instability. During the 1970s employers and trade unions sought to formalize the shift in power that had taken place from full-time union officials to shop stewards in multi-union workplaces who were beyond the direct control of their national organizations. As a Warwick University study observed, by 1978 single employer agreements covering one or more factories within a company had become the norm for two-thirds of manual and three-quarters of all non-manual workers. It explained:

> Pay is increasingly fixed by a single bargain for a single bargaining unit, rather than added to on successive bargaining levels. It is also more likely to be covered by job evaluation and by work study. Formal disputes procedures at the place of work have become almost universal. The accumulation of these reforms means that adherence to multi-employer agreements is generally both impractical and unnecessary.[46]

The consequence of this important change in the workplace was dramatic in transforming the strategic importance of the shop steward, who had 'moved from the wings (or prompt box) to the centre of the negotiating stage'. The Warwick study stressed the crucial role being played by management in this extension in shop steward responsibilities in the collective bargaining system. It pointed to the spread of closed shop arrangements with the strong backing of employers and the managerial encouragement for the growth in the use of 'check-off' for the payment of union dues to three-quarters of manual workers by 1978. The study also calculated that the number of full-time stewards had quadrupled during the 1970s so that they now outnumbered full-time union officials for the first time in union history.[47] The Warwick study explained that the growth of the full-time stewards was 'particularly dependent upon managerial policy' and warned that many shop steward organizations in sectors of industry with little tradition of workplace bargaining owed 'more to the administrative needs of management than to the bargaining achievements of the workforce'. 'It remains to be seen how they will fare in a worsening economic climate', argued the study.

A more comprehensive, partly government-commissioned, survey of workplace industrial relations during the late 1970s – but not published until 1983 – confirmed many of the important trends discerned by the Warwick study. Here was a portrait of British trade unionism at its illusory high watermark of power and influence. The most important conclusion of the study was to underline the growth of formalism in shopfloor trade unionism in the large companies employing over a thousand workers, through the spread of joint multi-union consultative committees dealing with substantial issues which had occurred without any outside pressure from government. The study also emphasized the expansion of the closed shop until it covered an estimated 27 per cent of all workers, and the emergence of the full-time shop steward and convenor paid for by the employer to carry out trade union work on company premises and in company time.[48] The study also highlighted the boost provided by the 1974 Health and Safety at Work Act to the spread of joint health and safety committees on the shop floor and the greater formalization of disciplinary procedures stimulated by the 'various legislative initiatives' of the 1970s.

This decentralized and increasingly formalized system with its emphasis on shopfloor autonomy and independence was an uncomfortable reality that both union leaders and above all ministers were forced to recognize. As Healey admitted in the calm reflection of his memoirs, 'In Britain it is difficult to operate a pay policy even with the co-operation of the union leaders. For the real power lies not in union headquarters but with the local shop stewards who tend to see a rational incomes policy as robbing them of their functions.'[49] But at the same time he accepted that he had no option but to try and contain wage pressures. It was a task that consumed an extraordinary amount of his time amounting to 12 hours a week for 12 months of the year as he examined 'the smallest details of the individual negotiations in progress at the time'. As Healey revealed:

> I spent two thirds of my time dealing with the disastrous consequences of free collective bargaining and the other third dealing with the distortions and anomalies caused by my own pay policy. Adopting a pay policy is rather like jumping out of a second-floor window: no one in his senses would do it unless the stairs were on fire. But in post-war Britain the stairs have always been on fire.

The successful conclusion of a second year of voluntary wage restraint in the early summer of 1976 failed to reassure the volatile foreign exchange markets and sterling continued to fall in value. In June 1976 the Cabinet had agreed to accept a six month $5.3 billion standby loan from the Group of Ten central banks as a precaution to stave off difficulties. Ministers also accepted Healey's demand for £1 billion worth of public spending cuts coupled with a further £1 billion tax increase through a 2 per cent rise in employers' national insurance contributions. Now the Labour government was being forced to face international economic realities. As Callaghan told the 1976 Labour party conference, in words written by his son-in-law Peter Jay that would become famous:

We used to think you could spend your way out of a recession and increase employment by cutting taxes and boosting spending. I tell you in all candour that this option no longer exists and that in so far as it ever did exist, it only worked by injecting a bigger dose of inflation into the system.[50]

He warned delegates the 'cosy world' had gone where a Chancellor could guarantee full employment with a stroke of his pen.

When it came to negotiations five months later over a standby credit from the International Monetary Fund to finance Britain's £3 billion balance of payments deficit, ministers found the going much tougher than they had expected. The resulting so-called IMF 'crisis' proved to be a crucial turning point for the Labour Cabinet as it was forced to come to terms with unpalatable facts and cut back still further – albeit temporarily – on cherished public spending programmes to meet the IMF's loan conditions. Throughout that period Callaghan was anxious to keep in close contact with Murray and Jones in order to ensure there was no rupture with the TUC which could have damaged the IMF talks. Congress House lost no time once the government had reached agreement with the IMF in throwing its support behind the Prime Minister even if it still insisted the trade unions were intent on 'an orderly return to collective bargaining'.

Ministers tried unsuccessfully to secure the TUC's cooperation for a third year of pay restraint in the spring of 1977 with the aim of keeping the average rise in earnings to no more than 10 per cent over the twelve months from 1 July, but they were told that the best that Congress House could do was ensure that trade unions honoured their existing collective agreements and would negotiate only when they came to an end. The most dramatic indication of the troubles ahead came in early July 1977 when Jones was overturned by his own union's biennial conference as he sought to convince delegates that an attempt should be made to at least ensure a responsible attitude to pay bargaining in the next wage round. Jones's very public failure came as a sad blow to the government's counter-inflation efforts. It meant ministers could no longer rely on his powerful and constructive influence inside the TUC. His retirement in March 1978 deprived the Labour Movement of one of its most formidable and impressive post-war figures.

Efforts were made through the Liaison Committee to restore a sense of unity between the TUC and the government despite the strains. A broad policy statement, *The Next Three Years and into the Eighties*, was agreed in 1977 by both sides which spoke optimistically about reaching 'the end of a period of falling living standards' as the benefits from North Sea oil began to flow and make the British economy self-sufficient in its energy resources. 'Our task is to ensure that the sacrifices of recent years have not been in vain', argued the Liaison Committee. 'We can look forward to the time when the IMF arrangement will no longer be necessary.'[51]

Nobody could have been left in any doubt by the 1977 Congress, however, that the trade unions were determined on a return to free collective bargaining as fast as realistically possible. But Murray sought to reassure the government that this would not precipitate a wage explosion:

> Bigger pay packets all round are not going to buy us out of our personal troubles if inflation snatches back the gains that we make and we know it. . . . The brutal fact is that living standards are bound to be undermined if the economy sinks into a run–down condition, which is what is happening. These problems cannot just be swept away on a big tide of wage increases. . . . The motto of 'Every man for himself' was taken down from the wall when the first trade union was formed and it does not become an acceptable motto if we change it to 'Every union for itself'.[52]

The new mood was not to be one of confrontation, however, and Healey tried to assuage shopfloor discontent through an October 1977 package that boosted economic growth. In fact, the TUC did its best to hold the line in the 1977–8 wage round and prevent a pay explosion. It insisted that affiliated unions should stick to a 12 month interval between pay settlements and should negotiate responsibly so as not to increase un-employment and worsen industry's competitiveness. 'In the absence of an agreement the government could hardly have asked for more', reflected Callaghan.[53] 'Ten per cent was not agreed but tacitly accepted by the unions', admitted Jones. 'By and large there wasn't too much evasion and trouble.'[54]

Just how far the TUC general council was prepared to go in continuing to help the government was made clear in December 1977 when it voted by 21 to 19 not to throw its support behind the firemen's strike. For their part, ministers adopted an *ad hoc* pragmatism with promises of delayed settlements and special wage deals for troublesome groups like the firemen. The outcome was rather ragged but with considerable patience, flexibility and more than a touch of luck the 1977–8 wage round was weathered. The government claimed the Social Contract had held, and at least ministers did not believe they had been humiliated. Yet between August 1977 and August 1978 earnings rose not by 10 per cent as the govern-ment's own guidelines had called for but by 14.2 per cent, while prices over the same period increased by 7.9 per cent. The improvement in money wages amounted to 6.3 per cent, which was a substantial figure in the circumstances. The government's wage restraint efforts were clearly failing to achieve a positive response from pay bargainors. Indeed, as many as 57 private sector companies were deprived of government financial assistance for breaking the government's 10 per cent pay rise guidelines.

Towards discontent

With increasing difficulty, a semblance of wage restraint had continued since July 1975 but the prospects for yet a further round of moderation in the 1978–9 wage round looked decidedly unpromising, particularly as improvements in the economy began to increase labour market pressures from skilled workers who believed their squeezed earnings were falling behind those of others. Apparently, however, Callaghan did not appear to share the pessimism of employers and union leaders about the possibilities of further pay restraint. On 22 December 1977 the Cabinet discussed the economic prospects for 1978 and it was at that meeting the Prime Minister first made it clear he wanted to have a 5 per cent wage limit in the next pay round. On 1 January 1978 the 5 per cent norm 'hardened' when the Prime Minister 'tempted by the interviewer popped out' in a radio interview that he wanted to see wage increases over the twelve months from August to be no more than 5 per cent.[55] The Treasury calculated that with such a norm it would be possible to contain the average earnings figure for the next pay round at around 7 to 8 per cent. But there had been no serious Cabinet discussion about the size of the pay target, let alone any ministerial soundings about it with Congress House. Yet many months before August 1978 when the next pay round was due to begin, Callaghan had decided to close down the government's options. It was a dangerous high risk strategy and explanations of how it came about still remain unsatisfactory. In his memoirs Healey admitted that the government was 'blind' to the warnings of impending trouble and he admitted ten years later that the 5 per cent pay limit was 'typical of the hubris which can overcome a successful government towards the end of its term'.[56]

It was not just Callaghan's low 5 per cent figure for pay rises that was difficult for the trade union leaders to swallow. They were opposed to any attempt by the government to limit pay bargaining. But by the early months of 1978 the Prime Minister was convinced that Britain needed a permanent coordinated national incomes policy, not just a temporary one to deal with an immediate crisis. As he explained:

Influenced by the West German experience I preferred tripartite discussions to take place each year between the government, unions and employers in an attempt to create a consensus about the national level of earnings that would be compatible with keeping inflation at a low level; both sides would then work within such an understanding in their pay negotiations.[57]

In its July 1978 White Paper, *Winning the Battle against Inflation*, the government suggested that the country 'should aim at a long-term approach in which collective bargaining is based on a broad agreement between government, unions and employers about the maximum level of earnings compatible with keeping inflation under control in the following twelve months'.[58] The TUC through its membership of the Liaison Committee endorsed the government's opinion that there needed to be 'a thorough discussion with the trade union movement each year' so there was a 'broad understanding' over pay.[59] Callaghan recalled in his memoirs that TUC leaders were 'conciliatory and helpful' when he met them that summer to discuss the government's counter-inflation programme. Murray told him that they all 'shared the same objectives and acknowledged that without the efforts the government had made unemployment and inflation would have been higher',[60] adding that the unions 'were anxious to avoid a wages explosion but employers were increasingly blaming the government for their failure to pay higher wages with the result that beating the "norm" was becoming a challenge'.

In fact, most union leaders refused to take seriously Callaghan's 5 per cent pay rise target for the 1978–9 round. They were not consulted about it and they believed the figure was simply based on a Treasury economic forecast print-out that bore no relation to shopfloor realities. 'This figure came right out of the blue', recalled Murray, and he believed Callaghan's fixation with 5 per cent stemmed from his wish to get the price rise level down to 5 per cent by the middle of 1979.[61] Union leaders also thought that the government could not really expect to achieve what would amount to a fourth year of wage restraint by trying to establish a smaller pay increase for workers than the previous three wage rounds. In any event, they reasoned, the Prime Minister was going to call a general election for October 1978 now the government lacked an overall parliamentary majority with the end of its pact with the Liberals in the summer. They expected that if the Labour party won that contest there would be plenty of time afterwards to reach an understanding with the TUC over more flexibility in wage bargaining. But in July 1978 the Cabinet endorsed the 5 per cent figure, albeit with some doubts and little enthusiasm. Ministers believed – like the TUC – that Callaghan would go to the country in October and they saw no point in having a pitched row over the exact size of the pay limit figure. Callaghan teased the 1978 Congress when he spoke to it about when he intended to dissolve Parliament. As TUC delegates were packing their bags to return home on the final day of Congress he announced on television – to the astonishment of union leaders and many Cabinet ministers – that there would be no autumn general election after all and he intended to soldier on into 1979. His decision was a serious political mistake, but the Prime Minister – on the basis of private polling – believed the Labour party would stand a better chance of victory if it stayed in office through the winter, when it could expect to benefit from a falling inflation rate and improved living standards. However, Callaghan had angered the TUC unnecessarily. Congress House believed that he had misled union leaders. They had united together in a public display of support for the Labour government in what they thought was pre-election fraternity at the Brighton Congress.

There was now little hope of avoiding a confrontation over the Prime Minister's 5 per cent pay limit target. Murray had already warned the government that it could not expect to win cooperation from the unions for any further wage restraint. He told delegates at the 1978 Congress: 'There must be sufficient flexibility if unions and employers are to sort out difficult problems and anomalies and to take account of profitability without splash headlines about defeats or surrenders or nonsense of that sort.'[62] Murray was convinced that the government had underestimated the determination of the unions to avoid any irresponsible pay offensive because he believed they had learned the lessons from the self-destructive inflation of 1974–5. In fact, there was little support among the unions for any form of wage understanding with the government. A resolution at the 1978 Congress that called for the creation of a concerted action approach over pay on West German lines went down to heavy defeat without the need for a card vote.

Callaghan certainly believed his position was also made worse by the retirement in 1978 of both Jones and Scanlon. The two men – despite their contrasting styles – had formed a strong partnership inside the TUC through an 'amalgam of gritty integrity, strength and subtlety'.[63] Ten years earlier the media had described them as the 'terrible twins', but now they had become a vital ballast to ensure the prolonged life of a Labour minority government. It is unlikely that the events of 1978–9 would have been any different if Jones and Scanlon had remained in charge of their unions through the period, but their absence from the scene certainly revealed a serious power vacuum at the centre of the TUC. Moss Evans as General Secretary of the TGWU was a sad disappointment who lacked the vision and the authority of his predecessor. A verbose Welshman, he often sounded and acted like a man out of his depth. Terry Duffy, the AUEW's new right-wing President, could not be faulted for his unstinting loyalty to the Labour government. A product of the 'take no prisoners' factionalism of his union, Duffy was decent and friendly but he lacked Scanlon's intuitive grasp of events and his political sophistication.

The 1978 Labour party conference turned into a disaster for Callaghan. A militant resolution from the Liverpool Wavertree constituency was passed which 'demanded' that the government must 'immediately cease intervening in wage negotiations and recognise the right of trade unions to negotiate freely on behalf of their members'. It went on to declare 'the planning of wages' would only be acceptable when prices, profits and investment were also planned' within the framework of a Socialist planned economy'.[64] Joe Gormley, the NUM President, told the Prime Minister: 'For God's sake trust us', while the normally moderate Gavin Laird, General Secretary of the AUEW, declared to loud applause that the Cabinet did not 'have the sole prerogative of intelligence in economic thinking' and his union would 'certainly not accept a 5 per cent pay norm'. Only Sid Weighell, the NUR's General Secretary, dissented, with a ferocious attack on free collective bargaining which he described as 'the philosophy of the pig trough – those with the biggest snouts get the biggest share'. The Wavertree motion was carried by a crushing 4,017,000 votes to 1,924,000.

Once again the issue of pay determination was returning to haunt the Labour Movement and the tensions between the sectionalist aspirations of the unions and the political imperatives of a Labour government could not be glossed over easily by Liaison Committee statements of good intentions. Callaghan found himself back to where all his post-war Labour predecessors had found themselves at critical moments. As he explained to the 1978 Labour conference:

> We must find a better way to resolve the issue of pay levels. The power of the organised worker in society today demands that we do. The power workers can shut off our lights. The sewage workers can stop work too with all the consequences. Yes, society today is so organised that every individual group almost has the power to disrupt it. How is that power to be channelled into constructive channels? That is the question for the government but it is a question for the trade union movement too.[65]

In the six weeks that followed the 1978 Labour party conference intensive negotiations were held between the TUC and the government to try and find a way out of the impasse. Callaghan believed that all was not yet

Table 7.2   Strikes in the age of the Social Contract, 1974–1979

	Number of stoppages	Working days lost per 1,000 workers
1974	2,946	647
1975	2,332	265
1976	2,034	146
1977	2,737	448
1978	2,498	413
1979	2,125	1,273

Source: Employment Gazettes.

lost. Certainly, Moss Evans seemed anxious to try and be as helpful as possible. He told the Prime Minister that 'most negotiators in the TGWU were thinking of settlements below 10 per cent because they recognise that if wage increases generated price increases, inflation would take off again'.[66] Evans suggested that both sides should have a 'common goal, namely not to increase prices by more than an agreed percentage figure'. A form of words was cobbled together. In return for the government's strengthening of the Price Commission's powers, the TUC was to issue guidance to union negotiators 'on the need to maximise efficiency and to contain unit costs'. There was also to be an examination of the low pay problem and the work of the Wages Councils and it was agreed that 'the principle of comparability should be given a more central role in pay negotiations'.[67] However, this did not mean that the TUC would abandon free collective bargaining and it is doubtful whether the formula would have avoided the industrial excesses of the 'Winter of Discontent'. It had been proposed that pay negotiators should negotiate settlements that did not lead to price increases; and the interests of the consumer as well as the need for new investment were also to be taken into account in pay bargaining to ensure productivity improvements were not all swallowed up in fatter wage packets. Although there were no pay figures in the document, Callaghan recognized that at best its acceptance 'might ensure a helpful neutrality from the TUC as a whole (similar to their stance in 1977) when the going became rough later on'.[68]

Hopes for even that 'modest' deal in fact turned out to be short-lived. On 14 November the TUC general council tied by 14 voted to 14 over the agreed document and its chairman Tom Jackson of the UPOW declared it was lost. Evans – one of the main drafters of the documents – was absent. Told the deal would go through easily, he had decided to go off to Malta on holiday. It was symbolic of the state of the TGWU at the time that two of his three colleagues on the TUC general council voted different ways and the third abstained. The last chance of achieving at least a semblance of a settlement between the TUC and the government had gone. Murray was not sorry that the vote went against a deal in which he placed little faith. 'It is a real kick in the teeth for the corporate state', Benn noted in his diary.[69] But Healey believed the failure dealt a mortal blow to the Labour government. 'This shambles was of course a triumph for Mrs Thatcher', he wrote later. 'The cowardice and irresponsibility of some union leaders in abdicating responsibility at this time guaranteed her election.'[70]

Three days later came a further but long-expected blow to the credibility of the government's 5 per cent pay limit when the Ford Motor Company settled the nine week long strike of its employees with a wage agreement that brought average rises of 16.5 per cent, far beyond the government's flimsy pay limit. The government tried to impose financial sanctions against the American multinational, but that move was defeated by a Commons majority of two when the Commons passed a Conservative party motion calling for the abandonment of any sanctions against companies who broke the 5 per cent limit. The government was left defenceless in the face of escalating wage demands.

The TGWU now became the 'spearhead of a frontal attack on the Government'.[71] The wages offensive revealed a serious power vacuum at the top of the union which was occupied by the shop stewards who tried to turn many of their full-time officials into little more than messenger boys between government departments and themselves. The full flavour of the disintegration inside the TGWU is conveyed in the pages of Tony Benn's diary. Although a strong supporter of the union's position, Benn was too honest a diarist not to reveal the inability to establish a firm and clear line of authority between the TGWU and the government. This was particularly apparent when the oil tanker drivers threatened an all-out strike in pursuit of a 25 per cent pay rise. The Cabinet instructed Benn as Secretary of State for Energy to inform the TGWU leaders that the government hoped the union would allow essential services to continue as normal if the oil tanker drivers stopped work. The alternative would have been the use of troops and the calling of a State of Emergency. Benn explained to Evans:

Look Moss, we are in a hell of a jam because the timetable for the use of troops is such that I will have to make a move this week if I can't get the TGWU's agreement. . . . We have got to find a way through particularly now pay sanctions are over. I can't give a nod and a wink to the oil companies; the Government can't now push the companies to settle – that's asking too much.

Evans appeared to 'appreciate the terrible political damage of using troops' and Benn expressed some hope that the union would comply with the government's request. Later in the day, however, Benn was told the TGWU could not ensure essential supplies in the event of an oil tanker drivers' strike. Evans phoned Benn and told him: 'They've [the shop stewards] have turned me down; there is no point in seeing you. They won't accept the essential supplies.' Benn insisted that Evans came to see him about the situation. The union officers explained what had happened:

> We gave the Texaco shop stewards the list of supplies. Jack Ashwell [the full-time national officer covering the oil tanker drivers] argued for emergencies but the only emergencies they will accept are fire, ambulance, police, hospitals, old people, British Oxygen gases and livestock. Beyond that any discussion about who should get what would be a matter for local decision. The men had turned it down because they thought the emergency supplies defined on our list would prolong the dispute and they were determined not to supply any oil to power stations or for gas and electricity operations. They said there was no prospect of deferring the date of the strike beyond 3 January. Indeed, the men had increased the overtime ban to bring forward the crunch. Moss said, 'The plain truth is we can't deliver'.[72]

It took much arm-twisting and behind the scenes negotiations before the oil tanker drivers were eventually bought off with average pay rises of around 20 per cent. This brought little respite in the pay offensive. The start of the New Year led to a sharp escalation in labour militancy. Road haulage drivers who were mainly TGWU members struck from 3 January and extended secondary picketing to try and disrupt the movement of food supplies and other essential goods around the country. The government tried to convince Evans and his full-time union officials to exercise some control over the strikers by at least agreeing on a voluntary code of conduct but nobody seemed to be taking any notice. All Transport House was prepared to do was recommend exemption from picketing of essential supplies to local strike committees, but left it to their 'discretion' what they did. The brutality of the dispute came as an unpleasant surprise and did much to antagonize public opinion. The lasting television image of that time was of picket lines of 'bearded men in duffel coats huddled around braziers'.[73] After three weeks of conflict the road haulage drivers achieved pay rises of around 21 per cent. There was no apparent stomach for resolute government action in the face of such aggressive industrial disruption. As Bill Rodgers, Labour's transport minister at the time, noted: 'the Prime Minister had no taste for a fight to the finish and hoped for an early settlement and no direct confrontation with the unions'.[74]

The most serious outbreak of worker militancy, however, and one which has etched itself indelibly onto the national memory of the so-called 'Winter of Discontent', came on 22 January when the public service unions with NUPE in the lead launched their jointly organized campaign for a £60 a week minimum wage for their low paid manual worker members in local government, the health service and other parts of the public services sector. The resulting scenes – of refuse piling up in the streets, pickets turning away sick patients including children from hospitals, the dead left unburied and schools closed – inflicted incalculable moral damage on the Labour Movement. 'Even with the passage of time I find it painful to write about some of the excesses that took place', Callaghan wrote in his memoirs.[75] The scars have still not entirely healed. This was no heroic struggle of workers against their employers. The victims of the strikes were those who could least help themselves like the old, the sick, the bereaved, children and the poor. Moreover, the public sector campaign was not one which the low paid could really hope to win, for if they had secured £60 a week it would have provoked the demand for the restoration of pay differentials for more skilled workers and white collar staff. Indeed, at the end of the 1970s it was skilled manual workers rather than the low paid in the public services sector who had most grounds for complaint, as their relative wage position had been eroded as a result of the distortions of two years of flat rate incomes policies.

In his prophetic and seminal 1978 Marx Memorial lecture, Professor Eric Hobsbawm had posed the question: 'The forward march of labour halted?' In his opinion, the Labour Movement had reached a critical point in its evolution. Out of the proletarianism and class consciousness of the early twentieth century, under the influence of structural and occupational changes, had risen a new sectionalism. 'We now see a growing division of workers into sections and groups, each pursuing its own economic interest irrespective of the rest', he explained. What was novel, he contended, was the ability of each group or section to mobilize its bargaining strength not so much by placing pressure on their employer but on the general public. 'In the nature of things such sectional forms of struggle not only create potential friction between groups of workers but risk weakening the hold of the labour movement as a whole.'[76] This 'economist militancy' meant a corresponding decline in social solidarity. It is possible to question just how much strong working class or labourist consciousness there was at any time in British industrial society. Sectionalism was always a potent force for dividing worker against worker. But the attack on the community by public service workers was new in the Winter of Discontent, and its ferocity irrational. The sour rancour of that time came as a shock to many in the Labour government. It is true more working days were lost later in 1979 during the national engineering workers' strikes for shorter working hours than in the pay offensive against the 5 per cent wage limit, but the turbulent and often callous events of January to March sealed the fate of the Labour government.

The cumulative impact of industrial conflict almost paralysed government for a short time at the end of January 1979, after Callaghan had returned sun-tanned and seemingly complacent from a summit conference on the French island of Guadeloupe. The Prime Minister's chief aide Lord Donoughue provided a graphic account of the atmosphere in 10 Downing Street. Apparently, Callaghan was for a time 'worryingly lethargic' as he appeared to be 'sitting in a sinking Titanic without music'. 'He was clearly very tired, both physically and mentally', recalled Donoughue. 'It was equally clear that he was very unhappy at having to confront the trade unions. His whole career had been built alongside the trade union movement and he seemed to find it quite impossible to fight against it'.[77] Frank Chapple, the EETPU's General Secretary, recalled one meeting the TUC inner group had with Callaghan at that time in which the Prime Minister declared: 'We are prostrate before you – but don't ask us to put it in writing.'[78] On a number of occasions a State of Emergency was nearly called and Callaghan regretted later that he had not used troops to deal with essential supplies, but he was not very willing at least in public to condemn the callous behaviour of too many pickets. As Bill Rodgers wrote:

> the Prime Minister could not stop the strike [of lorry drivers] or prevent a final settlement way out of line with pay policy. But he could have condemned the abuse of trade union power and distanced his Government from those responsible. This he signally failed to do. He was a prisoner of his own trade union past – which had often served him well – and the conventional wisdom that the Labour Party remained the political wing of the trade union movement and must ultimately bow to it.[79]

In fact, slowly but surely the Prime Minister began to move away from his own 5 per cent pay limit policy in what turned eventually into a humiliating surrender. A new Standing Pay Commission on Comparability in the public sector was established by the government under the chairmanship of Professor Hugh Clegg from Warwick University, in a belated attempt to construct an independent institution that could find solutions to the sensitive issue of public–private sector pay comparisons. The claims of the striking local government manual workers, ancillary hospital workers and nurses were presented at once to the Clegg Commission, which was given until 1 August 1979 to come up with recommendations. In the meantime, the government agreed to honour whatever the Clegg Commission's binding awards would cost in stages and gave down-payments on top of already agreed 9 per cent general wage increases. The Clegg Commission could have been a serious attempt by the government to escape from the normal hand to mouth and *ad hoc* responses to the persistent troubles caused by public service pay, but unfortunately the new body had come into being too late as a hasty solution to a serious conflict. It is possible that if the Commission had been proposed and formed six months earlier it might have prevented the damaging public service pay offensive that more than any other strike alienated public opinion.

Negotiations were also started again between the government and the TUC on a new economic understanding, and on 23 February the so-called Concordat emerged. This politically inspired document was an attempt to repair the severely damaged relationship. Efforts were made to convince senior union leaders of the need for a more structured approach to pay bargaining. The TUC and the government committed themselves to bring down the rate of inflation to below 5 per cent within three years. Ministers would have liked to see the Concordat provide the basis for a national incomes policy agreed each year between the government, trade unions and employers, but the TUC would go no further than to accept the need for an annual economic assessment and to say it was committed to reducing the inflation rate. Both sides also agreed to publish TUC guidelines on the conduct of industrial disputes, negotiating procedures and union organization. Congress House had grown as alarmed as anybody by the aggressive picketing tactics of the striking lorry drivers and low paid public service workers, and the apparent lack of trade union control being exercise over their behaviour. The document was full of sound advice. It even suggested that unions ought to consult their members by secret ballot before calling them out on strike, and it advised trade unions to exercise greater authority over the number of people they deployed on picket lines, especially in so-called secondary actions.

But it was all too little, too late. The Winter of Discontent undermined the credibility of the Labour Movement. As Healey wrote in his memoirs, it 'destroyed the nation's confidence in the Labour party's ability to work with the unions'.[80] Above all, the unpleasant face of sectionalist trade unionism disgusted public opinion and inflicted lasting moral damage on the cause of organized labour, not least among many rank and file trade union members. The war against the 5 per cent limit also paved the way for Margaret Thatcher's May 1979 general election triumph. Her populist appeal of acquisitive economic liberalism with its promise of an end to statutory incomes policies, as well as tax cuts for everybody evoked a favourable response, especially among many skilled manual workers in the industrial West Midlands and south east of England, more of whom voted Conservative than Labour for the first time in the post-war period. As many as 33 per cent of all trade unionists voted Conservative in the 1979 general election. Opinion surveys also found that there was widespread sympathy among Labour voters for Conservative policies like the cuts in social benefits being received by strikers' families, an end to secondary picketing, and the sale of council houses. The old appeal of Labourism to social equity and class solidarity made little impression on the 1979 electorate. As Callaghan admitted to Donoughue on the eve of his defeat, there was 'a sea-change' taking place in British politics and it was moving in Mrs Thatcher's direction.[81] 'Seldom can a major party have penetrated the political thinking of the other side's staunchest supporters', claimed Professor Anthony King.[82]

In 1979 – as in 1951 and in 1969 – a Labour government had again found itself unable to resolve the underlying tensions of its traditional organic relationship with the trade unions. The turbulent events of the 1974–9 period highlighted in a particularly painful way just how difficult it was in Britain to reconcile an essentially decentralized collective bargaining system based on voluntarist principles and little legal enforcement, with the need for the creation of industrial stability and consensus through a jointly agreed national economic policy which involved some degree of wage restraint. From Attlee to Callaghan, no Labour Prime Minister could find a way of working for more than a short time in harmony with the TUC on the management of an ailing economy. But then the trade unions were always being called upon by hard-pressed Labour governments to take on responsibilities they were not in existence to shoulder. The Social Contract – for all its high-minded rhetoric – was a much more modest arrangement than its critics recognized, but it still gave the misleading impression that the trade unions were somehow the equal of the government in running the country. In fact, the TUC lacked – as always – the collective power and authority to establish any long-term economic pact with a Labour government that could bind together its diverse affiliated unions, most of whose rank and file members did not share the ideological assumptions made by Congress House. Indeed, the early 1970s in many respects looked less promising for the success of a Labour–TUC Alliance than the immediately post-war period, as any sense of social cohesion between workers grew increasingly weaker. The decentralization of power inside trade union structures and the formalization of shop steward authority in an uncoordinated pay bargaining system made national tripartite agreements look increasingly ineffective.

At the end of the 1970s many people believed Britain's trade unions were much too powerful and posed a serious threat to constitutional government. Professor Brown was particularly critical of the damaging legacy bequeathed by this particular myth:

> Unions are reactive, bargaining organisations, ill-prepared for writing the agenda for government. . . . In attempting to placate, for tactical economic reasons, a largely unprepared trade union movement, the government did that movement lasting damage. It perpetuated the myth of the centrality of trade unions to the British inflationary process when, as the CBI itself was aware, a fragmented bargaining structure was a major contributor. By placing unions so centrally on the political stage, it prepared the way for the devastating Conservative reaction.[83]

But these criticisms could apply with equal force to the other post-war relations between Labour governments and the TUC. The problem lay in the inability to reconcile the increasingly decentralized and fragmented system of collective bargaining with the need for national pay restraint to provide stability for a weak economy highly vulnerable to external pressures in an increasingly integrated global market. What the events of the late 1970s highlighted was the strength of work group power in a mixed economy suffering from relative decline. The intractable nature of the so-called trade union 'problem' stemmed not from the supposed overweening strength and pretensions of organized labour at the national level, whether inside or outside the TUC, but from the TUC's fundamental weaknesses, which grew more apparent under conditions of high inflation and dominant workplace bargaining in the private manufacturing sector. As Professor Beer observed: 'The lack of co-ordination in wage bargaining in Britain stems from having a system which is too highly organised for market forces to prevail but not organised enough to yield overall sensible and lasting bargains with employers and governments.'[84]

Other European market economies before the 1980s, most notably those of Sweden and West Germany, were able to demonstrate that it was possible for trade unions to work in partnership with governments in the achievement of national strategies for economic growth combined with social justice. But in Britain – for all Callaghan's 'vain hopes' – such an arrangement was not possible. Back in 1948–50 a tentative move had been made in that direction at a time when a strong sense of moral purpose and collective solidarity bound at least the activists of the Labour Movement together in defence of the post-war social settlement. Yet over the intervening thirty years, under conditions of full employment and growing worker affluence, notions of solidarity and equality lost whatever faint resonance they may have had. In fact, the devolution of power down through union structures to the shop floor made it harder not easier to bind unions and workers together in common cause. Tragically, Jack Jones, probably the most far-sighted and imaginative trade union leader in the post-war years, was unable to see that his idealization of the shop stewards gave an ideological justification for the resurgence of old-style acquisitive sectionalism that had nothing to do with fairness. Moreover, the weakening and denigration of full-time union officials in the 1960s and early 1970s made it impossible to reform trade union structures to ensure that they grew more professional and innovative. The conundrum over pay and employment debated in 1943–4 between Beveridge and the TUC was still unresolved, partly because of the failure of union structural reform.

Notes

1   T. Balogh, *Labour and Inflation*, Fabian Society, October 1970, p. 34.
2   Labour Party Conference annual report, 1970, p. 164.
3   Ibid., p. 176.
4   Ibid., p. 121.
5   Labour Party Conference annual report, 1971, pp. 168–9.
6   J. Jones, *Union Man*, Collins 1986, p. 237.
7   *Economic Policy and the Cost of Living*, TUC–Labour party Liaison Committee, 1975, p. 6.
8   H. Wilson, *Final Term*, Weidenfeld & Nicolson, 1979, p. 43.
9   Labour Programme, 1973, p. 3.
10 S. Dunn and J. Gennard, *The Closed Shop in British Industry*, Macmillan, 1984, p. 89.
11 D. Healey, *The Time of My Life*, Michael Joseph, 1989, p. 394.
12 TUC Congress report, 1974, p. 34.
13 Ibid., p. 291.
14 J. Barnett, *Inside the Treasury*, Deutsch, 1982, p. 49.
15 P. Johnson, *The Recovery of Freedom*, Basil Blackwell, 1980, pp. 15–16.
16 Barbara Castle, *Diaries 1974–1976*, Weidenfeld & Nicolson, p. 10.
17 Ibid., p. 20.
18 TUC Congress report, 1974, p. 398.
19 Ibid., p. 289.

20 Ibid., p. 423.

21 TUC Congress report, 1975, p. 349.

22 'Industrial Relations', in M. Artis and D. Cobham (eds), *Labour's Economic Policies 1974–1979*, Manchester University Press, 1991, p. 59.

23 D. Healey, *The Time of My Life*, p. 394.

24 TUC–Labour Liaison Committee, 1975, p. 6.

25 TUC Congress report, 1975, p. 354.

26 P. Whitehead, *The Writing on the Wall*, Michael Joseph, 1975, pp. 148–9.

27 B. Castle, *Diaries*, p. 283.

28 TUC Congress report, 1975, p. 460.

29 J. Jones, *Union Man*, p. 256.

30 J. Monks, 'Gains and Losses after 20 Years of Legal Intervention', in B. McCarthy (ed.), *Legal Intervention in Industrial Relations: Gains and Losses*, Basil Blackwell, 1992, p. 213.

31 W. Daniel and E. Stilgoe, *Impact of the Employment Protection Laws*, Policy Studies Institute, 1978, p. 74.

32 L. Dickens, *Disclosure of Information to Trade Unions in Britain*, discussion paper, Warwick University Industrial Relations Unit, 1980, p. 41.

33 *Response to the Government Working Paper on Trade Union Recognition*, Warwick University, 1979, p. 8.

34 R. Clifton and C. Tatton-Brown, *Impact of Employment Legislation on Small Firms*, Department of Employment, 1979, p. 33.

35 W. Brown, 'Industrial Relations', in M. Artis and D. Cobham (eds), *Labour's Economic Policies*, p. 219.

36 G. Bain and L. Dickens, *Response*, Warwick University, 1979, p. 12.

37 R. Lewis, 'Collective Labour Law', in G. Bain (ed.), *Industrial Relations in Britain*, Blackwell, 1983, p. 378.

38 J. Jones, *Union Man*, p. 315.

39 J. A. G. Griffith, *The Politics of the Judiciary*, Fontana, 1991, pp. 105–6.

40 TUC Special Congress report, 1976, p. 43.

41 J. Jones, *Union Man*, p. 307.

42 TUC Congress report, 1976, p. 30.

43 J. Callaghan, *Time and Change*, Collins, 1987, p. 416.

44 TUC Congress report, 1976, p. 523.

45 W. W. Daniel, *The Next Stage of Incomes Policy*, PEP, 1976, p. 28.

46 W. Brown (ed.), *The Changing Contours of British Industrial Relations*, Basil Blackwell, 1981, p. 120.

47 Ibid., p. 142.

48 W. W. Daniel and N. Millward, *Workplace Industrial Relations in Britain*, Heinemann, 1983, p. 156.

49 D. Healey, *The Time of My Life*, p. 399.

50 Labour Party Conference report, 1976, p. 188.

51 TUC–Labour Liaison Committee, *The Next Three Years and into the Eighties*, 1977, p. 6.

52 TUC Congress report, 1977, pp. 357, 470.

53   J. Callaghan, *Time and Change*, p. 470.
54   M. Holmes, *The Labour Government 1974–1979: Political Aims and Economic Reality*, Macmillan, 1985, p. 110.
55   J. Callaghan, *Time and Change*, p. 519.
56   D. Healey, *The Time of My Life*, p. 462.
57   J. Callaghan, *Time and Change*, p. 521.
58   Ibid., p. 474.
59   TUC Congress report, 1978, pp. 437–8.
60   J. Callaghan, *Time and Change*, p. 523.
61   Labour–TUC Liaison Committee document, p. 34.
62   TUC Congress report, 1978, p. 543.
63   *Contemporary Record*, 1 (3), Autumn 1987, p. 36.
64   TUC Congress report, 1978, pp. 242–3.
65   Labour Party Conference report, 1978, p. 214.
66   Callaghan, *Time and Change*, p. 65.
67   TUC Congress report, 1979, p. 272.
68   J. Callaghan, *Time and Change*, p. 527.
69   T. Benn, *Conflicts of Interest 1977–1980*, Hutchinson, 1990, p. 391.
70   D. Healey, *The Time of My Life*, p. 64.
71   W. Rodgers, 'Government under Stress – Britain's Winter of Discontent 1978–79', *Political Quarterly*, 155 (2), 1984, p. 173.
72   T. Benn, *Conflicts of Interest*, pp. 419–20.
73   D. Healey, *The Time of My Life*, p. 463.
74   W. Rodgers, 'Government under Stress', p. 176.
75   J. Callaghan, *Time and Change*, p. 537.
76   E. Hobsbawm, *The Forward March of Labour Halted?*, Verso, 1981, p. 14.
77   B. Donoughue, *Prime Ministers*, Cape, 1987, p. 177.
78   F. Chapple, *Sparks Fly*, Michael Joseph, 1984, p. 150.
79   W. Rodgers, 'Government under Stress', pp. 177–8.
80   D. Healey, *The Time of My Life*, p. 467.
81   B. Donoughue, *Prime Ministers*, p. 191.
82   *Observer*, 6 May 1979, p. 10; and in D. Lipsey and D. Leonard (eds), *The Socialist Agenda*, Cape, 1981, pp. 50–1.
83   W. Brown (ed.), *Changing Contours*, p. 66.
84   S. Beer, *Britain against Itself*, Faber & Faber, 1982, p. 50.

8 The Taming of the Trade Unions, February 1975 to January 1993

Rolling back the unions: An overview

The taming of Britain's allegedly powerful trade unions was widely regarded as being the most impressive and permanent of Mrs Thatcher's political achievements during her premiership between May 1979 and November 1990. Even when contemporary opinion was divided over many of her other 'successes' during her protracted period in office, a virtual consensus exists, at least among political commentators, that she solved the post-war trade union 'problem'.

As Peter Riddell, *The Times*'s political editor argued, 'The trade union issue has largely disappeared from the centre of the political stage – with the annual exception of Congress week in early September when there is much despairing introspection on the theme of whither the unions.'[1] Hugo Young, the *Guardian* political columnist, concluded that Mrs Thatcher's industrial relations strategy was 'remarkably successful'. Among her policies, apparently 'the remorseless shrinking of trade union power' was 'almost universally accorded prime place'.[2] 'The government's legislation on industrial relations has taken hold', wrote Professor Denis Kavanagh. 'Here is an area where the balance of advantage has changed since 1979, from union to employers and managers and from the consultative role granted to the unions to one in which they are virtually ignored by the government'.[3] Mrs Thatcher herself liked to emphasize that marginalizing Britain's trade unions was one of the undoubted successes of her years in power. A number of her Cabinet ministers in their memoirs have expressed a similar conviction. Even her most articulate opponents inside the Conservative party accepted that Mrs Thatcher's handling of the trade union 'question' proved singularly effective. 'Successful trade union reform was Margaret Thatcher's most important achievement', admitted an otherwise highly critical and leading Tory Wet, Sir Ian Gilmour.[4]

Industrial Relations in the 1990s, a Department of Employment White Paper published in July 1991, asserted:

> Without doubt, the government's reforms of industrial relations have played an essential part in transforming Britain's industrial relations since 1979 . . . many of the worst abuses of trade union power have been curbed; union leaders are more accountable to their members than ever before; and the role of the law in industrial relations is widely accepted. Strike levels are at an all-time low. Industrial relations in the UK have now achieved both maturity and stability.[5]

The undoubted relative tranquillity of Britain's industrial relations after the end of the miner's dispute in February 1985 – as measured by the number of working days lost by strikes – was contrasted with the previous two turbulent decades when trade union 'power' was supposed to be at its height. The 1991 White Paper gave cogent expression to the prevailing orthodoxy when it argued that:

> Britain's poor industrial relations were generally acknowledged to be a fundamental cause of the weakness of the British economy. British industry's record of strikes, restrictive practices and overmanning seriously and persistently damaged its ability to compete in the markets of the world. The balance of bargaining power appeared to have moved decisively and permanently in favour of the trade unions. In many cases union leaders were seen to be both irresponsible and undemocratic in exercising their industrial power. British industrial relations were increasingly disfigured by scenes of intimidatory picketing and by strikes aimed directly at the life of the community.[6]

Apparently, many employers and managers during the 1970s:

> had become demoralised by the bias in the law which gave trade unions such power. The law had provided trade unions virtually unlimited protection to organize strikes and other forms of industrial disruption. By giving positive encouragement to the closed shop, the law allowed the trade unions in many sectors of employment to dictate whom an employer could recruit and whom he could not.

The White Paper went on to argue that successive governments in the 1960s and 1970s had attempted to reform industrial relations by legislation only to be 'frustrated by trade union opposition':

Direct intervention in collective bargaining through various forms of incomes policy had failed to tackle the problem of rising earnings unmatched by improvements in productivity. By the end of the 1970s 'incomes policies' were discredited both in theory and practice. Many people had come to believe that Britain's industrial relations problems were insoluble and that, as a result, continuing economic decline was inevitable.

The TUC on the fringe

It would be hard to deny that the years since 1979 have seen the political influence of organized labour reduced gradually to a minimum. Certainly, the TUC ceased to be in any meaningful sense an Estate of the Realm and lost most of its post-war importance; and it will experience enormous difficulty in making any kind of serious comeback during the early 1990s. The Prime Minister rarely met TUC delegations at 10 Downing Street to discuss the economy, industrial relations or anything else. It is true she did not seek to destroy outright or at a stroke most of the innumerable tripartite organizations that were established in the employment area and grew into maturity, mainly during the 1960s and 1970s. Congress House continued to appoint its own nominees to participate as the TUC's representatives on statutory tripartite bodies like ACAS, the HSC and the EOC. But the union nominees exercised at best only a very limited influence over the direction and content of the government's economic and social policies, though they were still able to make an impact on the technical details of an issue under discussion. The NEDC, that worthy bastion of tripartism, was spared the Thatcher axe and only abolished finally by John Major's government on 1 January 1993. But its monthly meetings had been reduced to only four a year after June 1987, while the scope of its work was restricted and its secretariat reduced to a pitiful rump. Norman Tebbit could not bother to conceal his contempt for the senior trade union leaders from the TUC who sat around the table with him at NEDC meetings during his period as Employment Secretary. As he explained in his memoirs: 'I scarcely saw the union leaders at all except at meetings of NEDC. Somehow this old corporatist tripartite forum escaped the axe, much to my personal irritation as I detested wasting a morning in an agony of boredom when I had better things to do'.[7]

The sorry story of the demise of the tripartite Training Commission (formerly the MSC) underlined the erosion of TUC influence over government policy-making. During the early 1980s, the TUC was able to retain an important role in the formulation and implementation of the government's training and manpower strategies. Its support was seen as vital for the successful operation of the Youth Training Scheme, and the TUC members of the MSC's board pressed and won the argument that the young workers on the scheme should be paid an allowance higher than the level of their social benefit entitlement. As Lord David Young, the MSC's chairman from 1981 to 1984 and later Secretary of State for Employment, made clear in his memoirs, he was keen to try and keep party politics out of manpower policy as far as possible and that meant working in a friendly way with the TUC. Indeed, he regarded the TUC's consent as crucial for the government's efforts in tackling the mounting unemployment crisis, even if he did not share the TUC's views about how to cut the jobless total. But in September 1988 the TUC Congress voted to boycott any further participation in the government's revamped Youth Training Scheme. As a result, Norman Fowler, the then Employment Secretary, lost no time in closing down the MSC in retaliation at the TUC's decision and transferring all its functions back to the Department of Employment.

At the beginning of the 1980s, TUC leaders were convinced that Mrs Thatcher would have no policy alternative but to change economic direction – as Heath had done before her in 1972 – if she hoped to survive as Prime Minister in the face of mounting unemployment, which had climbed to more than 3 million by the early months of 1984. Through a mixture of arrogance and short-term miscalculation, the TUC general council behaved as if Mrs Thatcher was merely a nightmarish interlude who would be swept away within a brief period amidst the ruins of her economic failures. In the often complacent expectation that they could defeat her legislation designed to weaken trade union power, the TUC general council decided not to cooperate with the Conservative Employment Acts of 1980 and 1982, just as they had done so successfully with the 1971 Industrial Relations Act. Blind to the different and bleaker realities of the early 1980s they became prisoners of their own recent history and refused to recognize that the labour market had changed significantly during the previous ten years. No amount of bellicose rhetoric could restore their old but lost illusions of power.

The 1983 Conservative election triumph slowly began to change trade union attitudes. TUC General Secretary Len Murray questioned the wisdom of the TUC's non-cooperation strategy at Congress that autumn. He argued in favour of what came to be known as 'New Realism'. 'We cannot talk as if the trade union movement is some sort of alternative government, Brother Bonnie Prince Charlie waiting to be summoned back from exile', he told delegates. Moreover, Murray added that the TUC would also have to 'win back ground' it had 'assumed was safe for ever' now a Conservative government had been re-elected to office – a government that unlike any other since 1945 did not regard the maintenance of full employment as a 'dominant objective' of policy nor the welfare state as a 'binding force' in British society.[8] As Frank Chapple, the EETPU's robust right-wing General Secretary, warned in his TUC presidential address that year, the unions had to 'look reality in the face' and 'confront the truth'.[9] Murray won Congress's backing for his wish to seek a discussion with ministers on a wide-ranging policy agenda but his sincere efforts at achieving a rapprochement between the TUC and the government proved to be futile, mainly because Mrs Thatcher did not want to provide the TUC with even a limited advisory role in the governance of the country. Indeed, the Prime Minister lost little time in underlining the hopelessness of Congress House's belated attempt to adopt a more reasonable attitude.

On 25 January 1984 Sir Geoffrey Howe, the Foreign Secretary, outlawed trade unionism at the government's intelligence gathering centre at Cheltenham in the name of national security. The move may have been purely coincidental with the TUC's attempt to try and restore a dialogue with the government, but when Mrs Thatcher rejected out of hand the TUC's offer of a no-strike agreement for GCHQ workers in return for allowing them to remain as trade union members it was clear that little real prospect existed of any new and positive relationship developing between the trade unions and a Conservative government that made no secret of its determination to destroy Britain's post-war efforts at building an industrial consensus based on voluntarism. The Prime Minister actually told a TUC delegation who came to meet her in Downing Street during the GCHQ crisis that she believed there was an inherent conflict between the structure of trade unions and their loyalty to the state.

As a result of government hostility – at best indifference – by the end of the 1980s the TUC was a shadow of its former self, prone to understandable bouts of bitter introspection and unsure of its role as the focus of its activities moved inexorably away from economic policy-making with the state into the gloomy problems of inexorable trade union decline, organization and inter-union relations. From being men with names that enjoyed instant household recognition, Britain's trade union leaders disappeared almost completely from the glare of public view.

Step by step

The TUC's growing impotence was evident from the effortless evolution of the Conservative 'step by step' industrial relations strategy to shift the power balance in industry decisively away from organized labour No less than six specific pieces of industrial relations legislation were passed between 1980 and 1993. The measures, when taken together, represented the most fundamental transformation in Britain's labour laws since the passage of the 1906 Trade Disputes Act. Cumulatively, the legislation imposed severe restrictions on the ability of trade unions to act freely, which brought strong criticism on nine occasions from the International Labour Organization in Geneva for the alleged British defiance of ILO conventions. More often than not, the strategy was developed in a piecemeal and *ad hoc* manner with the policy-makers being greatly influenced – as has happened so often in the past with industrial relations law – by their instant reaction to a specific event or the search for electoral popularity.

Legal restraints alone, however, were not enough – as most Conservatives realized – to shift the power balance away from the trade unions. As Nigel Lawson explained in his memoirs: 'the transformation of industrial relations' during the 1980s also depended on the government's 'abandonment of the unfulfillable commitment to full employment' and its 'eschewing of pay policy which conferred undue importance on trade union leaders while creating unnecessary grievances among their members'.[10]

Unlike Heath in the spring of 1972, Mrs Thatcher was in no mood for turning in the face of soaring dole queues which might threaten her government's standing with the voters. Despite the enormous political pressures on her to do so she refused to abandon her monetarist strategy with any move to reflate the economy and reverse the unemployment trend. Between May 1979 and its peak in July 1986 the official registered number of people out of work in Britain rose from 1.09 million to 3.3 million, despite the thirty government changes in the way that the statistics were compiled that reduced the jobless total significantly by perhaps as much as one million.

The deepest recession since the inter-war years cut swathes through the ranks of organized labour, especially in the old industrial sectors of steel, engineering and shipbuilding. Many commentators expressed gloomy fears about the country's deindustrialization. Others convinced themselves that manufacturing would emerge leaner and fitter from the squeeze. In its seminal 1985 White Paper, *Employment: The Challenge for the Nation*, the government explicitly dropped the post-war government commitment to the state's responsibility to maintain or seek to achieve full employment. The laudable bipartisan aspiration contained in the famous 1944 Employment White Paper was longer regarded as valid. According to the Thatcher government, 'Jobs come from customers and from nowhere else. That simple and enduring truth must underlie any useful discussion

Table 8.1 Unemployment under the Conservatives, 1979–1992

	Average number out of work	*Percentage of the labour force*
1979	1,234,000	5.4
1980	1,513,000	6.9
1981	2,395,000	10.7
1982	2,770,000	12.1
1983	2,984,000	11.7
1984	3,284,000	11.7
1985	3,346,000	11.8
1986	3,289,000	11.8
1987	2,870,000	10.3
1988	2,370,000	8.4
1989	1,799,000	6.3
1990	1,665,000	5.8
1991	2,292,000	8.1
1992	2,778,000	9.8

Source: Employment Gazettes.

of employment.' The White Paper went on to insist there was 'no basic lack of demand in the economy'. Apparently, the reason why there was such a large number of people without work in the early 1980s stemmed from the fact that the jobs market had 'not adapted well enough' to change. This did not mean that the state had no role to play but it was to be 'though crucial, inescapably limited'. Indeed, the White Paper believed government had three interlocking parts to play in 'guiding and supporting the national effort for jobs'.[11] These were to control the rate of inflation; to remove obstacles to employment and encourage skill training; and to help the long-term jobless through direct state schemes.

The government also made moves during the 1980s in the name of competitiveness and efficiency to dismantle the old legal protections in the labour market which covered millions of lower paid workers and the unorganized. This involved not merely the repeal of what flimsy legal advances were made to safeguard such workers in the 1975 Employment Protection Act during the period of the Social Contract, but also the abolition of the Fair Wages Resolution which covered the tendering of contracts by public authorities to the private sector – first introduced in 1891 by a Conservative government. In 1988, a significant weakening was also achieved in the legal position of the 26 tripartite Wages Councils, the first of which were created in 1909 by Winston Churchill when Liberal President of the Board of Trade. This was done by simply removing all young workers between the ages of 16 and 21 from the operation of the Wages Councils. In 1993 the government went much further and decided simply to abolish all the Wages Councils.

The government's abandonment of any attempt to maintain even the semblance of an industrial consensus during the 1980s was also seen in Mrs Thatcher's consistent and firm refusal to accept the need for either a statutory or voluntary prices and incomes policy. She was even hostile to any suggestion there should be a pay norm in the public sector. The Prime Minister was determined that there must be no return to what she regarded as the discredited post-war attempts to curb wage-push inflation through the establishment by the state of an incomes policy with its resulting distortion on the free play of market forces. In this respect, Mrs Thatcher accepted the merciless logic of free collective bargaining. But in practice, her policy towards the unionized public sector was more prag- matic and not ideological. She was willing to avoid potential trouble by accepting high wage settlements for public sector workers with proven muscle power such as those employed in electricity supply, but with groups with less effective bargaining strength, like the teachers and hospital ancillary workers, she was prepared to resist their wage increase demands. Treasury-imposed cash limits laid down a seemingly tight ceiling on the level of permitted public sector pay settlements, and for the most part those working in the public sector found their pay and conditions relative to the private sector deteriorate for most of the 1980s.

But this did not pave the way for an all-out state assault on the very existence of public sector unionism. Contrary to understandable fears at the time, the government's outlawing of trade unions at its Cheltenham intelligence gathering centre did not lead on to similar draconian moves by the government to roll back the trade unions from anywhere else in the public services sector. While there was a noticeable lack of ministerial enthusiasm in the promotion of trade union principles and collective bargaining inside the public sector, at least up until 1991 demands from radical right pressure groups for an actual state ban of strikes in 'essential services' failed to secure much ministerial approval.

In the nationalized industries Mrs Thatcher seemed generally intent on allowing commercial market pressures to determine the outcome of pay bargaining. As a result, a number of set-piece industrial conflicts took place during the early years of her rule from the 1980 national steel strike, through the 1982 rail showdown over the restrictive practice of flexible rostering used by drivers, and ending up with the epic and tragic

Table 8.2   Trade union membership decline, 1979–1991

	Number in unions	Percentage of workforce
1979	13,289,000	53.0
1980	12,947,000	51.8
1981	12,106,000	50.4
1982	11,593,000	49.1
1983	11,236,000	48.2
1984	10,994,000	46.3
1985	10,821,000	45.0
1986	10,539,000	43.8
1987	10,475,000	42.8
1988	10,376,000	41.0
1989	10,158,000	39.2
1990	9,700,000	38.0
1991	9,500,000	34.4

Source: Employment Gazettes.

showdown with the miners in 1984–5. Unlike in the previous bouts of post-war industrial unrest, these battles did not result in many victories for the forces of organized labour. On the contrary, Mrs Thatcher herself emerged more resolute and triumphant than ever from the selective industrial measures of the early 1980s.

The government's crusade to privatize state owned industry which grew in intensity only after the Conservative election victory in June 1983 was also partly motivated by a determination to weaken the trade unions. It was claimed that they enjoyed monopolistic powers of bargaining in the highly politicized nationalized sector of the economy.

Lost union bargaining power

But outside appearances were not all what they seemed. Indeed, it was by no means clear that the industrial as opposed to the political strength of the trade unions had really declined dramatically as a result of government action during the years of Thatcherism. It is true that the size of the unionized workforce fell from a historic high of 58.9 per cent in 1979 to 32 per cent by 1992, and the TUC's affiliated unions together lost a third of their members. In the private sector, union density among those in work dropped from just over one in four in 1980 to less than one in three ten years later. However, this sharp contraction was much more due to the high level of unemployment and occupational and structural change inside the labour market, with the sharp cut in jobs in traditionally unionized sectors of manufacturing, than to any coherent state strategy which was single-mindedly intent on emasculating the trade unions. Concerted union recruitment drives may have failed to make any dramatic inroads into the burgeoning private services, but the public services sector continued to remain a stronghold of trade unionism through the 1980s.

Collective bargaining also persisted despite the government's increasingly explicit rhetorical support for more individualized systems of wage determination, at least in the early part of the 1980s. In the words of the 1990 ACAS annual report: 'Collective bargaining still remains, directly or indirectly, the prime determinant of the terms and conditions of employment for the majority of people at work.'[12] But the 1990 government-sponsored workplace industrial relations survey revealed that a more ominous trend for the trade unions was gathering pace by the end of the decade, when it estimated the proportion of the labour force covered by collective bargaining agreements had fallen from 68 per cent to only 54 per cent between 1984 and 1990. In the private sector the proportion declined from 52 per cent to only 41 per cent, while in the public sector the fall was from 95 per cent to 78 per cent.

In the summer of 1991 the Conservatives raised what was potentially the most devastating reform of industrial relations law designed to weaken the trade unions, when the government proposed for the first time to change the 'check-off' arrangement under which employers paid trade unions the subscription rates for their members from their wage packets. This was a system that had grown more widespread through the greater formalization of labour practices during the late 1970s and 1980s under the enthusiastic direction of employers, and undoubtedly it helped to strengthen the financial position of the trade unions at a time when their memberships were falling. In 1989 it was estimated that 72 per cent of all Britain's trade unionists had their union subscriptions paid for by their employer through the check-off system compared with only 58 per cent ten years earlier. Some estimates suggested that the trade unions could lose up to 15–20 per cent of their existing members as a result of the change in the law that was introduced in 1993. This required individual trade unionists every three years to give their approval to their employer to agree to allow the check-off of union dues from their pay packet.

Contrary to Conservative assumptions that the existence of the closed shop was a primary reason why workers belonged to trade unions, a government-commissioned study in 1989 found only one in ten workers gave as a reason for belonging to a union that it was 'a condition of having the job'. By contrast, just under 40 per cent said the most important reason they were in unions was 'to protect' them 'if problems come up in the future', while a further 23 per cent claimed they belonged to trade unions in order 'to get higher pay and better conditions'. Only 7 per cent said they were in unions because unions were a 'way of creating a more just society'.[13] But the closed shop became virtually extinct in Britain by the end of the 1980s when it was made in effect illegal. Between 1984 and 1990 the number of establishments with closed shop agreements covering their manual workers fell from 20 per cent to only 4 per cent. The number of workers in closed shop arrangements dropped from 5 million in 1980 to only 500,000 ten years later. But there were no signs that the demise of the closed shop stimulated employers to adopt more overtly anti-union strategies in their workplaces. As the 1990 workplace industrial relations survey went on to point out, managers still found it was in their interest to have most of their workers represented by trade unions, and many took positive steps to encourage them to join.

Moreover, although the industrial relations climate grew more difficult for the trade unions during the 1980s, some of the reforms carried out under Mrs Thatcher actually strengthened unions rather than weakened them, even if this was not always the real intention. The extension of democratic procedures into the trade unions through the use of workplace and later postal ballots under Conservative legislation certainly helped to legitimize their activities. The introduction of the secret ballot before the calling of official strikes was often used by the trade unions to improve their bargaining stance with employers. Up to 1989 an estimated 92 per cent of such ballots had resulted in Yes votes by members for strike action in pursuit of union demands and brought an improved employer offer as a result. However, it is true on the other hand that there was a marked decline in strike activity during the 1980s, and the risk of sequestration by the courts of trade union funds certainly became a major deterrent to those unions who were threatening the use of the strike weapon. Trade unions that used secondary action as a tactic in industrial disputes had to think more seriously than before about doing so.

The wages 'problem' continues

More crucially, however, Mrs Thatcher's government was unable to do very much to resolve Britain's underlying and persistent post-war problem of high unit labour costs, caused by inflationary wage settlements that

Table 8.3   Strikes under the Conservatives, 1979–1992

	Number of strikes	Workers involved	Working days lost
1979	2,125	4,608,000	29,474,000
1980	1,348	834,000	11,964,000
1981	1,344	1,513,000	4,266,000
1982	1,538	2,103,000	5,313,000
1983	1,364	574,000	3,754,000
1984	1,221	1,464,000	27,135,000
1985	903	791,000	6,402,000
1986	1,074	720,000	1,920,000
1987	1,016	857,000	3,546,000
1988	781	790,000	3,702,000
1989	701	727,000	4,128,000
1990	630	298,000	1,903,000
1991	369	176,000	761,000
1992		148,000	528,000

Source: Employment Gazettes.

plagued the economy for much of the time after 1945, and sluggish productivity performance. For the majority of trade unionists who remained in employment, the 1980s turned out to be a prosperous decade of rising living standards as the increase in their real post-tax earnings remained firmly above the rise in the Retail Price Index for every year between 1982 and 1991, despite the stubborn existence of relatively high unemployment. Between 1979 and 1989 real earnings rose on average by 21 per cent and money wages by a huge 145 per cent, while consumer prices over the same period increased by 103 per cent. The stubborn refusal of real or nominal earnings to fall and rise in line with improved productivity suggested that the political marginalization of trade union leaders and the passage of a plethora of industrial relations legislation designed avowedly to weaken workplace trade union power were not sufficient in themselves to create the preconditions necessary for the long-awaited economic take-off that had eluded Britain ever since 1945.

Limited success on supply side problems

The overall impact of Mrs Thatcher's government on industrial relations and the labour market during the 1980s appeared limited, uneven and ultimately inconclusive. But the vulnerability of organized labour in the face of a determined government was real enough. What success Mrs Thatcher enjoyed in her handling of the trade union 'problem' stemmed from her willingness to abandon what remained of the post-war social settlement, most notably by forsaking any explicit commitment to the maintenance of 'full' employment, and also through the rejection of statutory controls to restrain wage rises and of market-distorting economic measures like subsidies and price restrictions designed to pacify shopfloor discontents.

The most important legal change she made was to reform Britain's unique legal immunities system of industrial relations to the tactical disadvantage of trade unions. Unlike Edward Heath, Mrs Thatcher sought not to change industrial relations through a single comprehensive legal measure but moved much more cautiously in stages so as to work along with rather than against the grain of the voluntarist tradition. Like Britain's trade union leaders she also believed in 'free' collective bargaining and a minimalist role for the state in industrial relations. Often her ideological zeal was tempered by hesitancy and prudence. In an area which had defeated her three predecessors Mrs Thatcher moved with understandably pragmatic caution. She was willing to retreat from time to time better to fight another day, as she did for example in February 1981 when the threat of a premature showdown with the miners on Britain's coalfields appeared to threaten her authority to govern. But on the other hand she never lost sight of her ultimate objective, which was to weaken the trade unions and prevent them from thwarting her avowed attempt to turn Britain into a dynamic free market economy much closer in spirit and practice to that allegedly created by President Reagan in the United States during the 1980s than to the successful social market capitalism of western Europe.

It is questionable whether the weakening of the trade unions through changes in the law or barring the entry of their leaders into 10 Downing Street did much to remove the deep-rooted labour market troubles that really lay at the heart of Britain's post-war industrial malaise. Mrs Thatcher's surprising failure to give a high priority to dealing with genuine supply side problems like Britain's inadequate education and industrial training systems was much more significant than her symbolic headline-catching victories in reducing so-called trade union power in the early 1980s. So was her short-sighted resistance to the creation of a 'social Europe' based on economic liberal principles to complement the European Community's free single internal market from 1 January 1993. Nor did Mrs Thatcher display much interest in forms of employee involvement like German-style works councils and co-determination, which she believed were mere political corporatist devices designed to bring about the return of trade union power. The fact that the more consensual industrial relations approach was the norm in northern European countries like West Germany and Sweden, which had achieved much better records of industrial success and higher living standards than Britain's since the end of the Second World War, failed to impress her.

By treating the relationship between the state and trade unions as a zero-sum struggle of winners and losers, Mrs Thatcher lost the opportunity to stimulate the creation of a high wage, high output economy where industrial relations were based – for the most part – on a framework of positive law. By the early 1990s it was unclear whether the Iron Lady had indeed transformed worker attitudes and trade union practices in any fundamental way, but her intention was clear enough and it represented a dramatic abandonment of the One Nation Conservatism that had dominated her party's post-war strategy towards the trade unions apart from the unhappy period of Heath's ill-fated 1971 Industrial Relations Act.

The start of the step by step strategy

During their years in opposition between March 1974 and May 1979, the Conservatives were unsure and divided about how to resolve the trade union 'problem'. The unexpected election of Margaret Thatcher to the party leadership in February 1975 led to no immediate emergence of a coherent anti-union strategy. Indeed, for the most part, perhaps because she felt uncertain about the security of her own political position, Mrs Thatcher seemed willing at least to tolerate the benevolent paternalism of the emollient Jim Prior who remained as the party's shadow Employment spokesman although he had been appointed to the post by the discredited Heath. His deliberate attempt to conciliate the national union leaders reflected his own sober assessment of the mistakes alleged to have been made by the last Conservative government in its relations with organized labour during the early 1970s. To many of the party's right-wingers, however, like Norman Tebbit, who although on the back benches worked closely with Mrs Thatcher in her robust parliamentary tactics, Prior's attitude was nothing less than one of rank appeasement. 'They are willing not only to tolerate evil but to excuse it', declared Tebbit and likened by implication the Prior policy to the 'morality of Laval and Petain'.[14] During the notorious 1977 Grunwick strike, Prior was criticized openly by many leading Conservatives for his refusal to throw the party's whole-hearted support behind the cause of Mr George Ward, the owner of the North London photographic processing company, in his resolute stance against recognizing the clerical trade union APEX to bargain on behalf of his employees. Indeed, Prior found himself in serious disagreement with other members of the Shadow Cabinet who were much closer than he was to Mrs Thatcher's opinions on the trade unions – notably Sir Keith Joseph, the party's Industry spokesman, and shadow Chancellor of the Exchequer Sir Geoffrey Howe.

Prior's attempt to revive the benevolent One Nation Toryism of the pre-1964 era in his handling of industrial relations coexisted often uneasily with his new leader's more ideologically hostile instincts for a much more robust approach to curb alleged trade union power. It was clear that Mrs Thatcher had no wish to establish any close cooperation with the TUC in a future Conservative government. She denounced Heath-style corporatism in unequivocal language. There would be no return to a statutory prices and incomes policy under a future Conservative government led by her. Nor would she seek a Conservative version of the Social Contract. Mrs Thatcher was determined to destroy what remained of the post-war social settlement, not to revive it. Moreover her economic convictions – that the cure for inflation lay through a tight control of the money supply and the country's economic revival would come through a mixture of tax cuts to stimulate the work ethic and stiff curbs on government expenditure – were unlikely to find any favour among trade union leaders, particularly as she seemed willing to tolerate a substantial increase in the level of unemployment, at least in the short term, to discipline the labour market.

Mrs Thatcher's dislike of trade unions was not just a reflection of her natural combative personality. It also stemmed from her strong conviction that they were primary obstacles to the kind of successful free market economy she wanted to create. Her views about industrial relations were derived not from any direct experience in running a business, but mainly from the influential writings of that formidable neo-liberal economist Professor Friedrich von Hayek. His intellectual impact on her economic thought should never be underestimated. Unfortunately, in his academic approach to industrial relations Hayek was at his most dogmatic. He regarded trade unions as monopolistic threats to the free market who prevented 'competition from acting as an effective regulator in the allocation of all resources'.[15] In his influential *Constitution of Liberty* published in 1960, Hayek warned that trade unions as 'open enemies threatened the whole basis of our free society'. Hayek argued that trade unions were 'coercive' organizations who raised workers' wages above a free market level, thereby causing unemployment, restrictions on labour mobility, and inefficiencies through the control they exercised over the labour supply. He recommended transforming trade unions into 'friendly societies' by removing all of their legal protection for picketing and also their ability to stop employers hiring non-unionists through a ban on the closed shop, by the outlawing of all secondary strikes and boycotts, and by making 'the responsibility for organized and concerted action in conflict with contractual obligations or the general law firmly placed on those in whose hands the decision lies, irrespective of the particular form of organized action adopted'. Hayek argued:

> If we want to preserve the market economy our aim must be to restore the effectiveness of the price mechanism. The chief obstacle to its functioning is trade union monopoly.

But he also argued that:

> A monetary policy that would break the coercive powers of the unions by producing extensive and protracted unemployment must be excluded, for it would be politically and socially fatal.[16]

In his opinion,

> the acquisition of privilege by the unions had nowhere been as spectacular as in Britain where the 1906 Trade Dispute Act – in the words of the eminent legal expert Professor A. V. Dicey – conferred 'upon a trade union a freedom from civil liability for the commission of even the most heinous wrong by the union or its servant and in short conferred upon every trade union a privilege and protection not possessed by any other person or body of persons, whether corporate or incorporate'.

Hayek claimed that the legalized powers conferred on Britain's trade unions by that legislation had 'become the biggest obstacle to raise the living standards of the working class as a whole'.[17] He explained – without a shred of evidence – in 1980 that: 'They are the chief cause of the unnecessarily big differences between the best- and worst-paid workers. They are the prime source of unemployment. They are the main reason for the decline of the British economy in general.' Hayek argued that 'all the most harmful practices of British trade unions' like 'intimidatory picketing, preventing non-members from doing particular jobs such as demarcation rules and the closed shop' derived from 'their being allowed forcefully to prevent outsiders from offering their services to the public on their own terms'. In his opinion such a development had made 'the average level of attainable real wages of British workers as a whole' substantially lower than they would otherwise have been and reduced labour productivity. 'They have turned Britain, which at one time had the highest wages in Europe into a relatively low wage economy', he claimed. He went on to assert that the country's economic recovery was 'impossible so long as general opinion makes it impossible to deprive trade unions of their coercive powers'.[18]

Professor Hayek's strictures against the state's intervention in wage fixing were welcome to many Conservatives, after the dismal and traumatic experience of Heath's statutory prices and incomes policy. He suggested that the trade union desire to 'see wages determined by some conception of "justice" rather than by the forces of the market' would lead inevitably to state control of pay determination and the destruction of free trade unionism. As he argued:

> In no workable system could any group of people be allowed to enforce by the threat of violence what it believes it should have. And when not merely a few privileged groups but most of the important sections of labour have become effectively organized for coercive action, to allow each to act independently would not only produce the opposite of justice but result in economic chaos.

As a result government would have to decide wage levels and this meant workers would be in 'complete subjection to the control by a corporative state'. Hayek asserted that 'The present position of the unions cannot last, for they can function only in a market economy which they are doing their best to destroy.'[19]

Hayek's trenchant critique of trade unionism may have first been fully formulated at the end of the 1950s, but to Mrs Thatcher and other likeminded Conservatives it seemed more valid than ever after the Heath government's period of interminable industrial conflict. Moreover, the Social Contract between the Labour party and the TUC strengthened their conviction that the Hayekian analysis provided a valuable insight into the character of the British 'disease'. Sir Keith Joseph – the party's industry spokesman – was influenced strongly by such thinking:

> Our unions have been uniquely privileged for several decades but Labour's recent legislation – all at the TUC's request – seems designed to ensure a strong union can almost always win any dispute regardless of its economic case. . . . The predictable result has been the growing use of strikes and the strike threat. In a trade dispute most things seem permitted for the union side – breaking contracts; inducing others to break contracts; picketing of non-involved companies; secondary boycotts. A trade dispute can be between workers and workers; it can concern matters of discipline, membership, facilities; it may even relate to matters overseas. All this is unique to Britain; there is nothing like it in other countries.[20]

Joseph contrasted the allegedly greater trade union powers acquired under the Social Contract with the loss of centralized control by trade union leaders over the way their members behaved in industrial disputes. In his opinion, 'national economic failure and the militants' charter' had combined in the mid-1970s to provide 'a supreme opportunity to the left-wing minority whose instincts are destructive and bitterly opposed to the free enterprise economy most people want'. To Joseph the end result was 'confusion' with the breakdown of trust between full-time trade union officials and shop stewards as well as between shop stewards and workers. 'We now face an unstable situation', he warned. 'The collapse of Socialist expectation; increasingly ruthless efforts by big unions to escape the consequences; inter-union warfare and the fruits of the militants' charter.' In his opinion, trade union strength had weakened the ability of employers to resist:

> The enterprise cannot count on subsidy to help survive the dispute, as strikers can. Its financial haemorrhage starts immediately as its hard-earned savings bleed away. Other companies may have to pay guaranteed lay-off pay to their workers who are not involved in the strike at all. Secondary picketing may force them to halt operations altogether. If after surrender to strike action, the struck-against company has to reduce its workforce, it must add to the cost of the strike and of increased wages, substantial redundancy payments to workers it has been forced to lay off. The militants' charter looks increasingly like a charter for the systematic destruction of law-abiding, job-creating free enterprise in the name of Socialism.

Such strictures were not confined to the neo-liberals in the Conservative party. The leading intellectual Tory Wet Sir Ian Gilmour, whom Mrs Thatcher was to dismiss from the Cabinet in September 1981, was also critical of the trade unions. In the late 1970s he likened the trade union movement to the late medieval Church on the eve of the Reformation:

> Much as Luther believed that the Church of his day was a barrier between the Christian and his God, so trade unions are now an obstacle to the prosperity of their members. By their insistence on restrictive practices, overmanning, government pourboires and inflationary wage claims and strikes, trade unions have slowed economic growth, fuelled inflation, increased unemployment and undermined the authority of the state. Whatever the other reasons for Britain's economic failures, strong trade unions are certainly one of them. Although they did so in the past, these costly antiques do not now further the interests of their members.[21]

Despite the clear hardening of Conservative attitudes towards the trade unions during the 1978–9 Winter of Discontent, the party's 1979 general election manifesto was not a Hayekian clarion cry to roll back trade union power. Prior was able to hold his own in the Shadow Cabinet behind a prudent industrial relations strategy. The Conservatives promised to make immediate legislative changes in only three specific areas of labour practice. Picketing was to be confined to strikers at their place of work and nowhere else. 'Violence, intimidation and obstruction cannot be tolerated', asserted the manifesto. 'We shall ensure that the protection of the law is available to those not concerned in the dispute but who at present can suffer severely from secondary action.'

Action was also promised to weaken the closed shop by ensuring that future ones would need the support by secret ballot of an 'overwhelming majority' of the workers involved to come into force. Workers 'arbitrarily excluded or expelled from any union' were to be given the right of appeal to a court of law for redress with 'ample compensation' if they lost their job as a consequence of the imposition of a 100 per cent union membership agreement. Secret ballots were to be encouraged in the holding of union elections and on 'other important issues' such as strikes by the provision of public funds towards their administration. 'Every trade unionist should be free to record his decisions as every voter has done for a hundred years in parliamentary elections', argued the manifesto. 'Too often trade unions are dominated by a handful of extremists who do not reflect the common-sense view of most union members.' There was just a hint that these proposals might not prove to be sufficient. 'Further changes may be needed to encourage people to behave responsibly and keep the bargains they make at work', argued the manifesto and it mentioned in particular action to review the financial support provided by the state for strikers and their families in the belief that unions should 'bear their fair share of the cost in supporting those of their members who are on strike'.[22]

Although the Conservative agenda for changes in labour law were limited and specific, the party's manifesto suggested there were no inhibitions about going further. 'Labour claims that industrial relations in Britain cannot be improved by changing the law. We disagree', declared the party. 'If the law can be used to confer privileges, it can and should also be used to establish obligations. We cannot allow a repetition of the behaviour that we saw outside too many of our factories and hospitals last winter.'

However, the proposed changes in the law fell far short of any root and branch confrontation with organized labour. They were pragmatic, cautious and undoubtedly enjoyed the approval of the vast majority of people at the time, including that of most trade unionists. But, as so often, labour law was being shaped not by adherence to any universalist principles of right and wrong but by the muddy issues of the moment. In the summer of 1979 Mrs Thatcher was not yet self-confident enough to press for more drastic change in industrial relations in the face of Prior's likely resistance. Moreover, she was keen to avoid suffering the dismal fate of her hapless predecessor Heath at the hands of organized labour. A 'step by step' strategy made much more sense than an anti-union blitzkrieg that could well provoke a confrontation with the TUC in her first year in office that she could not hope to win.

As a sign of her willingness to move slowly, Mrs Thatcher decided to make Prior her first Employment Secretary – much to his own evident surprise. As a conciliatory One Nation Tory he did not share her enthusiasm for Hayek's views on trade unions and he sought valiantly to keep open Conservative government channels to the TUC. Despite some misgivings, however, Prior won his argument for cautious change and at least initially for only limited changes in industrial relations law. His 1980 Employment Act was very much a minimalist measure, though it met with the TUC's predictable opposition. As Prior explained in his memoirs:

> It would have been easy for the Government to go too far in changing the law and to do so too fast; we would then find that not only the unions but also business and most of the country would unite in saying that we had produced a scheme of law that was unworkable. A more cautious step by step approach would also make it virtually impossible for the unions to whip up an effective campaign of opposition since the measures being introduced could scarcely be portrayed as draconian.[23]

He was also keen to play down any suggestion that the measure was part of any grand strategy, motivated by anti-union ideology. 'Our approach is essentially a pragmatic one. We are not in the business of change for change's sake', he assured the Commons during its second reading.[24]

In fact, both Prior and Mrs Thatcher agreed they must try and avoid any repetition of the humiliating experience of the 1971 Industrial Relations Act. The resulting 1980 Employment Act restricted picketing to a striker's own place of work. So-called 'sympathy' strikes as well as blacking and blockading were to be confined only to the first direct suppliers and customers of the firm in dispute. Moves were also made to weaken the existence of the closed shop. Any future 100 per cent union membership agreement would need to acquire an 80 per cent majority vote of approval in a secret ballot from the workers involved before becoming legally acceptable. The conscience and personal conviction grounds for exclusion from a closed shop were widened and compensation was to be provided to workers who lost their jobs because they refused to join a trade union in a closed shop. A Code of Practice called for a 'periodic review' of existing closed shop agreements and laid down specific conditions on how those reviews were to be conducted. Government funds were also to be made available to trade unions who wished to ballot their members before calling strikes, and for the costs involved in the election of their officials or changes they wanted to make in their own union rule books, while employers were obliged to provide premises for the holding of such ballots. This was a voluntary provision and indeed no trade unions took up the state offer of financial assistance until 1984, when both the EETPU and AUEW defied the TUC's boycott and accepted retrospective payments from the Department of Employment.

Prior insisted the 1980 measure was concerned with 'balance' in industrial relations between the 'rights of the individual' and the 'right of individuals to act together'. Essentially, it was a limited reform designed not to roll back trade union power but to strengthen responsible voluntarism. 'Our proposals are designed to improve industrial relations but to do so by working with the grain rather than against it', he explained.

During the passage of the Employment Bill through Parliament, Prior introduced a new and important clause into the measure after a House of Lords judgement in the case of *Express Newspapers* v. *MacShane*, which reaffirmed that trade unions enjoyed comprehensive immunity in tort from legal action for breaches of commercial as well as employment contracts. As Prior explained:

> The Lords' ruling had shown that union immunities, as defined by the 1976 Trade Union and Labour Relations Act, were unnecessarily and dangerously wide. The law gave unions virtual carte blanche for any action they chose to take – it did not matter what anyone else thought or what the objective facts were, the sole criterion of any action was the subjective view of the trade unionists who were carrying out the industrial action.[25]

The 1980 steel strike compelled Prior to act quickly, after the steel unions decided to extend their conflict with the state-owned British Steel Corporation to cover the country's private steel producers who were not directly involved in the strike through the use of mass picketing outside their premises as well as other secondary action. He was under enormous Cabinet pressure, particularly from Thatcher and Howe, to amend his Bill passing through Parliament in order to make all secondary action unlawful. But Prior resisted this move, 'believing anything more restrictive at that stage simply would not stick'.[26] However, it took an enormous effort to restrain Mrs Thatcher, who wanted to rush a one-clause Bill through Parliament to outlaw all forms of secondary picketing and even tried to mobilize Conservative peers behind her on the issue despite the opposition of her own Lord Chancellor Lord Hailsham.

The 1980 Employment Act failed to go anywhere near far enough in curbing the power of the trade unions to satisfy most Conservatives. The Prime Minister did not disguise her determination to press ahead with a further measure to weaken trade union power as quickly as possible. However, Prior was less convinced about the need for more immediate industrial relations legislation. Instead, he sought to assuage the pressure for further reform by launching a national debate on the future of labour law. As he recalled in his memoirs: 'It seemed to me that if Labour's legislation had been unbalanced in one direction favouring the unions, we had to be wary of not tilting the balance too far back in the other.'[27] In January 1981 his Department published a cogent and well-argued Green Paper on legal immunities, which examined the intricacies of the problem. But this scholarly and reasonably objective document stimulated rather than terminated demands for more radical industrial relations legislation. Indeed, it provided a useful catalyst for action among the numerous right-wing pressure groups who were busy agitating behind the scenes for Prior's removal from his post at the Department of Employment. During the summer of 1981 a number of such organizations – most notably the Institute of Directors, Aims of Industry, and the Centre for Policy Studies, who worked together through a dining club called the Argonauts – coordinated their written responses to the Green Paper with a list of like-minded demands which they wanted to see included in the next piece of industrial relations legislation.

First and foremost, they wanted the government to take a decisive step forward by making the trade unions liable – for the first time since 1906 – to damages in civil actions taken out against them by employers or other aggrieved parties in what the courts deemed to be unlawful industrial disputes. They also favoured the removal of immunities from the organizers of strikes that breached an existing procedure agreement between an employer and unions, as well as the abolition not only of the pre-entry closed shop, but of all forms of secondary action as well as the existence of union-labour-only clauses in commercial contracts. The groups also proposed that workers in essential services such as gas, water and electricity should lose their legal immunity in strikes in return for some form of wage protection against inflation. The Engineering Employers' Federation and the Association of British Chambers of Commerce joined forces with the Argonauts in the coordinated lobbying which was encouraged by

Sir John Hoskyn, then the head of Mrs Thatcher's Downing Street policy unit and a regular attender at Argonaut lunches.

Prior remained unsympathetic to the orchestrated pressure building up on his party's right wing. He was opposed in particular to any change in the law that would make trade unions liable to damages for the actions of their officials in disputes:

> I had fought to prevent this as once again it would have risked taking us back to the 1971 Act in which unions were made liable for their member's actions: I feared it could become the cement of union solidarity. . . . I would not have curbed union immunities any further than they had already been restricted in the 1980 Act. I wanted to see the main provisions in our first Act given time to be accepted and not to try to rush ahead too fast.[28]

All that Prior seemed prepared to do was tighten up the existing legislation on the closed shop by increasing compensation and providing for regular reviews of them through secret ballots of those workers covered. However, a number of unsavoury cases hit the newspaper headlines during 1981 that intensified the pressure for further government action over the closed shop issue. The most notable concerned the dismissal of six dinner ladies by Walsall council for their refusal to join a trade union, and the case of Joanna Harris, a poultry inspector who lost her job with neighbouring Sandwell district council for refusing to join NALGO in a closed shop. Three British Rail employees won their case and secured financial damages from the European Court of Human Rights when they argued successfully that they had been unfairly dismissed for refusing to join a trade union.

By September 1981, Prior found his modest ideas for more industrial relations legislation were much too timid for the Prime Minister's liking. Moreover, he had shown his strong distaste for the controversial 1981 Budget, with its firm determination not to change course from a tight control over the money supply despite a deepening recession and rising unemployment. Further cuts in government spending threatened to worsen the already deepening slump. Prior found himself increasingly out of favour with the whole direction of the government's economic policy. As a leading Tory Wet, he disliked the human harshness of monetarism and feared rising dole queues would endanger social stability.

Mrs Thatcher decided in a wider Cabinet reshuffle to remove him from the Department of Employment. In effect, he was demoted and marginalized by being sent to the Northern Ireland Office. As his replacement she promoted Norman Tebbit, the rising right-wing star with an abusive turn of phrase and no sense of guilt about trade unions. He lost no time in moving where Prior had feared to tread and drew up a further piece of industrial relations legislation which met with Mrs Thatcher's strong approval. 'I was determined to form public opinion and then to be always just a little behind rather than ahead of it as I legislated', he recalled later when summing up his approach to industrial relations reform as a 'mixture of menace and reasonability'.[29] In this, he was a stark contrast to Prior whom he feared had grown 'dangerously behind the mood of the nation'.

Not all the coordinated demands of the right-wing lobbyists found favour in Tebbit's 1982 measure. He was against making procedure agreements legally enforceable nor was he in favour of outlawing disputes in the 'essential services'. Tebbit was also unwilling to bow before pressure from the Engineering Employers Federation who wanted to see a change in the law which would allow their members to lay off workers in disputes without having an obligation to pay them lay-off compensation when they did so.

However, Tebbit did decide to include what turned out to be the most important change of all in the Conservatives' 'step by step' strategy of the 1980s. The funds of trade unions themselves were to be open to damages in the civil courts for unlawful actions carried out by their officials. 'We do not believe that it is right or necessary for trade unions to continue to enjoy an immunity which, as the Donovan commission pointed out, is wider than that of any other organisation or person, even the Crown', declared Tebbit on 23 November 1981.[30] He proposed therefore to repeal Section 14 of the 1974 Trade Union and Labour Relations Act which in the words of the Employment Department gave 'trade unions as such virtually unlimited immunity from actions in tort, even when they organized industrial action outside a trade dispute. This meant that trade unions cannot be sued for their unlawful acts done on their behalf by their officials.'[31] The government argued that:

> The breadth of the immunities is no longer necessary in modern conditions to enable trade unions to represent their members effectively. It is unfair and anomalous that while trade union officials may be sued for organising unlawful industrial action on behalf of a trade union, the union itself can escape liability altogether. In these circumstances there is a lack of incentive for trade unions to ensure that their officials operate within the law and that industrial action is restricted to legitimate trade disputes and is otherwise lawful.[32]

Tebbit proposed to bring trade union immunities into line with those covering individuals who organized or took part in industrial disputes under Section 13 of the 1974 Act. This meant that trade unions themselves would be liable to be sued in tort where they were responsible for 'unlawful acts' which were not – in the words of the golden formula – 'in contemplation and furtherance of a trade dispute', and for actions that were also unlawful for individuals like secondary picketing, indiscriminate secondary and industrial action to compel union membership, and any other changes proposed in the future.

The Employment Secretary also promised that guidance would be provided to indicate when trade unions were to be held 'vicariously liable for unlawful acts committed by their officials' based on the common law principles adopted in the 1972 case of *Heatons Transport (St Helens)* v. *TGWU* and *General Aviation Services (UK) Ltd* v. *TGWU* in 1976. This meant trade unions would be vicariously liable 'only if a trade union's national executive committee had specifically authorized or ratified the action complained of ', or if

[the union's] subordinate body or official of the union whose action was complained of had authority for the action under the union's rules or was acting on instructions from a body or officials who had such authority and if his action had not been repudiated by a more senior authoritative body or union official.[33]

Where union rules were ambiguous on this point, Tebbit declared then the 'trade union official should be liable unless a more senior authoritative body of officials has repudiated the action'.

The 1982 Employment Act stipulated that trade unions which were found liable of carrying out unlawful actions in disputes could be fined heavily by the courts and even have their funds sequestrated and assets seized for contempt. Limits were set on the size of financial penalties depending on the size of the trade union involved. For any trade union with over 100,000 members the limit was set at £250,000, and others on a sliding scale down to £12,500 for those with fewer than 5,000 members. As Lord Wedderburn argued, the opening up of trade union funds to civil damages was 'the key' that made the 'new' step by step strategy 'work'.[34] This change needed no radical transformation in the industrial relations system. On the contrary, it stemmed logically from the old common law tradition with its distaste for autonomous collectivist organizations like trade unions which blocked the free play of economic market forces. 'In the 1980s the sweeping reductions of the immunities readmitted the tides of the common law and put the union, its property and its organisation increasingly at risk', explained Lord Wedderburn. 'A law based and judicially developed upon those very principles which saw unions as an improper restraint of trade in the market and industrial action as an unlawful interference with contracts and property rights, parallel to the Hayek formula.' The 'exposure of union property to civil liability under that common law' avoided the danger of trade union martyrs going to prison for contempt of court.

Indeed, the importance of exposing trade union funds to legal attack and terminating the 1906 settlement was not lost on Tebbit. He admitted in his memoirs that he doubted he would have been able to achieve that proposed drastic change if he had not enjoyed Mrs Thatcher's unyielding support in the face of a hesitant Cabinet. Section 15 of the 1982 Employment Act indeed represented a return to the past, which is why it slotted so easily into the existing legal framework of industrial relations. As Lord Wedderburn argued. 'The "vision" of the Thatcher/Hayek industrial relations programme fitted hand in glove with that mixture of individualism and artificially enforced, spontaneous social order which has often characterized the dominant strain' of the common law tradition.[35]

The rest of the clauses in Tebbit's Employment Bill were far less important than this formidable change. Further steps were taken to undermine the closed shop. Existing union membership agreements that had not been approved in the previous five years were required to secure the support of as many as 80 per cent of the workers concerned or 85 per cent of those voting in a secret ballot. It was also to be deemed an unfair dismissal if an employer fired a worker for not belonging to a trade union in any closed shop which had failed to win membership approval through a secret ballot, and the trade union could be joined in the subsequent legal action and thereby also face severe financial damages. A step was also taken to outlaw union-labour-only subcontracts with employers by making it unlawful for any company to be excluded from a tender list or to fail to win a contract simply on the grounds that they did not employ trade unionists. Tebbit claimed his Bill provided 'the most comprehensive statutory provision for non-union employees we have ever had in this country'.[36]

The legal definition of what was a 'trade dispute' was also narrowed considerably to ensure that only strikes between employees and their own employer enjoyed the protection of legal immunities. Four amendments were proposed to Section 29 of the 1974 Trade Union and Labour Relations Act to tighten up the law in this regard. All strikes had to be related 'wholly or mainly' to pay, conditions and matters of an industrial character rather than merely 'connected with' these elements. Strikes of workers in support of other workers also lost their legal immunity, as did 'disputes relating solely to matters occurring outside Great Britain'. This was a clear move to make solidarity actions unlawful. So-called political strikes also lost their legal immunity. On top of this, disputes involving an employer and a trade union where the employer was not in conflict with his own employees were also made illegal. Employers were also empowered under the 1982 Act to decide for themselves which of their workers they should re-employ after the end of a strike without falling foul of the law. This enabled them to be selective in their rehiring policy so they would not face legal trouble if they refused to take back workers they regarded as trouble-makers.

Tebbit insisted his proposals amounted to a 'modest measure' which was 'demanded' by the majority of trade union members. 'The Bill is noteworthy as much for what it has left out as for what it contains', he told a *Financial Times* conference on 29 April 1982.[37] 'And believe me it would have been very easy to have succumbed to the extensive pressures and made the Bill more comprehensive than it is. But I don't believe in miracles or that it is possible to transform industrial relations overnight.' He pointed out that the 1982 Employment Act had 'not interfered with the internal workings of trade unions in any respect'. In his memoirs he confessed his Act:

> was carefully designed and did not of itself compel the unions to do anything – so there could be no mass refusal to comply with what came to be known as Tebbit's Law. Nor did it create a complex legal statute. It simply tilted the balance of power away from the unions by clipping away the privileges and legal immunities which gave them their ability to ride roughshod over the legitimate rights of the general public.[38]

In fact, Tebbit was dissatisfied at the way in which employers conducted their industrial relations and he often criticized them for a failure to inform their own employees on the most elementary information about their company's performance. He also wondered how hard managements tried to persuade their workers to support the benefits of technological change. 'Employees have to be given a greater stake in the success of the company than simply their wage packet', he insisted. 'If the wage packet is the limit of the employee's consideration it is no wonder that we have so often suffered from irrational and ugly wages explosions'. But Tebbit did not suggest legislative action might be needed to change those deep-seated management attitudes. Apparently, only the trade unions were to be the subject of further legal restriction. This was to set the pattern for the whole of the 1980s. The full rigour of statute law was to be made available for use by aggrieved employers or other parties injured in disputes to order to improve trade union and worker behaviour, but ministers were content merely to express verbal exhortation for employers to behave sensibly and fairly in their industrial relations strategies.

The miners' strike, 1984–1985

The coal strike of 1984–5 was the longest national dispute in post-war Britain and it turned into the seminal domestic event of Mrs Thatcher's years in office. The decisive defeat of the NUM at the hands of a determined government was of crucial importance in the declining power of organized labour. For Mrs Thatcher, the outcome was a personal triumph. Her resolute approach against what she described as the 'enemy within' brought a reaffirmation of the state's authority after the humiliations suffered by Heath in 1972 and in 1974 and by Mrs Thatcher herself in 1981 at the hands of the militant miners. The bitter dispute witnessed violent scenes on picket lines as the police fought pitched battles on some occasions with ranks of angry young miners. Less than a harbinger of brutal conflicts to come, the strike brought a tragic end to the NUM's ability to paralyse the economy.

There was a sad inevitability about the coal dispute. Under the leadership of its far-left president Arthur Scargill, the NUM seemed set on a collision course with Mrs Thatcher's government. From the moment of his landslide election to the top position in the union in April 1982, Scargill made no secret of his ultimate intentions. He demanded a written undertaking from the government and the state-owned National Coal Board that no pit should ever close because it was uneconomic. The only circumstances for a colliery shutdown should be when there was no more coal left to extract from it without endangering the men. Scargill also demanded that annual coal output must be doubled to 200 million tons, with an immediate decision to open 30 to 40 new pits. Scargill also called for the construction of new coal-fired power stations to replace those being planned to use oil or nuclear energy. Miners working on the surface were to have a £100 a week minimum wage paid on a salaried basis, a four day working week, and voluntary retirement at 55 on a big pension. There was to be no pay restraint. The NUM was also to be transformed into a vanguard union which would seek to radicalize the rest of organized labour by force of example. 'The union must never shirk its responsibilities by continually negotiating compromises', Scargill argued in his election manifesto. 'We must neither fear the employer nor the government when the interests of our members are at stake'.[39]

There seems little doubt that Scargill and his Broad Left allies wanted to subvert Mrs Thatcher's government through the use of industrial muscle. Their programme was impossibilist, an inflexible list of extravagant non-negotiable demands. But with memories of the glory days of 1972 and 1974 still fresh in their minds they were convinced the NUM could restore its waning fortunes by the pursuit of a militant strategy. Unfortunately, a majority of miners did not agree with them. In three pit head ballots between 1981 and 1983 the rank and file rejected strike calls in what was seen as clear evidence that they were in no mood to become Scargill's shock troops in a new vanguard union.

For her part, Mrs Thatcher was anxious not to be dragged into a showdown with the miners before she was ready for an effective resistance. In early 1981 she made a strategic retreat over pit closures in the face of a sudden industrial disruption that threatened to turn into a national official strike. At that time the Prime Minister feared it would have been difficult to defeat a stoppage on the coalfields. But she was also preparing the ground for when the moment was ripe to resist. Her appointment of the tough minded Ian MacGregor as chairman of the National Coal Board from 1 September 1983 indicated that Mrs Thatcher was ready to stand firm in the face of any further unrest in the mining industry. The self-made Scot who became a successful capitalist in the United States was a worthy combatant to take on the NUM. He was determined to bring an end to the cosy consensus that had dominated NUM–NCB relations ever since the industry's nationalization in 1947 and to run coal as a commercial business, not as part of the post-war social settlement. MacGregor came to his new post from the chairmanship of the British Steel Corporation, where he had gained a not altogether justifiable reputation as a heartless butcher of the industry. He was intent on cutting the Coal Board down to a viable size to fit its market prospects even though this meant substantial pit closures and job losses.

At a fatal meeting on 6 March 1984 at Coal Board headquarters in London, MacGregor spelt out when asked by the union's leaders what this would mean in practice. To Scargill and many of his executive committee colleagues the proposals were nothing less than a provocation with the suggestion that up to 20 pits and 20,000 jobs would have to go.

But the NUM leadership was unsure how their members would react to the bad news. Scargill did not intend to find out. Since the previous autumn, the union had been enforcing a national overtime ban over its 1983 wage demand and it had recently given its backing for a strike by miners at Cortonwood colliery in Yorkshire who were fighting against the sudden decision to close their pit. The Broad Left on the NUM executive decided to press for an all-out strike, but this time avoiding the use of a

Table 8.4   Public opinion in the 1984–1985 miners' strike

'Are your sympathies with the employers or mainly with the miners in the dispute
which has arisen in the coal industry?'

(%)	Employers	Miners	Neither	Don't know
July 1984	40	33	19	8
August 1984	43	32	18	6
November 1984	52	26	17	5
December 1984	51	26	18	5

'Do you approve or disapprove of the methods being used at present by the miners?'

(%)	Approve	Disapprove	Don't know
July 1984	15	79	6
August 1984	11	85	4
November 1984	4	92	4
December 1984	7	88	5

Source: Gallup poll surveys.

national strike ballot as stipulated in the NUM's own rule book. Communist vice-president Mick McGahey asserted the union would 'not be constitutionalized' out of a strike. The decision not to secure the support of rank and file miners for a strike against pit closures through a secret ballot was a crucial mistake that has haunted the NUM leadership ever since. By rejecting its own constitutional provisions for strike action Scargill and his supporters on the NUM executive split the union at the very moment when it needed genuine rank and file unity. The clear alternative strategy that the leadership followed was to force less militant areas of the NUM out on strike by the use of flying mass pickets and appeals to miners' solidarity. But the traditionally moderate Nottinghamshire miners refused to join in the struggle. They held their own strike ballot and 70 per cent of them rejected the call for a stoppage. The huge police contingent on the Nottinghamshire coalfield and elsewhere – co-ordinated through the police's National Operating Centre in London's Scotland Yard – made sure that the working miners were not intimidated by the ranks of flying pickets.

Scargill displayed enormous ingenuity in outwitting the pathetic rump of right-wingers on the NUM executive committee, but it was clear from the strike's early days that the union's leadership was out of touch with the divided mood on the coalfields. Scargill fired the enthusiasm of the young miners with his wild oratory, and from NUM headquarters in

Sheffield he planned his summer campaign like an industrial Napoleon, convinced that the union would be able to prevent the movement of coal to the power stations as it had done in 1972 and 1974 and that it would force the government to surrender or face the grim prospect of an eventual return to three day working in industry and a paralysed economy. But this time Scargill was unable to mobilize worker opposition to the government. Faced by the fact that many miners continued to work, he found it hard to win the backing of workers in other industries to take solidarity action in support of his own members. At the 1984 Trades Union Congress, national union leaders in the name of TUC unity pledged their public support for Scargill and the miners but they were unable (as many of them knew full well at the time) to win the approval of their rank and file for any sympathy stoppages. Public opinion – appalled by the picket line violence that Scargill would not repudiate – failed to sympathize with the NUM, but Scargill made little serious attempt to win people over to his own point of view.

It was also clear from the beginning of the strike that the NUM faced a much more resolute and better prepared government than it had done in the early 1970s. A perceptive leaked memorandum written by Nicholas Ridley, one of Mrs Thatcher's most devoted right-wing ministers, during the late 1970s when the Conservatives were in opposition had set out what ought to be the state's strategic response to any renewed threat of a coal strike. This suggested building up coal stocks at the power stations in a pre-emptive move, making preparations to import foreign coal, recruiting non-union lorry drivers to convoy coal to the power stations when necessary, and switching from coal to oil firing to save coal stocks. It was also proposed to establish greater police coordination at national level to ensure they were in a better position to counter any mass picketing action by striking miners.

Thanks in part to the pre-emptive plans of Nigel Lawson when energy minister, coal stocks were built up deliberately from 42.2 million tonnes to 58 million tonnes at the power stations. There was to be no repetition of the panic that had gripped the Heath Cabinet during the early months of 1972, when ministers realized the miners had brought the movement of coal to a standstill and industry faced the prospect of a shutdown for lack of energy. The only period of genuine anxiety for Mrs Thatcher came in the early autumn of 1984 when it looked as if the pit deputies' union NACODS would also go on strike and thereby threaten maintenance at the pits, but that moment of crisis soon passed. For most of the dispute, the government remained in an impregnable strategic position to confront and defeat a divided and weakened NUM, though this did not often appear to be so at the time. The trouble was that MacGregor turned out to be a surprisingly inept and blundering figure with little ability to articulate the NCB's rational case. Moreover, for many months he seemed to have convinced himself that a mere form of words could be agreed with Scargill that would satisfy all sides on the issue of pit closures. Well-thumbed copies of *Roget's Thesaurus* were used to find the magic formula that would end the strike. What MacGregor failed to recognize was that Scargill was not like any other union leader but hated compromise and conciliation. As a class warrior, the NUM president had no time for half measures. It was the irrational element in Scargill's militancy that ensured there could not be any fudge to settle the dispute. It had to be all or nothing. In every sense the miners who stayed out on strike for over twelve months were foot soldiers in an unwinnable conflict. No government or employer could have accepted Scargill's inflexible terms that there must never be any pit closures except on grounds of physical exhaustion. In his defiance of economic logic and common sense, the NUM president condemned his members to total defeat.

Indeed, Scargill's reckless adventurism played into the hands of the government. The strike was not only called at the wrong time in the spring when the demand for coal was declining, but on the wrong issue of pit closures over which the miners were by no means united. By refusing to ballot the rank and file in defiance of his union's own constitutional requirements, the NUM president also ensured that the miners would remain fatally split. The failure to ballot reflected a clear lack of self-confidence in the attitude of the leadership about the mood of the rank and file. It meant that Scargill and his allies had to try and use physical coercion to force many reluctant miners into the dispute. But once the majority of Nottinghamshire miners, protected by a vast police presence on their coalfield, rejected the NUM strike call and defied the mass pickets by going to work there could be little expectation that key workers elsewhere in other industries would be prepared to throw their weight behind the NUM leadership by taking sympathy action to help the miners' cause. To an unfortunate degree Scargill was over-influenced by his own rank and file experiences as a flying picket in the unofficial strikes in Yorkshire in 1969 and above all in the national strike of 1972 when miners backed up by thousands of other workers had closed down Saltley coke depot in Birmingham. That kind of working class solidarity did not reappear in the gloomier industrial climate of 1984–5. On the contrary, union lorry drivers as well as dockers, steel workers and railwaymen defied their own union instructions and refused to put their own jobs at risk to assist those miners on strike.

The stoical suffering of miners and their families left a bitterness on the defeated coalfields, but tens of thousands were soon to leave the industry as it went into the fastest and deepest contraction in its history. The NUM as a union was broken by the dispute. Its membership shrivelled from over 200,000 to less than 40,000 in five years, while it was forced to compete for members with the Union of Democratic Mineworkers, founded by working miners in the summer of 1984. Scargill – true to his own impossibilist attitudes – claimed the NUM had won a great victory and he rejected the back to work terms that were passed narrowly by a union delegate conference. In fact, the once all-powerful union – the praetorian guard of the Labour Movement – was marginalized as an ineffective force in the late 1980s.

For Mrs Thatcher revenge must indeed have been sweet. The recognition that behind the hapless antics of MacGregor stood an implacable Prime Minister was important in ruling out any serious possibility of one of those 'shoddy, shabby compromises' that tended to settle most postwar industrial conflicts. But it was also true that her victory owed next to nothing to the government's 'step by step' strategy to weaken union power by changes in the law. Indeed, the NCB and its business customers were actively discouraged by ministers from using the new labour laws against the NUM for fear that such action might detonate widespread mass support for the miners. It was the traditional common law not new employment legislation that in the words of John Lloyd and Martin Adeney 'in the end choked much of the life' out of the union, and it was its 'own members and not the state who were the most active agents' in using the law.[40] Mrs Thatcher and her Cabinet colleagues were, of course, not to know that Scargill backed up by the union's executive committee and delegate conference would deny their own rank and file their democratic and constitutional right to a secret ballot over whether or not to go on strike against pit closures. But his contempt for the views of the rank and file played into the government's hands. It ensured above anything else that the slogan of the militants of the 1980s – 'the workers united shall never be defeated' – became a hollow pretence.

But the defeat of the miners also underlined that the use of industrial muscle to bring about political change was a dangerous, self-defeating delusion in a society as complex, democratic and tolerant as Britain's. It is true there was little triumphalism, even inside the government, at the end of the strike. In the closing weeks of the dispute public sympathy began to grow for the sad plight of the striking miners and their families. Public opinion did not want Scargill to win, but it did not want to see the miners humiliated either. However, the lesson for the government seemed at the time clear enough: never again would a Conservative Cabinet tremble before the prospect of an industrial confrontation with the miners or anybody else. Scargill's strike had revealed that the NUM was no longer a mighty power in the land as it had appeared to be during the 1970s. In its reckless tactics to stage a rerun of those glory days, the NUM leaders revealed the union's own tactical weaknesses. By doing so they laid to rest what many miners had convinced themselves was true: that they enjoyed the collective strength to paralyse the economy. The miner's strike turned out to be the last, almost primeval scream of a dying proletariat. To many young miners it was a great drama, perhaps bringing the most memorable days of their lives. It was also a national tragedy of often heroic proportions.

The defeat of the NUM in 1985 did not turn out to be the end of the matter. By a curious twist of fate the miners recaptured the sympathy of the British people yet again in the winter of 1992–3. In October 1992, John Major's Conservative government announced that the remnants of the coal industry would have to be halved with the loss of up to 30,000 jobs and 31 pit closures. The reason seemed clear enough to industry minister Michael Heseltine. There was simply a lack of demand for the amount of coal being produced, mainly because of the decision of the newly privatized electricity companies to invest in gas fired power stations as an energy alternative to coal. But the decision shocked Britain and caused a fire-storm in public opinion. The government was seen as heartless and incompetent in its utter lack of awareness. Under a welter of popular protest that even included a crucial number of Conservative MPs, the government was forced to make a strategic, if perhaps temporary, retreat. The TUC organized a mass demonstration in London against the pit closures on 25 October 1992 which attracted more than 200,000 people. It was the largest gathering of its kind since the TUC's march against the Industrial Relations Bill more than twenty years earlier. From being a figure of defeat and derision, Scargill staged an improbable personal comeback as the cause of the miners won widespread mass support. The NUM alone might no longer be a mighty force in the land but the miners' cause continued to strike a chord of national solidarity, albeit temporarily. This could not, however, alter the economic logic for a declining industry; in the spring of 1993 the government announced only a partial and temporary reprieve for some of the doomed pits.

Giving the unions back to their members

Tebbit did not regard the 1982 Employment Act as the final step in the government's industrial strategy. Within weeks of its completion he was hard at work on the next piece of legislation, designed this time to reform the internal organization of trade unions and in the words of Mrs Thatcher 'to give the unions back to their members'. As the resulting White Paper, *Democracy in Trade Unions*, argued in January 1983:

> Trade union power which springs from legal immunities and privileges can be used not just against employers but against individual members of unions. As the law has granted these privileges, it is necessary to consider whether the rights of individual members of trade unions are adequately protected and whether those who exercise power in the name of the membership are properly accountable to the members.[41]

The document went on to suggest that 'the unique legal status' enjoyed by trade unions and the alleged power in the hands of their leaders to call disputes made it 'essential for their internal affairs to be conducted in a manner which commands public confidence'. 'That confidence is bound to be lacking if individual members are denied a fair opportunity to register their views on all matters which directly concern them', it suggested.

The subsequent 1984 Trade Union Act was condemned by the TUC as a direct assault by the state on trade union autonomy and on the freedom of trade unions to decide for themselves how they should be organized, and therefore in contravention of ILO Convention 87. Certainly, it represented a far more detailed intervention by the state into forms of trade union self-government than had occurred in any other Western industrialized country except for the United States and Australia. But Tebbit argued that the measure would mean the liberation of individual trade union members from the potential danger of autocratic control by ossified trade union bureaucracies, and anyway that its proposals were popular with the rank and file. Under the 1984 Act, trade unionists were given the legal right to participate through a secret ballot and to agree by a simple majority in a bargaining unit before being called out on strike if the stoppage was to enjoy the protection of legal immunities. Trade union executive committees (but not general secretaries unless they exercised a vote on the executive) were to be elected at least once every five years through a secret ballot of the members. Trade unions that possessed political funds were also to hold secret ballots at periodic intervals to find out whether or not their members approved of them. Tebbit had wanted to change the method of payment of the political levy to require trade unionists to contract in rather than contract out, as had been the case between 1927 and 1946, but such a move was seen by the Conservative whips' office as too being partisan. They also feared it might lead to future legislation by a Labour government aimed at cutting off corporate contributions to the coffers of the Conservative party. Tom King, who replaced Tebbit as Employment Secretary in October 1983 and who piloted the Trade Union Bill onto the statute book, accepted a TUC compromise offer under which the trade unions agreed to inform their members of the legal regulations allowing them not to pay the political levy. The means of enforcement for the allegedly democratic changes enshrined in the 1984 Trade Union Act were through depriving trade unions of their legal immunities and leaving them vulnerable to fines and sequestration if they sought to defy the law.

Initially, many trade unions continued to express their defiance of the legislation but the TUC's negative attitude was not to last for very much longer. In November 1984 the TGWU was fined £200,000 by the High Court for failing to carry out a ballot of its members in connection with a dispute at Austin Rover car plants. This was followed by a High Court fine of £25,000 on the print union SOGAT as well as the sequestration of its assets during the News International dispute in early 1986 when the union refused to withdraw an instruction to its members employed in the wholesale trade (who had not been balloted) not to handle the distribution of News International titles. In the three year period to 1987, interim injunctions were won by employers in 73 out of 77 cases but only three resulted in damages being paid.

On balance, however, the 1984 Trade Union Act turned out to be far more of a help than a hindrance to the trade unions. The use of the secret ballot before the calling of official strikes tended to strengthen their negotiating stance. ACAS noted in its 1986 annual report that there had been 246 strike ballots organized by at least 30 unions under the measure during the first 15 months of the legal provision and of those 246 had resulted in a majority to support industrial action with high turnouts of between 75 and 85 per cent. There were 1,030 officially recorded stoppages in 1986 alone; less than a quarter were covered by ballots. ACAS believed the use of the secret ballot before strikes was becoming 'a permanent part of the negotiating scene'.[42] Moreover, it seemed to be strengthening the hand of trade unions against employers as it demonstrated the strength of feeling among members 'in ways which some managements have found difficult to counter'. By 1989 the ACAS annual report was reporting that it had become 'a universal practice' for trade unions to ballot their members before taking industrial action and in 92 per cent of those occasions the rank and file vote backed the union-recommended disruption call.[43] Moreover, it was also clear that the longer term consequences of strike ballots could well intensify industrial conflict by raising rank and file expectations of an improved wage offer. As Professor Brown and Sushil Wadhwari argued:

> The importance of continuity for the maintenance of effective bargaining relationships between managers and union leaders would suggest, on balance, that where the rank and file decide a matter by direct vote they will tend to respond more timidly in adversity and more aggressively in prosperity than their elected leaders. In an economic upswing the greater use of strike ballots is thus likely to result in wage claims that are more extravagant and in negotiators with less room for manoeuvre than would otherwise be the case. In times of rising expectations governments may come to regret that the 1984 Trade Union Act was born of the politics of recession.[44]

The political fund ballots required under the 1984 Trade Union Act also turned into an unexpected triumph for the trade unions. Of the 53 unions which balloted their members over the question to mid-1989 in only one was there a No majority for a political fund. Indeed, 20 further unions acquired political funds for the first time as a result of the balloting process, an outcome not envisaged by the government when it decided to introduce the provision. Tebbit was furious at what happened and claimed later that the political fund ballots had been conducted unfairly but the shattering results were entirely the government's own fault. The impressive rank and file majorities in support of their unions having political funds did not endorse, however, the existing organizational and financial links between most of them and the Labour party, but they reflected the strong support from the rank and file for their unions who feared any form of political action by them such as lobbying Parliament over public spending cuts would become unlawful under section 17 of the 1984 Trade Union Act. As David Grant wrote, 'the Act was a major coup for the trade union movement.'[45] The political fund ballots revived trade union morale and through a brilliantly coordinated campaign confounded the Labour Movement's enemies. Perhaps even more importantly in the longer run, the use of secret ballots for strikes and the election of union executives compelled the trade unions to modernize themselves internally. It gave them greater credibility as representative organizations and a new legitimacy with many workers:

> The social processes associated with balloting have helped to maintain collective cohesion at the workplace. . . . At the same time the linkage between the workplace and the union hierarchy has been strengthened, especially between the workplace and district level to maintain institutional integration against possible legal action officials have increased supervision over the conduct of local industrial action.

Apparently, there was 'little evidence that ballots had the anticipated effect of decollectivising unions'. 'Instead ballots have been absorbed into the repertoire of union bargaining tactics and have helped to legitimise union decisions'.[46] The sheer professionalism of trade unions and their willingness to communicate more openly with both their own members and the outside world improved enormously. Moreover, they also benefited directly from the provision of state financial support to the tune of £4.2 million to the end of 1990 as the government agreed under its own legislation to help meet some of the costs borne by the trade unions in holding pre-strike and election ballots.

Marginalizing the unions

Between 1984 and 1988 there was a respite from the government's 'step by step' industrial relations strategy as it directly affected trade unions – much to the frustration of the radical right who wanted to keep on pushing ahead with yet further legal measures designed to weaken the power of organized labour. The primary reason for the period of legal consolidation was that neither Tom King, nor Lord David Young his successor as Secretary of State at the Department of Employment, were particularly interested in introducing yet further industrial relations legislation. King was essentially a consolidator, content to uphold the status quo, while Young – a self-made businessman and close friend of Sir Keith Joseph and the Prime Minister – wanted to transform the Department of Employment so that its primary aim should be to 'encourage the development of an enterprise economy'. Its new priorities were to help businesses grow through a strategy of deregulation, improved training and the encouragement of small firms and the self-employed. In his memoirs Lord Young had almost nothing to say about trade unions and the traditional agenda of industrial relations. Indeed, the words 'trade union' do not even appear in its index. What he sought to do – with the enthusiastic backing of Mrs Thatcher – was to lift the fashionable pessimism about the labour market and invigorate the Department of Employment with schemes and plans to create jobs – not through Keynesian demand management, but through a shake-up of the employment services. Young brought an entrepreneurial drive to the Department of Employment. Yet he enjoyed relatively friendly relations with national trade union leaders. During his period as MSC chairman he had won the confidence of the TUC's General Secretary Len Murray with his clear commitment to take action to reduce unemployment and reform the industrial training system. For a time it seemed that the Conservative appetite for further trade union legislation had been satisfied. Certainly, Young did not appear to believe that further legislative assaults on organized labour were justified. This did not mean he intended to return to the One Nation approach of Prior. But he seems to have reached the conclusion that trade unions as institutions were irrelevant to the creation of the enterprise society.

The return of step by step

After Young's move to become Secretary of State at the Department of Trade and Industry in June 1987 after the Conservative election victory, there was a return to the 'step by step' industrial relations strategy under Norman Fowler. But it was hard to detect any burning industrial reasons why this should have been so. Increasingly by the late 1980s the primary motive behind the formulation of yet more trade union legislation was political. Indeed, senior civil servants at the Department of Employment during that time began to recognize that ambitious ministers who wanted to catch Mrs Thatcher's eye were intent on scraping the bottom of the barrel in search of anti-union measures to win approval. Little attempt was made any longer to justify the introduction of yet more labour law as a necessary state response to widely perceived shopfloor evils or employer needs. As a result, there was a noticeable deterioration in the intellectual rigour of Department of Employment publications, written to justify further legislation designed to curb union power. Increasingly, those documents read like propagandist tracts for the converted, and Whitehall traditions of impeccable scholarship and objectivity were abandoned.

It is also apparent that after 1987 the 'step by step' strategy was gradually being replaced. Instead, with increasing boldness of language and action, ministers began to denounced collective bargaining and the old agenda of industrial relations. They were no longer content simply to push the power balance further in the employer's direction. Now the emphasis was on the individualization of workers as the tide of collectivism was to be turned back. With little empirical evidence to justify legislative reform, Fowler and his successor Michael Howard resorted to unproven assertion to justify ever more sweeping reforms to erode trade union freedoms. By 1993 Britain had the most restrictive industrial relations laws of any western European market economy. It is true that the Conservatives had not gone all the way to the radical Hayekian position where trade unions would have been reduced merely to the status of friendly societies with the loss of all their legal immunities. But the aggressive evocation of worker individualism by the government went hand in hand with an increasingly open contempt for collective bargaining and voluntarism. For the first time since the early nineteenth century and the passage of the Combination Acts, the British state appeared to see no merit in the continuing existence of trade unionism. It did not go so far as to outlaw them but it sought to undermine and weaken their activities and at the same time strengthen the cause of non-unionism. As the January 1992 White Paper *People, Jobs and Opportunity*, declared:

> There is every reason to be confident that by the end of the 1990s we will
> have moved decisively away from the collectivist pay arrangements which
> restricted individual choice and damaged employment growth to a situa-
> tion where the pay of the great majority of employed people will reflect
> their individual contributions at work.[47]

Under the provisions of the 1988 Employment Act a number of important and controversial changes were made in industrial relations law. The
post-entry closed shop was abolished outright. Trade union members
were given the statutory right to vote in postal instead of workplace secret
ballots for the periodic election of their leaders and not just members of
their union executive committee, as well for political funds. The measure
also broke new ground through the introduction of a number of restrictive provisions aimed at weakening the power of organized labour. Trade
unionists were to enjoy legal protection from being disciplined by their
own union for refusing to go on strike or for crossing a picket line to
work, even if the majority of their fellow workers had agreed to strike in
a secret ballot and it was therefore a lawful dispute. The Employment
Department argued that:

> The government believes that a decision to take industrial action should be
> a matter for the individual. Every union member should be free to decide
> for himself whether or not he wishes to break his contract of employment
> and run the risk of dismissal without compensation. No union member
> should be penalized by his trade union for exercising his right to cross a
> picket line and go to work.[48]

As Auerbach commented, the new Act gave 'clear and unequivocal expression' to the central conception that 'the protection of individual rather
than union membership rights' enjoyed primacy under the law.[49] But this
provision was opposed strongly and unavailingly not just by employer
organizations but even by the Organization of Conservative Trade Unionists. It is also clear that the balance of power strategy had been changed

into one that sought to subordinate collectivism to individual preference. Lawyers regarded Section 3 of the 1988 Act more any other provision as a clear breach of the post-war consensus on the value of collective decision-making and a clear indication in legislative form of Hayekian values.

Trade union members were also provided with the legal right to take action in the courts against any attempt by their union to call a strike involving them that had not been approved of by a secret ballot. A Commissioner for the Rights of Trade Union Members was also established with the task of assisting trade union members with any legal action proposed against their union with the provision of public funds for legal advice and representation. This was hardly a balanced move. There was no suggestion that the Commissioner might also help trade unionists and other workers with finance and legal advice in any action they might consider against an employer for an alleged breach of the law by him.

The second part of the 1988 Employment Act signalled the government's intention to begin diluting the TUC's influence on employment policy. Jobcentres were transferred back from the MSC to the responsibility of the Department of Employment so that help for the unemployed to find jobs could be coordinated with the payment of their benefit. At the same time, the MSC was renamed the Training Commission and more employer representatives were added to its board. Labour employment spokesman Michael Meacher accused Fowler of transforming the MSC from being 'an independent body into the government's pliant poodle, centralising power in the hands of the Secretary of State for Employment'.[50]

Fowler went on to pilot a further industrial relations measure onto the statute book in the following year. The 1989 Employment Act was mainly concerned with provisions to extend the government's labour market deregulation programme, but it also contained clauses designed to weaken the trade unions still further. Lay trade union officials had their rights restricted for paid time off in carrying out their duties or for union training that they had enjoyed under the 1975 Employment Protection Act. Fowler was also responsible in 1989 for the abolition of the National Dock Labour scheme, created in 1947 by the Labour government to try and bring stability to dockland through the decasualization of the industry. The TGWU called a national dock strike to oppose the refusal of the employers to negotiate an alternative to the national scheme and it won the necessary majority (74 per cent for and only 26 per cent against on a 90 per cent turnout) among the dockers in a secret ballot. But the result failed to make the government change its mind and the dock employers were able to delay the onset of industrial action through the shrewd use of the courts and the imposition of interlocutory injunctions. By the time the House of Lords upheld the TGWU's lawful right to call a strike over the scheme it had become legally necessary for the TGWU to hold a second ballot on the same question. This produced a convincing three to one majority for strike action. The strike then went ahead but within a few weeks it had collapsed without having made much impact on the economy. The days when striking dockers could paralyse Britain were at an end. The demise of the National Dock Labour Scheme was a convincing demonstration of the new realities. In the early 1980s even Mrs Thatcher had hesitated from making such a drastic move. Now the changing industrial relations climate was more conducive to such bold state action.

In 1990 yet another Employment Act went on to the statute book. This one was purportedly introduced to 'limit the abuses of industrial power and to guarantee the democratic rights of trade union members'. Michael Howard, the new Employment Secretary, told the Commons that this was 'the culmination of the long process of reform' begun by Prior eleven years earlier. The main provisions introduced further restrictions on the freedom exercised by organized labour. Trade unions were made legally responsible in the organization of industrial disputes not just for the behaviour of their own full-time officials but also of the shop stewards unless they were unequivocally repudiated by the union when behaving unlaw-fully. The law stipulated that for the repudiation to be 'effective' the trade union was required to notify all of its 'relevant' members in writing. As an estimated three quarters of strikes in Britain were unofficial, this provision made trade unions liable for civil damages in all such disputes un-less those organizing them had been disowned clearly by their own union.

The 1990 Employment Act went even further in weakening the trade unions. Any worker dismissed by their employer for taking part in an unofficial strike and refused re-engagement would be unable to claim damages or even reinstatement for unfair dismissal before an industrial tribunal. Up until then only an employer faced a risk before an industrial tribunal if he tried selectively to rehire those who had broken their employment contracts by going out on strike rather than everybody who had taken part in the stoppage. The Act also provided a right of complaint to an industrial tribunal for anyone who was refused employment on the grounds of union membership or non-membership. Howard described this as 'a hammer blow for the freedom of the individual to choose for himself whether or not he wishes to become a member of a trade union'. 'It puts paid once and for all to the tyranny of forced association', he asserted. It meant in effect the final outlawing of the closed shop in Britain.

Industrial dispute secret balloting provisions were also tightened up by requiring on the voting paper the name of the specified persons who would call the industrial action if the vote was affirmative. Finally, legal immunities were removed for those organizing secondary industrial action or action in support of an employee dismissed while taking unofficial action. This meant the outlawing of all secondary action, a step that Prior – now in the House of Lords – thought unreasonable.

Not even this measure turned out to be the final step in the Conservative industrial relations strategy. In *Industrial Relations in the 1990s*, a White Paper published in August 1991 – nine months after Mrs Thatcher's resignation – further legal restrictions were proposed against trade unions of a potentially sweeping character. Howard suggested his latest proposals were 'designed to consolidate and build on the improvement in the country's industrial relations over the last 13 years' and 'ensure an effective and up to date framework of law in order to maintain that progress through the 1990s'.[51] In line with Prime Minister John Major's well-publicized Citizens' Charter it was proposed that customers in the public services covered by the Charter (health, housing, education, transport, employment, social security, the post office, taxation, the police and criminal justice) would be given the right to bring proceedings to prevent or restrain any unlawful organization of industrial action affecting those services where the employer or a union member failed to use the legal remedies already open to them. Fines or sequestration of union funds would follow if the resulting court orders preventing or restraining the unlawful action were defied or ignored. The White Paper also proposed the introduction of a seven day strike notice to an employer once a ballot had produced a majority of his employees in support of official industrial action. The notice would be required for each individual period of stoppage where one day stoppages or other intermittent disruption was planned. 'This requirement will help to protect the general public from the hardship caused by lightning strikes in public services', explained Howard. 'It will also allow employers to take steps to safeguard jobs and business.'

In yet a further tightening up of the secret ballot provisions required for the trade unions it was also suggested that all such ballots of more than 50 workers would have to be independently scrutinized. Employers with employees entitled to vote in a strike ballot would also have to receive notice of intent to hold the ballot, a sample of the voting paper supplied to the unions' members, details of the result, and the scrutineer's report. Union members were also to have the statutory right to inspect their union's entire register of members not just their own entry in order 'to combat fraud and vote-rigging' in union elections. In a move scarcely designed to ensure shopfloor peace the White Paper proposed an individual worker should be given the right to join the trade union of their choice where more than one union organized employees of similar qualifications and occupations. Union merger ballots were also to be conducted by postal voting and subject to independent scrutiny, bringing their legal requirements into line with those covering union ballots. The document also proposed a potentially devastating blow against the organization of trade unions and their financial viability. Union members would have the right to decide whether or not to pay their union subscriptions by check off by making it unlawful for employers to make deductions from pay without the employee's written consent renewable at least once every three years. It was estimated that by the end of the 1980s as many as six million workers had their union membership subscriptions paid out through their employers. On top of this the Certification Officer would be empowered to carry out wide ranging investigations into trade union finances where there may have been alleged 'serious or widespread irregularities'. A maximum fine of £2,000 would be imposed for 'certain criminal offences relating to union accounting records, accounts and annual returns'. Individuals found guilty of such an offence would be debarred from holding or standing for office within the union for a specific period of time. The time limit for legal proceedings stemming from such offences would be extended from six months to three years after the offence. A union would also be required by law to provide each of its members with a written summary of its financial affairs every year. And last but not least Howard suggested that employers and unions should be encouraged to consider the merits of making collective agreements legally enforceable by revising the present presumption in law that agreements are not binding. Apparently, agreements would then be enforceable between unions and employers unless they contained an expressly contrary provision. But the White Paper hastened to add that 'no employer or trade union would be obliged to enter into a legally enforceable agreement unless they wanted to do so'.[52]

After their April 1992 general election victory the Conservatives insisted they would push ahead with legislation to implement the White Paper's proposals, even if most employer organizations expressed little enthusiasm for them. Mrs Gillian Shephard, the new Employment Secretary, announced in November 1992 that the government intended to carry out what it had promised to do in its Green Paper. The Trade

Union Reform and Employment Rights Act reached the statute book a year later.

Deregulating the labour market

The legislative assault of the Conservative party's 'step by step' industrial relations strategy during the 1980s and early 1990s was not confined merely to weakening the legal powers of the trade unions. During the Thatcher years there was also a substantial deregulation of the labour market through the systematic removal of many of the often long-standing legal safeguards that the Prime Minister and her Cabinet regarded as obstacles to competition. This process began tentatively enough under Prior who was determined to repeal what most Conservatives saw as the excesses of the 'militants' charter' in the Social Contract legislation. This meant the early demise of Schedule 11 of the 1975 Employment Protection Act which was criticized as an inflationary device that forced up wage rates. A study by Warwick University industrial relations research unit found 'little or no evidence to validate the government's assertion that recourse to unilateral arbitration (through the Central Arbitration Committee) constrained the development of bargaining',[53] and suggested there was a 'high level of satisfaction expressed by both employers and trade unionists with the outcome of Schedule 11 claims and the by the majority of managers who either mentioned an improvement in industrial relations as a result of a CAC award or stated that there were no consequential effects whatsoever'. But empirical research did not form the basis for much of the Conservative industrial relations legislation during the 1980s. The government considered in the mid-1980s the outright abolition of the Wages Councils established in 1909 to provide statutory minimum wage rates to the unorganized at the bottom of the labour market, but instead ministers decided under the 1986 Wages Act to abolish the Truck Acts and to exclude workers under the age of 18 from the protective provisions of the Wages Councils. The numbers employed in the government's own Factory Inspectorate to ensure that employers honoured Wages Council awards were cut back, hardly a move designed to uphold the rule of law. In the summer of 1992, ministers condemned the continuing existence of Wages Councils and announced their intention to abolish them in 1993–4.

The 1989 Employment Act was also designed to 'bring down the barriers standing in the way of developing employment',[54] by opening up the competition in jobs equally for all workers. The measure in fact destroyed most of the legal protections, many of which went back to the

Factory Acts of the early nineteenth century, that sought to prevent employers from being able to exploit young people and women in the workplace. Under its provisions employment restrictions on women were repealed in favour of a general principle of equal treatment in terms of access to work. While controls continued for children under the minimum school leaving age of 16, restrictions were also lifted on the employment and working hours of young workers aged between 16 and 18. The 1989 Employment Act also chipped away further at the individual employment rights contained in the 1978 Employment Protection (Consolidation) Act. Under the measure, workers in companies employing less than 20 on their payrolls were not entitled to a written statement of disciplinary procedures nor were they entitled to a written explanation from their employer if they were dismissed within two years of the qualifying period rather than six months as previously. The Act also sought to discourage workers from taking unfair dismissal cases before industrial tribunals by granting those bodies the power to require an applicant to pay a £150 deposit as a condition for proceeding with their claim.

Despite such erosions in individual employment rights the government insisted it had no intention of dismantling the whole framework of employment protection. Apparently, ministers sought merely to achieve 'an appropriate balance; a balance between safeguarding employee's rights and enabling employers to improve their competitiveness and create new job opportunities'. As Simon Deakin argued; 'The weak and fragmented system of labour law in Britain is decreasingly capable of conferring basic levels of security upon the low paid and non-unionized workers who need legal protection most.'[55] The 1989 Employment Act indeed took Britain even more out of line from recognized international labour standards, particularly in comparison to the codified systems of rights existing in almost all other European Community countries.

The enormous outpouring of legislation by Mrs Thatcher's government in the 1980s which was continued by John Major in the early 1990s, designed to restrict trade union behaviour and liberate the labour market from its supposed obstacles to improved competitiveness, was not paralleled by the provision of any corresponding statutory obligations being imposed on Britain's employers to encourage an actual improvement of their industrial relations strategies. Here confidence continued to be expressed in the merits of the voluntarist tradition. As Norman Fowler, the Employment Secretary, explained in his introduction to a departmental guide to good employer practices published in 1989:

> Successful employee involvement is best developed on the basis of voluntary agreement. It depends on a spirit of co-operation, not on legal

requirements. You cannot free people by law to co-operate with one another. It has got to be suited to the specific circumstances of the particular firm and its employees.[56]

There was no question of trying to introduce any statutory provisions on Britain's employers to consult or even inform their workers about their management strategies. The unilateral right to manage was not to be questioned by anybody, least of all by those who worked for the company. The document argued that:

The government believes that it is important to preserve the freedom of firms to choose for themselves the policies and practices that they wish to develop. No single blueprint can be suitable for every company. Forcing employee involvement into a legal straitjacket would destroy the diversity which in Britain has allowed a thriving, effective voluntary system to take root.

Apparently, legislation in this area would 'direct a firm's energies into trying to satisfy irrelevant new statutory requirements instead of developing policies which suited them best'. Moreover, 'managers do not have unlimited resources to devote to employee involvement'. The trouble with 'formalism and legalism' was that they had 'often been found to be the enemies of effective employee involvement, which depended on co-operation and mutual trust' for 'regulation was not the way to implement good employment practices'.

By 1989–90, the target of the Conservative industrial relations attack was no longer just the British trade union movement but also the European Commission in Brussels under its dirigiste French Socialist president Jacques Delors. The emergence of the Social Charter and the subsequent social action programme of minimalist rights for workers alarmed Mrs Thatcher, who viewed such developments as a new dangerous collectivist threat to the deregulated market economy and strong state she was seeking to create in Britain. She resisted with vigour the modest social rights that the EC wanted to introduce as a complement to the creation of the 1993 single market with its commitment to economic liberal values. John Major continued to oppose the so-called 'social' dimension of the EC. Indeed, he persuaded his 11 prime ministerial colleagues in December 1991 to accept that Britain should be excluded from the social chapter of the EC's Maastricht treaty.

The radical right were still insistent in the early 1990s that yet more legislative steps were needed to reform the labour market in a competitive direction. It seemed that the plethora of laws already passed had failed to cure the country's underlying industrial relations problems so further action by the state was vital. Charles Hanson lamented in 1991 that 'unit costs were rising too fast', 'labour productivity was far too low' and the government had been moving away from 'the obsolete, collectivist approach to employment relations' in the public sector. The fact that ACAS still had the statutory obligation 'of encouraging the extension of collective bargaining' reflected in Hanson's opinion 'major doubts about the government's commitment to a radical reform of the traditional system'.[57] This was dropped in a clause of the 1993 Act. Hanson also proposed that the remaining legal immunities for trade unions should be abolished in two stages. As the argument went: 'Trade unions would then operate under the jurisdiction of the common law and the excuse sometimes advanced that Britain's economic problems were largely the fault of the unions would disappear.'[58]

Despite Howard's assertion that the 1990 Employment Act was to be the 'culmination' of the government's 'step by step' strategy, a further measure was promised with the publication in the spring of 1991 of yet another Green Paper with a wide-ranging number of proposals to tighten the law even more firmly against trade unions. Most were included in the Trade Union Reform and Employment Rights Bill that reached the statute book in 1993. There was little evidence of much support among employers for more legislation and the sixth industrial relations measure since 1980 received a generally lukewarm reception from the media.

But many of its clauses looked like causing further severe difficulties for the trade unions. A provision to allow an individual worker to join the union of his or her choice unless the union rules explicitly restricted membership to workers employed in a specified trade or industry, was a grave threat to workplace stability and the continuation of the TUC's 1939 Bridlington rules which were designed to avoid inter-union conflicts over membership rights. The decision to tighten up the administration of check-off arrangements posed a sizeable problem for many unions with the danger of a dramatic decline in individual union membership. Under the Act a worker must authorize union membership deductions every three years and has the right to complain to an industrial tribunal if an employer deducts union subscriptions from his or her pay packet without permission. But the measure was passed without much fuss, despite TUC criticisms.

Shopfloor realities

The Thatcherite 'step by step' industrial relations strategy appeared to make much more of a political impact than it seemed to do on the realities of collective bargaining at the workplace, at least until the end of the decade. The government-commissioned 1984 workplace industrial relations survey stressed considerable continuity and stability on the shop floor five years after the Conservatives had returned to power. Indeed, some of its conclusions must have provided unpalatable reading for ministers. Apparently there were 'as many full-time lay representatives in 1984 as in 1980'[59] and 'the proportion of workplaces in which the pay of at least some workers was determined by negotiation with trade unions increased' over the period. A further study from the same data published in 1986 by the Policy Studies Institute tended to question the well-entrenched views of the government about the obstructiveness of trade unions. It asserted: 'There was no sign that the general effect of trade unionism was to act as an obstacle to any form of change.' On the contrary, workers and their unions had been so positive in their support for technical innovation that managers had not needed to 'use consultation, participation or negotiation to win their consent to change'.[60]

However, a comprehensive government-commissioned 1990 workplace survey published in 1992 suggested that significant changes had taken place in the British industrial relations system by the end of the 1980s. As we shall see later in this chapter, it suggested only 53 per cent of 'establishments' had recognized trade unions to represent any of their workers compared with a figure of 66 per cent only six years earlier, describing the fall of collective bargaining as an institution as 'stark, substantial and incontrovertible'.[61]

There was no need for any aggressive employer counter-offensive to roll back the trade unions through a persistent recourse to the new legislation. Indeed, very few cases of union derecognition in British companies were recorded over the period. One research study found there had been only 56 such cases up to the end of 1988 and these were confined mainly to the newspaper and book publishing industry, coastal shipping and the docks. While it was suggested derecognition might 'become more widespread', the process was expected to 'be piecemeal and possibly temporary'.[62] However, there were also some signs that employers were ready to derecognize trade unions in certain areas but not across the whole of their plants. Another research study discovered 13 per cent of companies examined withdrew some recognition from the trade unions between 1984 and 1990 while 6 per cent had extended recognition over the same period. The 1990 industrial relations survey found only 3 per cent of workplaces without recognized unions that had previously had them at some stage between 1984 and 1990.[63]

On the other hand, the closed shop contracted dramatically during the

1980s due in part to the hostile climate created to a large extent by Conservative legislation but also to occupational change with the run-down of employment in sectors like dockland where the closed shop had been endemic. In 1978 just over 5 million workers were covered by union only employment agreements – about 39 per cent of everybody employed in manufacturing industry – but by 1989 that figure had dropped to no more than about 1.3 million and it continued to fall to only around 500,000 by 1990, according to the government-commissioned workplace survey.

Although the government placed a formidable amount of restrictive legislation on the statute book for employers or injured parties to use if they wished to do so against trade unions or workers, it was also clear that very few companies were ready to resort to the use of the law in industrial disputes. It was calculated that only 114 interlocutory injunctions were taken out against trade unions in disputes between 1983 and 1987, though there were an average of 1,000 strikes a year over that period. However, these statistics are liable to misinterpretation. They fail to take into account the strenuous efforts made by trade unions to prevent potential conflicts erupting and thereby dragging in the law. The mere existence of a battery of legislation acted as a clear deterrent to trade unions and workers in pursuing actions that might lead them into legal difficulties, though this does not provide a satisfactory all-embracing explanation for the decline in the use of the strike threat weapon after 1985. All over the Western industrialized world resort to stoppages became less frequent during the course of the decade, whether or not governments had introduced or enforced punitive legislation against trade unions.

What did become clear during the 1980s in British industrial relations was the extent to which the government's strategy worked in harmony with the more fundamental structural changes that were going on inside the labour market. The move away from any form of centralized collective bargaining at industry or national level, for example, was encouraged by ministers but it also fitted in closely with the corporate objectives of many enterprises in the private sector who were facing severe global competition in a more integrated and open world trading and financial system. The reduction in the incidence of multi-employer bargaining was best symbolized in 1990 by the end of national negotiations between the Engineering Employers' Federation and the Confederation of Shipbuilding and Engineering Unions. It was also apparent in other industries – notably cotton textiles, food retailing, cement and newspaper production, as well as in road passenger transport and the docks. The 1990 workplace study found that multi-employer collective bargaining was only the most important level for wage determination for 26 per cent of manual workers

Table 8.5 Productivity and labour costs in manufacturing, 1980–1991

	Wages per person employed	Output per unit of output increase
1980	22.3	−3.8
1981	9.3	3.5
1982	4.2	6.6
1983	0.5	8.6
1984	3.1	5.5
1985	5.8	3.4
1986	4.0	3.1
1987	1.8	6.3
1988	2.5	6.4
1989	4.6	4.6
1990	8.6	1.9
1991	8.2	−0.1

Source: Employment Gazette.

(compared with 40 per cent in 1984) and 24 per cent of white-collar staff (down from 34 per cent six years earlier).

By contrast, single employer bargaining had grown more predominant by the late 1980s and a decentralization of collective bargaining units also took place within companies. Purcell asserted that 'within these systems it would appear that the role of the trade union is marginalized as the employer focuses on the individual employee and the development of team work'.[64] But it was also clear that the changes in bargaining structures were motivated by reform in the corporate structures of companies rather than in their labour market circumstances.

Professor David Metcalf at the London School of Economics claimed Britain enjoyed a 'productivity miracle' at least until the mid-1980s, which he believed stemmed from the success of the government's industrial relations strategy. Certainly, an impressive improvement in output per head employed took place in the early years of the decade. Between 1979 and 1986 there was a 4.4 per cent rise in the annual rate of labour productivity but that figure has to be placed in a longer time perspective. While it was much higher than the 1.2 per cent output per head averaged during the 1970s, it was little better than the 4.3 per cent average productivity growth during the much-maligned decade of the 1960s when the trade union 'problem' was top of the British political agenda. It is also instructive to recognize that while labour productivity grew relatively faster in the early 1980s in Britain than in Germany, France and Italy, the productivity gap between Britain and its main European competitors still remained substantial by the end of the decade. As Peter Nolan argued:

> For many inefficient, low productivity enterprises, low wages and low social charges have become a precondition for survival. Over time low wages and low productivity have become self-reinforcing. The more employers and successive governments have seen pay restraint as the chief solution to the problems of British industry, the weaker has been the incentive for firms to innovate and modernize, to reduce costs by implementing more efficient technologies.[65]

Towards the end of the 1980s, Britain's productivity growth began to slow down perceptibly, suggesting that the 'miracle' was due to the closure of obsolete plant and inefficient machinery with resulting redundancies rather than a widespread restructuring and investment in new productive capacity which would have produced more on-going improvements.

Brown and Walsh concluded that:

> The attack on collectivism and the steady increase in income inequality have not been accompanied by a competitive turnaround. Britain's key economic problem remains one of low labour productivity, a problem the magnitude of which can no longer be accounted for in terms of idle employees or obstructive unions. The explanation for it is far more likely to lie in a history of low investment in capital equipment and probably more importantly in employees' skills.[66]

Contrary to government assertion, there was no reliable evidence to suggest trade unions were an obstacle to productivity improvements in the 1980s. In fact, productivity actually rose faster in unionized than in non-union companies where technological innovation was also more likely to be introduced. 'The driving force behind changes in industrial relations practices in the 1980s was not government policies aimed at increasing competition in the labour market and at weakening trade unions but increased product market competition, precipitated by a variety of circumstance, which has driven employers to put their own houses in order'.

Can Britain's unions survive?

In February 1992 the Department of Employment published a White Paper, *People, Jobs and Opportunity*, that cast serious doubt on the future of the traditional system of British collective bargaining. It asserted:

There is a new recognition of the role and importance of the individual employee. Traditional patterns of industrial relations, based on collective bargaining and collective agreements, seem increasingly inappropriate and are in decline. Many employers are replacing outdated personnel practices with new policies for human resource management which put the emphasis on developing the talents and capacities of each individual employee. Many are also looking to communicate directly with their employees rather than through the medium of a trade union or formal works council. There is a growing trend to individually negotiated reward packages which reflect the individual's personal skills, experience, efforts and performance.[67]

In the so-called new age of workplace individualism, there seems almost no role left for trade unions to play. 'Successive surveys have shown that the presence of trade unions in the workplace had very little influence on people's choice of jobs or on job satisfaction', asserted the White Paper. 'Given the difficulty trade unions have experienced in recruiting outside traditional manufacturing industries, it seems unlikely that trade union membership will ever return to the levels of the 1970s. Current indications are that it may continue to decline.'[68] The Department of Employment predicted that, during the 1990s:

> successful industrial relations strategies will work with the trends in the labour market, widening individual choice and opportunity, moving away from collectivism and supporting the natural evolution of working arrangements and practices which suit both individual employees and the companies for whom they work. Attempts by national Governments or the European Community to impose rigid and uniform models from the centre or to treat people at work as an undifferentiated mass are likely to seem increasingly inappropriate.

The government's emphasis on individual workers – their rights as well as their obligations – represented a decisive shift in Conservative party industrial relations strategy that has outlived the end of the Thatcher era. There seemed little prospect of any return to the benevolent One Nation Toryism of the Monckton–Hare period, with its positive support for voluntarism, and the TUC as an Estate of the Realm. The abolition of the Wages Councils, and more anti-union legislation in 1993 confirmed the commitment of John Major's government to continue with the 'step by step' strategy of his predecessor. Just how much further there remains to go is unclear, though it still seems doubtful whether the Conservatives will carry through the whole Hayekian programme and finally strip trade unions of all their legal immunities. However, the transformation of industrial relations during the 1980s suggested the Conservatives were more than ready to limit trade union immunities to a minimum in the name of increased freedom and competition.

There has certainly been what will probably be an irreversible change in British industrial relations that even the return of a Labour government could do little to alter. As Sir Henry Phelps Brown observed, 'a new view of society' came to prevail during the 1980s:

> People are no longer dependent on society and bound by reciprocal obligation to it. Indeed, the very notion of society is rejected. Individuals are expected to shift for themselves and those who get into difficulties are thought to have only themselves to blame. Self-reliance, acquisitive individualism, the curtailment of public expenditure, the play of market forces instead of the restraints and directives of public policy, the prerogatives of management instead of the power of trade unions, centralisation of power instead of pluralism.[69]

In his opinion, Britain is witnessing the 'dissolution of the Labour Movement'. It is not just the Labour party's four consecutive general election defeats and the long slow net decline in union membership that pointed to this. As Phelps Brown asserted, the essence of the 'labour movement' was more than just institutional. It also existed 'in the sense of common interest and common purpose that animated its members', 'the faith of the workers in unity'. The Labour Movement was concerned through this century in 'substantial betterment through thoroughgoing changes in society' such as the 'substitution of orderly administration for chaotic competition, the redistribution of income and wealth toward greater equality and the substitution of self-government (or control by the people) in industry in place of the arbitrary authority of management operating in the interests of shareholders'. These objectives demanded 'action at the national level' through the Labour party or above all the work of the TUC. But now Britain has experienced a growth in a 'widespread localisation of interests' in both the home and the workplace which has weakened still further the older concept of solidarity. Phelps Brown pointed to the segmentation of the labour market and the decline in class divisions with the contraction in the numbers involved in manual work. With the 'new individualism' has come a change in the priorities of political action. Even without the experience of Thatcherism, the trend in Britain to a 'more independent way of life' for workers and their families would have grown stronger during the 1980s. After all, a similar structural development could be seen across most of the Western industrialized world; but it is also true that the process went faster and further in Britain than among its main competitor economies.

The 1990 government-commissioned workplace industrial relations survey published in the autumn of 1992 highlighted the transformation that was taking place. It concluded that the decline in both the level of unionization in the labour force and the proportion covered by collective bargaining indicated the end of what it called 'the traditional, distinctive system' of industrial relations which had dominated Britain for most of this century. But the survey also suggested 'no new pattern of employee representation' had emerged to replace trade unionism. New forms of consultation and employee participation schemes 'were more commonly a complement for trade union representation rather than a substitute filling a gap' left by the contraction in the size of organized labour, it argued.[70]

The empirical evidence on display in the survey suggested that Britain was entering a new era of industrial relations. It asserted: 'The fact that fewer workplaces had recognized unions in 1990 than in 1980 was our strongest evidence of the decline in collective bargaining as an institution. The fall was stark, substantial and incontrovertible'. It found only 54 per cent of the workers in the survey sample were covered by collective bargaining in 1990 compared with 71 per cent six years earlier. The workplace survey emphasized the transformation of the contours of British industrial relations but there were also signs of continuity at the beginning of the 1990s.

The academic debate about the consequences of Thatcherism for the labour scene might have been indecisive and conjectural but it would be myopic to suggest that during the years since 1979 the government had not had considerable influence at least on the climate of industrial relations. This did not mean a coherent employer counter-revolution. Few companies seemed to have any long-term strategies at all. But as Nigel Lawson indicated in his memoirs the Conservative agenda towards the trade unions was wide-ranging and radical and not confined to the mere passage of anti-union legislation. What Mrs Thatcher and her more like-minded Cabinet colleagues were intent on doing was to destroy once and for all the post-war industrial relations settlement. In every aspect of domestic policy the objective was to individualize the collective, to deregulate and stimulate competition, to diminish the public sector through privatizing industries and services, and to encourage personal ownership of shares, property and capital. The vision may often have become blurred in the flurry of events and the pace quickened and slackened, but the outcome was not in doubt. The world that Mrs Thatcher and John Major have sought to create has no obvious role for trade unions at all.

In some ways this ought to have satisfied the unions. After all – and as we have seen – they had fought to avoid taking on burdens from the state that undermined their basic purposes. The success that the Conservatives achieved during the 1980s stemmed from the fact that they did not seek to impose any alien measures on an unwilling trade union movement. On the contrary, they turned – with considerable tactical skill – the voluntarist tradition to their own advantage. The language of *laissez faire* individualism enjoyed a resonance on many a shop floor which proved to be far more potent than appeals to class action and solidarity. Increasingly it was union leaders and their militant activists who seemed out of touch with the times.

Moreover, Mrs Thatcher was also able to take advantage of the supposed shopfloor revolution of the 1970s to strengthen her own strategy to undermine collective bargaining and the authority of the trade unions. In a few years the Conservatives showed just how illusory the supposed power of the trade unions was in the period of the Social Contract. By formalizing and legitimizing workplace organization along the lines recommended by the Donovan Royal Commission, union champions of shopfloor democracy like Jones paved the way for a highly effective counter-attack by the state. Under conditions of recession, employers found they could much more easily restore lost authority over the workplace either by utilizing the shop stewards who were over-dependent on the companies for their sourcing and position or going over their heads to the shop floor. Far from being voices of the unions in the companies, the lay activists on the combine committees and the joint consultation bodies became conveyor belts for managerially imposed change.

By contrast, the unions outside the workplace were thrown onto the defensive. With a loss of political influence over government and facing the demise of national or multi-company bargaining, union leaders began to worry about their functions. In fact, strangely enough, Mrs Thatcher unwittingly threw them a life-line. The 1984 Trade Union Act forced the unions to become more accountable and professional organizations. It ensured the widening gap between the union bureaucracies and the workplace narrowed. By 1993, unions – under threat of financial ruin – had come to learn how to survive through adapting to external change. Of course, the cumulative restrictive industrial relations legislation has made it hard for the trade unions to function effectively. But they are not going to vanish, even though heavy losses of the 1980s may well continue through the 1990s.

In this respect, Britain may be coming into line with the experience of other Western countries outside Scandinavia. Through social and occupational change the manual industrial proletariat of the Labour Movement is a besieged and dwindling minority of organized workers. The highly educated salariat in the public sector are becoming the vanguard of modern trade unionism. No doubt, the underlying trends would have occurred if a Labour government had been in power since 1979. But the

Zeitgeist of self-interest and acquisitive sectionalism preached by Mrs Thatcher and her colleagues was all-important. Ever since the late 1940s brief glimpses of the rise of workerist individualism could be seen. It was apparent to those in the Labour party who debated its future after the third successive general election defeat in September 1959, and to John Goldthorpe and his colleagues who surveyed Luton manual workers in the late 1960s. In the early 1990s it is so-called Basildon Man who appears to rule supreme.

A guide to Conservative industrial relations legislation, 1980–1993

1980 Employment Act

1 Picketing was limited to strikers in lawful strikes at their own place of work.
2 Secondary action by strikers was lawful only if it concerned contracts of employment, was limited to the first supplier or customer of the goods and services of the employer in dispute, and where the principal reason for the action was to prevent the supply of goods and services during the period of the dispute.
3 Legal remedies were provided for workers against trade unions if they were unreasonably excluded or expelled from the union on the grounds of refusing to join a closed shop. This right was extended from workers with genuine religious convictions against closed shops to 'grounds of conscience or other deeply held personal conviction'.
4 New closed shops were only lawful where there was a majority support in a secret legally obligatory ballot where 80 per cent of those entitled voted.
5 The burden of proof was removed from an employer that he had acted reasonably in unfairly dismissing an employee. A worker had to be employed for two years to be able to bring an unfair dismissal case before an industrial tribunal.
6 The trade union recognition provisions of the 1975 Employment Protection Act were repealed. So was Schedule 11 of the same Act which had enabled unilateral action by workers to secure pay rises from their employers to bring them up to the general level of recognized terms and conditions with other workers in the area.
7 The government provided for financial support for trade unions that wanted money to assist in strike ballots and elections of union officials, as well as union rule changes.

1982 Employment Act

1   The key change was the repeal of Section 14 of the 1974 Trade Union and Labour Relations Act removing the immunity of trade unions from action in tort. This enabled, for the first time since 1906, the suing of a trade union for damages. Damage limitations were imposed in the law ranging from £10,000 for a union with under 10,000 members to £250,000 for one with more than 100,000. The union was liable for damages for any unlawful actions that had been authorized or endorsed by specific union officials.

2   Legal immunities were also removed from trade unions in specific cases: where the action was not taken 'in contemplation or further-ance of a trade dispute' under a new narrower definition of what constituted a 'trade dispute'; in cases of unlawful picketing or unlawful secondary action; and where trade union action was used to impose a closed shop or union recognition on another employer.

3   The definition of a trade dispute was narrowed to prevent solidarity actions at home or abroad, sympathy strikes, or inter-union disputes from being lawful.

4   Further action to limit the closed shop was introduced. Now all existing closed shops were required to be balloted if they had not been so for five years, and they required an 85 per cent majority of those voting to confirm their lawful existence. A worker could bring a claim against both the employer and the trade union jointly for unfair dis-missal in a closed shop where this legal provision had not been met.

5   The outlawing of trade-union-only commercial contracts. The provi-sion went on to prevent the existence of commercial contracts where the contractor had to recognize, or negotiate or consult with trade unions or their officials.

6   Trade unions and others organizing industrial action lost their legal immunities where they tried to force an employer to sign union-labour-only commercial contracts.

1984 Trade Union Act

This measure required:

1   The holding of secret ballots for the direct election of union executive committees at least every five years, where practicable by post but otherwise in the workplace.

2 The provision of a secret ballot before a union called workers out on strike. If this was not done the union lost its immunity from civil action in the courts. A majority had to agree to the strike and the ballot had to be held no more than four weeks before the stoppage was to begin. Other detailed provisions laid down the procedure for the holding of the ballot.

3 The provision of secret ballots for trade union political funds to ensure members approved of the use of union finances for political activities.

A trade union would lose its legal immunities from action in the courts if it defied any of these provisions.

1986 Wages Act

This measure sought to deregulate the labour market by:

1 abolishing the Truck Acts so manual workers did not have to be paid in cash; and

2 removing workers under the age of 21 from the provisions of the Wages Councils.

1988 Employment Act

This measure and those that have followed exposed the fiercely anti-union bias of Conservative industrial relations legislation. The so-called 'balance of power' justification was hard to sustain when many employer organizations made it clear that they were not particularly enthusiastic about the changes. The new legislation meant:

1 The abolition of all remaining legal protections for the post-entry closed shop. No strike would be lawful that tried to enforce such a closed shop.

2 Trade unionists in a lawful strike who cross picket-lines to work cannot be disciplined even if a majority of the workers involved supported the industrial action in a secret ballot.

3 No trade unionist can be called out on strike without the holding of a secret ballot.

4 All trade union members have the right to a postal ballot in all union elections and strike ballots.

5   The creation of a new body – the Commission for the Rights of Trade Union Members – which is designed to help trade union members with legal advice and financial support. Unfortunately, the Commissioner is not there to assist workers with unfair dismissal or other complaints against their employers. Nor was such a body envisaged to help people with their social security entitlements.

1989 Employment Act

This measure was a further stage in deregulating the labour market by the removal of more ancient protections for vulnerable groups of workers like women and young people.

1   Most of the laws that discriminated between men and women in employment were repealed. Legally, women can now be employed in coal mines. Young people above school age could be required to work limitless hours and at night.
2   The Training Commission was abolished and its functions taken over by the Employment Department. Unions lost their voice in what happened to industrial training boards, which were downgraded with non-statutory status.
3   Various provisions of legislation from the Social Contract period as affecting small companies were also repealed.

1990 Employment Act

This measure represented a further anti-union advance by the government, which had little positive employer support for it outside the radical right. Its main provisions included:

1   The abolition of the pre-entry closed shop by making it unlawful to refuse employment over the question of trade union membership.
2   Trade union officials were required to repudiate or take the responsibility for unofficial strikes.
3   Unofficial strikers could be selectively dismissed by an employer lawfully.
4   Legal immunities were removed from any industrial action taken to support people dismissed selectively for taking part in an unofficial strike.
5   All remaining forms of secondary action were made unlawful.

1993 Trade Union Reform and Employment Rights Act

The next measure made yet further assaults on trade union autonomy, including:

1 The check-off arrangement – the automatic deduction of trade union membership dues by an employer from employees – made unlawful unless there is written authorization every three years by each worker.
2 Workers have the right to join the trade union of their choice, which undermined the TUC's 1939 Bridlington Agreement that regulated which trade unions workers could join.
3 All pre-strike ballots are to be made postal and subject to independent scrutiny with at least seven days' strike notice given by the union after the ballot result to enable the employer to prepare for it.
4 Everybody who uses the public services has the right to try, by seeking injunctions, to prevent the disruption of those services by unlawful industrial action. Here the industrial relations law ties up with John Major's Big Idea of the Citizen's Charter.
5 Everybody who works more than 8 hours a day for an employer has to receive a clear written statement of terms and conditions of employment.
6 The terms of reference of the Advisory Conciliation and Arbitration Service are changed so that it has no longer to promote and encourage collective bargaining.
7 All Wages Councils to be abolished with an end to minimum wage fixing.
8 Industrial tribunals have their jurisdiction extended to cover breaches of employment contract.
9 All women to enjoy a 14 week continuous maternity leave. Protection for pregnant women from unfair dismissal.
10 Protection for workers who are victimized and dismissed by an employer over a health and safety at work issue where they seek to protect themselves and other workers.
11 Employers allowed to offer workers financial inducements to leave unions.

Notes

1 P. Riddell, *The Thatcher Era and its Legacy*, Blackwell, 1991, p. 44.
2 H. Young, *One of Us*, Macmillan, 1989 p. 533.

3   D. Kavanagh, *Thatcherism and British Politics: The End of Consensus?*, Oxford University Press, 1987, p. 243.
4   I. Gilmour, *Dancing with Dogma: Britain under Thatcherism*, Simon and Schuster, 1992, p. 79.
5   *Industrial Relations in the 1990s*, Cm 1602, HMSO, July 1991, p. 6.
6   Ibid., p. 8.
7   N. Tebbit, *Upwardly Mobile*, Weidenfeld & Nicolson, 1988, p. 193.
8   TUC Congress report, 1983, pp. 463–4.
9   Ibid., p. 402.
10 N. Lawson, *The View From No. 11*, Bantam Press, 1992, p. 437.
11 *Employment: Challenge for the Nation*, Department of Employment, Cmnd 9474, 1985, p. 6.
12 ACAS annual report, 1986, p. 18.
13 *Employment Gazette*, June 1991, p. 100.
14 Tebbit, *Upwardly Mobile*, p. 153.
15 F. von Hayek, *The Constitution of Liberty*, Routledge & Kegan Paul, 1960, p. 276.
16 Ibid., p. 302.
17 Ibid., p. 316.
18 Ibid., p. 286.
19 Ibid., p. 000.
20 Sir K. Joseph, *Solving the Trade Union Problem is the Key to Britain's Recovery*, Centre for Policy Studies, February 1979, p. 34.
21 Sir I. Gilmour, *Inside Right*, Hutchinson, 1984, p. 215.
22 Conservative party general election manifesto, 1979, in F. W. S. Craig (ed.), *British General Election Manifestos 1959–1987*, Dartmouth, 1990, pp. 269–72.
23 J. Prior, *A Balance of Power*, Hamish Hamilton, 1986, p. 158.
24 Hansard Parliamentary Debates, Vol. 974. 17 December 1979, cc. 59–61.
25 J. Prior, *A Balance of Power*, p. 158.
26 Ibid., p. 159.
27 Ibid., p. 166.
28 Ibid., p. 169.
29 Tebbit, *Upwardly Mobile*, p. 184.
30 Hansard Parliamentary Debates, Vol. 13, 23 November 1981, c. 631.
31 *Trade Union Immunities*, Green Paper, Department of Employment, Cmnd 8128, January 1981, pp. 29–30.
32 Ibid., p. 44.
33 Ibid., p. 56.
34 W. Wedderburn, 'Freedom of Association and Philosophies of Labour Law', *Industrial Law Journal*, 118 (1), March 1989, p. 31.
35 Ibid., p. 35.
36 Department of Employment Press Release, 29 April 1982.
37 Department of Employment Press Release, 29 April 1982.
38 Tebbit, *Upwardly Mobile*, p. 186.

39 A. Scargill's election manifesto, 1981, p. 4.

40 M. Adeney and J. Lloyd, *The Miner's Strike: Loss without Limit*, Routledge & Kegan Paul, 1986, p. 6.

41 *Democracy in Trade Unions*, Green Paper, Department of Employment, Cmnd 8778, January 1983, p. 1.

42 ACAS annual report, 1986, p. 8.

43 ACAS annual report, 1989, p. 6.

44 W. Brown and S. Wadhwari, 'The Economic Effects of Industrial Relations Legislation since 1979', *National Institute Economic Review*, February 1990, p. 63.

45 D. Grant, 'Mrs Thatcher's Own Goal: Unions and the Political Fund Ballots', *Parliamentary Affairs* 40 (1), January 1987, pp. 69–70.

46 R. Martin, P. Fosh, H. Morris, P. Smith and R. Undy, 'The Decollectivisation of Trade Unionism? Ballots and Collective Bargaining in the 1980s', *Industrial Relations Journal*, 22 (3), Autumn 1991, p. 206.

47 *People, Jobs and Opportunity*, Cm 1810, HMSO, February 1992, p. 39.

48 *Trade Unions and their Members*, Green Paper, Cm 95, HMSO, February 1987, pp. 7–8.

49 S. Auerbach, *Legislating for Conflict*, Oxford University Press, 1990, p. 164.

50 Hansard Parliamentary Debates, Vol. 166, 29 January 1990, c. 78.

51 *Industrial Relations in the 1990s*, Green Paper, Department of Employment, July 1991.

52 Ibid.

53 Warwick University Industrial Relations Unit, Response to Green Paper, 1981, p. 4.

54 Hansard Parliamentary Debates, Vol. 144, 11 January 1989, c. 854.

55 S. Deakin, 'Equality under a Market Order: The Employment Act 1989', *Industrial Law Journal*, 19 (1), March 1990, p. 2.

56 *People and Companies: Employee Involvement in Britain*, Department of Employment, HMSO, 1989, p. 2.

57 C. G. Hanson, *Taming the Trade Unions*, Macmillan, 1991, pp. 88–9.

58 C. G. Hanson and G. Mather, *Striking out Strikes*, Institute of Economic Affairs, 1988, pp. 89–90.

59 N. Millward and M. Stevens, *British Workplace Industrial Relations in Britain 1980–84*, Heinemann, 1983, p. 305.

60 W. W. Daniel, *Workplace Industrial Relations and Technical Change*, Heinemann, 1986, p. 260. Also see E. Batstone and S. Gourlay, *Unions, Employment and Innovation*, Basil Blackwell, 1986, for added confirmation.

61 N. Millward et al., *Workplace Industrial Relations in Transition*, Dartmouth, 1992, p. 352.

62 T. Claydon, 'Union Derecognition in Britain in the 1980s', *British Journal of Industrial Relations*, 27 (2), 1989, p. 222.

63 N. Millward et al., ibid., p. 306.

64 Purcell, 'The Rediscovery of the Management Prerogative: The Management of Industrial Relations in the 1980s', *Oxford Review of Economic Policy* 17 (1), 1991, p. 41.

65 P. Nolan, 'Walking on Water? Performance and Industrial Relations under Thatcher', *Industrial Relations Journal* 20 (2), Summer 1989, p. 84.

66 W. Brown and J. Walsh, 'Pay Determination in Britain in the 1980s', *Oxford Review of Economic Policy*, 17 (1), 1991, p. 57.

67 *People, Jobs and Opportunity*, p. 6.

68 Ibid., p. 11.

69 H. Phelps Brown, 'The Counter-Revolution of Our Times', *Industrial Relations Journal*, 29 (1), Winter 1990, pp. 1–2.

70 Millward et al., *Workplace Industrial Relations in Transition*, p. 350.

Conclusion Governments and Trade Unions since 1945: An Assessment

Every British government from 1945 until the arrival of Margaret Thatcher in 10 Downing Street in May 1979 tried to establish a close working relationship with the trade union movement. It was believed – rightly or wrongly – that organized labour's cooperation was essential for the successful management of the economy. At the beginning of the period the TUC was regarded as an Estate of the Realm, the undisputed representative voice of working people. Its leaders were treated by the state as important public figures whose consent and advice was needed not just for the achievement of stable and effective industrial relations but in wider policy areas. Under the Labour government from July 1945 to October 1951, a close working alliance existed between the state and the TUC built upon the foundations of social solidarity created during the war years. Union officials regarded the Labour government as 'their' government, implementing a post-war domestic settlement of full employment, the nationalization of key industries and the creation of a more comprehensive welfare state. As a result, an inner cohesion and sense of common purpose was established between the industrial and political wings of the Labour Movement. This helped to sustain the TUC's voluntary implementation of the 1948–50 wages freeze in the battle to save the vulnerable British economy.

Inevitably, that first ambitious attempt at national pay restraint fell to pieces after just over two years. But it proved to be much more successful in the short term than many union leaders had believed was possible. Despite the existence of a tight labour market and inflationary wage pressures, the trade unions kept a check on the pay demands of their members and did not pressurize employers as hard as they could have done for fatter wage packets. But there were severe limitations on just how long such a strategy could be sustained. Ministers were disappointed when union leaders insisted they were unable to persist with the national wages policy beyond the summer of 1950. By that time most of the Labour Cabinet were convinced that the British economy needed not just a temporary wage standstill in response to a transient crisis but a permanent system of pay bargaining which would involve an annual agreement between the state, employers and the trade unions on what the country as a whole could afford in overall wage increases. The bitter experience of the first years after the war convinced ministers and their civil service advisers that the state could not hope to regulate the economy in a suc-cessful way while leaving the voluntarist industrial relations system alone. Unfortunately for the government, union leaders were unable or unwilling to accept the government's analysis, and ministers – both Labour and Conservative – were reluctant to endanger the post-war social consensus by introducing any compulsory incomes policy. But most union leaders were in no position to coerce or persuade their members to contain their wage rise expectations in the broader national interest as defined by the Treasury. Under pressure from a slowly fragmenting and decentralized shop floor, where particularly in the private manufacturing sector shop stewards were able to maximize workgroup bargaining strength in a tight labour market as a way of achieving higher earnings, even the most loyal of the trade union leaders at national level were forced to accept that they could not perpetuate voluntary pay restraint for more than a limited period.

Yet during the early 1950s there was no wages explosion in a self-destructive free-for-all, as some economists had feared. The Conservative government under Churchill's benign paternalism was determined to establish friendly working relations with the TUC and uphold the cherished principles of voluntarism. Until 1955–6 this strategy of industrial appeasement proved to be relatively successful, with Sir Walter Monckton's enlightened impartiality reigning at the Ministry of Labour and National Service. Contrary to the critics with hindsight who have suggested the period was a lost opportunity for dealing with trade union power, there was only mild wage–push inflation. National union leaders continued to urge their own members to behave with self-restraint and responsibility. They feared a more militant posture would have only provoked damaging inflation and a probable return to mass unemployment. This was why so many of them took a hostile view of shop stewards, who were seen not only as threats to the existing structure of authority in trade union organizations but as undisciplined promoters of sectionalist pay bargaining.

The social cohesion of the war years between the TUC and the political world did not really start to pass away until the late 1950s. After

Monckton's long stint of industrial conciliation a period of uncertainty followed as the state and TUC sought to establish a new relationship in increasingly difficult political and economic circumstances. The sudden and unexpected election victory of Frank Cousins as the TGWU's General Secretary in the spring of 1956 signalled a partial change of mood and direction inside the TUC. The trade union movement did not reject overnight the government's blandishments for a national consensus, but the end of the era of political dominance in the TUC by the post-war right-wing junta took place at a time when the public's view about the role of organized labour in the economy was starting to grow more critical. From being viewed in a positive way as essential and responsible partners in the creation of a more competitive economy, trade unions were now increasingly being judged as obstacles to growth with their defence of restrictive practices and opposition to genuine productivity improvements, and as unprofessional oligarchies incapable of modernizing themselves.

Sir Anthony Eden followed by his successor Harold Macmillan tried to draw the TUC into forms of national economic cooperation with little success. It is true that in 1962 at the behest of TUC General Secretary George Woodcock, the TUC general council agreed to participate in the tripartite National Economic Development Council and there was a greater willingness by the TUC to accept the need for positive state action in improving industrial training and encouraging union mergers. But for the most part the TUC was unready to help any Conservative government – however well-intentioned it might be – to achieve wage restraint and encourage genuine productivity agreements through the abolition of restrictive practices. Union leaders preached the virtues of free collective bargaining and insisted on the preservation of the voluntarist approach to industrial relations. While willing to agree with governments on ambitious growth targets to transform Britain's relatively stagnant economy, the trade unions were less enthusiastic about reforming themselves if it involved making painful decisions that might compromise their autonomy. The sense of drift and complacency that dominated the TUC at the end of the 1950s made the trade unions a particular focus for criticism in the wave of self-criticism that swept across much of British society at the time. Among venerable institutions under attack, the trade unions were vulnerable to the new mood of modernization. Undoubtedly, the iconoclasm exaggerated the perception that trade unions were responsible for economic stagnation. They were visible and easy targets for attack and they found it hard to respond effectively. The trouble was there was a serious lack of empirical evidence to justify isolating the behaviour of the trade unions as a primary cause of Britain's relative decline during the period. Anecdotal and journalistic assertion was an unconvincing foundation for the making of public policy.

For a brief moment in the early 1960s it looked as though the trade unions and the Labour party had found common ground in a national strategy for the 'planned growth of incomes' which would reconcile the short-term demands of trade union bargainers with the government's commitment to economic expansion. Unfortunately, Labour's promise of growth failed to materialize once the cabinet decided not to devalue sterling. Within weeks of taking office in October 1964 Harold Wilson's government accepted the need for deflation and leaned heavily on the TUC to deliver wage restraint as a crucial way of convincing the outside financial world that the pound would be held at the fixed exchange rate value it had kept since 1949. Holding back real and even nominal pay rises became an end in itself, and the underlying loyalty of the trade unions to a Labour government which had promised so much began to evaporate rapidly. After the July 1966 measures with the resulting wage pause, it was only a matter of time before the two wings of the Labour Movement divided in bitter recrimination. Within two years a new more militant generation of union leaders came to power in the country's two largest trade unions who were determined not to see their organizations used by the government to enforce any kind of wage restraint. The early years of dominance by Hugh Scanlon of the AEU and Jack Jones of the TGWU reflected the growing shopfloor unrest and disillusionment at the failure of a Labour government to deliver its economic objectives of growth and redistribution. Relations were stretched to breaking point in the spring and summer of 1969 when Wilson and Barbara Castle, his zealous Secretary of State for Employment and Productivity, tried to confront the trade unions with legislation designed to put an end to unofficial strikes. In the end Wilson and Castle were forced to back down and they suffered a public humiliation, not because of trade union resistance but because they lost the vital support of their Cabinet colleagues and the majority of the Labour parliamentary party. However, the extraordinary episode underlined Labour's inability to make any reforms in industrial relations without winning trade union consent.

As a result, by 1970 it looked as though trade union 'power' had become the dominant issue in British politics. Many commentators began to question whether any democratically elected government would be allowed to govern as it wished in the face of the TUC's implacable opposition. Edward Heath and the Conservatives refused to believed such a notion. They were determined to modernize Britain by encouraging the rapid development of a much more managerialist and competitive economy. For a brief period after coming to office in June 1970 it seemed as if this would bring about a complete break with the post-war social settlement. Union leaders accused Heath of declaring war on them with his determination to stand up to damaging public sector strikes and to implement the huge Industrial Relations Act, designed to bring organized labour within a new codified legal framework. The divisive rhetoric of the time, however, belied the underlying attempts to maintain a semblance of tripartite cooperation. Faced by the permanent prospect of more than a million unemployed, the Heath Cabinet changed course sharply in the spring of 1972 and adapted a more expansionary economic policy as well as seeking a new more positive relationship with the TUC. The government's genuine attempts at conciliation failed, mainly because the politically partisan TUC was in no mood to reach a *modus vivendi* with the Conservatives. Instead, union leaders like Jones looked to the tangible benefits from the emerging Social Contract that had just been established between the TUC and the Labour party. This was designed to bind the two wings of the Labour Movement together in a much closer workable alliance based on a blend of shared idealism and mutual self-interest.

After the chastening experiences of the 1966–70 period, Wilson and his senior party colleagues appeared content – when returning as a minority government in March 1974 – to accept most of what the TUC wanted from the state but without bargaining any *quid pro quo* for their agreed pro-union strategy. Jones insisted that the issue of incomes policy should not even appear on the agenda of Social Contract discussions. Apparently, a Labour government had to trust the ability of the trade union leaders themselves to bargain for their members in a responsible manner without any direct government interference. Instead, Labour ministers were supposed to create a more positive industrial relations climate through the extension of limited trade union rights of recognition and other statutory assistance to strengthen trade unions and by using subsidies and price controls to stabilize living costs and thereby lower wage rise expectations. But between July 1974 and July 1975 Britain suffered the horrendous consequences of a wages free-for-all that threatened to propel the country into Latin American levels of hyper-inflation. On the political right this period was condemned as the height of unacceptable trade union power. Jones became a hated Emperor figure and for a moment a majority of people even believed he had grown more powerful than the Prime Minister himself. Feverish and irrational discussions took place at the time about the dangers of a military coup in response to the alleged lurch towards left-wing extremism epitomized by Tony Benn's brief and colourful period at the Department of Industry.

After July 1975 the picture changed almost overnight. Under Jones's important influence a flat rate voluntary incomes policy was introduced and accepted by the TUC. It was followed by a further year of wage norm restraint and then twelve months of an 'orderly' return to 'free' collective bargaining. There is little doubt that the TUC's action in 1975 was decisive. Enough union leaders were alarmed at the dire consequences for employment and living standards of a further bout of irresponsible wage bargaining to ensure support for a voluntary incomes policy, backed up by the threat of penal sanctions to be imposed by the government if it became necessary. But such drastic intervention in collective bargaining under conditions of national crisis could only be a crude and temporary response to the underlying collective bargaining problem caused by fragmented wage structures and leap-frogging pay claims in an increasingly decentralized industrial relations system. The years of national wage restraint between July 1975 and July 1977 severely squeezed pay differentials and built up a substantial resistance among skilled manual workers in the private manufacturing sector. What Jones and others did not appreciate was that flat rate wage policies with their explicitly redistributive approach to pay bargaining were bound to inflame shopfloor discontents. The resulting 'Winter of Discontent' in 1978–9 witnessed a tragic convergence of rank and file frustrations. On one side, groups of workers with proven muscle sought to acquire huge pay deals to enable them to recover what they regarded as their lost relativities. On the other side were the massed ranks of the public service sector's low paid, who thought the moment had come to make a breakthrough in achieving from a Labour government under stress a recognized minimum position of two-thirds of national earnings.

The climactic months of early 1979 paved the way for Mrs Thatcher's 'step by step' industrial relations strategy. For the first time since the Second World War a majority of skilled manual workers did not vote Labour, when the party went down to defeat in the May 1979 general election. Elected partly on a national wave of anti-union feeling, the Conservatives believed that this time they should move with caution in trying to transform industrial relations through changes in the power balance of the law away from the trade unions. Under Mrs Thatcher, industrial relations legislation was introduced which accepted the legal immunities approach but turned what had been traditionally a defence of trade union freedoms into a weapon to restrict the lawful ability of organized labour to act freely in strikes. After five separate pieces of industrial relations legislation between 1980 and 1990 the alleged 'balance' between trade unions and employers had shifted decisively away from organized labour. But it was less the exact changes in the law that mattered than the spirit in which Mrs Thatcher and her Cabinet handled the trade unions. The marginalizing of the trade unions and encouragement of individualism as part of the creation of the opportunity state reflected the Prime Minister's determination not to bow the knee to militants like Arthur Scargill, the NUM president, or to accept any of the TUC's dirigiste agenda. The election of Mrs Thatcher to power in May 1979 represented a decisive break by the state with the post-war industrial consensus.

No British government after 1945 really challenged directly the voluntarist inheritance of industrial relations practice. Historically, for the Labour party and the TUC it was the best of all systems in the best of all possible worlds and many believed it had stood the supreme test of total war. There was therefore little consistent interest displayed anywhere across the political spectrum in the creation of the kind of industrial relations systems that became commonplace in post-war democratic northern Europe. The insular British Left took an often arrogant and misguided view of German works councils and co-determination, of the value of centralized collective bargaining based on principles of solidarity or concerted action. Nor did the trade unions seek the establishment of new institutions to solidify their position in a burgeoning corporatist state. For the most part, Britain's trade union activists continued to worship at the shrine of free collective bargaining where the state was to play only a minimalist role in the conduct of industrial relations.

This blinkered, parochial but understandable outlook began to break down slowly from the end of the 1950s in the wider national debate about incomes policy, but it never disappeared entirely, even when it had become increasingly clear that workplace organization alone could not hope to bring about a better deal for the low paid, women workers, the unskilled and those suffering from bad health or injuries at work. Slowly and hesitantly but in mostly an ad hoc way, governments after 1960 turned to the use of legislation as a way of introducing some long overdue minimum standards at work. It was a belated recognition that the state would have to take the initiative and shoulder some direct responsibilities for improving the effectiveness of workplace performance. The initial reforms were aimed at giving workers a greater sense of security in the workplace by modifying the still predominantly *laissez-faire* attitudes of employers towards their labour market needs.

What was crucial was to arm the trade union activists with the necessary legislation to complement, not duplicate, their workplace efforts. The later legislation of the Social Contract period stemmed perhaps from more than a half-hearted recognition by idealists such as Jack Jones that shopfloor power was not enough in itself unless it was coordinated with a much wider bargaining perspective that transcended the familiar sectionalist mentality upon which so much of the shop steward movement was based in theory and practice.

So often voluntarism became the ideological excuse for inertia. It was a highly conservative, often unthinking, instinctive acceptance of a legacy from an earlier age when *laissez faire* attitudes of mind were much more dominant. Unfortunately, the tradition was stubborn in its longevity because it preserved workplace autonomy and the multi-union realities which made successive TUC efforts after 1927 to reform trade union structures so futile. Organizations as vested interests are slow to move, even under the pressures of technological change. So many of the country's industrial relations problems stemmed from that unpalatable fact.

But in post-1945 Britain the employers were as like-minded as the trade unions in their fundamental lack of interest in industrial relations reform – at least until the 1970s when more formalized systems began to emerge in a belated response to the main recommendations of the Donovan Royal Commission, with the growth of full-time lay representatives, combine committees, single company agreements, and the check-off system. However, no coherent or unified employer view of the issues involved was to emerge. The diversity of employer attitudes reflected an *ad hoc* pragmatism rather than an enlightened commitment to any unified and socially responsible corporatist strategy. In fact, in the years after the Second World War there were few signs of any concerted employer position on the so-called trade union 'problem'. The CBI and EEF both reflected the confusions and the divisions that prevented the emergence of an aggressively anti-union offensive by the forces of capital, either in the early 1970s under Heath or again during the era of Mrs Thatcher's political dominance.

It is hard, therefore, to avoid drawing the conclusion that employers and trade unions sought to insulate their own mutual relationships from the realities of the outside political world where governments tended to react in an *ad hoc* manner to the events of the moment in an economy in relatively slow decline. Employers were particularly aware, at least until the 1980s, that any moves to reform industrial relations by one government would lead inevitably to changes in the opposite direction by its successor. The chopping and changing that was a feature of so many policy areas in post-war British politics was particularly acute in the industrial relations area. As the EEF argued in June 1981:

Under the British political system it is virtually certain that immunities taken away by a government of one complexion will be at least restored by another government more sympathetic to the cause of union power. There is no merit therefore in initiating this kind of debilitating struggle in industry merely to make use of a temporary political advantage. However desirable in principle the wholesale radical reform of union immunities may seem to be, there is no advantage in attempting it unless the British political system can deliver the prospect of its durability.[1]

With the political hegemony of the Conservative party in the 1980s and early 1990s, that reservation no longer applied but it reflected a widespread feeling among British employers that state interference in industrial relations should be limited and circumspect. Astonishingly, most demands for radical legislative reform designed to weaken the trade unions came not from employers but from a quixotic alliance of Conservative party lawyers imbued in the common law tradition of legal immunities, politicians in search of instant electoral popularity, newspaper editorial writers, neo-liberal economists in search of an easy scapegoat for Britain's undoubted post-war economic ills, and from time to time the general public when inconvenienced by strikes as in the Winter of Discontent of 1978-9 when they became the hapless victims of a workerist offensive.

The resulting legislation of the 1980s underlined the fragility of the position of the trade unions in the British industrial relations system. In 1969 with the *In Place of Strife* White Paper, and again with the 1971 Industrial Relations Act, tentative moves were made by the state to bring the trade unions into a more comprehensive framework of law. The primary purpose was to make them more accountable organizations. But union leaders argued that the bodies they represented could not be transformed into centralized institutions with clear-cut command structures capable of shouldering national responsibilities and turning their members into obedient workers. As always in Britain, it came back to a question of where power should lie in the trade unions. Organized labour's traditional support for voluntarism stemmed from a deep-rooted sceptical attitude born of historical experience about the use of the law in industrial relations. Such doubts among the trade unions about the merits of state action encouraged a desire to be left alone. Trade unions did not demand – nor were they given by the state – positive legal rights and obligations to make them more responsible to interests wider than those of their own members.

In the late 1890s and early 1900s when a number of adverse High Court decisions threatened the very legal existence of trade unionism, an important but short-lived debate took place inside the Labour Movement about the best way to safeguard collective bargaining – legal immunities or positive rights? After the passage of the 1906 Trade Disputes Act the point at issue appeared to have been closed in favour of legal immunities.

It was only at the end of the 1980s that the TUC began to reassess the value of moving towards a system of rights and obligations in line with its commitment to the 1989 Social Charter and subsequent Social Action programme of the European Community. This process of intellectual conversion was by no means complete, but it did appear that the severe setbacks suffered by Britain's trade unions during the 1980s began to shift deep-seated trade union attitudes on this fundamental question.

A number of important general conclusions can be drawn from the tangled story of state–union relations since 1945. First and foremost, the voluntarist traditions of British industrial relations were incompatible with the kind of state interventionism required in the post-war economy to achieve the virtuous circle of full employment, low inflation, high productivity and a balance of payments surplus. Bluntly, trade unions in Britain were not organized nor did they have the resources to become social partners of any government. The more burdens the state sought to impose upon them, the more dangerous grew the prospect of their internal disintegration. Lord Callaghan, the tragic victim of trade union 'power' in 1979, put his shrewd finger on the trouble in his 1980 Jim Conway lecture. He pointed out that after 1945 there was a clear change in the status of the trade unions as it was accepted that the state should 'step more then ever previously into areas which had been left before to collective bargaining'.[2] The passage of legislation to ensure equal pay at work, stronger health and safety provisions, statutory redundancy requirements and employment protection with minimum standards of maternity leave and time off for union work, all emphasized that the law could be a useful supplement to voluntary collective bargaining and most of those reforms originated from TUC pressure. However, as Lord Callaghan argued: 'The very success of the trade unions and their consequential incorporation into the machinery of government consultation and decision-making led to a lessening of the bonds of solidarity between the union hierarchy and the membership.' He exaggerated when he added that trade unions between 1945 and 1979 became 'one of the corporate institutions that helped to shape the future' but they were certainly encouraged by governments to involve themselves in wider concerns than the narrow, often sectionalist self-interests of the workplace.

The real problem was that trade unions were ill-suited by attitude and structure to accept and carry through incomes strategies on behalf of the state. The Social Contract period, in particular, imposed enormous strains on trade union organization. The demands on organized labour proved to be far too ambitious. The years between 1974 and 1979 may have been a logical evolution of the kind of state–union alliance envisaged during the Second World War by men like Citrine in his more visionary moments, but they threatened trade union autonomy and intensified the genuine tensions between national union leaders, the activist minorities in their organizations and the passive but troubled mass membership. The state's economic imperative was to enjoin the trade unions into a social partnership but the pressure from below worked strongly in a different direction.

Nobody with any understanding of industrial relations before 1945 should have been surprised at the outcome. The difficulties and arguments that dominated state–union relations for so much of the time after 1945 stemmed from the historic and confused ambivalence of the British trade unions towards the role of the state in industrial relations. On the one hand they hankered for freedom and autonomy, asking of governments only to provide them with a minimalist legal framework to practise collective bargaining with employers untrammelled by hostile courts imbued with common law traditions of absolute property rights. Unlike most continental European countries in the twentieth century, Britain did not go down the road to positive legal rights for trade unions and workers. But nothing was ever so clear-cut. Trade unions in Britain from their origins fought for a welfare state for all, a progressive tax system and increasingly during the first half of this century the public ownership of private industry and finance. Their leaders claimed to be democratic Socialists and they provided a crucial ballast of common sense and stability for the Labour party they helped to create after 1900. Outside the area of industrial relations, trade unions took a benevolent view of state action. They proclaimed dirigiste economic strategies, especially after the inter-war depression destroyed an earlier faith in the virtues of free trade. In the 1960s and 1970s the TUC and leading trade unions broke down the self-imposed barriers that had held them back in the past from demanding legislative reform on labour market issues. Under the initiative of Jack Jones, for a short period there was even trade union interest in using the law to spread industrial democracy into private sector manufacturing.

But at no stage did the rhetoric for a social contract measure up to the reality of a fully-fledged corporatist system as in Austria, Sweden and West Germany. The TUC – like the Confederation of British Industry – lacked and was never allowed to have the necessary powers of accountability that would have been necessary to ensure national bargains between governments and the representative institutions of labour and capital could have been honoured. In this, for much of the post-war period, the state matched the trade unions and employers in the lack of interest, the sheer indifference, to the creation of a social corporatism. Indeed, the state did not have a coherent, unified view of trade unions. It was divided about what to do about them. The Ministry of Labour remained the most articulate and effective defender of the voluntarist tradition while the Treasury yearned for measures to curb wage-push inflation through reforming the trade unions or at least establishing constraints on wage bargaining. Yet even the Labour government of 1945–51 had by the end of its life moved decisively away from the concept of centralized economic planning. During the 1960s, and for the 1970s after Heath's U-turn in the spring of 1972, governments favoured national incomes policies to restrain wage-push inflation and assist in ensuring economic growth. Unfortunately, they became instruments of deflation, hitting living standards, and not prerequisites for self-sustained expansion. Rank and file trade unionists were unimpressed by the growth in the so-called 'social wage' in universal state benefits when they were funded by ever higher marginal rates of taxation that pressed particularly hard, not on the rich, but on those earning average and below-average incomes. The pressures of steep rises in taxation coupled with inflationary expectations made it increasingly hard to maintain any voluntary pay restraint, particularly among the skilled manual working class. Nor did the return of mass unemployment in the middle to late 1970s make much difference to the upward push on wages that brought persistently high unit labour costs, relative to Britain's main global competitors.

The lack of institutional development in post-war Britain, at least until the creation of NEDC in 1962 and later the voluntary tripartite bodies of the 1970s like the MSC, the HSC and the EOC, reflected a deep-rooted scepticism, if not downright hostility, inside the trade unions as well as the state about the wisdom of social corporatism. Delegations of union leaders reported favourably on the wonders of the Swedish model in the 1950s and 1960s but this led to only half-hearted and sporadic attempts to emulate such a success in the British scene.

The failure of a social market economy to emerge in post-war Britain on the Swedish or German pattern was due predominantly to the attitudes inside the Labour Movement. It also stemmed in part from the increasingly fragmented and decentralized character of so much of the industrial relations system. But then in the last resort, union leaders could not forget their primary purpose was to serve the short-term, materialistic interests of their members not the needs of the state. 'If members ever ceased to speak of "our union" and regarded it as no more than an institution to which they must pay a subscription in order to hold a union card or keep a job then it would be a failure', warned Lord Callaghan.

There are other important conclusions that should be drawn from the history of post-war Britain's industrial relations. Not enough public attention has been focused on the real, as opposed to the alleged, contribution of trade union inadequacies to the wider issue of Britain's relative economic decline. As the TUC General Secretary Len Murray argued in his 1980 Granada lecture:

> It is less difficult for unions to win from their members acceptance of temporary wage restraint than it is for them to win agreement to changes in manpower practices. Indeed, Britain's poor economic record since the war is due much more to the ineffective use of resources than to excessive wage settlements.[3]

The way to ensure a much more productive use of labour lay less through the use of legislation to curb trade unions than in the introduction of government measures, designed to encourage or force employers to start taking their employment responsibilities seriously. By the standards of continental western Europe, British companies in the early 1990s still lagged far behind in their lack of consistent interest in the long-term problems of manpower planning. In crucial areas like work flexibility and industrial training they continued to take a restricted and short-term view even of their own limited needs.

For many commentators, politicians and economists in the post-war period, Britain's trade unions proved to be useful scapegoats in helping to explain the country's relative economic decline. But too often these observers mistook the cause for the effect. The troubles of the economy certainly required urgent remedial action in the labour market, but by seeking to deal one-sidedly with alleged trade union inadequacies, public attention was diverted away from more fundamental reasons for the Britain's lamentable productivity performance at least until the early 1980s. As a recent analysis of trade union performance since 1945 observed: 'The limited hard evidence that was and is available, as opposed to anecdotes and newspaper headlines, gives surprisingly slender support to the view that trade unions or industrial relations arrangements were themselves major contributors to our economic difficulties.'[4]

Much more relevant was the consistent failure of will to tackle the protracted problem of an inadequate industrial training and education system. Complaints about the limited skills of most of Britain's workers began almost from the beginning of the country's first industrial revolution. Over the generations since then, innumerable public inquiries revealed what has become a familiar and lamentable picture of an ill-trained and inflexible workforce. Here was the worst example of the consequences of the *laissez faire* voluntarist system as the state took a minimalist view of its responsibilities, employers confined their limited training efforts to the short term for fear that their competitors would poach away their best workers, and the craft trade unions sought to limit the numbers with skill to maximize their bargaining power. As it has been argued Britain's industrial relations system 'undermined attempts to improve the skills of the workforce' because of the lack of solidaristic authority among employers' associations and the 'historical neglect' of placing the training issue on the collective bargaining agenda.[5]

There was also a lack of political courage by the state to change national attitudes in the face of a decentralized education system and a stubborn determination by employers and trade unions alike to uphold a voluntarist view of training needs. Training failed to establish the high priority it needed on the agenda of post-war British politics. The 1964 Industrial Training Act seemed to presage a new more corporatist approach to the subject but its very tripartite structure of industrial training boards proved to be its own undoing and it failed to provide a coordinated approach to the skill shortage problem. During the 1980s, there was a sharp decline in traditional apprenticeships and most training boards were wound up in favour of an Employment Training (ET) scheme that led in turn to the creation of employer-dominated, underfunded and ineffective Training and Enterprise Councils (TECs). By the beginning of the 1990s, Britain had fewer workers with skills than ten years earlier. Government indifference to the use of its own financial resources to boost training continued as spending cuts were made in what limited contribution the state was making to training budgets.

The history of state–union relations since 1945 also underlined the tenacity of traditional attitudes of mind, in the political world as well as in industrial relations, which went back far into the nineteenth century. The *laissez faire* presumptions of political economy triumphed over those who wanted Britain to develop a much more dirigiste industrial strategy like that of Wilhelmine Germany after 1871. Keeping the state as far as possible out of the relations between employers, trade unions and workers was an instinctive response to the peculiar legal structure and organizational pattern of bargaining that developed towards the end of the Victorian era. Of course, voluntarism had its imperfections and the state began to intervene in areas like health and safety at work from the early part of the nineteenth century. But even when notions of a collectivist social policy began to emerge from the 1880s onwards, trade unions remained determined to uphold the traditional system of voluntarism. The defence of union autonomy coupled with an arm's-length attitude towards the state was seen by many in the Labour Movement as fundamental to its well-being, even after the collectivist ideology of democratic Socialism became dominant among trade union activists. To many observers the defence of *laissez faire* practices in industrial relations coexisted uneasily with an emerging trade union belief in a planned state-owned economy. But even during the Second World War such inconsistencies failed to bring any TUC reappraisal of its basic belief in voluntarism. This was why Britain after 1945 did not become a centralized democratic corporate state. As David Marquand has asserted:

> The British approach to industrial relations has usually been one of benign neglect, tempered by a common law tradition of hostility to the whole notion of collective action. . . . No government has contemplated organising the system even-handedly on neo-corporatist lines.[6]

The forces of individualism and the free market proved to be much stronger than the countervailing tendencies towards centralization and planning. In the struggle between the competitive pull of workplace pressures and the demands imposed on trade unions by national economic perspectives, there could be little doubt which tendency would emerge the more dominant.

This was understandable. After all, whatever politicians and employers might have desired, Britain's trade unions continued to remain in the post-war world what they had always been – insecure, voluntary bodies at the mercy of the often fickle and divided moods of their own members and the uncertain and often harsh fluctuations of the labour market. The country's trade unions and workers were still imprisoned by attitudes of mind that they inherited from long ago in the country's first industrial revolution when Britain was the workshop of the world. Too often critics of the labour scene blamed trade unions when so often those vulnerable institutions reflected the instinctive views of their members. Professor Otto Kahn-Freund – with his contrasting experience of the more rigid, formalized German Labour Movement in the Weimar Republic – liked to emphasize the direct democracy of British workplace organization with its fluid spontaneity, an almost anarchic mentality among the sectionalist-minded work groups. As Kahn-Freund explained:

> In this country the unions have remained a 'movement' more than elsewhere abroad, the process of institutional petrification has not gone as far as in some other industrial societies, the unions have remained 'we' and not become 'they' quite as much as elsewhere or, if this must be expressed in proper language: integration is still over wide areas a more prominent characteristic of the unions than alienation.[7]

The much-maligned shop stewards of post-war Britain tried to reflect as best they could that unpredictable work group mentality. And so often contrary to popular myth, they strove to bring a semblance of order and stability, not conflict, to the workplace at a time when the small overworked cadres of full-time trade union officials lacked the authority or the time to manage the unsettled shop floor. The decentralization of trade union authority was a recognition of a reality that was hidden by national agreements and the social consensus forged during the war years. But it returned much trade union activity to its earlier workplace practices where work group power was of crucial importance.

Self-regarding sectionalism is nothing new to British industrial relations. It was a dominant feature of the labour scene in Victorian Britain. The craft unions, with their restrictive control over entry to the skilled trades and desire for job control through closed shops, were keen to defend their privileged position against both the unskilled and technological innovation. A strong class consciousness could not mask the real and complex social status and occupational divisions that separated workers from each other. The rhetoric of a Labour Movement – an industrial army of the working class of one mind – made little sense beyond the rostrum of union and party conferences. So did any real sense of discipline among workers to achieve a greater good. It is debatable whether social solidarity was ever strong across the working class as a whole. The impressive days of the General Strike in 1926 and the critical period of mid-1940 were perhaps exceptional. Many workers may have called for a 'fair day's work for a fair day's pay' but vague notions of social justice made little impact on the hallowed defence of established and inherited wage differentials and relativities. Here was the strange paradox that post-war British trade unions were forced to grapple with in difficult circumstances. Their members were so often in divided mood. Instinctively suspicious of authority and bloody-minded in defence of the status quo in the workplace, and yet at the same time they were modest in their aspirations and posed no real challenge to managerial prerogatives. This volatile mixture of disdain for organization and compliance with those in power may help to explain a phenomenon that bewildered so many trade union leaders and politicians in the post-war period – namely how the majority of workers tended to back incomes policies in general devised at national level but resisted them when applied to their own wage packets.

What is clear is that the pressures placed upon the trade unions by the post-war realities of relative economic decline proved insufficient to transcend those deeper instinctive feelings and beliefs. This was why the ambiguous triumph of Thatcherism over organized labour during the

1980s seemed unlikely to bring an end to the long-debated trade union 'problem' in British politics. The never-ending dialectic between freedom and control, between workplace autonomy and state intervention, will continue to ravage the country's industrial relations. The experience of state–union relations in the years since 1945 suggests there can be no end to the process of change and continuity. The old Labour Movement, with its collectivist convictions and an ethos of social justice and fraternity, may have passed away but nothing coherent or settled looks set to take its place. The so-called 'new' agenda of British industrial relations with its focus on individualism and hostility to the collective cannot provide a satisfactory solution to the problems of the labour market raised and debated so clearly by Beveridge and the TUC in the final years of the Second World War. The historic tensions between the British state and labour will not easily be spirited away during the 1990s.

Notes

1 Response to the 1981 Green Paper on Legal Immunities, Engineering Employers' Federation, June 1981, p. 2.
2 See R. Taylor, 'Trade Unions and the State', in *Trade Unions: The Thatcher Years*, Jim Conway Foundation, 1993, p. 96.
3 *The Role of the Trade Unions*, Granada, 1980, p. 75.
4 R. Richardson, 'Trade Unions and Industrial Relations', in Crafts and Woodward (eds), *The British Economy since 1945*, Oxford University Press, 1991, p. 417.
5 D. Finegold and D. Soskice, 'The Failure of Training in Britain: Analysis and Prescription', *Oxford Review of Economic Policy*, 4 (3), 1988, p. 29. Also see D. King, 'The Conservatives and Training Policy: From a Tripartite to a Neoliberal Regime', *Political Studies*, December 1992.
6 D. Marquand, *The Unprincipled Society*, Jonathan Cape, 1988, p. 161.
7 O. Kahn-Freund, *Labour Relations: Heritage and Adjustment*, Oxford University Press, 1979, pp. 9–10.

Abbreviations

ACAS	Advisory, Conciliation and Arbitration Service
AESD	Association of Engineering and Shipbuilding Draughtsmen
AEU	Amalgamated Engineering Union (later AUEW)
ASLEF	Associated Society of Locomotive Engineers and Firemen
ASTMS	Association of Scientific, Technical and Managerial Staffs
AUEW	Amalgamated Union of Engineering Workers
CAC	Central Arbitration Committee
CBI	Confederation of British Industry
CIR	Commission on Industrial Relations
CSEU	Confederation of Shipbuilding and Engineering Unions
DEP	Department of Employment and Productivity
EAT	Employment Appeals Tribunal
EEF	Engineering Employers' Federation
EETPU	Electrical, Electronic, Telecommunication and Plumbing Union
EOC	Equal Opportunities Commission
ETU	Electrical Trades Union
GMWU	General and Municipal Workers' Union
HSC	Health and Safety at Work Commission
IRSF	Inland Revenue Staff Federation
ISTC	Iron and Steel Trades Confederation
MSC	Manpower Services Commission
NACODS	National Association of Colliery Overmen, Deputies and Shotfirers (the mine overseers' union)
NALGO	National and Local Government Officers' Association
NATSOPA	National Association of Operative Printers and Assistants (later SOGAT)
NCB	National Coal Board

NEDC	National Economic Development Council ('Neddy')
NGA	National Graphical Association
NIRC	National Industrial Relations Court
NUM	National Union of Mineworkers
NUPE	National Union of Public Employees
NUR	National Union of Railwaymen
NUS	National Union of Seamen
NUVB	National Union of Vehicle Builders
SOGAT	Society of Graphical and Allied Trades
TGWU	Transport and General Workers' Union
TUC	Trades Union Congress
UCS	Upper Clyde Shipbuilders
UCW	Union of Communication Workers
UPW	Union of Post Office Workers
USDAW	Union of Shop, Distributive and Allied Workers

Appendix 1
Dramatis Personae

DAVID BASNETT (1921–89) General Secretary of the General and Municipal Workers' Union from 1973 to 1986, was a sad disappointment. Self-consciously determined to lead his Labour ultra-loyalist union politically from the Right to the Centre, he failed to fill the power vacuum in the TUC after 1978. Neither effective as an orator nor persuasive on television, he became a grey eminence with a Hamlet reputation for dithering. His lack of decisiveness did little to halt the drift inside the TUC and the self-destructive antics that convulsed the Labour party in 1980–2.

TONY BENN Industry Minister from 1974 to 1975 and then Energy Minister until the defeat of the Labour Government in the May 1979 general election. Back in the 1960s he was known as Anthony Wedgwood Benn and enjoyed successful stints as Postmaster General and then Minister of Technology under Harold Wilson. A centre-left figure who voted for Hugh Gaitskell as Labour leader in 1955 he had few close contacts inside the trade unions before 1969. Indeed, he supported the controversial *In Place of Strife* White Paper in 1969 designed to reform the unions through the force of the law, and he was one of the last Cabinet ministers to switch sides and oppose the proposed curbing of unofficial strikes. Thereafter he transformed himself into Tony Benn and built up links with left-wing shop stewards.

WILLIAM BEVERIDGE (1879–1963) Social reformer, economist, high-minded Liberal, he is a key figure in the history of British social policy. Director of the London School of Economics and Political Science, 1919–37, then Master of University College, Oxford, 1937–45, his 1942 report on social insurance turned him briefly into a popular figure – the People's William. His debate with the TUC on wages and jobs in 1943–4 was the first important quasi-public discussion on a vital post-war economic problem.

ERNEST BEVIN (1881–1951)   Foreign Secretary in the Labour Government from 1945 to 1950, he was the most impressive British trade union leader of this century. A big man in every sense of the word, Bevin created the Transport and General Workers' Union almost single-handed and was its General Secretary from 1921 to 1940. Between the wars his practical creativity gave a sense of direction to the TUC, and as Churchill's Minister of Labour and National Service between 1940 and 1945 he was one of the country's saviours. In his own words he was 'one in a million'. A staunch working class patriot with a flair for organizing, he upset armchair intellectuals on the Left like Richard Crossman who disliked his authoritarian tendencies. But Bevin was loyal to Attlee, hated intrigue and more than any other senior figure of his generation he embodied the ethos of the Labour Movement during its brief mid-century period of national dominance.

GEORGE BROWN (1914–85)   Secretary of State for Economic Affairs from October 1964 to July 1966 and deputy leader of the Labour party from 1963 to 1970, he was an *enfant terrible*. Many regarded him as impossible – bullying, over-emotional and self-indulgent. Others thought he was a brilliant, energetic man whose talents were wasted through bouts of destructive argument made worse by over-drinking. He was a fervent champion of economic growth and British membership of the European Community. A firm right-winger, however, he radiated a deep sense of insecurity and succumbed easily to the rumours and innuendo that are part of political life. His later years were depressing, as he left the Labour party but found it hard to settle down in old age as a foot soldier in the Social Democrats.

JIM CALLAGHAN   Labour Prime Minister from April 1976 to May 1979 and before that Home Secretary, Chancellor of the Exchequer and Foreign Secretary, he was once described as the 'keeper of the cloth cap' for his sturdy resistance in 1969 to Barbara Castle's plans to reform the unions by law. A former official with the tax officers' union, he was a pragmatic right-winger who turned into a more impressive Prime Minister than many of his contemporaries were ready to accept. Tragically, however, he fell foul of his former trade union allies, who rejected his belief in incomes policy and launched a savage wage offensive in the winter of 1978–9 that ensured Labour went into the political wilderness for more than a generation. A moral and social conservative, suspicious of radical ideas, he was the articulate voice of homespun Labourism.

ROBERT CARR   Secretary of State for Employment in the Heath Government from June 1970 to April 1972, he was responsible for the passage of the 1971 Industrial Relations Act onto the statute book. A reasonable and quietly spoken man, and former One Nation group Tory, Carr was hardly a union-basher. He was later to admit that the measure to reform the trade unions was so complex he could not understand all of it himself.

BILL CARRON (1902–69)   President of the Amalgamated Engineering Union from 1956 to 1978, he was a devout Roman Catholic and a tough right-winger in the Labour Movement who was prepared to manipulate his union's block vote to an extent that discredited its existence even when his behaviour was designed to save the Labour Establishment from the ravages of the Left. He finished up in the House of Lords.

BARBARA CASTLE   Secretary of State for Employment and Productivity from 1968 to June 1970. Her fervent attempt to force the trade unions to reform themselves through the stimulus of the law was met with bitter hostility from union leaders who regarded her intervention in industrial relations as maladroit and ignorant. But a former Bevanite who regarded herself as being on the left of the Labour party, she became convinced that the trade unions needed to be shaken up and modernized if they were to turn themselves into effective institutions. Her attempt to force through legislation to curb unofficial strikes almost split the Labour Movement in June 1969. She was never really forgiven by the trade union leaders of the time for what she did.

FRANK CHAPPLE   General Secretary of the Electrical, Electronic, Telecommunication and Plumbing Union from 1970 to 1983. A fierce former Communist who became an equally fierce anti-Communist, he was uncomfortable with the high-ups at the TUC. He despised the Broad Left ideology that dominated so much of the general council's attitude, but he was unprepared to organize an effective counter-force. Slightly apart from the rest of the right-wing he was a strong supporter of free collective bargaining for his members with a genuine scepticism towards incomes policies. Chapple was in many ways a man before his time as a champion of the market economy and individual benefits for his members. A pungent debater who took no prisoners, he was never really forgiven by many in the TUC for his part in the exposure of the scandalous election rigging organized by the Communists in his own union.

SIR WALTER CITRINE (1887–1983)   General Secretary of the Trades Union Congress from 1926 to 1946 and chairman of the Central Electricity Authority from 1947 to 1957. An impressive administrator, he worked to make the TUC into an Estate of the Realm with some success in an unlikely partnership with Bevin. Articulate and authoritative, he did much to ensure that the TUC did become a respected and respectable institution. After the trauma of the 1926 General Strike and the TUC's brief flirtation with syndicalism, Citrine created the essential structure of the TUC which lasted until the end of the 1980s. He made the impossible position of General Secretary into a crucial one in the Labour Movement. His diplomatic skills meant he was able to balance the interests of affiliated member unions with the wider objectives of the whole.

JACK COOPER (1908–88) General Secretary of the General and Municipal Workers' Union from 1960 to 1973. A convinced supporter of incomes policies and an admirer of the Swedish system of industrial relations, he proved to be a thoughtful bastion of the Labour Right. Ennobled, he was even prepared to contemplate working with the hated 1971 Industrial Relations Act. He was a modernizer inside his union whose recruitment policy ensured that some of the best and brightest university graduates manned the union's research department including Rupert Pennant-Rea, appointed in 1993 to be the deputy governor of the Bank of England, Giles Radice, the Labour MP for Chester-le-Street, John Edmonds who was elected General Secretary in 1986, and Dianne Hayter, once General Secretary of the Fabian Society. Made a life peer in 1966.

FRANK COUSINS (1904–86) General Secretary of the Transport and General Workers union from 1956 to 1969. A rather confused and angry man who was described even by his admiring biographer Geoffrey Goodman as 'the awkward warrior', he led his union decisively away from its position on the right wing of the Labour Movement. But his fierce rhetoric belied his caution as a union leader, especially after the fiasco of the London busmen's strike in 1958. He seemed often more interested in politics than industrial relations, as a passionate if muddled nuclear disarmer and believer in the state ownership of industry. But his short stint as Minister of Technology from October 1964 to July 1966 was an unhappy experience and he was relieved to get back to the TGWU.

LAURENCE DALY General Secretary of the National Union of Mineworkers from 1968 to 1983. In his prime he was one of the most impressive union leaders of the post-war period – articulate, well-read, a romantic Socialist from the Fife coalfield. At the 1972 Wilberforce Inquiry he presented the union's case with all the forensic skill of a polished advocate. But after that he drifted downhill, a sad embarrassment to many of his supporters. Many on the left such as Scargill regarded him as a traitor. Tragically, like some other union leaders he succumbed to the seductions of the good life.

ARTHUR DEAKIN (1890–1955)   General Secretary of the Transport and General Workers' Union from 1946 to May 1955. He held the post as caretaker from May 1940 when Bevin joined the Churchill wartime coalition. A fierce but effective right-winger of integrity, he was a vital force in keeping the TUC loyal to the Labour Government of 1945–51. Hated by the Left as the epitome of the union boss, who ran his union with a suffocating authoritarianism, he was a man of moderate opinions, pungently expressed. Increasingly he found it hard to uphold his central authority inside his union with the rise in shop steward discontents in the early 1950s.

TERRY DUFFY (1922–85)   President of the Amalgamated Union of Engineering Workers from 1978 to 1987. A Roman Catholic right-winger whose ruling creed was 'I am my brother's keeper', he was a friendly, disarming and honest man who could often seem gauche in the power game but whose views were closer to the membership of his union than many realized. A staunch anti-Communist, he worked hard against the left-wing tide in the TUC of the early 1980s to rally support behind moderate causes. In 1979 he led his union in the successful campaign to cut the 40 hour week in the engineering industry.

MOSS EVANS   General Secretary of the Transport and General Workers' Union from 1978 to 1987. A verbose and rather insecure but friendly Welshman, he was too often swayed by the pressures. Incapable of filling the admittedly large boots of Jack Jones at a very difficult time for the union on the eve of the 1978–9 Winter of Discontent, he left the impression of being overwhelmed by events, lacking either authority or persuasive skills to rise to the occasion. During his period at the top his union became convulsed by bitter internal faction-fighting, about which he could do little.

VIC FEATHER (1908–1976)   General Secretary of the Trades Union Congress from 1969 to 1973. A jolly Yorkshireman, he was an arch-fixer who seemed to spend his entire life making deals and trying to maximize the limited powers he enjoyed as a latecomer to the top job at Congress House. But he was more successful than his predecessor Woodcock even if he lacked Woodcock's brains. Indeed, his frenetic workaholic activities were helpful to Wilson and later Heath who came to like and trust him. A stalwart Labour man, he aroused the doubts of left-wingers like Jones and Scanlon who thought he was prepared to go too far in seeking a deal with the Conservative government in 1972.

MICHAEL FOOT Secretary of State for Employment from March 1974 to April 1976, he was a welcome reassurance to the TUC in the implementation of the Social Contract. His critics argued that he became little more than a rubber stamp for Congress House decisions. Certainly, he did his best to placate the TUC but he also turned out to be, when Leader of the House of Commons from April 1976 to May 1979, a crucial go-between for the government with the TUC. A middle-class romantic who as a Tribunite in the 1950s despised the union bosses, he mellowed in later life and came to take a rather uncritical view of the excesses of the trade unions. However, he was a genuine champion of workplace rights and proud of his work in particular to give safety and health at work issues a much higher political priority.

NORMAN FOWLER Secretary of State for Employment from September 1987 to September 1989. A partisan figure, who later became Chairman of the Conservative party. He was responsible for two of the five anti-union legislative measures passed during the 1980s. Perhaps more importantly it was Fowler who in 1989 brought an end to the controversial dock regulation scheme of registered ports.

JOSEPH GODBER (1914–80) Minister of Labour from September 1963 to October 1964. He was the last of the One Nation Tory occupants of the Ministry during the thirteen consecutive years of Conservative rule. A cautious and moderate man, his wise advice not to rush too fast into comprehensive change in labour law after 1964 was not accepted by his colleagues. But he turned out to be shrewder than they did in his assessment and understanding of the trade union 'problem'.

JOE GORMLEY (1917–93) President of the National Union of Mineworkers from 1971 to 1981. A canny Lancastrian right-winger, he led the union through two strikes in a tumultuous period of its history. Never an ideologue, he was an arch-pragmatist who believed his members should be the best-paid workers in the country. He disliked the idea that the union might be a battering ram to destroy governments and never accepted the Scargill view of the NUM as the vanguard union. As long as the lads had fat pay packets, Gormley was satisfied. A manipulator of the union rule book, he manoeuvred his way out of many a corner as he kept the increasingly assertive Broad Left in his union at arm's-length. But he made little impact inside the TUC and he distrusted Labour leaders. His closest ally often seemed to be National Coal Board chairman Sir Derek Ezra. Certainly, the two of them were very successful in ensuring the coal industry in the 1970s revived with the help of a massive injection of taxpayers' money.

RAY GUNTER (1909–77) Minister of Labour from October 1964 to April 1968. He once called his job a 'bed of nails'. Not close to the inner group of the Wilson government, he was one of the few working class Cabinet ministers and even he had been active in a white-collar union, the Railway Staffs' Federation. A pungent Welshman, he was an above-average orator but he failed to carry much influence with the high-ups of the TUC.

JOHN HARE (1911–82) First Viscount Blakenham. Minister of Labour from October 1959 to October 1963, he was a faithful and effective supporter of One Nation Toryism who preached the virtues of voluntarism against the mounting attacks inside his party from the right who wanted tough action to curb union power. He was not content, however, to remain inactive when it came to formulating labour law. Under his initiative a number of important measures were prepared and reached the statute book, including the enforcement of written contracts of employment and a measure to make it easier for unions to amalgamate with each other.

DENIS HEALEY Chancellor of the Exchequer from March 1974 to May 1979. A rumbustious Yorkshireman who was one of Labour's lost leaders. Brilliant but brutal he made enemies more than friends in politics. A down to earth intellectual, he did not suffer fools gladly even when they were in his own party and on his own side. He did his best to humour the TUC through the period of the Social Contract, though regretted later he had given away too many concessions in its early years in return for fine promises from the trade union leaders that were not delivered on wage restraint. Contrary to Left fiction he was not an iron Chancellor but rather a soft one, and a reluctant and temporary believer in monetarism. His relations with the trade union leaders were often stormy even if he was keen to defend their interests.

EDWARD HEATH Prime Minister from June 1970 to March 1974 and Conservative party leader from May 1965 to February 1975. A tragic and misunderstood figure who was destroyed in part by the trade unions. He wanted to modernize labour relations and give union leaders more control and authority over their members through a comprehensive reform of the legal framework of industrial relations. But in public a humourless and unbending figure, he gave the misleading impression until the spring of 1972 that he was anti-union. After that in his search for agreement with the TUC he went further than any other Prime Minister to give them a role in the management of the economy. But the union leaders spurned his offer and rejected his policies. In the short run they helped to humiliate him, but their behaviour served to pave the way for Mrs Thatcher's much tougher policies.

MICHAEL HOWARD   The combative Secretary of State for Employment from March 1990 until May 1992. A right-wing lawyer who was adept at getting under the skin of union leaders. He did not disguise his basic distaste for trade unions and collective bargaining and championed the cause of worker individualism. He was responsible for two large measures designed to curb union power still further, despite the lack of pressure for doing so from employers. He seemed keener to make a political splash with his attacks on the unions than take a serious view of industrial relations.

SIR GEOFFREY HOWE   As Solicitor General in 1970–1 he played a key role in the drafting and passage of the 1971 Industrial Relations Act. Twelve years earlier as a young Bow Grouper and lawyer he had taken part in the writing of *A Giant's Strength*, the influential pamphlet written in support of legal reform of industrial relations. But throughout his long and distinguished public career, he took a sustained interest in the trade union 'problem' and in the need to make organized labour accountable for its actions within a framework of law. As Chancellor of the Exchequer from May 1979 to June 1983 he was a strong supporter of dealing with union power and an occasional source of irritation to Jim Prior.

GEORGE ISAACS (1883–1979)   Minister of Labour and National Service from July 1945 to January 1951. General Secretary of the National Society of Operative Printers and Assistants (NATSOPA) for 40 years, he was a conservative, reassuring presence for the TUC at the heart of the Labour government. With Bevin, he strongly resisted ministerial attempts at wages policy. A doughty defender of voluntarism, his greatest success was in carrying through the demobilization of the armed forces after 1945 with the minimum of social disruption. But under his tutelage the Ministry of Labour remained firmly non-interventionist. As a result, it became marginal to the Attlee government's economic and industrial strategy.

JACK JONES   General Secretary of the Transport and General Workers Union from 1969 to 1978. One of the most formidable British trade union leaders of the century after Bevin. As District Secretary in Coventry during the Second World War and afterwards he came to believe that the shop stewards should be given an enhanced role in industrial relations at the expense of full-time union officials. Over the years he came to have a rather romanticized view of shopfloor power. But he believed passionately in industrial democracy. In running his union he was less libertarian. Indeed, Jones was a worthy successor to Bevin, Deakin and Cousins in the way he wielded power inside the union. He had a fertile mind with keen and successful advocacy of the Social Contract, the tripartite Advisory Conciliation and Arbitration Service, and other institutions to promote the interests of labour. The trouble was nobody dared to contradict him. A fierce advocate, he found it hard to tolerate opposition. But he was also a man who was incorruptible, a strong champion of the old age pensioners. The 1974–9 Labour government came to value his loyalty and willingness to try and sustain it in office. He did so without really diluting his Broad Left brand of Labour politics.

SIR KEITH JOSEPH   Secretary of State for Industry under Mrs Thatcher from 1979 to 1981. He took a keen intellectual interest in the British trade union 'problem'. As his views on economic affairs became more neo-liberal, he began to view the unions as a primary cause of the country's relative economic decline. He was influential in shaping Mrs Thatcher's views on the subject of trade unions reform, though was never given responsibility himself for dealing with them. A sincere, anguished figure, he may have lacked a sense of reality but he grappled with the problem of British post-war decline with a serious intent shared by few of his contemporaries.

WILL LAWTHER (1889–1976)   President of the National Union of Mineworkers from 1939 to 1954. He was a stalwart member of the right-wing junta that dominated the TUC for the ten years after the end of the Second World War. A former Communist, he became a ferocious enemy of the Left and unofficial strikes. A loyal stalwart of the Labour Movement, he was one of the union leaders Mr Attlee could rely on to keep the block votes in line behind Labour government policy at party conference and the TUC. His rumbustious style was well expressed by his 'Shut your gob' outburst to his howling left-wing opponents at the infamous 1952 Labour conference at Morecambe.

IAN MACLEOD (1913–70)   Minister of Labour from December 1955 to October 1959. A One Nation Tory, he was a brilliant orator and competent administrator. He did not bring any original ideas to his handling of industrial relations but remained content to espouse the voluntarist tradition and combat right-wing elements in his party who wanted more robust action to curb the trade unions. But he was no emollient conciliator like Monckton had been under Churchill. At times he could be tough and unbending as he was when he dealt with the famous 1958 London bus strike.

HAROLD MACMILLAN (1894–1987)   First Earl of Stockton. Prime Minister from February 1957 to October 1963. The epitome of the

One Nation Tory. Despite his private gloom about union power, he was an economic expansionist at heart and favoured incomes policy, bringing the trade unions into tripartite decision-making and ensuring that full employment continued. He often took a rather benevolent if paternalistic view of the trade unions and on more than one occasion he succumbed to their moral pressure to concede higher wage deals than made economic sense. But Macmillan was an Edwardian romantic whose view of the working class stemmed in part from his experience on the Western Front during the Great War and also from his period as MP for the depression town of Stockton on Tees between the wars.

MAURICE MACMILLAN (1921–84)   Secretary of State for Employment from February 1972 to December 1973. He proved to be a sad disappointment. His early months were spent grappling with the consequences of the 1971 Industrial Relations Act. A well-meaning gentleman, he was regarded by the TUC as rather a weak figure. But he was highly strung, shy and rather diffident. His qualities were conciliatory but perhaps he was not in the best ministry to reveal his political talents. Nor did he carry sufficient weight in Cabinet. In the great crisis of 1973–4 he was bundled out of the job to make way for Willie Whitelaw.

SIR WALTER MONCKTON (1891–1965)   Minister of Labour from October 1951 to November 1955. An arch-conciliator, he was an apolitical figure who was given the explicit job of appeasing the trade unions. He did so with charm and panache, though his encounters with union leaders could often arouse his nervous tension and make him ill. Wrongly denounced with hindsight for his soft treatment of the trade unions, he was able to maintain friendly relations with union leaders at a time of relative industrial peace. His gentlemanly ways appealed to the inner group of the TUC and he was a good host.

LEN MURRAY   General Secretary of the Trades Union Congress from September 1973 to September 1984. A shrewd, likeable and cautious man, he did his best to enhance the role of the TUC through the Social Contract. In the shadow of Jones and Scanlon in his early years, he was perhaps over-conscious of the need to keep the TUC general council marching at the speed of the slowest. But he was a good administrator and faithful civil servant of the Movement that thrives on order and protocol. In the 1978–9 Winter of Discontent he was not impressive but then neither was anybody else. Moreover, as TUC General Secretary he could not fill the power vacuum left by the loss of Jones and Scanlon. After Labour's 1983 election defeat, he became the New Realist, keen for the TUC to drop its boycott of talking to government. His stance in the printing dispute in Warrington in the autumn of 1983

aroused criticism from the Left but he won little encouragement from
Mrs Thatcher for his efforts.

JIM PRIOR   Secretary of State for Employment from May 1979 to
September 1981. A One Nation Tory after being hawkish to the trade
unions during the period of the Heath government, he was a jolly and
intelligent politician who wanted to do as little as possible to offend
union leaders. Remembering the experience of the Heath years, he did
not want to provoke confrontation. His scepticism about changes in
labour law and his clear dislike for monetarism when it began to force
up unemployment alienated him from Mrs Thatcher after two years at
the Employment Department, though he was responsible for the modest but important 1980 Employment Act. In retrospect, he expressed
surprise that he was given that job in the first place as during the years
in opposition he did nothing to disguise his opposition to the more right
wing demands of party colleagues who wanted to neuter the unions.

HUGH SCANLON   President of the Amalgamated Union of Engineering Workers from July 1967 to September 1978. He came to office
as an aggressive and articulate champion of the Broad Left who cut
his teeth at GEC's plant in Manchester's Trafford Park as a militant
Communist. Later on he mellowed rapidly and ended up accepting a
peerage with a seat in the House of Lords. To MI5 he was a security
risk and many Conservatives thought he put politics first before collective bargaining. It was under his leadership that the union spearheaded
the destruction of the 1971 Industrial Relations Act. Ambivalent when
not hostile to incomes policies, he became an eventual faithful champion of the Social Contract. In his final years he turned into a persuasive
backer of reviving manufacturing industry and in later life repudiated
his former radicalism.

ARTHUR SCARGILL   President of the National Union of Mineworkers from November 1981. Elected by a landslide, the unbending Yorkshireman took his union through the trauma of the 1984–5
miners' strike and continued thereafter to urge the miners to take
industrial action in defence of their interests. Under Scargill the union's
membership was cut by more than three-quarters as the coal industry
went into steep decline. An uncompromisingly militant Socialist, he
despised the TUC and Labour party leadership for weakness and class
collaboration. His demagogic style appealed to the wilder elements at
Congress. But attempts to implicate him in financial irregularities during the miners strike failed to stick. Never admitting his mistakes, he
became an incorrigible if increasingly humourless figure on the lunatic
fringe of the Labour Movement even though – unlike many other
union leaders – he could still fill an assembly hall and was instantly

recognizable on television. In October 1992 he staged an unexpected comeback after the Conservative government announced plans to axe half of what remained of the coal industry. Many people began to reassess their view of Scargill. Almost overnight he was feted as a man of sense and moderation who had been proven right in his campaign against pit closures.

NORMAN TEBBIT   Secretary of State for Employment from September 1981 to September 1983. A rough self-made man who was once a trade union militant in the Airline Pilots' Association, he soon acquired a well-earned reputation for his sardonic but deadly humour as he carried through the crucial 1982 Employment Act that exposed union funds to damages through their loss of legal immunities in unlawful strikes. He was also responsible for preparing the 1984 Trade Union Act which introduced statutory secret ballots for union executive elections and the calling of strikes. Unlike One Nation Tories, he had no guilt complex towards manual workers. His earthy cynicism made him despise union bosses with their perks and privileges. He disliked corporatism as intensely as any Trotskyist. But his populist views were very much those of 'Essex Man' in the saloon bar and found an echo among many rank and file trade unionists.

SIR VINCENT TEWSON (1898–1981)   General Secretary of the TUC from November 1946 to September 1960, after being Assistant General Secretary since 1931. A mediocre figure who failed to make much of an impact on the TUC. It is a pity, because he administered the organization at a time when it had the opportunity to make positive advances as an Estate of the Realm. An orthodox right-winger, he was keen to work with Conservative governments during the 1950s. Like his senior colleagues, he worried about shop stewards and unofficial strikes and wanted to be responsible. But he failed to take any initiatives, being content to consolidate. His complacency was harder to justify as the years went by and the favourable view of trade unions began to change.

TOM WILLIAMSON (1897–1983)   General Secretary of the General and Municipal Workers' union from November 1946 to July 1961. A loyal part of the TUC junta, he kept his union closely in line with official Labour orthodoxy. Under his leadership the GMWU became a stalwart part of the Labour Establishment. A friendly if autocratic Lancastrian from St Helens, he was a protagonist of the Bevanites. Made a life peer in 1962.

NORMAN WILLIS   General Secretary of the Trades Union Congress from 1984 to 1993. A man for the times. A surprisingly inarticulate man with a rich repertoire of jokes but an apparent lack of seriousness, he was of no harm to the government. During his time in the office Congress House fell into steep decline as an Estate of the Realm.

GEORGE WOODCOCK (1904–1979)   General Secretary of the Trades Union Congress from 1960 to 1969. A sad disappointment, he came to the top post too late in life when the iron had already entered his soul. A rather aloof working class self-made intellectual who started work at the age of 13 as a cotton weaver near Preston, Lancs, and graduated from New College, Oxford, with a first class honours degree. He could hardly conceal his contempt for the lesser brethren on the TUC general council, preferring the company of journalists from the quality newspapers. He was regarded by Labour governments in the 1960s as a moody and despairing pessimist who could always see good reasons for not doing anything. Lacking the ability to glad hand, he was more aware of the difficulties than the opportunities of his thankless job at the TUC. His half-hearted efforts to interest other union leaders in modernizing the Labour Movement failed to win many enthusiasts. As a member of the Donovan Royal Commission on the Trade Unions and Employer Associations from 1965 to 1968, he made sure the final report was mainly to the liking of the TUC. But he was also one of the few major figures in the post-war Labour Movement who wrestled with the central problem of how to reconcile free collective bargaining with low inflation and full employment. If Woodcock was unable to find a lasting solution to that conundrum, at least he did more than most to agonize over it. Moreover, in posing the question 'What are we here for?' to the unions, he forced them – however reluctantly – to reappraise themselves.

Appendix 2
A Chronology of Key Events in Industrial Relations since 1945

1945

July   The Labour party wins the general election with an overall majority of 146.

1946

May   Repeal of the Trade Union and Trade Disputes Act.

1947

January   Nationalization of the coal industry.

July   Sterling made convertible into dollars on foreign exchanges.

November   Stafford Cripps replaces Hugh Dalton as Chancellor of the Exchequer.

1948

January   Nationalization of the railways.

February   Government White Paper *Incomes, Costs and Prices* leads to a TUC Agreement on wage restraint.

April   Nationalization of the electricity supply industry.

June   State of Emergency called in the dock strike.

July   National Health Service begins.

1949

June   Troops used in London docks.

September   The pound is devalued from $4.03 to $2.80. The TUC backs further wage restraint.

November   The TUC agrees on a wage standstill.

1950

February   General election leaves Labour with an overall parliamentary majority of 5.

July   The TUC announces the end of wage restraint.

1951

February The nationalization of the steel industry.

August Withdrawal of Order 1305 which prohibited the right to strike.

October The Conservatives win the general election with an overall majority of 20. The emollient Sir Walter Monckton appointed Minister of Labour and National Service, with express job of conciliating the TUC.

1952

July Monckton refers back 12 Wages Council pay awards for being too generous, but the TUC pressurizes Churchill and the government caves in.

1955

May Dock, rail and newspaper strikes at the time of the general election that ends with an overall Conservative majority of 58. Government calls State of Emergency.

November Ian Macleod replaces Monckton as Minister of Labour and National Service.

1956

March White Paper on full employment and its economic implications blames wage pressures for rising inflation.

September Frank Cousins, the new left-wing General Secretary of the Transport and General Workers' Union, takes his first Congress by storm with a fiery speech denouncing pay restraint. It marks the end of an era.

1957

January to *March* Engineering and shipbuilding strikes.

August The Council of Productivity, Prices and Incomes created by Harold Macmillan's government. The so-called 'three wise men' led by Lord Cohen, a High Court judge, were given the task of exhorting responsibility in pay bargaining.

1958

June to *July* London bus strike.

1961

July The pay pause introduced in the public sector by Selwyn Lloyd, Chancellor of the Exchequer.

November Power workers break through the pay pause.

1962

February Formation of the tripartite National Economic Development Council.

February to *March* Engineering and shipbuilding strikes.

July   The National Incomes Commission created by the government to monitor wage increases. Also replacement of Selwyn Lloyd by Reginald Maudling as Chancellor of the Exchequer in a Cabinet purge described as the 'night of the long knives'.

1963

February   Unemployment climbs briefly to 900,000.

August   Contracts of Employment Act passed.

1964

October   A narrow general election victory for the Labour party. Harold Wilson forms the new government with a Commons majority of only five.

November   Joint Declaration on Growth and Productivity announced.

1965

February   National Prices and Incomes Board created. Royal Commission on Trade Unions and Employers' Associations formed.

August   Redundancy Payments Act comes into law.

September   National Plan announced.

1966

March   General election brings Labour an overall majority of 103.

May   State of Emergency called by the government over seamen's six week long strike.

July   Pay freeze introduced for six months after the British economy is 'blown off course' following a strike by the country's merchant seamen.

1967

November   Devaluation of the pound.

1968

June   Royal Commission on Trade Unions and Employer Organisations published. Ray Gunter resigns and is replaced by Barbara Castle at Department of Employment and Productivity.

1969

January   *In Place of Strife* White Paper to reform trade unions published.

March   Legislation introduced to deal with unofficial strikes.

June   A 'solemn and binding' agreement between the TUC and the Labour Government ends crisis over union legislation.

1970

June   Edward Heath's Conservative party wins the general election with a surprise defeat for Labour. N minus one pay policy by the government to reduce each settlement by 1 per cent.

July   Government introduces State of Emergency in response to a national dock strike, which ends with a Court of Inquiry under Lord Pearson and a large pay deal.

October   Heath tells Conservative conference his government has embarked on 'a change so radical, a revolution so quiet and yet so total that it will go far beyond the programme for a Parliament'.

October to *November*   Local government manual workers' dispute ends after six weeks with a victory for them after Sir Jack Scamp conciliates.

December   Work to rule by electricity power workers which leads the next February following an inquiry under Lord Wilberforce to a big pay deal.

1971

January to *February*   Post office workers strike for pay rises of 15–20 per cent. They receive 9 per cent in May.

25 January   TUC march in London against the Industrial Relations Bill in the largest demonstration it has ever organized.

February   Ford car workers strike for two months and secure 33 per cent pay rise over two years.

April   Rail drivers go slow for 15 to 25 per cent pay rise and secure 9.5 per cent.

August   Industrial Relations Act reaches the statute book, the most comprehensive measure to deal with the issue since 1906.

1972

January to *February*   National coal strike leads to a humiliating defeat for the government.

January   Unemployment exceeds the 1 million figure for the first time since before the Second World War.

March   Transport and General Workers' Union fined by the National Industrial Relations Act for not stopping the blacking of non-dockers loading containers.

April   Railmen threaten strike for 16 per cent pay rise. Government compels a ballot under the Industrial Relations Act after a cooling off period which brings six to one majority in favour of stoppage. Railmen achieve what they want.

May   Industrial Relations Court says union officials are responsible for the unlawful actions of their shop stewards but on *13 June* Court of Appeal overturns the judgement.

June   Three dockers sent to jail for contempt and 30,000 dockers strike. Official Solicitor intervenes to gain their release. House of Lords overturns Court of Appeal judgement.

April to *October* Marathon tripartite talks that attempt to establish an agreed economic strategy for the country between the government, TUC and employers end in failure.

November Conservatives introduce a 90 day wage freeze as start of a new statutory prices and incomes policy.

1973

April Phase Two of the incomes policy starts with limited rises to £1 a week and 4 per cent.

October Yom Kippur War breaks out – followed by a quadrupling of oil prices.

November Phase Three of the incomes policy starts. *12 November* Miners start a national overtime ban. *13 November* government declares a State of Emergency.

December Heath announces three day working will start on 1 January. Emergency budget on 17 December.

1974

January to *February* Second coal strike in two years begins. On *14 January* TUC offers to make miners a special case but government rejects the idea. On *7 February* Heath calls a general election. This leads to the defeat of the Conservatives.

March Return of a minority Labour government. Pay Board provides miners with 29 per cent wage increase to end their dispute.

May First threshold payments made under Stage 3 of the statutory incomes policy.

June TUC agrees to voluntary incomes policy.

July Repeal of the Industrial Relations Act and end of the statutory incomes policy.

October General election provides Labour government with an overall majority of only three.

1975

February The miners accept a 35 per cent pay rise.

May Jack Jones of Transport and General Workers' Union calls for a maximum flat across the board pay rise in the next wage round.

July £6 a week flat rate maximum incomes rise introduced by the TUC under the Social Contract. Accepted by the TUC general council by only 19 votes to 13. Unemployment goes over one million figure for only the second time since 1940.

August Employment Protection Act passed.

1976

March Wilson resigns. Jim Callaghan elected Prime Minister by 176 votes to 137.

May   TUC and the government agree on a further twelve months of pay policy with £4 a week maximum and £2.50 a week minimum.

June   Special TUC Congress backs the incomes policy by 9.3 million votes to only 500,000 against.

September   TUC votes to return to 'free' collective bargaining at the end of Stage 2 of the incomes policy on 1 August 1977.

December   The government introduces a package of cuts to ensure a loan from the International Monetary Fund.

1977

January   IMF agrees to $3.9 billion of standby credits for Britain. Bullock committee on industrial democracy favours equal worker representation on the boards of private companies employing over 2,000.

May   Engineering Union rejects a third stage of pay policy.

July   TGWU votes at its biennial conference for a return to free collective bargaining.

September   TUC Congress votes to support 12 month rule between pay settlements and return to 'free' collective bargaining.

November   National firemen's strike begins in support of 30 per cent pay rise.

December   TUC General Council vote by 20 to 17 not to support the firemen in dispute.

1978

January   Callaghan says in a radio broadcast he hopes in the next wage round to keep pay rises to around 5 per cent. Firemen call off their strike after government promises them a special index-linked pay system from 1979.

February   The retail price index is down to less than 10 per cent for the first time since October 1973.

March   Jack Jones replaced by Moss Evans as TGWU General Secretary.

May   Terry Duffy elected as President of the Engineering Workers' union to replace Hugh Scanlon.

July   Government announces 5 per cent pay limit policy to get inflation down in 1979 to 7.5 per cent.

September   TUC votes against pay restrictions. Callaghan decides against calling an autumn general election. Ford car workers start strike.

October   Labour party conference votes by 4.0 million to 1.9 million against to reject the government's 5 per cent   pay policy.

November   Ford car workers accept a 16.5 per cent pay rise after a nine week long strike.

December   The House of Commons vote by 285 to 283 against allowing government to use discriminatory sanctions against companies who break the 5 per cent pay policy.

1979

January Lorry drivers' strike begins and made official by TGWU on 11 January. Government relaxes pay policy but fails to stop the start of the low paid public services workers' strike in pursuit of a £60 a week minimum wage. Hospitals, schools and other institutions hit badly by a concerted union offensive.

February Callaghan backs down from the 5 per cent pay limit. Low pay comparability commission created under Lord Clegg. The TUC agrees with the government on a so-called concordat with guidelines on how strikers should behave on picket lines.

March The House of Commons votes by 311 to 310 for no confidence in the government.

May The Labour party loses the general election. Conservatives are returned with an overall majority of 43 in the Commons.

September Trade union membership peaks at 13 million, 55 per cent of the workforce.

1980

January National steel strike, which ends with a 16 per cent pay rise for the steel men with strings attached – but seen as a government victory.

August Employment Act becomes law.

1981

January Department of Employment publishes consultative document on Legal Immunities.

September Norman Tebbit becomes Employment Secretary after Prior.

1982

July Rail dispute over flexible rostering leads to defeat of ASLEF, the footplatemen's union.

August Second Employment Act becomes law.

1983

May Mrs Thatcher and the Conservatives win a landslide general election victory.

September TUC General Secretary Len Murray calls for New Realism at the TUC Congress.

November National Graphical Association strike at the Stockport Messenger newspaper group leads to massive defeat for the union as it faces heavy fines and sequestration of funds.

1984

January The government bans trade unions at its intelligence gathering centre at Cheltenham.

March   National coal strike begins.

August   Trade Union Act passed that introduces compulsory workplace secret ballots before unions can call strikes and to elect their executive committees.

1985

February   National coal strike ends with complete defeat of the miners.

1987

February   Wapping dispute ends at News International with the complete defeat of the print unions.

June   Third successive general election victory for the Conservatives.

1988

August   Third Employment Act passed with virtual outlawing of the closed shop and legal protection for workers who want work in defiance of a lawful strike.

September   TUC Congress rejects cooperation with the government's Youth Training Scheme, so the government winds up the Training Commission depriving the TUC of a role.

1989

June   The government abolishes the National Dock regulation scheme and a short-lived dock strike fails to make ministers change their minds.

1990

August   Fourth Employment Act passed with further restrictions on the trade unions.

November   Mrs Thatcher defeated in Conservative leadership election. John Major becomes party leader and Prime Minister.

1991

July   Government publishes latest plans to curb the powers of the trade unions still further.

1992

April   Fourth consecutive Conservative general election victory. Gillian Shephard, the new Employment Secretary, promises to introduce more legislation to reduce union power, giving workers the right to choose for themselves which union to join, and requiring them to be informed of the right to opt out of union check-off through their pay packets.

October   Michael Heseltine, President of the Board of Trade, announces plans to close 31 pits and dismiss 30,000 miners, but the government is forced to back down in the face of nationwide protests. The TUC organizes a mass demonstration in London that is the biggest for twenty years.

Appendix 3
Public Opinion and
Trade Unions

Table A3.1 Do you agree or disagree that 'trade unions have too much power in Britain today'?

	Agree (%)		Disagree (%)	
	All	Union members	All	Union members
October 1975	75	65	16	28
August 1977	79	68	17	27
September 1978	82	73	16	25
September 1979	80	69	16	28
July 1980	72	58	19	31
November 1981	70	58	22	31
August 1982	71	62	21	34
August 1983	68	56	25	39
August 1984	68	55	24	37
August 1989	41	26	42	62
August 1990	38	22	45	66
February 1992	27	14	64	82

Source: Market and Opinion Research International (MORI), 1992.
Unfortunately, MORI did not ask this crucial question before October 1975.

Table A3.2　Do you think that the trade unions are becoming too powerful, are not powerful enough or are about right?

	Too powerful (%)	Not powerful enough (%)	About right (%)	Don't know (%)
August 1972	63	8	21	8
August 1973	52	13	26	9
August 1974	61	6	19	13
August 1975	73	4	17	6
August 1976	65	5	23	7
August 1977	75	5	16	4
August 1978	69	3	23	5
January 1979	84	3	9	3
August 1979	77	5	14	4
August 1980	70	6	21	4
August 1981	60	10	23	4
August 1982	63	9	23	5
August 1983	59	10	27	4
August 1984	64	9	23	4
August 1985	49	11	34	4
August 1986	45	13	36	3
August 1987	36	15	42	7
August 1988	32	19	42	6
August 1989	33	22	42	4
August 1990	30	19	44	7
August 1991	23	17	54	7
August 1992	21	21	53	6

Source: Gallup.

Table A3.3 Changing attitudes to whether trade unions are a 'good' or a 'bad' thing

	Good (%)	Bad (%)	Don't know (%)
December 1952	69	12	19
August 1954	71	12	17
May 1955	64	12	24
August 1956	61	20	19
August 1957	53	21	26
August 1958	61	15	24
August 1959	60	23	17
September 1960	56	17	27
August 1963	62	21	17
August 1964	70	12	18
August 1965	57	25	18
August 1966	63	20	17
August 1967	60	23	12
August 1968	66	18	16
June 1969	57	26	18
August 1970	60	24	17
August 1971	62	21	17
May 1972	56	32	12
August 1972	55	30	16
August 1973	61	25	14
December 1973	57	24	19
February 1974	60	25	14
August 1974	54	27	19
July 1975	43	41	16
August 1975	51	34	16
August 1976	60	25	14
August 1977	53	33	14
August 1978	57	31	12
January 1979	44	44	12
August 1979	58	29	13
August 1980	60	29	11
August 1981	56	28	16
August 1982	59	30	11
August 1983	63	25	12
August 1984	61	30	10
August 1985	65	24	10
August 1986	67	22	12
August 1987	71	17	12
August 1988	68	21	11
August 1989	68	24	8

Table A3.3 (*cont.*)

	Good (%)	Bad (%)	Don't know (%)
August 1990	67	21	12
August 1991	70	17	13
August 1992	62	26	13

Source: Gallup.

Unsurprisingly, popular attitudes to the trade unions tended to fluctuate in the degree to which strikes were prominent. In the Winter of Discontent of 1978–9 those who though unions were a 'good thing' divided evenly with those who thought they were 'a bad thing'. However, 41% thought they were a 'bad thing' in July 1975 after a pay free-for-all that took inflation to nearly 30 per cent.

Table A3.4 Do you approve or disapprove of the government's plans to reform trade union law?

	Approve (%)	Disapprove (%)	Don't know (%)
October 1970	46	22	32
March 1971	53	25	22
August 1979	54	20	26
August 1980	49	28	23
August 1981	43	26	30
August 1982	43	32	25
August 1983	52	28	37
August 1984	40	37	23

Source: Gallup.

Table A3.5 How Britain's trade unionists voted in general elections, 1964–1992

	Labour (%)	Conservative (%)	Others (%)
1964	73	22	5
1966	71	25	4
1970	66	28	6
1974 (February)	55	30	15
1974 (October)	55	27	16
1979	51	33	13
1983	39	31	29
1987	42	31	25
1992	46	31	19

Source: Market and Opinion Research International (MORI).
Before 1964 the opinion surveys did not disaggregate how trade unionists voted in general elections.

Appendix 4 Main Public Appointments in the British Industrial Relations Scene since 1940

Government

Ministers of Labour and National Service

May 1940 – May 1945	Ernest Bevin
May 1945 – August 1945	R. A. Butler
August 1945 – January 1951	George Isaacs
January 1951 – April 1951	Aneurin Bevan
April 1951 – October 1951	Alfred Robens
October 1951 – December 1955	Sir Walter Monckton
December 1955 – October 1959	Ian Macleod

Ministers of Labour

October 1959 – July 1960	Edward Heath
July 1960 – October 1963	John Hare
October 1963 – October 1964	Joseph Godber
October 1964 – April 1968	Ray Gunter

Secretary of State for Employment and Productivity

April 1968 – June 1970   Barbara Castle

Secretary of State for Employment

June 1970 – April 1972	Robert Carr
April 1972 – December 1973	Maurice Macmillan
December 1973 – March 1974	William Whitelaw
March 1974 – April 1976	Michael Foot
April 1976 – May 1979	Albert Booth
May 1979 – September 1981	Jim Prior
September 1981 – October 1983	Norman Tebbit
October 1983 – September 1985	Tom King
September 1985 – June 1987	Lord David Young
October 1987 – September 1989	Norman Fowler
September 1989 – April 1992	Michael Howard
April 1992 – May 1993	Gillian Shephard
from May 1993	David Hunt

The Civil Service

Permanent Secretaries since 1940 (Ministry of Labour)

1939–44	Sir Thomas Phillips
1944–56	Sir Godfrey Ince
1956–9	Sir Harold Emmerson
1959–62	Sir Laurence Helsby (from the Treasury)
1962–6	Sir James Dunnett
1966–73	Sir Denis Barnes
1973–6	Sir Conrad Heron
1976–82	Sir Kenneth Barnes
1982–8	Sir Michael Quinlan (from the Ministry of Defence)
1988–92	Sir Geoffrey Holland
from 1993	Nicholas Monk (from the Treasury)

The TUC

TUC General Secretaries since 1945

September 1926 – October 1946   Walter Citrine (knighted 1935)
October 1946 – September 1960   Vincent Tewson (knighted 1950)
September 1960 – September 1969   George Woodcock
September 1969 – September 1973   Victor Feather (peerage 1973)
September 1973 – September 1984   Lionel Murray (peerage 1984)
September 1984 – September 1993   Norman Willis

The leaders of the main trade unions since 1945

Transport and General Workers' Union (TGWU)

General Secretary
1940–55   Arthur Deakin (Acting General Secretary until 1946 during Ernest Bevin's absence in government)
1955–6   Jock Tiffin
1956–69   Frank Cousins (Harry Nicholas was Acting General Secretary from October 1964 to July 1966 when Cousins was in government)
1969–78   Jack Jones
1978–85   Moss Evans
1985–92   Ron Todd
Since 1992   Bill Morris

General and Municipal Workers' Union (GMWU)

General Secretary
1934–46   Charles Dukes
1946–62   (Sir) Tom Williamson (peerage 1962)
1962–72   Jack Cooper (peerage 1969)
1972–86   David Basnett (peerage 1986)
Since 1986   John Edmonds

Amalgamated Engineering Union (AEU, later AUEW)

President
1939–54   Jack Tanner
1954–6   Richard Openshaw
1956–67   (Sir) William Carron (peerage 1967)
1967–78   Hugh Scanlon (peerage 1978)
1978–88   Terry Duffy
Since 1988 Bill Jordan

National Union of Mineworkers

President
1944–55   Sir William Lawther
1955–60   Ernest Jones
1960–71   (Sir) Sid Ford
1971–81   Joe Gormley (peerage 1981)
Since 1981 Arthur Scargill

General Secretary
1932–44 Ebby Edwards
1946–59 Arthur Horner
1959–68 Will Paynter
1969–84 Laurence Daly
1984–92 Peter Heathfield

National Union of Public Employees (NUPE)

General Secretary
1934–62   Bryn Roberts
1962–8   Sid Hill
1968–81   Alan Fisher
Since 1981 Rodney Bickerstaffe

Appendix 5
Key Labour
Market Indicators,
1945–1992

Table A5.1   Unemployment, 1945–1992

	Number out of work	Percentage
1945	100,000	0.4
1946	400,000	1.7
1947	300,000	1.3
1948	298,000	1.3
1949	328,000	1.4
1950	332,000	1.4
1951	264,000	1.1
1952	368,000	1.5
1953	356,000	1.5
1954	303,000	1.2
1955	244,000	1.0
1956	258,000	1.9
1957	327,000	1.3
1958	451,000	1.8
1959	480,000	2.0
1960	377,000	1.5
1961	347,000	1.4
1962	467,000	1.9
1963	558,000	2.2
1964	404,000	1.5
1965	347,000	1.4
1966	467,000	1.9
1967	559,000	2.2
1968	586,000	2.3
1969	581,000	2.3

Table A5.1 (*cont.*)

	Number out of work	Percentage
1970	612,000	2.4
1971	792,000	3.1
1972	837,000	3.3
1973	596,000	2.3
1974	600,000	2.3
1975	941,000	3.6
1976	1,302,000	5.0
1977	1,403,000	5.4
1978	1,383,000	5.2
1979	1,296,000	4.9
1980	1,665,000	6.2
1981	2,520,000	9.4
1982	2,917,000	10.9
1983	3,105,000	11.7
1984	3,160,000	11.7
1985	3,271,000	11.8
1986	3,289,000	11.8
1987	2,953,000	10.6
1988	2,370,400	8.4
1989	1,798,000	6.3
1990	1,664,400	5.8
1991	2,291,900	8.1
1992	2,778,600	9.8

Sources: The Economist, *One Hundred Years of Economic Statistics*; Employment Gazette.

Table A5.2 Strikes, 1943–1992

	Number of workers involved	Aggregate number of working days lost
1943	557,000	1,808,000
1944	821,000	3,714,000
1945	531,000	2,835,000
1946	526,000	2,158,000
1947	620,000	2,433,000
1948	424,000	1,944,000
1949	433,000	1,807,000

Table A5.2 (*cont.*)

	Number of workers involved	Aggregate number of working days lost
1950	302,000	1,389,000
1951	379,000	1,694,000
1952	415,000	1,792,000
1953	1,370,000	2,164,000
1954	446,000	2,457,000
1955	659,000	3,781,000
1956	507,000	2,083,000
1957	1,356,000	8,412,000
1958	523,000	3,462,000
1959	645,000	5,270,000
1960	814,000	3,024,000
1961	771,000	3,046,000
1962	4,420,000	5,798,000
1963	590,000	1,755,000
1964	872,000	2,277,000
1965	868,000	2,925,000
1966	530,000	2,398,000
1967	732,000	2,767,000
1968	2,256,000	4,690,000
1969	1,656,000	6,846,000
1970	1,793,000	10,980,000
1971	1,175,000	13,551,000
1972	1,726,000	23,909,000
1973	1,513,000	7,197,000
1974	1,622,000	14,750,000
1975	789,000	6,012,000
1976	670,000	3,284,000
1977	1,155,000	10,142,000
1978	1,003,000	9,405,000
1979	4,583,000	29,474,000
1980	842,000	11,964,000
1981	1,499,000	4,266,000
1982	2,103,000	5,312,000
1983	574,000	3,753,000
1984	1,464,000	27,135,000
1985	792,000	6,399,000
1986	721,000	1,923,000
1987	888,000	3,545,000
1988	790,000	3,702,000
1989	727,000	4,128,000

Table A5.2 (*cont.*)

	Number of workers involved	Aggregate number of working days lost
1990	298,000	1,903,000
1991	176,000	761,000
1992	148,000	528,000

Source: Employment Gazettes.

Table A5.3   Trade unions and union membership, 1945–1991

	Number of unions	Total membership	Percentage of labour force
1945	781	7,875,000	42.2
1946	757	8,803,000	44.4
1947	734	9,145,000	43.4
1948	749	9,362,000	43.3
1949	742	9,318,000	42.8
1950	732	9,289,000	42.1
1951	735	9,535,000	42.9
1952	723	9,583,000	43.3
1953	720	9,523,000	42.7
1954	711	9,556,000	42.2
1955	704	9,741,000	42.4
1956	685	9,778,000	42.2
1957	685	9,829,000	42.4
1958	675	9,639,000	41.8
1959	668	9,623,000	41.5
1960	664	9,835,000	41.5
1961	646	9,897,000	41.3
1962	626	9,887,000	41.4
1963	607	9,934,000	41.5
1964	641	10,218,000	41.6
1965	629	10,325,000	41.6
1966	621	10,262,000	41.1
1967	602	10,190,000	41.5
1968	582	10,193,000	41.7
1969	561	10,472,000	42.8

Table A5.3 (cont.)

	Number of unions	Total membership	Percentage of labour force
1970	538	11,179,000	45.8
1971	520	11,127,000	46.0
1972	499	11,349,000	47.0
1973	519	11,456,000	46.3
1974	507	11,764,000	47.4
1975	501	12,193,000	48.6
1976	473	12,386,000	50.5
1977	481	12,846,000	52.3
1978	462	13,112,000	53.1
1979	454	13,498,000	53.0
1980	438	12,947,000	51.8
1981	414	12,106,000	50.4
1982	408	11,593,000	49.1
1983	394	11,337,000	48.2
1984	375	11,086,000	46.3
1985	370	10,716,000	45.0
1986	335	10,539,000	43.8
1987	330	10,475,000	42.8
1988	315	10,387,000	41.0
1989	309	10,158,000	39.2
1990	287	9,947,000	38.0
1991	275	9,585,000	34.4

Source: Department of Employment.
There is no official series for union density, so this has to be derived from published Certification Officer union membership data combined with published employment data. The density calculations use workers in employment (excluding the jobless) plus the self-employed as a base.

Table A5.4 Output per person employed, 1948–1987

	Whole economy (%)	Manufacturing (%)
1948	52.7	46.8
1949	54.5	48.9
1950	56.1	51.0
1951	56.3	51.3
1952	56.0	49.2
1953	58.0	52.3
1954	59.5	53.8
1955	60.9	55.8
1956	60.9	55.3
1957	62.0	56.8
1958	62.6	57.1
1959	65.2	60.3
1960	68.6	63.2
1961	69.0	62.7
1962	69.6	63.5
1963	71.8	66.5
1964	75.2	71.6
1965	76.5	72.6
1966	77.6	73.9
1967	80.0	76.5
1968	83.8	82.5
1969	85.5	84.6
1970	87.3	85.1
1971	89.7	86.9
1972	92.1	92.0
1973	95.5	100.0
1974	93.7	98.5
1975	92.4	95.9
1976	94.9	100.9
1977	97.6	102.5
1978	100.6	103.6
1979	102.2	104.1
1980	100.0	100.0
1981	101.9	103.5
1982	105.7	110.4
1983	110.0	119.8
1984	111.7	126.4
1985	114.2	130.6
1986	117.0	134.6
1987	120.4	144.4

Source: Employment Gazettes.

Table A5.5   Output per person employed, 1988–1991 (1985=100)

	Whole economy (%)	*Manufacturing (%)*
1988	105.2	116.2
1989	107.8	120.8
1990	108.5	121.9
1991	105.4	122.5

Source: The Economist, *One Hundred Years of Economic Statistics*, 1989 edn, p. 45; Employment Gazette.

Table A5.6   Britain's price and wages spiral, 1950–1992

	Retail price index (%)	*Weekly earnings (%)*
1950	3.2	5.8
1951	9.2	10.2
1952	9.1	7.5
1953	3.0	5.4
1954	2.0	7.4
1955	4.4	9.0
1956	4.9	7.3
1957	3.7	5.8
1958	3.1	2.3
1959	0.5	5.1
1960	1.1	6.6
1961	3.4	5.4
1962	4.3	3.2
1963	1.9	5.3
1964	3.2	8.3
1965	4.8	8.5
1966	3.9	4.2
1967	2.5	5.8
1968	4.7	7.8
1969	5.4	8.1
1970	6.4	13.5
1971	9.4	11.1
1972	7.1	15.7
1973	9.2	15.1
1974	16.0	20.0
1975	24.2	23.4
1976	16.5	13.2
1977	15.8	8.6
1978	8.3	13.8
1979	13.4	16.0
1980	18.1	20.7
1981	11.9	12.9
1982	8.6	9.4
1983	4.5	8.5
1984	5.0	6.0
1985	6.0	8.5
1986	3.4	7.9
1987	4.2	7.8
1988	4.9	8.7
1989	7.8	9.3
1990	9.3	10.6
1991	4.5	9.2
1992	2.6	7.2

Source: The Treasury, *Economic Trends*.

Bibliography

The contemporary history of British industrial relations and politics since 1945 is vast but patchy. The best general overview accounts can be found in Henry Pelling, *The History of British Trade Unionism*, Penguin, 1992 edition; and Ben Pimlott and Chris Cook (eds), *Trade Unions in British Politics*, Longman, 1991 edition. Also see S. Bornstein and P. Gourevitch in *Unions and Economic Crisis*, Allen and Unwin, 1984; and R. Taylor, *The Fifth Estate: Britain's Trade Unions in the Modern World*, Routledge & Kegan Paul, 1978, and Pan, 1980.

The most stimulating books that have influenced me in my own assessment of the subject over the years are: Robert Currie, *Industrial Politics*, Oxford University Press, 1976; Alan Fox, *History and Heritage: The Social Origins of the British Industrial Relations System*, Allen & Unwin, 1985; Henry Phelps Brown, *The Origins of Trade Union Power*, Clarendon Press, Oxford, 1983; David Marquand, *The Unprincipled Society*, Jonathan Cape, 1988; and above all Allan Flanders, *Management and Trade Unions*, Faber & Faber, 1970.

On the trade unions and the British state since 1945 see Denis Barnes and Eileen Reid, *Governments and Trade Unions: The British Experience 1964–1979*, Heinemann, 1980. There is also Keith Middlemas, *Politics in Industrial Society*, Deutsch, 1979, and his more recent interesting and formidable if densely written trilogy, *Power, Competition and the State* (Vol. 1, *Britain in Search of Balance 1940–1961*, Macmillan, 1986; Vol. 2, Macmillan, 1990; and Vol. 3, Macmillan, 1991). Also see D. F. MacDonald, *The State and the Trade Unions*, second edn, Macmillan, 1976; Eric Wigham, *Strikes and the Government 1873–1974*, Macmillan, 1976; and V. L. Allen, *Trade Unions and Governments*, Allen & Unwin, 1960.

The general impact of trade unions on post-war British politics are well covered by Professor Samuel Beer's two impressive books: *Modern British Politics*, Faber & Faber, 1965, and *Britain against Itself*, Faber &

Faber, 1982. But also see James Cronin, *Labour and Society in Britain 1918–1979*, Batsford, 1984.

Trade unions and the Labour party in the 1950s are covered splendidly in Martin Harrison, *The Trade Unions and the Labour Party since 1945*, Allen & Unwin, 1960; and the more recent period by Lewis Minkin, *The Contentious Alliance*, Edinburgh University Press, 1991. Also see Andrew Taylor, *The Trade Unions and the Labour Party*, Croom Helm, 1987. There are perhaps surprisingly no books at all on the Conservative party and the trade unions.

On trade unions and the law there are many impressive publications. The most formidable are the various editions of W. Wedderburn, *The Worker and the Law*, Penguin, 1969, 1972 and 1986 editions. But also see Otto Kahn-Freund, *Labour Relations: Heritage and Adjustment*, London, 1979; W. Wedderburn, R. Lewis and J. Clark, *Labour Law and Industrial Relations*, Clarendon Press, 1983; and J. A. G. Griffith, *The Politics of the Judiciary*, Fontana, 1991 edition. For more recent legal events there is W. Wedderburn, *Employment Rights in Britain and Europe*, Lawrence and Wishart, 1991; and Bill McCarthy (ed.), *Legal Intervention in Industrial Relations*, Basil Blackwell, 1992.

There are a number of general overviews of post-1945 industrial relations. The best are Hugh Clegg, *The System of Industrial Relations in Britain*, Basil Blackwell, 1970; and George Bain (ed.), *Industrial Relations in Britain*, Basil Blackwell, 1983 and 1986 editions.

There is surprisingly little of serious value on the economic impact of British trade unions – at least, not before the 1980s when the many and important articles of Professor David Metcalf at the London School of Economics were of particular interest. This has not stopped innumerable voices across the ideological spectrum from making assertions about the alleged inefficiencies of British trade unions and their key role in the relative post-war decline of the country.

Polemics can be found in, for example, Sidney Pollard, *The Wasting of the British Economy*, Croom Helm, 1982. A formidable missive against the defenders of the post-war social settlement can be found in Correlli Barnett's controversial book, *The Audit of War*, Macmillan, 1986. But there are also authoritative studies in the Brooking Institution's *Britain's Economic Prospects*, Allen & Unwin, 1969; and Andrew Shonfield, *Modern Capitalism*, Oxford University Press, 1969. An effective riposte to criticisms about work-shy Britain can be found in Theo Nichols, *The British Worker Question*, Routledge and Kegan Paul, 1986.

The books on economic policy and British politics since 1945 that provide the most useful background for understanding industrial relations during the period include Michael Stewart, *The Jekyll and Hyde Years*, Pergamon Press, 1978; Frank Blackaby (ed.), *British Economic Policy 1960–1974*, Cambridge University Press, 1979; Bernard Elbaum and William Lazonick (eds), *The Decline of the British Economy*, Clarendon Press, Oxford, 1987; and N. F. R. Crafts and N. W. C. Woodward, *The British Economy since 1945*, Oxford University Press, 1991. On the labour market see R. Taylor, *Workers and the New Depression*, Macmillan, 1982.

A number of published primary sources are also well worth reading. These are *The Royal Commission on Trade Unions and Employers' Associations 1965–1968*, Cmnd 3623, HMSO, 1969; and the TUC's evidence to that Commission, *Trade Unionism*, TUC, 1966; see also *Trade Union Immunities*, Green Paper, Cmnd 8128, HMSO, 1981. For the triumph of Thatcherism see the Employment Department's propagandist publications *Industrial Relations in the 1990s*, Cm 1602, HMSO, 1991; and *People, Jobs and Opportunity*, Cm 1810, HMSO, 1992.

Anybody interested in Britain's post-war industrial politics needs to consult the annual reports of the Trades Union Congress. Not only do they contain the debates of Congress verbatim, but also highly detailed reports from every TUC department that provide a glimpse of government–TUC relations behind the doors of Whitehall and Congress House, at least until Mrs Thatcher shut out the TUC after May 1979.

Trade unions and the making of the post-war settlement, 1940–1945 (Chapter 1)

No book has yet been written that deals directly with the trade unions during the Second World War. But Angus Calder, *The People's War*, 1969, provides some useful insights. Paul Addison, *The Road to 1945*, Jonathan Cape, 1975, is an excellent overview. Also see Stephen Brooke, *Labour's War*, Oxford University Press, 1992.

Labour and the honourable alliance, July 1945 to October 1951 (Chapter 2)

There are no books directly on union–government relations in the Attlee years. However, good overviews of the period can be found in Kenneth Morgan, *Labour in Power 1945–1951*, Oxford University Press, 1987 paperback reprint; and Peter Hennessy's, *Never Again*, Jonathan Cape, 1992. The best economic study of the period is Sir Alec Cairncross, *Years of*

Recovery: British Economic Policy 1945–1951, Methuen, 1985; but also see J. C. R. Dow, *The Management of the British Economy 1945–1960*, Cambridge University Press, 1970.

Only a slight biography exists of George Isaacs, the Minister of Labour, written by G. Eastwood, and published by Odhams in 1952. There is no book about Sir Vincent Tewson, the TUC General Secretary of the period. As his more influential and interesting predecessor Sir Walter Citrine also lacks a biography, it is perhaps not surprising. The only trade union leader of the immediately post-war period who is well covered in the literature is Arthur Deakin in Vic Allen's *Trade Union Leadership*, Allen & Unwin, 1957. Plenty of large biographies have been published since 1980 covering all but one of the giants of the Attlee Cabinet – Sir Stafford Cripps still awaits his biographer – but few have much to say about union–government relations. Paul Addison's *The Road to 1945*, Cape, 1975, provides a brilliant portrait of the ethos of the Labour Movement of the time, and he has some shrewd reflections to make on the post-1945 social settlement in his essay 'The Road from 1945', in Peter Hennessy and Anthony Seldon (eds), *Ruling Performance: British Governments from Attlee to Thatcher*, Basil Blackwell, 1987.

Three contemporary books help to provide a picture of the trade unions in the aftermath of war. The most interesting is Ferdynand Zweig, *The British Worker*, Penguin, 1952; but also see N. Barou, *British Trade Unions*, Gollancz, 1946; and *British Trade Unionism*, PEP, 1949.

The Conservatives and industrial relations, July 1945 to October 1964 (Chapters 3 and 4)

Useful sections on the subject can be found in Nigel Harris, *Competition and the Corporate State: The British Conservatives, the State and Industry 1945–1964*, Methuen, 1972; Andrew Gamble, *The Conservative Nation*, Routledge & Kegan Paul, 1974; and J. D. Hoffman, *The Conservative Party in Opposition*, MacGibbon and Kee, 1964.

Few biographies or autobiographies of the prominent Conservatives of the period contain anything useful about industrial relations. Even Lord Birkenhead's *Walter Monckton*, Weidenfeld & Nicolson, 1969, devotes more space to his role in the Abdication crisis than on his four years at the Ministry of Labour. There is next to nothing about Churchill's attitude to labour questions in Martin Gilbert's biography (Vol. 8, *Never Despair: 1945–1965*, Heinemann, 1988). But this is made up for in Paul Addison's perceptive study, *Churchill on the Home Front*, Jonathan Cape, 1992. As

Chancellor of the Exchequer, R. A. Butler worried continually about trade union wage pressures but there is not a line about that in Anthony Howard's *RAB: The Life of R. A. Butler*, Jonathan Cape, 1987. The best account of the 1951–5 government is in Anthony Seldon, *Churchill's Indian Summer*, Hodder & Stoughton, 1981. On economic policy see Andrew Shonfield, *Economic Policy since the War*, Penguin, 1960; and Samuel Brittan, *The Treasury under the Tories*, Penguin, 1963.

There are a few references to industrial relations in Eden's memoirs *Full Circle*, Cassell, 1960, or in Robert Rhodes James, *Anthony Eden*, Weidenfeld & Nicolson, 1990, though Eden devoted much of his time as Prime Minister on the domestic front to worrying about the power of organized labour. The volumes of Harold Macmillan's memoirs provide a better recognition of the political importance of so called trade union 'power' in *Riding the Storm 1956–1959*, Macmillan, 1971, *Pointing The Way 1959–1961*, Macmillan, 1972, and *At the End of the Day 1961–1963*, Macmillan, 1973. His official biographer Alistair Horne has little to add on industrial relations in the second volume.

There are adequate chapters in Nigel Fisher's *Iain Macleod*, Purnell, 1973, about his period as Minister of Labour. On John Hare, perhaps the most creative of Ministers of Labour between 1945 and 1968, there is nothing.

On the trade union side, Geoffrey Goodman's *The Awkward Warrior: Frank Cousins, His Life and Times*, Davis Poynter, 1979, stands out as the exception. Most union leaders of the period neither wrote their own memoirs nor have they had biographies.

Harold Wilson and the 'great adventure', October 1964 to June 1970 (Chapter 5)

Harold Wilson's own memoirs of his years in office are a useful starting point: *The Labour Government 1964–1970*, Weidenfeld & Nicolson and Michael Joseph, 1971. Ben Pimlott, *Harold Wilson*, Harper-Collins, 1992, is a weighty and eloquent case in his defence, but it has surprisingly little to say about the trade unions or economic affairs, especially incomes policy, though this issue dogged the Wilson government for most of its life. The diaries of Barbara Castle for the period (Weidenfeld & Nicolson, 1984) and those of Tony Benn (*Out of the Wilderness 1963–1967*, Hutchinson, 1987, and *Office without Power 1968–1972*, Hutchinson, 1988) are invaluable. Richard Crossman's diaries have less to say about industrial relations. Roy Jenkins, *Life at the Centre*, Collins, 1991, is elegant but has next to nothing about the trade unions either. For their part, the union leaders of the period did not write their memoirs. Surprisingly, even TUC General Secretary George Woodcock failed to acquire a biographer. But Eric Silver's *Vic Feather*, Gollancz, 1983 is a lively account of the life of the TUC's arch-fixer.

The best book on the politics of industrial relations in the 1960s remains Peter Jenkins, *The Battle of Downing Street*, Charles Knight, 1970. But also see Leo Panitch, *Social Democracy and Industrial Militancy*, Cambridge University Press, 1976; and Clive Ponting, *Breach of Promise*, Penguin, 1990 edition. Barbara Castle, in *Fighting All the Way*, Macmillan, 1993, has little to add.

Edward Heath and modernizing the trade unions, October 1964 to March 1974 (Chapter 6)

The Heath years have so far been inadequately covered. Few of his Cabinet colleagues wrote interesting accounts, though Reginald Maudling, *Memoirs*, Sidgwick & Jackson, 1978, is worth looking at. The best insider sketch remains Douglas Hurd, *An End to Promises*, Collins, 1979.

There are three useful books on the rise and fall of the 1971 Industrial Relations Act: Michael Moran, *The Politics of Industrial Relations*, Macmillan, 1977; Brian Weekes et al. (eds), *Industrial Relations and the Limits of Law*, Basil Blackwell, 1975; and A. W. J. Thomson and S. R. Engleman, *The Industrial Relations Act: A Review and Analysis*, Martin Robertson, 1975. But strangely enough little of value exists on the 1972 national coal strike, and the political–economic international crisis of October 1973 to March 1974 lacks even a journalistic chronicler.

Labour and the Social Contract, June 1970 to May 1979 (Chapter 7)

Harold Wilson's memoirs in *Final Term*, Weidenfeld & Nicolson and Michael Joseph, 1979, are rather perfunctory. But Barbara Castle's *Diary 1974–1976*, Weidenfeld & Nicolson, 1980, provides a useful inside picture of the Social Contract in its early phase. Unfortunately, Jim Callaghan would not have Mrs Castle in his Cabinet so the only published insider diary for the post-1976 period appears to be Tony Benn, *Conflicts of Interest 1977 to 1980*, Hutchinson, 1990, which is particularly vivid on the 1978–9 'Winter of Discontent'. The best memoirs for those years are Denis Healey, *The Time of my Life*, Michael Joseph, 1989. But also of lvalue are Edmund Dell, *A Hard Pounding: Politics and Economic Crisis 1974–75*, Oxford University Press, 1991; Bernard Donoughue, *Prime Minister*, Jonathan Cape, 1987; Joel Barnett, *Inside the Treasury*, Deutsch, 1982; and Joe Haines, *The Politics of Power*, 1972. Also see C. Burk and A. Cairncross's study of the 1976 IMF crisis, *Goodbye Great Britain*, Yale University Press, 1992. There is a civil service view in Leo Pliatzky, *Getting and Spending*, Basil Blackwell, 1982.

Jack Jones, *Union Man*, Collins, 1986, is a good read. But there was nothing from Hugh Scanlon or TUC General Secretary Len Murray. As always, Britain's senior trade union leaders are absent from the literature, though we have had memoirs in recent years from the second tier in the Social Contract generation: Sidney Weighell, Clive Jenkins, Frank Chapple and Bill Sirs.

Among secondary material on the Social Contract years see Martin Holmes, *The Labour Government 1974–1979*, Macmillan, 1985; and David Coates, *Labour in Power?*, Longmans, 1980. The realities of industrial relations can be found in William Brown (ed.), *The Changing Contours of British Industrial Relations*, Basil Blackwell, 1981; and W. W. Daniel and Neil Millward, *Workplace Industrial Relations in Britain*, Heinemann, 1983.

The taming of the trade unions, February 1975 to January 1993 (Chapter 8)

The literature on the Thatcher years is already enormous. There are sections on industrial relations in Hugo Young, *One of Us*, Macmillan, 1991; and Peter Jenkins, *Mrs Thatcher's Revolution*, Jonathan Cape, 1987. Peter Riddell's *The Thatcher Era and its Legacy*, Blackwell, 1991, is very useful. Also worth reading is Stuart Hall and Martin Jacques (eds), *The Politics of Thatcherism*, Lawrence and Wishart, 1983.

Nigel Lawson has written the best inside account in *Inside Number 11*, Collins, 1992, with some fascinating chapters on the trade unions and labour markets. Among the other relevant memoirs so far published two have snippets of interest: Jim Prior, *A Balance of Power*, Hamish Hamilton, 1986; and Norman Tebbit, *Upwardly Mobile*, Weidenfeld & Nicolson, 1988.

For the 1975–9 period there are some interesting contributions in Zig Layton-Henry, *Conservative Party Politics*, Macmillan, 1980; and R. Behrens, *The Conservative Party from Heath to Thatcher 1974–1979*, Saxon House, 1980.

The secondary sources on trade unions under Thatcher include David

Marsh, *The New Politics of British Trade Unionism*, Cornell University Press, 1992; Neil Millward and Mark Stevens, *British Workplace Industrial Relations 1980–1984*, Gower, 1986; John Kelly, *Labour and the Unions*, Verso, 1987; John McInnes, *Thatcherism at Work*, Open University Press, 1987; John McIlroy, *Trade Unions in Britain Today*, Manchester University Press, 1988; David Coates, *The Crisis of Labour*, Philip Allan, 1989; and P. Bassett, *Strike Free*, Macmillan, 1986.

On the legislative changes see Simon Auerbach, *Legislating for Conflict*, Oxford University Press, 1990. The radical right's prescriptions can be found in Charles Hanson's *Taming the Trade Unions*, Macmillan, 1991, and his pamphlet for the Institute of Economic Affairs, co-authored with Graham Mather, *Striking Out Strikes*, IEA, 1988. *Workplace Industrial Relations in Transition*, edited by Neil Millward and others (Dartmouth, 1992) shows that by the late 1980s industrial relations had indeed been transformed under the impact of Thatcherism and structural change. A useful and succinct essay on the British industrial relations scene during the 1980s is 'Great Britain: Still Muddling Through', in Anthony Ferner and Richard Hyman (eds), *Industrial Relations in the New Europe*, Blackwell, 1992.

Index

402   *Index*